BOOKS BY MARK BEGO

The Captain & Tennille (1977)

Barry Manilow (1977)

The Doobie Brothers (1980)

Michael! [Jackson] (1984)

On the Road with Michael! [Jackson] (1984)

Rock Hudson: Public & Private (1986)

Sade! (1986)

Julian Lennon! (1986)

The Best of "Modern Screen" (1986)

Whitney! [Houston] (1986)

Bette Midler: Outrageously Divine (1987)

The Linda Gray Story (1988)

TV Rock [The History of Rock & Roll on Television] (1988)

Aretha Franklin: Queen of Soul (1989, 2001)

Between the Lines [with DEBBIE GIBSON] (1990)

Linda Ronstadt: It's So Easy (1990)

Ice Ice Ice: The Extraordinary Vanilla Ice Story (1991)

One Is the Loneliest Number [with JIMMY GREENSPOON OF THREE DOG NIGHT] (1991, 1998)

I'm a Believer: My Life of Music, Monkees and Madness [with MICKY DOLENZ OF THE MONKEES] (1993)

Country Hunks (1994)

Country Gals (1994)

Dancing in the Street: Confessions of a Motown Diva [with MARTHA REEVES OF MARTHA & THE VANDELLAS] (1994)

I Fall to Pieces: The Music & Life of Patsy Cline (1995)

Bonnie Raitt: Just in the Nick of Time (1995)

Rock & Roll Almanac (1996)

Alan Jackson: Gone Country (1996)

Raised on Rock: The Autobiography of Elvis Presley's Stepbrother [with DAVID STANLEY] (1996)

George Strait: The Story of Country's Living Legend (1997, 1998, & 1999)

Leonardo DiCaprio: Romantic Hero (1998)

LeAnn Rimes (1998)

Jewel (1998)

Matt Damon: Chasing a Dream (1998)

Will Smith: The Freshest Prince (1998)

Vince Gill (2000)

Madonna: Blonde Ambition [Updated Edition] (Cooper Square Press 1992, 2000)

Cher: If You Believe (Cooper Square Press 2001)

Cher
IF YOU BELIEVE

MARK BEGO

Introduction by
Mary Wilson

Cooper Square Press

First Cooper Square Press edition 2001

This Cooper Square Press hardcover edition of *Cher: If You Believe* is an original publication. A portion of the material contained herein appeared in a work by the author entitled *Cher!*, first published as a mass market original paperback in New York in 1986. *Cher: If You Believe* is published by arrangement with the author.

Published by Cooper Square Press
An Imprint of the Rowman & Littlefield Publishing Group
150 Fifth Avenue, Suite 817
New York, New York 10011

Distributed by National Book Network

Library of Congress Cataloging-in-Publication Data

Bego, Mark.
    Cher : if you believe / Mark Bego.
        p. cm.
    Includes bibliographical references (p.) and index.
    Discography: p.
    Filmography: p.
    ISBN 0-8154-1153-7 (alk. paper)
    1. Cher, 1946– 2. Singers—United States—Biography. 3. Motion picture actors and actresses—United States—Biography. I. Title.

ML420.C472 B44 2001
782.42164 '092—dc21
[B]

                                                                                        2001017206

♾ ™ The paper used in this publication meets the minimum requirements of American National Standard for Information Sciences—Permanence of Paper for Printed Library Materials, ANSI/NISO Z39.48-1992.
Manufactured in the United States of America.

To Mary Wilson,

My most "Supreme" friend!

XXX

⁓Bego

CONTENTS

FOREWORD

I have known Cher since the very beginning of her career. The first time we met, the Supremes and Sonny & Cher were both performing at the Cow Palace in San Francisco. This was around 1965, when "I Got You Babe" was still on the charts. It was one of those multi-act shows. That was the only time we performed with them in concert, other than appearing on their TV show.

The next time we worked with Sonny & Cher, it was 1966 and we were all on the television series *Hullabaloo*, which we taped in New York City, with Sammy Davis Jr. as the host. Cher, for me, has always been the same sincere person. She was always very down-to-earth. I would say that she is—and always has been—very much outgoing, no pretense, very warm, and genuine. She was always "real."

Then, in the 1970s, the Supremes were guests on *The Sonny & Cher Comedy Hour* several times. It was a different era then. Cher was different than she was when we first met her. At that point, she had attained more of a high-profile position, and a demeanor about her. Still, on the sidelines, after the cameras stopped rolling, she was the same Cher I had always known, greeting me warmly. To her friends she was still a real and very down-to-earth person. On the stage she was more in control, but offstage—she was totally herself. She didn't carry her onstage persona into her offstage life. Some people are "on" when they're "off" and "on" when they're "on." When she was offstage, she was not "on," she was just herself—the Cher I'd always known.

One of the things that has always impressed me the most about Cher is the fact that she's always been like "one of the girls"—like an advocate for "the girls." I identify with her, because I think I'm the same way. I think she was definitely a "girl's girl." Whenever she sees me, she always says, "Hey Mare! How you doing, MARY?" and she gives me a big hug. All the time. It never fails, no matter where we are in the universe, if it's in England, or wherever it is, she's always the same. She never lets protocol get in the way of saying, "Hey MARY! Girl, it's so nice to see you!"

No one is happier than I am about her big comeback with the album *Believe*. In my mind, Cher and Tina Turner are the only two who've come across and showed the industry that what show business executives think is "it" is not always correct. They have both proven them wrong—Tina and Cher. Tina broke down age barriers, and Cher trailblazed the way for all of us by doing the Broadway play, and then all the movies—she's proven them all wrong about her talent.

When the industry has labeled Cher as being "too this" or "too that," she's come out and shown everyone that the individual can overcome those labels. The same things that she has done are things that I thought that I should strive to do. I've not been able to do it on the same scale—but she has, and she's done it bigger. I applaud her for that. Prior to *Believe* a lot of people didn't think she could come back, bigger than ever—but she pulled it off. I think that's the brilliance of Cher.

—MARY WILSON

ACKNOWLEDGMENTS

The author would like to thank the following people for their help, insight, and assistance:

Bart Andrews
David Andrews
Anne Bego
Catherine Bego
Mary & Bob Bego
Fred Bernstein
Cindy Birdsong
Angela Bowie
Michael Bradley
Joe Canole
Mark Chase
Cher
John Christe
Rita Coolidge
Sarah Dash
Daphne Davis
Michael Dorr
Daniel Eastman
Alf Elkington
Bob Esty
Gino Falzarano
Sasha Goodman
Randy Jones

Jan Kalajian
David Kelly
Sally Kirkland
Mark Lasswell
Walter McBride
Michael Messina
Marie Morreale
Bob Noguera at Strider
  Records, NYC
Jim Pinkston
Ross Plotkin
Bobby Reed
Sherry Robb
David Salidor
Frank Sanello
Shea Scullin
Barbara Shelley
Andy Skurow
Mark Sokoloff
Leor Warner
Lori Weiss
Kelly West
Mary Wilson

PREFACE
Take Me Home

*I know for myself, if something happened to my face, or something hap-
pened that would change me physically, my career and my life would
pretty much be down the tubes.*—Cher to Mark Bego, 1979 (1)

In a very real sense, I have been working on this book for thirty-five years.
It was in 1966 that I bought my first Sonny & Cher album, the soundtrack for their film *Good Times.* Although it was years before I saw the
famed rock and roll movie, I loved the music, especially "It's the Little
Things." It fact, it is still my favorite Sonny & Cher song. I remember the
first time I saw them on a syndicated dance party–style TV program, *The
Lloyd Thaxton Show.* I'll never forget the fashion statement they made:
Sonny had his classic Caesar haircut, and Cher was wearing a pair of her
trademark bell-bottoms.

In the 1970s, when I went to college at Central Michigan University,
I wrote the record review column in the campus newspaper. One of the
first LPs I wrote about was the 1971 album *Cher,* which featured her first
solo Number 1 hit, "Gypsys, Tramps and Thieves." When I moved to
New York City, I began a career as a magazine writer, reviewing and
reporting about the music scene for *Billboard, Record World, Us,* and
anyone else who would purchase my writing.

When Studio 54 opened, on a night in 1977, I was there. My date that
evening was actress C. C. H. Pounder. Amidst all of the partying, at one
point I turned and pointed at someone in a straw cowboy hat, and said to
C. C., "Oh my God, we're dancing next to Cher!" That was my first live
and in-person encounter with the diva. (Since that time, C. C. has starred
as the owner of the title business in the movie *Baghdad Cafe* and was one
of the stars of Cher's film *If These Walls Could Talk.*)

From 1978 to 1980, I had one of the most exciting jobs of my Manhattan writing career. I was the nightlife editor of New York City's famed

CUE magazine. It was a guide to everything to do in Manhattan, and my "beat" included every discotheque, cabaret, nightclub, piano bar, and supper club in town.

In early 1979 I was informed by my editor, Daphne Davis, that I would be doing a big cover story interview with none other than Cher herself. She had just released her disco album *Take Me Home,* and I was invited to all of the festivities surrounding it. Two days before I was to interview Cher, I was a guest at the *Billboard* Disco Convention's late-night skating party in Brooklyn, hostessed by Cher.

Not only was that evening memorable for roller skating on the same rink as Cher, it also became memorable for the accident I was involved in. While I was skating, and craning my neck to follow Cher, someone skating behind me started to lose his balance and grabbed at the nearest thing he could find—me! Not only did he pull me down on the floor, someone else rolled over my right forefinger, damaging the cartilage in it.

Bob Weiner wrote in the *Soho Weekly News* gossip column (March 8, 1979), "*Cue* magazine's Mark Bego was one of the many casualties at Cher's Empire Roller disco party last week. Some stoned freak roller skated over his hand, which is now in splints. The party was the highlight of the fifth *Billboard* Disco Convention" (2).

Two days after the party, when I arrived at the Pierre Hotel for my one-on-one in-person interview with Cher, I had a metal splint holding the forefinger of my right hand in an extended position, and I was still very much in pain. Cher was upset when I told her how I was one of the casualties of her disco party, and I appreciated her concern. I found her to be warm and frank, and very relaxed when talking that day. She was standing at a crossroads in her high-profile career and was pondering the idea of getting into acting—both on Broadway and in the movies. Much of the material from our 1979 discussion is included in this book. Also present at our interview was a surprise guest star, Cher's boyfriend at the time, Gene Simmons of the rock group KISS.

My career focus shifted from magazines to books when I first hit the *New York Times* best-seller list in 1984, with a Michael Jackson biography I had written (*Michael!*). Now with forty books written, and ten million books in print, I became the biggest-selling rock and roll biographer ever! However, one of my biggest disappointments was the way my 1986 book *Cher!* was published and then promptly disappeared. Part of the problem was timing. I was simply ahead of the game. Cher's huge 1980s peak—winning the Oscar for *Moonstruck*—came two years after my book appeared, and no one seemed to want to listen to my suggestions to update *Cher!*

Undeterred, my passion for and interest in Cher continued. I twice saw her on Broadway in *Come Back to the Five and Dime, Jimmy Dean, Jimmy Dean*, I went to the press preview of *Mask*, I watched her reunite with Sonny on *Late Night with David Letterman* in 1988, and I continued to save every interview, article, photo, review, and detail I saw about Cher.

In January of 1998, when Sonny Bono was suddenly killed in a skiing accident, newspapers and television shows raced to cover the tragic event. That same month, the *New York Post* wrote an article about the fact that I was shopping for a publisher for this book. Days later, I received a phone call from the producers of the *Sally Jesse Raphael* TV show, asking me to be a guest on the program. They were assembling several of Sonny's family and friends to speak about him and give him a fitting tribute. I was honored to be invited to speak about the importance of his career in the music world. On the set of the show I met his mother, Jean Bono; his third ex-wife, Susie Coehlo; and a couple of his friends, including Tony Orlando.

As you read this book, you will discover just how thoroughly the lives of Sonny and Cher will forever be linked. Without Sonny Bono, the entertainment world would never have heard of the diva we have all come to know simply as "Cher."

Finally, in 1999, thanks to the song "Believe," Cher was back on top again, and I was ready to chronicle her latest career peak. This book, *Cher: If You Believe*, began as a reprint of my 1986 book, *Cher!*, with post-1986 updates. However, once I started entering the old book in my computer (the original manuscript was created on an electric typewriter), from the very start, I began rewriting the old material and giving it a whole new perspective.

I don't know a single author who wouldn't want a second chance to tinker with one of his or her previously written books. I always maintained that *Cher!* was one of my favorite books of those I have written. I made it my goal to eclipse that book with this one.

There are a few segments of the pre-1986 material that are from the book *Cher!*, as well as several of the original photos. Other than that, this is truly a whole new book. I got a big smile on my face recently when someone informed me that they saw a rare copy of my original *Cher!* book on the Internet auction site eBay, selling for $80. (The original cover price upon publication was only $3.50!)

Not only does this book contain material from my original interview with Cher, but it also encompasses several new interviews with many of her friends and coworkers, including record producer Bob Esty, Academy Award–nominated actress Sally Kirkland, Randy Jones of the Village People, Sarah Dash of LaBelle, and Mary Wilson of The Supremes. I have seen and photographed Cher's new Malibu mansion, attended the Phoenix opening night of her "Believe" tour, and was in the audience at the Grammy Awards in February 2000 to witness Cher's name being announced as one of that evening's winners.

The year 2000 began my fifth decade as a Cher follower and fan, and I am thrilled to be the first author of the new millennium to chronicle her roller-coaster–like story with all of the frankness and excitement that her life and career have encompassed.

I had a great deal of fun writing this book about the ever-colorful Cher, and I hope you enjoy it too.

AUTHOR'S EDITING NOTE

One of the biggest issues in this particular book concerned the very important look of the term "Sonny & Cher." Beginning in the 1960s all of the duo's albums and singles featured the use of the "ampersand" or "&" in the middle of their names. Whenever the "act" calling themselves "Sonny & Cher" are mentioned in this book, you will find that spelling. When action is taking place in a paragraph where both Sonny AND Cher are doing something as offstage individuals, we use the spelled-out "and" in the sentence.

Parenthetical numbers following quoted material refer to the numbered list of sources found in the back matter of the book.

—MARK BEGO
Los Angeles
August 2001

IF YOU BELIEVE IN LIFE AFTER LIFE

It is 6:00 p.m., Wednesday, June 16, 1999, and it is 106 degrees Fahrenheit in Phoenix, Arizona. In underground parking lots automobiles are so hot that stickers and decorative chrome pieces are melting loose. Above ground, as the sun begins its descent into the western sky, one can literally see waves of heat radiating up from the pavement in the downtown area. In spite of the excruciating heat, thousands of people are walking with determination, heading down the sidewalks toward one particular block, oblivious to the temperature. No matter how hot it feels outdoors, the inside of the air-conditioned America West Arena that they are heading toward is truly the hottest place on the planet tonight. Because tonight is the night Cher opens her sold-out "Believe" world tour.

This evening, America West Arena is in a virtual Cher time warp. Audience members are dressed in outfits representing every era of Cher's career. Several women are wearing bell-bottomed pants and sandals like the ones Cher made famous in the 1960s. One girl sports a bright purple shag wig, like the one Cher wore to Madonna's wedding in 1985. Another woman parades around with a headpiece of long strands of plastic tubing, like the one Cher wore in her "Believe" video. Men, women, and children of all ages have purchased and are wearing Cher "Believe" T-shirts. It is a gathering of Cher believers of all ages. Some are older, some are middle-aged, and some are decades too young to have even been born when the song "I Got You Babe" topped the charts on both sides of the Atlantic.

Tonight there is an air of excitement and sheer anticipation. After the two opening acts are finished with their musical sets, the members of the standing room–only crowd are at the edges of their seats. Tickets disappeared almost instantly at $60 and $75 apiece, and local scalpers were charging up to $600 per seat. "What is she going to wear?" "How will she sound?" "Which of her hits is she going to sing?" These were questions that were repeated throughout the crowd.

In true Cher fashion, the stage set is very gothic-looking. Rising about twenty feet above the huge stage, two nonsymmetrical staircases lead downward toward the stage floor. The stairways are encircled by fence posts topped with fleurs-de-lis linked with a guardrail of chain. The cyclorama backdrop is painted to look like it is made of stone. It's as though tonight's crowd is gathered in the secret cave of a mountain goddess, awaiting an audience with this deity.

On stage, musicians and technicians are scurrying about, checking lights, amps, and instruments. Finally, at 9:43 p.m. the house lights are dimmed. As the opening notes of a synthesizer-dominated song begin, it sounds more like *The X-Files* TV show theme than any recognizable Cher hit. It is hard to tell what song it is, especially through the resounding din of cheers, screams, clapping, and whistling that the audience is emitting. While huge video projection screens flash images of Cher's past, present, and future, there—from the central and highest point of the stage— where the two staircases join, something is rising up from the floor of the balcony walkway that is formed there. Hark, it is the pop goddess herself—Cher in all of her outrageous opening night glory.

The music is pulsing, the lights are flashing, and Cher is singing her heart out, but for the first few minutes of her performance it is impossible to hear a word she is singing, because the entire audience as one is on its feet, clapping and cheering at the top of its lungs. They have come to see the legendary pop goddess, and her flashy entrance delivers all that we had hoped for—opulence, spectacle, and the ever-radiant Cher.

Like a high priestess of some sort of video fantasy come to life, the music world's most enduring rock diva begins singing her impassioned version of U2's song "I Still Haven't Found What I'm Looking For." Although this isn't a song she has ever recorded before, it is a fitting choice for her. As in the lyrics of the song, Cher too has spent the last four decades in the public eye, morphing from one persona to another, like a restless seeker on a never-ending quest.

She is wearing her first of eight elaborate and over-the-top costumes that Bob Mackie has designed for this grand world concert tour. Known for wearing wigs ever since she was the star of *The Sonny & Cher Comedy Hour* in the 1970s, her tresses are to be changed with each and every costume change. For the opening number she is wearing a curly waist-length red wig atop her head, held in place by an elaborate beaded headband with side wings that hang at the side of her face.

Clad in a copper and bronze spangled outfit of crisscrossing beaded strips, a waist-cinching bustier, and slave bracelets, Cher looks like a Byzantine warrior woman, poised to conquer. And conquer she did.

After the wild cheering dies down after her opening number, Cher appears poised and in total command as she announces to her SRO legion of worshipers, "We've got a lot of territory to cover. . . . I'm gonna do songs I haven't done since the seventies." As promised, her 1999–2000 concert tour not only highlights her million-selling 1980s and 1990s hits, but for the first time in ages she is also to sing several of the songs from her past that she hasn't performed live in years: Number 1 hits like "Gypsys, Tramps and Thieves" and "Half Breed," to her million-selling disco smash "Take Me Home," through her 1980s rockers like "If I Could Turn Back Time" and "We All Sleep Alone," right up to the 1990s sound of "Believe." It is by far the most lavish concert tour mounted in years, and only Cher could pull it off with such style, flash, and sense of spectacle.

Since her hit-making career has literally spanned thirty-five years of musical memories, tonight she is prepared to touch on them all—from the very beginning of her career to "Believe" and beyond. She is the only pop or rock performer to have had Top Ten hits in the 1960s, 1970s, 1980s, AND 1990s. Tonight is a celebration for all who believe—in Cher.

No one in the history of show business has had a career of the magnitude and scope of Cher's. She has been a teenage pop star, a television hostess, a fashion magazine model, a rock star, a pop singer, a Broadway actress, an Academy Award–winning movie star, a disco sensation, and the subject of a mountain of press coverage. Her fans have followed her as one half of the pre-hippie duo Sonny & Cher, through her headline-grabbing divorce from Sonny, her disastrous marriage to drugged-out singer Gregg Allman, right up through her 1980s affair with the notorious "Bagel Boy" who was half her age.

We have watched her start fashion trends—like bell-bottomed pants—transform herself into a glamorous TV mannequin, and blossom as a serious film actress of legendary proportions. We have seen her through breast lifts, face peels, dental braces, puffed-up collagen-enhanced lips, talon-like finger nails, and enough plastic surgery and makeup to morph herself into a totally different person.

Outspoken since she was a young teenager, Cher can be called a lot of things. However, "helpless victim" has never been on that list. She is no creampuff when it comes to speaking her mind. She has publicly called Sonny Bono "a tyrant," David Letterman "an asshole," and Madonna "a cunt." Few could have gotten away with the things she has said.

Possessing a fabulous body—surgically altered as it may be—Cher has never turned the other cheek, but she has often shown her other cheeks. She has been banned by MTV, fought with TV censors, and "mooned" her fans with her tattooed *derrière*. Easy to get along with when you are her ally, she follows her own instincts and makes her own mistakes. She has often feuded with her film directors and thumbed her nose at any convention that displeases her.

As a singing star, her recording career has had five distinctively different phases. First, she was the in-tune half of the pop/rock duo Sonny & Cher, racking up million-selling hits like "The Beat Goes On" with her live-in lover/first husband Sonny Bono. Simultaneously, she had her own distinctively different solo career as a folk/rock balladeer, covering Bob Dylan songs like "All I Really Want to Do" in the 1960s. Her third incarnation found her singing melodramatic story-songs like "Dark Lady" and "The Way of Love" in the 1970s. She was reborn at the end of that decade as a roller disco queen with dance hits including "Take Me Home" and "Hell on Wheels." In the 1980s and early 1990s she embraced hard rock, producing three platinum albums and singing power ballads like "If I Could Turn Back Time" and "We All Sleep Alone." She astonished the world in 1998 and 1999 by staging the biggest career "comeback" since Tina Turner's 1984 resurrection, recasting herself as a dance music/techno-pop performer warbling the biggest hit of her entire career, "Believe."

She made three films in the 1960s with Sonny Bono, a short appearance in the surfing flick *Wild on the Beach*, followed by *Good Times* and *Chastity*. However, she longed to be taken seriously as a film actress. At the height of her musical fame, she literally turned her back on Las Vegas showrooms to establish herself as a movie star. Her films *Mask, Mer-*

maids, Suspect, and *The Witches of Eastwick* gave her the kind of screen career most actresses can only dream of obtaining.

Although she had proven her talent via TV ratings, million-selling hits, entertaining films, and creative record albums, she waited a long time for the kind of respect that she longed to receive from her peers. It came to her in an overwhelming fashion, when she won an Academy Award for her dazzling performance in the 1987 film *Moonstruck.* And—finally— in the year 2000, she won her first Grammy Award for her milestone global hit "Believe."

Likewise, she has managed to regain the momentum of her once-dazzling film career. Longing for more creative control, she made her filmdirecting debut with the 1996 HBO hit *If These Walls Could Talk.* In 1999 she received glowing reviews as one of the stars of Franco Zeffirelli's prestigious box-office hit *Tea with Mussolini.*

Meanwhile, her personal life has been a roller-coaster ride of tabloid newspaper headlines. Her divorce from Sonny and her irrational affair with heroin addict Gregg Allman all but eclipsed her mid-1970s television work. She was stricken with the debilitating Epstein-Barr virus in 1989, and nearly ruined her own film career by starring in a tacky 1990s television infomercial selling overpriced designer shampoo. Usually liberal-minded Cher was devastated when tabloid newspapers "outed" her daughter, Chastity, as a lesbian in the early 1990s.

By the middle of the 1990s her show business career was in shambles. Her 1996 film *Faithful* opened at theaters "dead on arrival." That same year, her album *It's a Man's World* scarcely made a dent on the American record charts. When her ex-husband Sonny Bono was killed in a tragic 1998 skiing accident, friends and fans alike wondered if that emotional loss would mark the end of her creative career as well.

She had no intention of producing a 1990s dance disc when she went into the studio to record the *Believe* album. She reportedly argued tooth and nail with the producers behind the project. Although she had a Number 1 hit in 1996 in England, singing "Love Can Build a Bridge" with Chrissie Hynde and Neneh Cherry, the rest of the world seemed to have written her off as a glamorous star of the past. When the song "Believe" became a Number 1 hit around the world in 1998–1999, she came back, bigger, better, and more excitingly revitalized than ever before. Her *Believe* album was certified either Gold, Platinum, or Multiple Platinum in thirty-nine different countries. It was as though the entire planet welcomed Cher back with open arms.

Cher is one of those rare individuals whose personal life, reputation, fame, and image often come to mind more readily than do thoughts of any of her accomplishments. She's still—in her fifties—that overgrown teenager who delights in flying in the face of convention like a pesky hornet. Who will ever forget the barely there Mohawk nightmare outfit she wore to the 1985 Academy Awards telecast, specifically designed to say "fuck you very much" for ignoring her acting in the movie *Mask*.

She is consistent only in her vast inconsistency, and she is a mass of internal and external contradictions. She's the serious actress who still balances her life as a rock and pop star. One moment she is the perpetual female Peter Pan who loves to dress down in jeans and claim that the world can simply take her the way she is. And the next moment she will turn around and make a grand entrance in a $5,000 beaded gown, a $500 manicure, and countless thousands of dollars of reconstructive body surgery.

She once proclaimed, "People regarded me as a clothes hanger more than an entertainer" (3). Yet, she has constantly allowed her wardrobe to make a statement for her.

From the mid-1970s one of the most collectable toys on the planet was the "Cher Doll." The new version of the Cher doll from Mattel caused another huge toy-store sensation when it debuted in 2001. But let's face the fact Cher IS the world's favorite real-life Barbie doll. We all delight in seeing what on earth it is that she is going to wear in public next. She stands only five feet, seven inches tall, yet in the eyes of the media and of the public, she is a larger-than-life giantess.

Sitting next to Cher on a sofa and having a conversation with her, one has to constantly remind one's self that this woman with the blasé attitude, saying "fuck this" and "fuck that," is the entertainment world's most famous spoiled-child-turned-goddess. The fact that she is so real, so down-to-earth in manner, and so at ease with herself is one of the reasons that she has endured the passing fads and fancies and emerged more undeniably beautiful than ever before. If we never had any memory of the Cher of the early 1970s, with her crooked teeth, not-so-perfect nose, and naturally pretty features, we would still find the Cher of the 2000s beautiful. However, since the metamorphosis of Cher has been such a public one—through nose peels, reported butt lifts, dental braces, dental caps, and seemingly countless nips and tucks—it is difficult not to think of her image in the past. Like a sleek cat, Cher has had at least nine lives by now.

This is what Cher's five decades as an international media star have been all about—spectacle. For her, the element of surprise is virtually "everything." Cher is not the most classically beautiful or most talented actress in Hollywood, nor is she the most gifted vocalist on record, but she is a celebrity of true "superstar" status.

She's the wisecracking pop princess whose success seems to be based as much on her unpredictability as upon her talents. Just when you think that she has done it all, sung it all, or accomplished it all, Cher recreates herself and takes on a whole new persona. She's an acknowledged pillar of self-determination, and her career has had both strength and longevity. As the reigning mannequin of the "me" generation, she has worn many labels, but she can only be described with one name that says it all: "Cher!"

As the consummate Renaissance woman, Cher calls her own shots, and she is in total control of her own destiny. She's forceful and direct, and she speaks her mind. In 1978, sick of being tagged with the surnames of her father, stepfather, and ex-husbands, Cherilyn Sarkisian La Piere Bono Allman legally shortened her name to just one word, Cher. To her it marked her independence from every one of the men in her life. In the 1980s she went through a succession of younger men, including actors Val Kilmer and Tom Cruise and ABC-TV executive Josh Donen. And then there was her famed affair with Robert Camilletti, the "Bagel Boy" who was only twenty-two when forty-year-old Cher started dating him. She also had her rock and roll boyfriend phases with Gene Simmons of KISS, Les Dudek, and Richie Sambora of Bon Jovi.

She is not a women's rights proponent by petitioning and picketing, but she is a "people's rights" symbol, simply by standing up and speaking her mind and saying what she feels. As she independently proclaimed, "This is my life—and I get to do everything I want to do. I don't really care what anybody thinks" (4).

According to her, "I'm a good performer, not a great performer. I don't know what I have, but I know I've got something, and I think people like me. I know I make mistakes, and I will continue to make mistakes, but I don't care if people agree with what I do. If I ever had a chance to be somebody better or prettier or whatever, I wouldn't want it. I love being me" (5).

"I don't answer to anyone except myself," she insists.

I can be very independent if necessary, and most of the time, I am. Basically, I think I'm a lot more moral than most people. I don't do drugs and

I don't drink—I've spoken out against them over and over again—and I think you must have a meaningful relationship with somebody, even if it's your dog. I don't think I really care if what I'm doing makes sense to every-body else. If it makes sense to me, that's all that's important (6).

Simultaneously, her ex-partner, Sonny Bono, had a post-Cher life that was as event-filled as that of the diva-in-the-making he had once married. He had found stardom with Cher, dressed as a Bohemian hippie in bob-cat fur vests in the 1960s, yet by the 1990s he had transformed himself into a conservative Republican congressman in Washington, D.C. He had gone from singer to restaurateur to successful actor in *Hairspray* to become the mayor of Palm Springs, and finally to the halls of Congress. Although they had reunited once in 1988 on network television, Sonny and Cher's once-inseparable friendship was strained at best. While Cher at first reluctantly embraced their daughter's lesbianism, it was Sonny who easily accepted the news. Although since the 1970s they had been estranged and combative with each other, Sonny's life and Cher's life will forever remain interwoven.

And yet, with all that is known about Cher, there are so many unan-swered questions. What was the truth about Cher sleeping with Warren Beatty when she was a teenager? What happened the night Cher saved the life of a drugged-out rock star at a Hollywood party? To what ends did she attempt to get Gregg Allman off of drugs? What role did Jackie Kennedy play in turning Cher into a *Vogue* magazine fashion model? How did Cher react when her daughter Chastity was "outed" by the tabloid newspapers, and then publicly "came out"? How did Cher feel when she heard the news of Sonny Bono's death—having spoken scathingly of him for years? Why have Cher and Sonny Bono's widow, Mary Bono, gone from "sisters in sorrow" to bitter enemies? The breakup of Sonny & Cher, who left whom? And, who was having the most extramarital affairs at the time of their top-rated television show? What is the truth about Sonny Bono being on prescription drugs at the time of his fatal skiing accident? Exactly what plastic surgery has Cher had done to herself in a constant race against time and aging? What are Cher's inse-curities? What is behind the obsession with her looks? What was the rea-son behind Cher's affair with openly gay record-company executive David Geffen? Did she hope she could make him go straight? In the 1980s, when Cher would have done anything to become a serious movie star, to what ends did she have to go? Which movie directors did Cher love, and which ones did she hate? Is she a pain in the ass to work with? What drove Cher to appear in those dreadful infomercials in the 1990s, the ones that nearly ruined her career? Cher made her brilliant return to movies in 1999 in *Tea With Mussolini*. What was her big gripe with director Franco Zeffirelli? Was Cher's eulogy at Sonny Bono's funeral from her heart, or was it just a brilliant opportunity for her to gain publicity? What went into Cher's un-"Believe"-able 1990s comeback? This biography will help to explain these mysteries, and the appeal of this one-of-a-kind pop icon.

For Cher, the story of her life, and of her brilliant career, has just begun. She has experienced vast heights of achievement and lived through low points of creative inactivity, but through it all she has remained true to only one person, herself. She is a triumphant survivor in a cutthroat business. She is a clever woman who can be defined by only one word: Cher!

CHERILYN SARKISIAN

About ten miles from the Mexican border and nearly a hundred miles east of San Diego lies the decidedly unglamorous little town of El Centro, California. The town is comprised of plain little houses made of stucco, nestled in the heat and dust of the desert—population 19,000. An unlikely spot for the birthplace of one of the most dazzling figures in show business, this is where Cherilyn Sarkisian was born, on May 20, 1946.

The daughter of a teenager named Jackie Jean Crouch and her often absent husband John Sarkisian, Cherilyn was named after Lana Turner's little girl Cheryl. Jackie Jean, who had aspirations of becoming an actress, later changed her name to Georgia Holt, and to date has been married eight times—three of those marriages were to Cher's father. According to Cher, "Even though my mother was married a whole bunch of times, I don't really remember very many times when there was a man in the house" (6).

When Cher was born, her mother could not even afford to take care of her. There was no such thing as daycare for the babies of working mothers, so Cher was placed in an orphanage for several weeks until her mother could save up enough money to support a child. "Honey, I worked in an all-night diner from seven at night until seven in the morning for $3.00," explained Holt. "I boarded Cher in a Catholic home at the time. I got a singing job in the Manilla Bar & Grill—a real dump—but in 1946 it paid $75.00 a week. That was a lot" (7).

Georgia was later to reveal, "That mother superior was a bitch to me. She wanted me to put Cher up for adoption. I would go over and look through this little window, and Cher would be standing at her crib crying. I didn't know how to buck authority them. But now, boy, I'm telling you, I'd go through that woman so fast she wouldn't know what hit her" (8).

John Sarkisian was not around when Cher was a little girl; in fact, she doesn't remember meeting him at all until she was eleven years old. "I hated him," she later recalled of her first encounter with her father. Following a stint in the Coast Guard, Sarkisian worked as a truck driver and became addicted to heroin. Explained Sarkisian, "I really didn't spend much time with her when she was a kid. I was away from home most of the time hauling produce. I'd only see Cher now and then because her mother, Georgia, was married several times in between all that. And, Georgia always told me that it was better if I stayed away" (9). He eventually ended up serving four prison terms for drug possession. In the 1970s, when Cher was asked about her father, she flippantly replied, "I don't even know what he's doing, but it's probably nothing legal" (10). He unsuccessfully sued her for slandering him, and their relationship rarely changed. He developed lung cancer in the late 1970s, and he and Cher spoke on the phone before he died, but he was more of a transient character in her life than a parent who was actively involved in her life or childhood development.

Cher's exotically dark features come from her varied ethnic background. Her father was Armenian; her mother was part Cherokee Indian. Georgia later married a man named John Southall and had another daughter, Cher's half-sister Georganne. Explains Holt, "Both Cher and Georganne were adopted by my fifth husband, Gilbert La Piere. He loved the girls. His name, of course, was French. At the time Cher married Sonny, her legal name was Cherilyn La Piere. But I can't seem to convince Cher we aren't French" (11).

Both Georgia and Georganne were fair-skinned and blonde, while Cher's coloring was darker. According to Cher, "My mother once told me something. 'Don't ever expect to be the most beautiful, the most talented, or even the youngest one around. But, what you do have is something special. Make that work for you" (12).

According to Georgia, her eldest daughter has been plagued by life-long insecurity about her looks. "I think Cher felt she was an ugly duckling," says Holt. "She never believed she was pretty. Of course, I never believed I was, either. My mother was highly critical of me, and even to this day I can't own beauty. Maybe that's what it is with Cher. She can't own it, either" (8).

Georgia Holt (Jackie Jean Crouch) was born in Arkansas, and when her alcoholic father separated from her mother, they headed west for California. Georgia and her father picked up money along their way by performing and passing the hat from town to town. Georgia would sing, and her father would play the guitar. After they arrived in Los Angeles, Georgia found a job as a maid, although she was only thirteen at the time. Energetic and determined to get ahead in life, she managed to hold down the job and attend junior high school.

> My father lived long enough to see Cher become a star. We sat together when she appeared at the Hollywood Bowl. He kept telling me, "That's you up there, Jackie, that's you!" I loved my father dearly. He had tremendous drive to be a somebody, to accomplish things. He never did. But I always told myself I was somebody—even when I cried myself to sleep as a maid. Since they were youngsters, I have told Cher and Georganne they were princesses, and I was a queen. They believed me. And I believed myself (11).

When she moved with her two daughters back to Los Angeles from El Centro, she changed her name to Georgia Holt and began making the rounds, looking for work as an actress. While she was out meeting casting agents, Cherilyn would baby-sit for her younger sister. Says Cher,

> I used to take care of "Gee" [Georganne] when my mother was working. One time I gave her a little toy car and she ate all the wheels off it. My mother came home and beat the hell out of me. I guess our life was strange. It wasn't like *The Donna Reed Show* or *Father Knows Best*. But my mother was real open and liberated. She was a combination of Auntie Mame and Florence Nightingale (13).

"Cher was very good with Georganne," her mother recalls, "We always had a lot of fun together when I got home. We moved around a lot, but the girls had birthday parties, nice clothes, and a real home to live in— not an apartment" (14).

According to Cher, her first memories of her childhood date back to when she was four years old. She remembers playing hide and seek with Maria, the Mexican girl who would look after her while Georgia was working. She recalls to this day getting lost one afternoon in the wooded area near their house in Laurel Canyon, and panicking.

It was around that same time that Cher recalls making her first trip to the cinema and into the magical world of the movies that opened up to her. The first movie she saw was the Disney film *Dumbo.* The theater was the famed Hollywood Boulevard landmark Grauman's Chinese Theatre. Cher claims that she was so entranced that when she had to go to the bathroom, she simply stayed in her seat and wet her pants rather than miss a moment of the movie.

She was hooked on cinema dreams. "That was the first time I ever thought whatever is inside this dark room is really what's happening. I don't care that much for what's outside. It was then and there that I knew what I wanted to be" (15). From that one experience, she became obsessed with the idea of becoming an actress.

Cher also remembers her mother and stepfather arguing. According to her, "My mother hated it when my father drank because it threw everything into turmoil. When they started arguing, I'd get sent to my room, but I could still hear the violent yelling. I hated those fights. They made me a nervous wreck at [the age of] four" (16).

When she was four years old, her grandparents, whom she called Mamaw and Pa, purchased their first television. Cher recalls being fascinated with the images she saw on it. When she was five, her mother got the family's first TV set, a maple cabinet with a black and white screen, and she recalls being fascinated by the movie *One Million B.C.* She fell head-over-heels in love with the movie's star, hunky Victor Mature.

Cher's other set of grandparents, Grandma Lynda and Grandpa Charlie, were her mother's parents. Grandma Lynda was only thirty-two years old when Cher was born. Grandpa Charlie worked for the Johnson Pie Company, and Cher recalls him bringing home samples from work. She still remembers the chocolate cream pie that he brought home one day as the best she has ever had.

Although Georgia Holt never became a star, she managed to land several small parts in films and on television.

No man ever paid me alimony or child support, so there I was a young mother with two small girls. I began working again in bit parts in television and movies. I worked as a cocktail waitress for a hundred dollars a week and hated it. It was the same feeling I had when I was a maid. But I had to feed my children. I was given a wonderful part in [the movie] *Asphalt Jungle.* My agent called to tell me it was mine. But later he told me a girl named Marilyn Monroe had been given the part. I had leads in the *Ozzie & Harriet* TV show, which was a big deal after doing one-liners on other programs. But I wouldn't go the casting couch route, so my career never did get rolling (11).

Georgia did several television commercials to make ends meet, and often took Cher and Georganne along with her. "David Janssen used to hold Cher on his lap when she was three—I couldn't get a babysitter—and when I did the old Ed Winchell/Speidel Watch commercials" (7). Holt remembers getting Cher and Georganne little walk-on parts on TV.

> I got the girls work on Ozzie's show whenever I could. But I wasn't a pushy stage mother. I did, however, push Cher into studying with Jeff Corey, the drama coach. And she was the youngest kid ever to qualify for the Pasadena Playhouse. But at the last minute she refused to join the group. I couldn't force her to go because she didn't know what she wanted to do with her life (11).

Cher insists that she had a pretty clear picture of what she wanted to be when she grew up—a star. According to her, "I thought I was an angel from heaven sent to cure polio. When Dr. Salk did it, I was really pissed off. From the time I could talk, I began to sing. Singing just came from the inside—something I'd do without thinking whenever I felt good or was really blue" (17).

"I always knew that I was going to be somebody," she continues.

> When I was little, my mom and I used to go to Hollywood Boulevard and buy a couple of hot dogs and sit in our car watching the interesting people go by, and I guess I thought about it even then. I grew up thinking I wanted to be a movie star, because they were happy; they wore diamonds. That life would take me away from all that was real and ugly. I always felt really embarrassed about being poor, because I thought it was punishment for something I had done wrong (18).

She also recalls, "My mother once told me something that has stayed with me through thick and thin. 'Honey, you're not the prettiest or the most talented, so make the most of what you got.' At the time, that hurt. I felt so ugly, while my sister was so beautiful, with this white-blond hair and green eyes, like my mom. Once we went to Mexico and they wouldn't let me back over the border because they thought I was a Mexican and my mother was trying to sneak me in" (18).

Still, Cher did not give up her dreams of becoming famous; in fact, she practiced her signature until it befit a movie star. "I got my autograph together when I was twelve. I worked out the way I'd write it when I was famous. My mother always told me, 'You have something, trust me!' I had no reason to believe her, but somehow I always did. Somehow, I always thought I'd become something fantastic" (19).

There were times when it didn't look like her dreams were going to come true. "I was a mess," proclaims Cher of her childhood self-image.

I knew I wanted to be famous, but I didn't know what I could do. I would look in the mirror and see a not very distinguished-looking person. I wasn't good looking. I wasn't even cute. I wasn't a Catholic, but I went to Catholic school and got A's on all my catechism tests. I never could get behind the idea of penance, though. Once, when I was a kid, I said, 'Mother so-and-so looks like Joe E. Brown.' That nun beat the absolute shit out of me; beat me to a pulp and made me say the Rosary on my knees across the schoolyard. It was a killer, but I still believe in God and America, even if it's bad for my image (20).

Georgia fondly recalls, "The girls always made me pretty little gifts of drawings. On Mother's Day, they'd steal a rose from a neighbor's garden and bring it to me on a tray with burned toast and runny eggs so I could have breakfast in bed. To this day, neither of them can cook" (11).

"I never expected Cher to do anything conventional," she attests. "As a child, she was incredibly strong-willed and never wanted to fit in with the crowd. She didn't kowtow to teachers or trends. Because she thought of herself as different she wanted to look different—she wore patent-leather shoes when teachers didn't permit it or wild-colored glasses. But the outside is a mask. On the inside, she's very conservative, straight, deeply emotional, and vulnerable," says her mother (21).

Cher has also always been very outspoken. Recalling one incident that took place when she was ten years old, she explains,

At the school I was going to then, you were supposed to share something in class, you know, your feelings, stuff like that. And I got up and said, "This is shit. I really don't enjoy it here, I really don't like any of you." And I walked out. I was ten. My grandmother kind of laughed. Eventually my family got used to the fact that I was a little bit strange. My mother invited that, because she thought it was much more interesting to be different. But she was never really comfortable with it, and I think she wanted me to be (22).

By 1957, rock and roll music was sweeping America, and the rest of the world. Ever since James Dean starred in the 1950s famed coming-of-age-film, *Rebel without a Cause*, he had young girls swooning for him. He defined an attitude, a love of rock music, and a restlessness that teenagers in America seemed to share. It was the era of Chuck Berry, Bill Haley & His Comets, Fats Domino, Little Richard, and Jerry Lee Lewis. But for Cher, and millions of other rock and roll fans, there was only one "King of Rock and Roll." According to Cher, "Well, Elvis was my first idol. I was a little bit young for it, but my mom took me to see him when I was 11, and the first time I ever saw him was on *Ed Sullivan*. Somehow, I really identified with him. Elvis was the beginning of rock & roll music for me" (23).

Looking back on this era, Cher was later to recall, "For me, Elvis was a singing James Dean, and I was very rebellious. When I was growing up in Southern California, the role models were Sandra Dee and Doris Day, and everyone but me was cute and perky and blond. I was dark and moody and strange looking" (24).

When she was in the fifth grade, Cher teamed up with four or five of her girlfriends, and they performed songs from the Broadway musical *Oklahoma!* Since none of the boys in her class was interested in such an activity, Cher ended up singing all of the boys' songs—that Gordon MacRea performed in the show—plus "Pore Jud Is Daid" and "Everything's Up to Date in Kansas City." Cher and her girlfriends gave their concert performance of the musical in front of their class on the last day of the fifth grade. Cher recalls thinking to herself, "If we'd only had costumes" (25). Already she had Broadway aspirations. This was truly the product of a creative mind in the making.

As a young girl, she grew up in a quite liberal household. Cher recalls her first exposure to homosexuals. "I think I was 11 or 12 years old," she says of her mother's lesbian friends Shirley and Scotty.

> We were at Shirley and Scotty's house. Shirley and my mom were in the living room talking all girlie stuff, and Scotty and I were making a salad in the kitchen. I was thinking how cool Scotty was, because she was the only person who treated me like I was a human being. We could just talk. I think I knew she was a lesbian, and I definitely sensed something different about her. But I liked her a lot. She was so much fun. My mom had a lot of gay friends, and I kind of thought, "Oh well, that's just the female counterpart" (26).

Georgia Holt specifically remembers Cher's first date with a boy. "It was hysterical," she claims. "I made her a new pink dress for a school dance and the boy brought a corsage. He was an ugly little fat boy, but

Cher was so excited she could hardly sit still when I did her hair" (11). Cher was thirteen years old at the time.

In the early 1960s, it wasn't long before teenage Cher came in contact with sex and drugs. She recalls, "When I was fourteen, I took four Benzedrine and I was up for the entire weekend. Chewed the same piece of gum for three days. When I came down, I was a mess, and went to my mom. She said, 'I hope you learned some kind of lesson from this.' And I said, 'I swear to God I have!' And that was the first and the last time for me" (18).

Cher claims that her views on sex have changed very little from her school days.

> I didn't drink or do drugs or any of the things people would consider wild now. I wasn't hopping into bed with everybody either. Of course, when I was fourteen, my girlfriends were all telling me how much fun sex was, and I could get away with it and that boys would respect me—as long as I didn't go all the way. But I thought stopping short was ridiculous. I wanted to find out what it was all about, so I just did it, all at once, with this little Italian guy next door I was madly in love with. When we'd finished, I said, "Is this it?" He said, "Yeah!" And I said, "Well, you can go home" (18).

> I still think sex is a dumb thing unless you love somebody. I mean, I see some of these magazines with naked guys standing around looking like real assholes and I wonder how any woman could get turned on. They all look like Ken dolls, you know? I would never make it with some guy I'd just met. The only thing that sees you through life is a relationship with someone, so to just fuck without feeling or love is stupid (18).

While growing up, she was never interested in academics.

> I hated school because I didn't fit into the right space. I kept thinking, "What's the matter with all these people?" They try to cut off your edges and make you round so you fit in the round hole. I occupied some space in a couple of buildings but I was never a part of it. I was always thinking about something else. I was thinking about when I was grown-up and famous, where I'd want to live or who I'd go out with or what kind of dresses I would wear. All these little scenarios—I'd be sitting in classes thinking I was going to save people. Childish things that people think about when they're children. I wasn't into high school at all. I saw a lot of movies and idolized Audrey Hepburn. I also used to stand in my room and act out all the parts to *West Side Story* (27).

Cher's fascination with Audrey Hepburn led her to want to be just like the character Holly Golightly, whom Hepburn portrayed in *Breakfast at Tiffany's*. In fact, in 1961, the first time she saw that famous movie, she was awestruck by Hepburn's performance. Up until that point, all of the female movie stars were statuesque blondes who were entirely different in look and manner from herself. When she saw Audrey up on the movie screen as the kooky brunette who had the ability to turn the lives of everyone around her upside down, young Cher had a new role model. She recalls running home and announcing to Georgia, "Oh, Mother, you've got to see this picture—I've just seen a girl who's exactly like me" (25). Cher's sense of doing whatever she feels like doing has helped to make her the real-life Holly Golightly of her generation. Sometimes fantasies do come true, and they certainly have come true in a big way for Cher.

For a while, in the early 1960s, Georgia and her daughters moved to New York City. Recalls Cher's mother, "When she got into junior high, yes, I really started worrying about her. Because she wouldn't date anybody her age. When we moved to New York City, she was 15, she was going with a trumpet player in Peggy Lee's band who was 26—who thought she was 18. Yes, I worried about her—a lot" (28).

When they moved back to California, due to one of her mother's financially advantageous marriages, Cher was able to attend Montclair Prep School in Van Nuys, which was considered quite affluent. One of her classmates, Terry Loeffler, recalls dating Cher in the tenth grade.

> She was nice but not especially pretty. She had a pair of legs that would scare you, they were so skinny. We always used to kid her about her legs. She was a hippie then. She and Judy Branch were superpals, really tight together. I remember that Cher didn't have a car, but Judy did. Cher was fun, kind of flighty. She wasn't particularly popular. There was definitely not a million guys around her. I remember she got in trouble a lot. Mrs. Young, the dean of girls, hated her (13).

In May of 1962 Cher turned sixteen years old, and like all teenagers, she couldn't wait to get her driver's license. With her newly acquired license, one day she borrowed Gilbert La Piere's Buick Skylark, for a drive to Hollywood from Encino. When she was in front of famed Schwab's Drugstore on Sunset Boulevard a young man in a white Lincoln convertible cut her off and ran her into the drugstore parking lot. Freaked out by what he had done to Cher, the young man followed her vehicle into the parking lot to apologize. He was wearing a pair of glasses, but even with them on, Cher recognized that he was none other than Warren Beatty. Cher asked him if he was nuts for driving so recklessly. He apologized profusely, and Cher nonchalantly asked him if he had a cigarette.

When he replied that he did not, he offered to go into a nearby gas station to get a pack of smokes. When he returned with the cigarettes, he asked her if she wanted to go up to his house to get something to eat. Since Warren was the first bona fide movie star that she had ever met, she accepted. He ended up serving her cheese and crackers and a Coke. Although she knew that Warren was dating Natalie Wood at the time, she had sex with him. When she came home at 2:00 a.m.—two hours past her parentally imposed curfew—Gilbert was waiting up for her and sent her immediately to bed.

The next morning, Cher told her mother about getting cut off on Sunset Boulevard by Warren Beatty, knowing that Georgia was a fan of Beatty's movies at the time. Naturally she omitted the part about having sex with the young movie star. Not long afterward, Warren telephoned Cher's mother in an attempt to get her out of trouble. According to Cher, Beatty charmed her mother into letting her off the hook. Warren seemed to like the fact that teenage Cher La Piere wasn't awestruck at his movie star status, and on more than one occasion, she went back to his house to talk, hang out, and have sex. They were to remain friendly over the years.

She was later to state that she really liked him, but she was not in love with him. "That was before Sonny," she was to explain in the 1990s.

> Warren has probably been with everybody I know and unfortunately, I am one of them. But since I was only sixteen, maybe I can get out of it with that. I don't know if I was a bimbo then, but I had a pretty low self-esteem, and I had never really been around men. I still don't know anything about them. But you want to know what? I honestly don't care what people think of who I choose to be with (8).

With her mother constantly working at one odd job or another, and an ever-changing array of father figures moving in and out of her life, Cher did not have an entirely stable home life to give her security. It was also at the age of sixteen that Cher decided to drop out of high school and go out into the world to discover for herself who she was. For Cher, this was the beginning of a wondrous new life, a life that would see all of her dreams of stardom turn into reality.

I GOT YOU BABE

It was in early 1963 that Cher said "goodbye" to high school and left her mother's house. While Georgia was a very well-manicured actress who was always beautifully made-up, her daughter Cher was on the decidedly unglamorous side. Charlie Greene and Brian Stone eventually became the managers of Sonny & Cher. Stone recalls of teenaged Cher, "She was a pimply-faced little kid" (29). According to Greene, she not only had a bad complexion, she had zero fashion sense, stringy hair, and was usually wearing worn-out blue jeans and a rumpled T-shirt.

Admitted Cher, "I was poor when I grew up, and I couldn't bear that—because I looked a certain way; before getting a chance to tell people what I had to say, they would know I was poor. I was ashamed that I was poor. I felt that somehow it was my fault. I didn't understand it, but I figured it was something I was doing wrong" (30).

Charlie Greene's wife, Marci, recalls,

> At the time, Cher didn't know the first thing about being a girl, which was strange because her mother's one of the most glamorous creatures I've ever seen. But Cher knew from nothing. I can't blame her. Her background had been very, very poor. She had very long hair and she used to iron it. That was what she did. She had none of the basics. No clothes sense; no clothes. She never wore anything. She'd take the same jeans off the floor she'd worn the day before and put them on—day after day (29).

According to Cher, "I was living by my wits. Belligerent. Sarcastic. People kept away from me. I was Sadie Thompson on the outside. But still a secret, heavenly star on the inside" (31).

She was staying with one of her girlfriends when she met the man who was going to change her life. His name was Sonny Bono, and he was working for the famous hit-making record producer Phil Spector. Sonny's claim to fame at that point was the fact that he and Jack Nitzsche wrote a hit song that was recorded by Jackie DeShannon—and later by the Searchers—called "Needles and Pins." It was the success of that song that helped land him the job as Spector's assistant.

Sonny Bono was born Salvatore Phillip Bono on February 16, 1935, in Detroit, Michigan. He moved with his parents to Los Angeles, and before he discovered that he had a knack for writing hit songs, he held several odd jobs as a waiter, a truck driver, a construction worker, and a butcher's assistant. When he was thirteen years old, Sonny was working in a grocery store, and while unloading boxes of Coco Joe's cookies, he jotted down a song idea he entitled "Koko Joe." It was first recorded by Don & Dewey, and a few years later, the Righteous Brothers recorded it.

Another one of his songs, "She Said 'Yeah,' " was recorded by Larry Williams in 1958. The Rolling Stones were later to revive it in 1965 on their *December's Children (and Everybody's)* album. At the time that he wrote these songs though, his track record for success was spotty at best.

However, he was totally hooked on music. According to Sonny, "As long as I can remember, I said, 'I'm gonna get into music.' I've always wanted to be involved in music—I never really had any other thought growing up. So it wasn't 'Do I wanna be a doctor? Do I wanna be a lawyer?' I just wanted to be in music. So I just kept doing it until I figured out how to get there" (32).

By 1958, Salvatore found himself married to Donna Rankin, and the couple had a daughter named Christy. Taking both of their first names, he called himself Don Christy, and began making the rounds of the record companies in a attempt to sell a song he had recorded called "High School Dance." Another song he penned and recorded, "Wearing Black," never went anywhere either. Instead of focusing on him as a singer, a company hired him as a record producer, and soon he was in the music business. By the time he hooked up with Phil Spector, his marriage had dissolved, and he was floating around from apartment to apartment.

In 1963, when Cher left home, she moved in with her girlfriend Melissa Melcher, and she landed a job at a See's candy shop. "A girlfriend

of mine said she wanted to introduce me to this nice guy who was supposed to be kinda famous," Cher remembers of her first encounter with
Sonny Bono (33).

> I was in a huge restaurant, and I didn't know him, but everyone else did.
> They said, "There's Sonny," and I swear to God, I saw him walk through
> the door, everyone else faded away. I just saw him—this thin guy with long
> black hair, Beatle boots, and a gold chain around his hand. I was knocked
> out. I didn't think he was handsome, but I'd never seen anyone with long
> hair and boots and stuff like that. All my girlfriends said, "He's kind of ugly,
> he has a big nose, and he's strange-looking. You could do a lot better." But
> there was something about him. He was good, stable, older—sweet. He
> was a record promoter. He had just left his wife and he liked my girlfriend,
> the one I was staying with, but she didn't like him at all (18).

Telling his side of the story, Sonny Bono recalled their first meeting
slightly differently. According to him, "When I met Cher, I was a [record]
promotion man. I went to a radio station, and then I went to Aldo's, where
we all went for coffee. There's Cher with her boyfriend. The only other girl
that was available was her girlfriend, who was a good looker too. Then we
all went out—me and the other girl. That didn't pan out at all" (32).

According to Sonny in his 1991 autobiography *And the Beat Goes On,*
the next night the foursome met again at Aldo's. Cher was with Sonny's
fellow promotion man, Red,[1] and Sonny was paired with Melissa. After
dinner and a lot of red wine, Melissa and Cher announced that they
wanted to go dancing at a place that neither Red nor Sonny had heard
of—it was called Club 86. However, they were game for a little dancing.
After the foursome arrived at Club 86, and were escorted to a table,
Sonny and Red realized that they were the only men in the whole place.
The girls had taken them to a lesbian bar! Sonny was even more confused
when Cher and Melissa got up and went to dance—with each other. Following a few uncomfortable minutes, the men announced to their dates
that they wanted to leave. Cher obliged, but Melissa decided to stay.
Sonny recalls that Cher, who was seated in the front seat of the car, kept
talking to him in the backseat, while Red drove the car. Sonny simply
assumed that he and Red had just had a joke played on them by the girls,
and figured that he would probably never see them again anyway.

1. In his autobiography *And the Beat Goes On,* Sonny Bono recalls that Red's last
name is Turner; in her autobiography *The First Time,* Cher gives Red's last name
as Baldwin.

Regardless of whose memory of their first meeting is clearer, or more accurate, it wasn't long before their paths did indeed cross again. Oddly enough, Sonny ended up renting the apartment next door to the one that Cher and Melissa were sharing. As Cher explains it, "This was when me and my girlfriend lived on Fountain Avenue, and well, Sonny moved in next door. He didn't know we were next door. So, I thought that was kind of neat. I went over to see him and we water-colored all day. He was really terrible too. So, that night, he asked me to go to Safeway [grocery store] with him. Yeah, real romantic" (33).

Sonny was to recall, "I was very attracted to her" (32). Due to the Club 86 adventure, Sonny also wondered about Cher's sexual preferences, although she denied that she was gay. He was also amazed by her use of foul language, which dotted her conversation as though she had learned English from a truck driver. Sonny chalked it up to her wanting to act more adult.

From the very start, Cher's affair with Sonny was unconventional at best. Yet there was a growing bond between them. Cher recalls, "I had a date with another guy that night, but I didn't want to get involved in that so I kind of cooled it. I got home around three o'clock that night and went over to see if Sonny was up. Well . . . he was in bed with some other girl and wouldn't even answer the door. That really pissed me off!" she remembers.

Then my girlfriend split and left me with all these bills, and I lost my job, and my mother was going to make me come home. So Sonny said, "Well, I'll tell you something. I don't find you particularly attractive, but you can stay in my house." He said, "Can you cook?" I said, "No," and he said, "All right, I'll pay everything and you keep the house clean and we'll do it." So I told my mother I was living with a stewardess, and it seemed like a good thing at the time. We stayed in the same room. I remember waking up one time, I'd had a really bad dream, and I said, "Sonny can I get in bed with you?" And he said, "Yes, but don't bother me." And I said, "O.K." And we just lived there together for ages. It took a long time for the relationship and if he can't he doesn't mess with you. It wasn't a fiery, sexy thing with us, but rather paternal, like we were bound together, two people who needed each other, almost for protection (18).

According to her, "It was platonic for a long while. I was more an annoyance to him, a silly kid, but I had a crush on him" (16).

Somehow, whenever Georgia was going to visit Cher at the apartment that she supposedly shared with a stewardess, she would call ahead. Says Cher of such hastily announced visitations, "I'd rush around, collect all of Sonny's clothes and dump them through the window into Melissa's place right across the way. One day Melissa was sitting at the table with some guests when a shower of Sonny's belongings descended on everyone. She just said, 'Oh, Cher's mother must be on the way' " (17).

Sonny Bono claimed that he was attracted to her simultaneous combination of maturity and immaturity. "When I met her she was sixteen and a waif," he explained.

> On one hand, she was a very mature kid. She had dealt with life and men on an adult level—she skipped the teenage stage. But on the other, she was a very naive little girl. She would walk around our house and sing her ass off. It drove me crazy. But in the first two weeks I knew her, I told her I felt that she would be a great star. That's what she wanted (17).

Although Cher had a bit of a rough exterior at the time, Sonny claimed that he spotted something special about her. "When I met Cher I knew she was going to be something great," he remembered. "I told her then that I thought she was a flower that hadn't blossomed yet but she would, and the whole world would know it. I knew then that if I didn't have something, it wouldn't work between us. I knew I had to do something, too, so I wouldn't just be a nebbish" (34).

Cher was the first to admit that she used to mask her insecurities with foul language and aggressive behavior; she developed a caustic attitude for protection.

> When I was younger, I was chicken and poor, which isn't hip, because you haven't got clothes and all that stuff. So I developed S.M.B. "Smart Mouth Bitch." Which meant, "Don't screw with me, because I may not have clothes or what everyone else has, but I can cut you to ribbons." When I met Sonny, I had that reputation; gave him the finger and all that. But after I'd been with him for about six months, I was so different. I wasn't allowed to say "fuck" or "hell" or "damn." With Sonny, that part of my personality was just tucked away (18).

In other words, Sonny and Cher inspired each other to refine themselves and get their acts together.

Cher's mother finally caught wind of her living arrangements with Sonny and decided to put an immediate end to their relationship. According to Georgia Holt, "Cher really had matured. Sonny just hung around the house. We didn't know he was married at first. At least I didn't. He and his wife were separated. When I found out Sonny was eleven years older than Cher and had a wife and a daughter, I didn't want him around my baby girl" (11).

Then, when Cher was suddenly absent, Sonny realized that he was really in love with her. According to Cher,

> Sonny and I kept going out and one day he's thinking, "Well, maybe I ought to ask you to marry me, huh?" I said, "I dunno." Then he bought this little diamond on a chain, just the cutest little thing, and he came home and got me out of the bath, and so he said, "Maybe I ought to propose to you, huh?" I said, "I still dunno." So that was kind of our engagement. Mother didn't like him and decided to take me to Arkansas to forget about him. Arkansas was a terrible place. It only made me think about him even more (33).

Recalls her mother of their Arkansas trip,

> We were gone for three weeks, but Cher didn't simmer down. It's strange, but at that time Sonny was the spitting image of her father, Johnny Sarkisian. I think the father image had a great deal to do with Cher's feelings, but I didn't think it would have helped it I'd told that to Cher. When a girl is as much in love with a man as she was, not much can be done about it (11).

Still determined, Georgia decided that the trip to Arkansas wasn't severe enough to shake Cher to her senses, so she took her to a home for wayward girls. Remembers Cher, "I had to move into this home for girls in El Centro. There were about ten truck drivers per room. Really heavy bull dykes. I was introduced to a few of them my first night there. One girl, Alex—I don't know what her real name was—she told me about this guy she loved and I told her about Sonny. I don't know what happened to her" (33). Anyway, Cher discovered that nothing could keep her and Sonny apart, and back to him she fled. "I was kind of impressed with Sonny," she says. "He was the first guy to ever treat me well, to hold doors open for me. He took me to nice little places, like this little pizza place" (34).

While Cher was out of town with her mother, Sonny had a one-night stand with a woman named Mimi. Sonny was lonely, and thought nothing of it at the time. However, a couple of months later, Mimi informed Sonny that she was pregnant, and it was his child. Sonny made a financial settlement, and Mimi gave birth to a son named Sean. According to Sonny, he told Cher the whole story, and she wasn't upset. "It was

strange," claimed Sonny, "Our relationship wasn't overly physical anyway, so maybe she felt some of the pressure was off her to perform" (35).
Yet, they were still very much in love.

Meanwhile, back at Phil Spector's Gold Star Studios, in Hollywood,
California, the producer was busy pumping out classic pop records by the
Ronettes, the Crystals, Darlene Love, and Bob B. Soxx & the Blue Jeans.
The interesting thing about the Crystals was the fact that although there
was a group of girls known as the Crystals, there could be any number of
different girls on each record. Frequently, the lead vocal would be sung
by Darlene Love. According to her, "My voice was on mostly all those
lead songs. Spector put the Crystals name on them, Bob B. Soxx & the
Blue Jeans, Darlene Love, nobody knew the difference" (13). Recording
under several different names, including her own, Darlene Love is
responsible for being the sound of more different acts' hits than any other
star in rock and roll.

Darlene recalls first meeting Cher at Gold Star Studios: "Sonny started
bringing this girl with him. She was tattered-looking with straight hair and
really dark make-up" (36). It wasn't long before Cher was a permanent fix-
ture at the studio. As long as Sonny was there, Cher was there too.

Songwriter Ellie Greenwich ("River Deep, Mountain High"), who
worked with Spector, explains of Phil Spector's operation, "He also
owned most of the names, so he had the right to make whoever he
wanted to be the Crystals" (13). This demonstrated very clearly to Sonny
how any one performer or group of performers could actually have several different personas—like he and Cher eventually did.

When Cher returned to Los Angeles, she and Sonny resumed their
unconventional but very strong love affair. Sonny was driven by a desire to
turn Cher into a singing star. Although at times she was painfully shy, she
kept telling him how much she wanted to be a huge star one day. He was
determined to make her dream come true. It became his top priority.

Together they completely meshed. Sonny and Cher were like two misfits who somehow fit together. Recalls Cher of their chemistry, "We were
both very strange people, very unmainstream, and when we came
together, we weren't freaky anymore for each other. We fit each other.
We both had the same kind of dreams, and we liked the same thing. We
thought the same thing was cool" (28).

One night at the recording studio Cher was hanging out with him and
watching all of the activity during one of Spector's sessions. That particular evening Phil was working on a new song by the Ronettes called "Be

My Baby." According to legend, Darlene Love didn't show up to record her background part of the song, and they needed another voice on the record. As Cher recalls, "Somebody said to me, 'Can you sing?' I said, 'No.' He said, 'Well, can you carry a tune?' I said, 'Yeah.' And he said, 'Well, get out there because we need some noise.' From that time on, I did all the dates" (37). Voila! Cher was on a hit record!

Although she was very shy in the recording studio, Cher loved the idea of making records and hanging out in the studio with Darlene, Ronnie Spector (lead singer of the Ronettes), and Sonny. As she was later to recall of Spector's music factory, "It was a time when girl singers were patted on the head for being good and told not to think" (24).

At Gold Star Studios, she also got the chance to meet several of the musicians. Remembers Cher, "I met Glen Campbell at one session when he was just a guitarist. He wanted to take me out and he asked Sonny if it was all right. Sonny said, 'Yeah, I don't care.' I thought, 'Wow, that's a fine way to talk with me right in front of him' " (33). According to Sonny, she was flirting with Glen just to make him jealous. Perhaps it was her way of retaliating for Sonny's affair with Mimi. Glen kept hitting on Cher, and she kept teasingly flirting with him. Finally Sonny and Cher had a big argument, and then they were back together again, stronger than ever.

Not long after she turned eighteen, Cher informed Sonny that she was pregnant. They were both very happy about the prospect of being parents. At the time, Cher kept this a secret from her mother. Unfortunately, Cher suddenly suffered the first in a series of miscarriages.

Cher claims that at the time, Sonny could have talked her into just about anything. She was in total awe of him. "I was the young student," she was to point out. "I took every opinion he had and made it my own" (16).

After Cher had sung on several of Spector's greatest hits—including "Da Doo Ron Ron" by the Crystals, "Be My Baby" by the Ronettes, and "You've Lost That Lovin' Feelin' " by the Righteous Brothers—Sonny hoped that everyone else at Gold Star Studios would see his skinny live-in girlfriend in a new light. He wanted to make her into a recording star and thought that Phil Spector would jump at the chance. It didn't happen immediately, but one night Phil invited Sonny out for a drive in his car. Sonny got into Phil's car, and during their drive, Phil told him that he had an idea for a song that could be recorded by Cher. The song was called "I Love You Ringo." Since the Beatles were currently dominating the radio airwaves in America, Phil figured that this would be a perfect way to capitalize on the whole Beatles craze. Sonny loved the idea.

Cher recorded the song, with Phil producing. The record was sold to Sceptor Records, and it was released under the fictional name "Bonnie Jo Mason." According to Cher, the name change was Phil's idea. It was his theory that in order to have a hit single in America, you had to have an all-American–sounding name. Unfortunately, the record was an instant flop. Still finding her solo singing voice, Cher sang the song in a very low key. "I sounded too much like a boy," says Cher of the recording. "Everyone thought it was a faggot song" (13). Back to the drawing board.

Not long after that, Sonny decided to take some of his own money and make a record with Cher. In October of 1964, Bono composed a song called "Dream Baby" for Cher. It was released on Imperial Records, and in order to leave the failure of Bonnie Jo Mason behind, this single was released as a solo recording by "Cherilyn." The song was also clearly produced to mimic Phil Spector's famous "Wall of Sound" method of recording. This formula would call for multitracking of the instruments and voices so that a handful of studio musicians would sound like a rock and roll orchestra. Although "Dream Baby" perfectly fit the formula, the single was not a success. More fine-tuning on the act was necessary.

Expounding upon what he had been taught by Spector, Sonny Bono was to explain,

I learned everything from Phil. I could never write commercially. I was writing, but I couldn't do it commercially. My favorite thing Phil used to say to me was "Hey Sonny, is it dumb enough?" And I'd go, "What's he saying to me?" What he meant was that it was simple and had a "hook." He termed that "dumb." I started to understand that in my writing, and that ingredient had to be there (32).

With regard to the trademark sound that all of Phil Spector's productions had, Bono said,

"The Wall of Sound" in itself is basically . . . [sound] leakage. What he'd do was line up three pianos and they would create their own echo. It [the sound] would come back down and wind up in another microphone, say the drummer's microphone. There was this echo going on in the room as we were performing and that basically was the "Wall of Sound," and he was able to control that. . . . I learned that and then just moved on when Phil and I stopped working together (38).

Sonny wanted to make Cher into a solo star, but she needed some exposure—and some self-confidence. According to legend, the first time she was in the recording booth, she was so frightened that she couldn't sing unless Sonny was standing right next to her, singing with her.

It was the session to record what turned out to be the duo's first single, "Baby Don't Go," which was recorded at RCA Studios using the musicians from Phil Spector's stable from Gold Star, including Leon Russell, Barney Kessel, and Don Randy. According to Cher, they were so broke that they convinced the musicians to play for free. It was intended to be a solo recording for Cher, but once she forced Sonny to sing along with her on the chorus, it became a Sonny & Cher classic. As long as Sonny was by her side, Cher felt that she could accomplish anything.

Cher was also mortified by the idea of singing live onstage in front of people, so they hit upon the idea that they could work as a team. With Sonny up on the stage with her, she would overcome her stage fright. They decided to call themselves "Caesar & Cleo." Explains Cher, "A lot of people [had] called Sonny's hairstyle a Caesar cut because there were no Beatles as a reference point at that time. And because Elizabeth Taylor had just come out with [the 1963 film] *Cleopatra,* everybody said we looked like Caesar and Cleopatra. So that's what we called ourselves at first, Caesar & Cleo" (6).

To complete the Cleopatra look, Cher began to wear her eye makeup in the exaggerated fashion of ancient Egypt. She would color her upper lash line with a fine black mascara brush, drawing the black line to the side of her face in points a good half-inch past her eye. Mimicking the Egyptian tradition of kohl-lined eye makeup, she had a look that was uniquely her own.

Caesar & Cleo were far from an instant hit. Their first public performance was at a roller rink and their second was at a bowling alley. They then landed a gig at the Hollywood club called the Purple Onion. The only reason they got the booking was that Georgia's brother Mickey was the owner. Cher remembers the outfit that she wore for their first performance as Caesar & Cleo: a shell beaded top, beige crepe pants, and high heels. "In the beginning we were trying to have this kind of 'Dick and Deedee' look. Sonny bought a suit, and I got a dress" (6).

Sonny even got a record deal for Caesar & Cleo with Reprise Records. The deal was for three singles only. If any of them became hits, the company could offer them a long-term deal. They proceeded to record three cover versions of other people's hits that were each released as singles by the company. The three songs were "Do You Wanna Dance," "Love Is Strange," and "Let The Goodtimes Roll." Somehow Caesar & Cleo weren't making any waves in the record world, so taking a lesson from Phil Spector with regard to changing the names of a recording artist to suit a project, Bono and Sarkisian went back into the recording studio and made a record under a different name: "Sonny & Cher." The record was a recording of a song that Sonny had written called "Baby Don't Go." He turned around and sold it to Reprise Records, who had no idea that "Sonny & Cher" were actually the Reprise Records unsuccessful duo, "Caesar & Cleo."

By this point Sonny had brought himself and Cher to the attention of two personal managers named Charlie Greene and Brian Stone. They believed in the fledgling singing duo so much that they were willing to financially go out on a limb to get a record released by the duo. According to Greene, "I hocked my typewriters for that first record, 'Baby Don't Go.' Got $168, you know. It was just a West Coast hit anyway" (33).

Another song, called "The Letter," also written by Sonny and recorded by Sonny & Cher, was released on Vault Records and also went nowhere. Then ATCO Records signed Sonny & Cher to their label and cut a single with "It's Gonna Rain" on one side and "I Got You Babe" on the other side, both of which Bono wrote.

According to Cher, she was not impressed with "I Got You Babe" the first time she heard it. Sonny used to compose all of his songs on an old upright piano he bought for $85. They were broke at the time, and they were staying with their managers, Brian and Charlie, and their respective girlfriends. Sonny had to keep the piano in their garage, because there was nowhere else to put it. Back then he did all of his best writing in the middle of the night, writing on used cardboards that the local cleaners would fold his shirts with. Cher was asleep when he came bounding into the house one night, waving some notes on one of his lucky shirt cardboards. Reluctantly, she accompanied him back to the garage. Cher had wanted him to write her a song that had a key modulation in the middle of it, similar to what had been done in one of Jackie DeShannon's recent hits. Sonny began singing the song, reading his notes and lyrics from the shirt cardboard it was inscribed upon. Although she wasn't thrilled with the lyrics of "I Got You Babe," Cher loved that he had put the modulation in the middle of it for her. She thanked him for putting the modulation in as per her request, but told him that she didn't think it was among his best work. Little did she know at the time, but that one simple pop ballad that Sonny sang to her that night was going to become the duo's instantly recognizable signature song.

Sonny was to recall that he got into a big argument with the president of Atlantic/ATCO Records, Ahmet Ertegun, as to which side of the single to promote as the "A" side. Regarding the evolution of Sonny & Cher's trademark hit, Bono explained,

> At the time, [Bob] Dylan was always going "Babe this, babe that." [The word] "babe" was all over the streets. I thought, "Man, that's a hook if you ever use it right." Philip [Spector] would always play that kind of 6/8 rhythm, so I could duplicate that 6/8 rhythm. You play and sing until a hook came in. . . . and "I Got You Babe" came in. I knew the hook was real strong. I knew that was the one. I was looking for a song that would get us past where we were with "Just You" and "Baby Don't Go"—those did well, but I was looking for that song that would create the rocket. We cut it and on the other side I cut "It's Gonna Rain." I wrote it in about four minutes and sent the demo to Ahmet Ertegun at Atlantic Records. So Ahmet goes, "Man, that's the greatest song!" He said he wanted to put out "It's Gonna Rain" right away. I said, "Ahmet, wrong song!" So he goes, "No, no." We had this big fight over that. He was gonna push "It's Gonna Rain." So we took "I Got You Babe" to [radio station] KHJ and [disc jockey] Ron Jacobs liked the right side. So I said, "Put it on the air," and he gave it an exclusive. Now the record company had to go with "I Got You Babe" (32).

The single was released, and "I Got You Babe" raced up the charts, hitting Number 1 in America. It eventually sold four million copies. In 1965, after trying to have a hit by Bonnie Jo Mason, Cherilyn, Don Christy, and Caesar & Cleo, Cherilyn Sarkisian and Salvatore Bono finally found overnight fame as Sonny & Cher. Their journey as pop stars had officially begun.

Around this same time, Sonny and Cher had decided that they needed a whole new "look" all their own, and Cher began designing her own bizarre-looking bell-bottom pants, and Sonny came up with this crazy idea of taking animal skins and making fur vests with them.

With regard to his own unique look, Bono was to recall,

> The "caveman" look came from Phil [Spector]! Phil had long hair before the Beatles and anybody—he was the first hippie that I had ever met. Phil was this real unique dresser. He had vests and he'd have this and that— Phil liked to be different than anybody. Then our clique—[Jack] Nitzsche, Nino Tempo, and me—all of us started dressing individually. We all personally had little contests to see who could come up with their own little clothes (32).

Out of their outlandish costume competition, "the Sonny Bono look" was born, and it is still one of the most indelible fashion images of the mid-1960s rock and roll era.

Due to the tremendous success of "I Got You Babe," Sonny & Cher were seen on all the hottest pop music television programs, sporting clothes and a fashion sense that were uniquely their own. No one had ever seen outfits quite like theirs. Between his fur vests and her unique one-of-a-kind bell-bottom pants, they created an instant fashion trend. Sonny & Cher were "Bohemians," nonconformists, and hippies, long before the term "hippie" was ever coined to describe the counterestablishment style that characterized the latter half of the 1960s. It was Cher who single-handedly popularized the whole fashion of wearing bell-bottoms, a fashion trend that lasted well into the 1970s.

Explains Cher of the evolution of their wardrobe, "We had these two friends, Bridget and Colleen. They were my girlfriends and they were real space cadets. I mean they were terrific, but they were really spacey chicks—and Bridget was into making clothes. We'd pool our money, I'd design things, and they'd make them. We were crazy dressers" (18). According to her,

> When I met Bridget, she had on these grommeted and laced up suede bell-bottoms, and I just said, well, that's what I want! I'd sent away to England for some pantsuits from the back of a magazine and the first thing I got was a tobacco-colored small-waled corduroy suit, double-breasted with stovepipe pants—real hip-huggers with big, wide belt loops, and a poor-boy shirt, the first one I'd ever seen. I got all of it from England and it was really cool, but when I saw the bell-bottoms I thought that was for me. They were nice, but then we developed something we called "elephant bells." I don't remember how many inches across they were, something like twenty-five or thirty inches [diameter at the widest point of the hem]. They were really ridiculous, because when you walked they just flapped back and forth. My mother [has] saved some of those for me (39).

Due to the success of their hit record, Sonny & Cher began appearing on a host of nationally broadcast American television shows like *Shindig, Hullaballoo, The Lloyd Thaxton Show,* and the most important record-launching program of them all, Dick Clark's *American Bandstand.* Even on *Shindig,* recalls Cher, they looked strange next to all of the groups in beaded dresses and suits. "We weren't really accepted there," she says, "because of the way we looked. It's weird, you know, people forget that the early sixties were still suffering from a bad case of Doris Day and Rock Hudson." Says Cher, "We were thrown out of every fucking place you can imagine. People were constantly trying to punch Sonny out because of the way he looked" (6).

While Sonny & Cher began producing a string of hits like "Just You," "But You're Mine," "What Now My Love," and "Little Man," Cher was simultaneously signed to a solo recording contract on Imperial Records. It wasn't long before her Sonny-produced hits like "All I Really Want to Do," "Bang Bang (My Baby Shot Me Down)," and "Where Do You Go" were also huge successes on the record charts. Since Sonny produced the "Sonny & Cher" records and the "Cher" records, owned publishing rights on all of his compositions, and was getting a percentage of the profits as a producer on the recordings, the couple was suddenly making a lot of money, in fact much more than most of their contemporaries on the pop charts.

In 1965, when Imperial Records sent out the official first "biography" to press members, the media got to know Cher La Piere. Describing her background, the bio explained,

> Cher, who has just turned 19, had seemed more destined for an acting career than one in music. Her mother has been acting in Hollywood for a number of years and started Cher off on a dramatic career a few years ago by engaging one of Hollywood's leading acting teachers, Jeff Corey, to tutor Cher. Aside from her two and one half years of study with Jeff, Cher also kept busy with dancing lessons. It has only been in the last year, working diligently with Sonny, that Cher has come into her own as a vocalist (40).

In an effort to tone down the impact of Sonny & Cher's outrageous outfits and unconventional appearance, it was decided that they be represented to the press and to the public as a wild-looking but very stable married couple. The only minor detail out of kilter was the fact that Sonny and Cher were not really married at all. In fact, they had been lying to the press whenever the question came up in conversation, claiming—falsely—that they had eloped in 1964.

To make it seem real in their own minds, Sonny and Cher had decided that they would perform their own ceremony and exchange vows. There was an old Indian trading shop near the corner of Hollywood and Vine, and Cher found a pair of cheap gold-plated rings in a basket there. For an extra twenty-five cents, names could be added to them. They splurged and bought the rings. The ceremony they performed was done in the bathroom of their apartment.

Remembers Brian Stone,

> We knew they were just living together, and they felt there was no reason to get married. But in mid-1965, when they became pop stars and the hottest young couple in America, role models for young marrieds around the world, we knew that they had to get married—legally. Sonny wanted nothing to do with it. He knew it would be impossible for them to walk into a Justice of the Peace and get married in secret. And if they were spotted going into a chapel, it would be like announcing that they'd been lying all along. So we came up with a scheme to go to Mexico and pay some registry official to backdate a marriage certificate for them for $7,500. But Sonny said, "You aren't going to waste my money on that." Sonny and Cher just never wanted to bother with marriage, even though they kept telling people they'd been married in September 1964. We had to remind them that, if they were going to claim they were married, they couldn't say it happened until at least October 1964—when Sonny's divorce from his former wife, Donna, took effect (41).

Brian claims that once things got started for Sonny & Cher, their success just snowballed. However, Cher hated getting on stage in front of an audience. Says Stone, "Sonny could just take a swig of bourbon before a show, but Cher hated performing in front of an audience. Sonny or Charlie or myself would coax her, but once we got her to the dressing room, it was O.K. Then Sonny would help her with her make-up and hair, and she'd be ready to go" (41).

In the summer of 1965, as "I Got You Babe" was logging two weeks at Number 1 on the American music charts, when the duo arrived in New York City for personal appearances and publicity, they were refused admittance to the Americana Hotel in Manhattan, because of their unconventional appearance. This ended up giving them even more publicity.

In August of 1965, ATCO Records released the duo's debut album, *Look at Us*. On the cover is Sonny with his now-famous bobcat vest and Cher with her flat, chest-length hair, cut into bangs at eyebrow level. Photographed between two tree trunks, in an instant frozen in time, Sonny & Cher gave the public its first image of themselves. The album features their first hit single, the impassioned "I Got You Babe." Exploring the subject of love, unrequited love, or devoted love, Sonny & Cher covered several hits of the day, including "Unchained Melody," "500

Miles," "Then He Kissed Me," "You've Really Got a Hold on Me," and even Phil Spector's "Why Don't They Let Us Fall in Love." Sonny also used the album to showcase four of his own compositions, including "Just You," "It's Gonna Rain," "Sing C'est La Vie," and of course "I Got You Babe."

For the sake of typeface and font trivia, on all of these first album releases, Cher spelled her name with an accent above the "e," appearing in print as Chér. The accent mark gave her name an exotic and classy European look . However, by the mid-1970s she began dropping the accent mark, which was usually neglected by media typesetters anyway. Viva la Chér!

On August 31, 1965, Sonny & Cher flew to London for the first time, and the British Isles have never been the same. Since "the British invasion" of musical acts was taking place in the United States in 1965, Sonny & Cher and their managers decided that they would use reverse psychology and head from America to England. Well, they were noticed in London, in such a big way that they were refused admittance to the Hilton Hotel when they went to register for their room. Sonny was wearing a "cavalier" or "pirate" shirt with puffy sleeves gathered at the wrist, a pair of striped pants, his Fred Flintstone–like bobcat vest, and a pair of calf-high, fur-covered boots. Cher was clad in a Union Jack–designed red, white, and blue top and pants, and on her feet she wore red leather Capezio shoes with thread-spool heels.

When Sonny and Cher strode into the lobby of the London Hilton at nine o'clock in the morning, two photographers popped up and began flashing shot after shot of the hit-making American singing duo. They were promptly escorted out of the front door and told not to return. When the newspaper, the *Daily Telegraph,* came out that afternoon, there was Sonny & Cher on the cover, being thrown out of the Hilton. Before the day was over, they were instantly famous from Trafalgar Square to Buckingham Palace. Four days later they were invited to appear on the hit ITV show *Ready, Steady, Go!,* which immediately propelled "I Got You Babe" into the stratosphere.

Remembers Cher of the fashion sensation they created in London,

No one knew who we were, but by the first night, our picture was on the cover of every newspaper because we'd been thrown out of the Hilton [hotel] for the way we looked. I had on one of my pride-and-joy outfits. It was red, white and blue striped bell-bottoms with an industrial zipper with a big ring on it. And a top with big bell sleeves and a pair of red shoes. And Sonny had a pair of striped pants and his dress Eskimo boots, real beautiful, and he had on his bobcat vest and a big shirt. The people in England loved it. They didn't even think we were American. You know, American rock & roll at that time was zilch. Everything was the Beatles, and Dave Clark, and the Stones (18).

Being tossed out of the Hilton Hotel was such a big publicity push for Sonny & Cher that Bono later immortalized the incident in the song "See See Rider," which Cher recorded on her 1965 solo debut album, *All I Really Want to Do*. In the lyrics of the song she sings, "I'm going to the Hilton, and I know I won't get in." They may not have let them in, but thanks to the Hilton incident, everyone in England instantly knew who they were.

While they were in London, Sonny & Cher performed at the 100 Club on Oxford Street and appeared in every magazine and newspaper in town, and their single "I Got You Babe" began a two-week run at the top of the British music charts. Their stay in London caused a huge splash of media attention, and overnight success. In a week they had gone from total unknowns to instant celebrities who were hanging out with the "who's who" of mid-1960s London.

According to Charlie Greene,

When we went to England with them, Sonny got upset with John Lennon. We were in a London club when Lennon sent his bodyguard over to ask Cher to join him. We all went over. Paul McCartney was there with a beautiful model. Sonny wanted to talk business, but Lennon and Cher were talking to each other, and Sonny didn't like it. You could see he was annoyed. There were other times on that concert tour of England when Sonny got angry because Cher was flirting with Roger Daltry, and she had an eye for Rod Stewart. Sonny wouldn't be a tourist with Cher, but she did have her sister Georganne along for the trip. Sonny preferred for Cher to stay at home at night and read magazines and watch TV (41).

One of the things that Sonny and Cher enjoyed the most about their trip to London was the trendy shopping. They shopped at the chic store Anello and David, where the Beatles were known to buy their distinctive-looking boots. And they shopped at Granny Takes a Trip, where Sonny stocked up on fashionable Carnaby Street–style shirts and pants, and Cher purchased her first-ever fur coat—a double-breasted rabbit pelt garment.

Greene also revealed of Sonny during this era,

> He liked to see other women. When we stayed at hotels, Sonny would take
> an extra suite, and when Cher was asleep, he'd go there and call out for
> hookers. Sonny would show them a big wad of bills, maybe $20,000, and
> he'd peel off $500 and give it to them. He would just talk to them—about
> himself. But he did have some unusual hobbies. He had a telescope and
> would peer into windows with it. The funny part was that although Sonny
> was so interested in women, we were always denying rumors he was gay.
> He had long hair, and he wore those flowered pants, and people asked
> questions (41).

In September of 1965, Sonny & Cher's debut album, *Look at Us,* was
certified Gold by the Record Industry Association of America (RIAA) for
over 500,000 copies sold. It peaked at Number 2, remaining in that position on the *Billboard* album charts for eight weeks.

Meanwhile, Cher's first solo album, *All I Really Want to Do,* peaked
at Number 16 in America, and Number 7 in England. In November of
1965 another single from the LP, "Where Do You Go," written by Sonny,
was released as a single. It peaked at Number 25 in the United States. In
September of 1965, Sonny's "Laugh at Me" hit Number 10 in the United
States, and Number 11 in England. Sonny, Cher, or Sonny & Cher were
all over the airwaves throughout 1965. They were on the first ascension
up the roller-coaster ride that was to be the nature of their professional
careers and their personal lives.

The story of "Laugh at Me" is entirely autobiographical, and has to do
with Sonny being expelled from a chic Los Angeles restaurant.

> Thanks to Martoni's. What happened, when we dressed like we did, and
> my hair was almost like it is now, and Cher's [long straight] hair, and the
> way we dressed. . . . we used to go into Martoni's all the time. They were
> friends of ours. But, to dress like that in '64, '65, it was a real conservative
> era. People would think you're strange or gay or weird or freaky or what-
> ever, and it was a real threat to people. We knew it caused a reaction and
> that's why we stuck to it. But, it would also cause a hostile reaction with
> some people. So when you went into a restaurant like Martoni's we'd get
> some tough times. One time, some guys just wanted to beat me up. I got
> on the phone while I was eating there, and we had friends then that were
> killers, so we threw them out of the restaurant! So Mario Antoni got mad.
> I said, "What are you getting mad for? They were gonna beat the hell out

of me. And I asked you to move the guys and you didn't." So they said, "Don't ever come back again." I said, "Come on, you're my friends." And they said "no." Both Cher and I felt real dejected. That night, we went home, she went to bed and I wrote "Laugh At Me," which was really over that incident. Then we recorded it. It was the only hit that I had as "Sonny Bono" (38).

In addition to "Laugh at Me," in 1965 Sonny released his second single, "The Revolution Kind." In December of that year it peaked at Number 70 on the *Billboard* charts in America.

It was also in 1965 that Cher and Sonny made their movie debut. The early 1960s witnessed a huge tidal wave of surfer movies like *Beach Party* (1963), *Beach Blanket Bingo* (1965), *Beach Ball* (1965), *Dr. Goldfoot and the Bikini Machine* (1965), and *Ride the Wild Surf* (1964). These films were usually light on plot, heavy on bikinis and bronzed bodies, and featured performers like Lesley Gore, the Supremes, the Four Seasons, James Brown, or other up-and-coming pop stars of the day who would make cameo musical appearances. Usually they would show up in a concert sequence at the local surfers' hangout. The movie that Sonny & Cher appeared in was entitled *Wild on the Beach*. The film starred Frankie Randall, Sherry Jackson, Cindy Malone, and Sandy Nelson, and the musical guests included Jackie & Gayle, the Astronauts, and last but not least Sonny & Cher. In the plot, the girls in the cast have rented a beach house, only to find that a group of boys have also leased the same house— with comical consequences. In a beachside club scene Sonny & Cher perform their song "It's Gonna Rain," which appeared on their first album, *Look at Us*.

Due to the media blitz that took place in London when Sonny & Cher were thrown out of the Hilton Hotel, they were considered big media stars in England. When Twiggy came to the United States with her boyfriend Justin, it was Sonny & Cher who led the Hollywood greeting committee. And when the Rolling Stones arrived in Los Angeles on their first visit to California, they were Sonny and Cher's houseguests. According to Cher, "When the Stones came to America for the first time, they wanted to stay with us. [I said,] 'We haven't got any furniture.' They said, 'That's O.K., we'll rent cots,' because they were really uptight around the people they were with over here. No one looked like them, and they felt insecure" (18).

Overnight success can be a strange thing to handle, especially when you've lived the majority of your life not having any money at all. Remembers Cher,

Being eighteen and walking on a stage and hearing ten thousand people screaming and yelling your name—the whole thing can make you lose all concept of who you are. Sometimes I'd get off the stage with my clothes and sometimes I wouldn't. But, overall, Sonny kept on top of the situation for me. I was like a worker in a beehive, mostly, just doing my gig (18).

Just after she became a singing star, Cher went on a shopping spree that she'll never forget, mainly for the lesson that she learned from it.

I went into this store one day, just in my regular duds, and I saw a Rudi Gernrich outfit that I wanted. I asked this saleslady "Can you tell me what colors you have this outfit in?" She said, "It's a very expensive outfit." I said, "O.K. What colors does it come in?" "Well," she said, "it comes in red and black, green and yellow, and purple and red." And I said, "O.K. I'll take all three." I never wore the outfits. I went home and told Sonny what I'd done. I said, "Sonny, I've really done a dumb thing." I was embarrassed, but I copped to it. And he said, "Well, now you did it once, and so it's not so important." But I did some other silly things. Like, if I'd go to buy a electric fry pan, I'd buy two, to put one away, in case someday we couldn't afford one. So I have this whole stockpile of stuff (18).

According to Cher, "There should be something like a school for stars. Nothing prepared me for all this" (10). Indeed, nothing that her mother told her, nor anything any of her teachers taught her, could have coached her for the lifestyle that she suddenly found herself amidst.

GOOD TIMES/BAD TIMES

In 1965 and 1966, directly following their smash hit "I Got You Babe," Sonny & Cher were a bona fide phenomenon in the record business. According to Cher, she really knew that she and Sonny had made it into the big time when they were booked to perform on America's traditional Sunday night television showcase, *The Ed Sullivan Show*. They sang three songs: "I Got You Babe," "But You're Mine," and "Where Do You Go?" Cher was comically pleased to be introduced to Sullivan's TV audience as his "dear little *paisans* . . . the current sensations of the recording field . . . Sonny & *Chur*" (25).

Every one of Cher's solo albums from the 1960s had at least one, and sometimes up to three, Bob Dylan songs included on them. In fact, Cher's first solo hit on the charts was the Dylan tune "All I Really Want to Do." The Byrds had also released their version of the same song. When a battle on the singles charts threatened to erupt between Cher and the Byrds, the group's record label—Columbia—simply began promoting the "B" side of the Byrds' single, "I Feel a Whole Lot Better." Roger McGuinn of the Byrds publicly conceded defeat to Cher. "We loved the Cher version. We just love the song, period. We didn't want to hassle. So we just turned our record over" (42).

Cher's version of "All I Really Want to Do" went on to become her first big solo hit, ultimately hitting Number 15 on *Billboard* magazine's charts, climbing to Number 9 in England. She sings one verse in a high register, and it is directly followed by a verse she sings in a lower range.

At first listening, one isn't certain whether it is all Cher, or if Sonny is singing the lower parts. Cher herself confirms that it was actually her singing both parts, and not overdubbing them; she had to simply switch back and forth in between the high parts and the low parts "live" in the studio. Not long after she had a hit with "All I Really Want to Do," Sonny & Cher were in New York City at a recording studio, and who should they run into but Bob Dylan himself. Much to her surprise, Dylan walked right up to her and told her what a great job she did with his song. She was totally knocked out by his compliment.

Throughout the 1960s Cher was to record an astonishing number of Bob Dylan compositions, ten in fact. In addition to "All I Really Want to Do," they include "Don't Think Twice, It's All Right," "Blowin' in the Wind," "Like a Rolling Stone," "I Want You," "The Times They Are A-Changin'," "Masters of War," "Tonight I'll Be Staying Here with You," "I Threw It All Away," and "Lay, Lady, Lay." It is a miracle that no one has released a compilation album entitled *Cher Sings Dylan!*

In April of 1966, ATCO Records released the second Sonny & Cher album, *The Wondrous World of Sonny & Cher*, which hit Number 34 in the United States and Number 15 in the United Kingdom. It opened with an exciting Wall of Sound interpretation of George Gershwin's "Summertime." Sonny & Cher's dramatic and bigger-than-life delivery excitingly kicked off this album, which was the strongest of their three original studio albums. Trading off choruses of this song from the musical *Porgy and Bess*, both Sonny and Cher sound great on this perfect opening cut. Their cover versions of the Exciters' "Tell Him," Sam Cooke's "Bring It on Home to Me," and the Zombies' "Leave Me Be" proved perfect choices for them vocally. As a songwriter, Sonny brought to this perfect Sonny & Cher set his compositions "But You're Mine," "I Look for You," and "Laugh at Me."

In June of 1966, the single "Have I Stayed Too Long" peaked at Number 49 in the United States and at Number 42 in the United Kingdom. The group's next single was the song "Little Man," which was released in October of 1966 and made it to Number 21 in America and Number 9 in Britain. Their next single, "Living for You," which was released in November of that year, made it to Number 87 in the United States and to Number 44 in the United Kingdom. Through it all, Sonny & Cher were permanently on the record charts on both sides of the Atlantic Ocean, month after month throughout the year 1966.

Their distinctively odd outfits made Sonny & Cher instant symbols of revolutionary *au currant* fashion. It wasn't long before bell-bottom pants *à la Cher* were the latest rage, and the couple was regular guests on such conservative middle-of-the-road television shows as *The Hollywood Palace, The Ed Sullivan Show*, and even TV specials starring Sammy Davis Jr. and Danny Thomas. One of the strangest invitations they received was a request to perform at a private party given by platinum tycoon Charles Engelhard that included such guests as Jacqueline Kennedy and Diana Vreeland, the editor of the fashion bible, *Vogue* magazine.

Recalls their former manager Brian Stone,

Ahmet Ertegun [of Atlantic Records] asked if Sonny & Cher would like to play at a very private party thrown in the Waldorf Towers by Charles Engelhard. It was to be very exclusive, only twelve people. We were all flown in from Los Angeles to New York, including the band, and taken to this suite in the Towers. We were going to play in what was a small living room of an apartment that rambled on and on, with platinum everywhere. The walls were covered with it. Cher should have been pleased she'd be meeting Jackie Kennedy but she was complaining about not being invited to dinner. She thought the entertainers should be treated like guests, too. But after the performance, Jackie and Cher got along just great. Jackie was talking in that whisper of a voice, and Cher was delighted Jackie enjoyed her music. Diana Vreeland, the fashion magazine editor, was also there that night and noticed Cher's clothes. Cher wore those old furs and bell-bottom pants. She never liked to wear dresses because she thought her legs were ugly. But Vreeland liked her look and started using Cher in her magazine (43).

Remembers Cher,

The very social Charles Engelhards had a party, and Jackie Kennedy was going. They asked her if there was anyone she'd like to have there and she wanted us! So we went and performed in their apartment. Sonny wore his bobcat vest, and we went after dinner because we weren't sure how to act. I met Diana Vreeland there. I was nineteen, and she said, "My dear, you have a pointed head and you're beautiful. Look at you, you're so skinny. Why aren't you in magazines?" All I could say was, "I don't know. . . ." I was like that then. I met Richard Avedon, whom I adore, and he wanted to photograph me. We were only supposed to do two pictures, but we ended up spending ten days and *Vogue* ran twenty pictures (34).

In a matter of months, the duo of Sonny & Cher went from nowhere to an act that was releasing chart hits on three different record labels. In October of 1965, Sonny & Cher's song "Baby Don't Go" was reissued by Reprise Records, credited this time to "Sonny & Cher" instead of to "Caesar & Cleo." It hit Number 8 in America and Number 11 in the United Kingdom. In November of 1965, the duo's second ATCO single, "But You're Mine," peaked on the charts, hitting Number 15 in America and Number 17 in England. Meanwhile, Vault Records reissued the song "The Letter," which—this time around—made it to Number 75 in America.

In February of 1966 clothing stores in America began selling a Sonny & Cher line of clothing. The line included bell-bottoms and blouses for girls and unisex bobcat vests. Suddenly Sarkisian and Bono were trendsetting fashion gurus.

Sonny & Cher began working on the feature film *Good Times* in March of 1966. The same month, a reissue of their song "What Now My Love" on Reprise Records entered the Top 20 on both sides of the Atlantic, peaking at Number 16 in America and at Number 13 in England.

On March 4, 1966, Sonny & Cher appeared on the NBC-TV pop music series *Hullaballoo*, with guest host Sammy Davis Jr., along with the Supremes and the Lovin' Spoonful. The show featured a great production number, with Sammy Davis Jr. singing and dancing with all of his musical guests, holding hands with Mary Wilson of the Supremes and Cher. Mary wore a pantsuit with a bell-sleeved top and "flats" on her feet. Cher was wearing a lace-covered pair of bell-bottomed pants, her trademark long, dark-brown hair hanging beyond her shoulders. It was the swinging sixties, and Sonny & Cher were an indelible part of it.

At the time they were pop music's number one couple. Magazines were filled with photo spreads of the Sonny & Cher mansion, Sonny and Cher modeling clothes from their outlandish closets, and Sonny and Cher on their expensive matching motorcycles or their George Barris–designed customized Mustang convertibles. They were America's hip-dressing, cool-acting young married couple—or so it seemed. Of course the reality was that the house cost them so much that they couldn't afford to furnish it properly, and they really weren't married at all but were just living together. However, in the eyes of their fans, and the press, they could do no wrong.

It was a time of *Hit Parader* and *Sixteen* magazines, *Hullaballoo,* and *Shindig,* and the "hip" and "cool" Bonos were very "in." Without a doubt, Sonny & Cher's fans truly loved them. It was an era in which the media helped to create teen idols like the Supremes, the Monkees, the Dave Clark Five, the Beatles, Martha & the Vandellas, and the Rolling Stones. When they landed at Kennedy Airport on their return from their initial trip to England, there was a mob of thousands of screaming fans waiting for their arrival. No one was more surprised than Cher. When the duo had left on that first trip to England, no one in America seemed to have any idea who they were. Now, they were suddenly front-page news. There was a era in which they couldn't leave a concert without being mobbed by their adoring fans, who would want to grab them or touch them or verbally let them know they were adored. One night fans got ahold of one of Sonny and Cher's car doors, and bent it on its hinges to the point where it couldn't be shut as they drove off. Their fans would also shower them with gifts, cards, and notes.

When Sonny & Cher's second album on ATCO Records, *The Wondrous World of Sonny & Cher,* was released in April of 1966, it included a reproduction of a signed "thank you" note from the number one "married" couple in pop music. It lovingly ended with

> There are so many things to thank you for, so many different things, that we would have to go on forever naming them—cakes that fans have baked for us, dolls that they have given us, poems, rings, or anything that they feel is close to them and that they want us to have. This is the only way we can tell you we appreciate you for your kindness.
>
> This is our second album and we hope you like it as well as the first.
>
> Love,
> Sonny + Cher (44)

On April 2, 1966, Sonny & Cher costarred along with the Mamas & the Papas, Jan & Dean, the Turtles, Donovan, Otis Redding, and Bob Lind at the Hollywood Bowl. It was Lind who wrote the songs "Elusive Butterfly" and "Come to Your Window," which Cher recorded on her *Sonny Side of Cher* album. The proceeds from that evening's box-office profits went to the Braille Institute.

Sonny & Cher were so big at this point that they even started receiving death threats from crazy stalkers. One crazed woman wrote threatening letters to Cher. In the past they had been dismissed, but for some reason Sonny & Cher's managers took a threat received the night of the Hollywood Bowl concert very seriously. To ensure Cher and Sonny's safety, the duo had to be brought to the gig in an armored Brinks truck. In spite of that potential danger, Cher recalls it as being "one of the highlights of the '60's for Son and me—headlining in at the Hollywood Bowl" (25).

That night Cher was truly in her "flower child" phase. She wore one of her trademark bell-bottomed pantsuits. On the top was stitched a huge colorful daisy, and the bells of her pants were covered in daisy appliques as well. Not to be outdone, Sonny wore a colorful flowered shirt, with its collar lapels over the laced-up vest that matched his stove-pipe trousers. It was a triumphant evening for Cher, especially since her mother and grandfather were in the audience that night. She was only nineteen years old, and she was headlining the famous Hollywood Bowl. In her eyes, and everyone else's who was there that evening, Sonny & Cher had truly made it. It was an evening that she would always fondly remember.

Also in April of 1966, Cher scored her first million-selling solo hit, the Sonny composition "Bang Bang (My Baby Shot Me Down)." With exotic-sounding Gypsy violins and a dramatic vocal delivery, this was to become Cher's first big solo trademark number. Backed with a wall-like vocal chorus, once timid Cher has a strength and intensity in her vocals on this cut that she had never before displayed. Released as a single, in America it hit Number 2, and in England Number 3, making it her highest-scoring solo hit of the 1960s.

At the same time, Cher was hot on the charts with her second album for Imperial, *The Sonny Side of Cher*. The album featured her current hit, "Bang Bang (My Baby Shot Me Down)," which propelled it up the LP charts to Number 26 in America and to Number 11 in England. Just as controversial in nature, the song "A Young Girl (Une Enfante)," which was written by Charles Aznavour, received Cher's effectively haunting interpretation. On this album she also covered a number of other people's hits, including Astrud Gilberto's "The Girl from Ipanema," Tom Jones's "It's Not Unusual," and Bob Dylan's "Like a Rolling Stone."

On May 20, 1966, Cher turned twenty years old, and as a birthday present Sonny bought her a twenty-karat, diamond and sapphire ring. The ring consisted of a nine-karat sapphire, encircled in eleven karats of teardrop and marquis-cut diamonds, in a platinum setting. Up until then, the couple's only conspicuous jewelry was confined to a gold band with the word "Cher" on it, which Sonny wore on the ring finger of his left hand, and the matching "Sonny" ring, which Cher wore. In many of their publicity photos from this era, Cher is seen with this very large and expensive ring on her right forefinger. The ring was in fact so large that one would assume it was an elaborate piece of costume jewelry worn by a bell-bottomed hippie girl. In reality it was worth tens of thousands of dollars.

Cher's next solo single was one that was literally fought over on the record charts, by three different singers. The song was "Alfie," from the 1966 film of the same name, which starred Michael Caine and Shelley Winters. In England, where the film originated, Cilla Black, a singer managed by Beatles manager Brian Epstein, was heard over the film's credits. However, when Cher covered the Burt Bacharach and Hal David composition, it was added to the credits of the American version of the film. Cher's interpretation of "Alfie" hit Number 32 in America. Cher's recording was such a hit in America that Dionne Warwick recorded the song on one of her albums. Dionne was to take her version of "Alfie" to Number 15 in America in 1967, but it was actually Cher who had the first stateside version of the popular song.

Just as big things were beginning to happen for Sonny & Cher, Cher's heroin-addict father, John Sarkisian, was released from prison following one of his several drug-related incarcerations. He threatened to sell his story to the press, so he was paid off to keep his mouth shut. The idea that he would do such a thing truly enraged Cher.

According to Charlie Greene, "John Sarkisian was just out of prison, and he started coming around looking for money. He was trying to blackmail her, and we did pay off—about $500 a week. It was worth it to keep the stories out of the papers" (43).

On August 26, 1966, Sonny & Cher made their British concert debut, at the Astoria Theatre, Finsbury Park, London. And on September 14, the duo had a special private audience with Pope Paul VI, in Rome, Italy.

After the notoriety that Sonny & Cher were receiving, it seemed like a natural progression to make a movie starring the two of them. Elvis Presley was at the time making the bulk of his income from his many films, which by 1967 encompassed twenty-five movies, including *Jailhouse Rock* (1957), *Blue Hawaii* (1961), *Fun in Acapulco* (1963), and *Viva Las Vegas* (1964). And the Beatles had successfully done it with *A Hard Day's Night* (1964) and *Help!* (1965). So Sonny & Cher began work on their own musical fantasy epic, which was ultimately to be entitled *Good Times*.

According to Brian Stone, the idea actually came from Elvis Presley's shrewd manager, the controversial Colonel Tom Parker.

> Parker told us how much he liked Sonny & Cher and then said, "I'm going to give you some advice—for free. How much are they getting per night?"

We told him maybe $2,500 a show. "From now on," he said, "don't take less than $15,000 a night. And have the kids do a movie. Do it fast and do it cheap. Nothing artsy-craftsy." So, we put together a musical called *Good Times*. We hired a relatively unknown director named William Friedkin, who went on to do *The Exorcist*. Unfortunately, we also had Sonny, who started to think he was a filmmaker, and that was the end of us with Sonny & Cher (43).

In October of 1966 Cher's single version of Bobby Hebb's hit "Sunny" reached Number 32 in England. Her third solo album, *Cher*, made it to Number 66 in America. Naturally, the song that Hebb wrote and sang referred to a "sunny"-dispositioned girl. When Cher sang it, it was heard as "Sonny," referring to her other half. Also included on the *Cher* album were her versions of Donovan's "Catch the Wind," the Shirelles' "Will You Still Love Me Tomorrow," Buffy Sainte-Marie's "Until It's Time for You to Go," Peter, Paul & Mary's "Cruel War," and Simon & Garfunkel's "Homeward Bound." Naturally, it also contained one of Sonny's originals, in this instance the controversial "Magic in the Air," which is about pregnancy out of wedlock. In Europe, it is credited as "I Feel Something in the Air." It only charted in the United Kingdom, peaking at Number 43.

By late 1966, Cher's solo singles weren't hitting the upper end of the recording charts either. Her single "Behind the Door" had an exotic Oriental sound, but the song only made it up to Number 97. The "B" side of the single, "Mama (When My Dollies Have Babies)," received some airplay, but never charted.

When things suddenly cooled off for them, no one was more surprised than Sonny. They needed a hit, and Sonny knew it. After a slight lull on the record charts, Sonny & Cher turned around and delivered one of the biggest hits of their career, "The Beat Goes On." Said Sonny,

We were real hot for awhile but we started cooling off as fast as we got hot. And I was looking for something, desperately. Psychedelic was in and everybody was going "psychedelic, psychedelic, psychedelic!" So I was looking for something that had kind of a psychedelic thing to it, but I didn't know how to write psychedelic. I just didn't understand it 'cause a lot of it was drug influenced. I didn't think in terms of what they did. Then I started fooling with this song, "The Beat Goes On." I thought, "great title." Then I called Billy Friedkin because we were shooting a movie, *Good Times*. And I sang it to him over the phone. Billy is vicious about his critiques. If he doesn't like something, you're real sorry you ever asked him.

But if he likes it, you're real glad you asked him. So, he just flipped over "The Beat Goes On." So I got a lot of inspiration from him being so excited, and I finished all the choruses of it 'cause he loved it. That was an instant hit. We put that out and people were going "Wow! Psychedelic" (45).

Their hold on their audience peaked around the time of the release of "The Beat Goes On." On December 11, 1966, Sonny & Cher made headlines by joining a picket line on Hollywood Boulevard. As part of a crowd of five hundred, they protested an enforced curfew. This certainly endeared them to their teenaged fans.

While Sonny and Bill Friedkin were working on the script for *Good Times,* they found the need to hire a secretary to help them with their various drafts of shooting scripts. They would work until late at night at Sonny and Cher's house, and Cher usually went to bed around 10 o'clock. One night Cher woke up in the middle of the night, and came downstairs, only to discover Sonny and his latest secretary having sex. According to Sonny, "Cher didn't scream; she just glared at me and walked out of the room. I got the cold shoulder treatment for the rest of the week, but that was it" (35). Sonny and Cher's relationship was an odd one, even then.

Things began to become strained between Sonny and his and Cher's managers. According to Charlie Greene, "Sonny began calling us at three in the morning, asking for writers' conferences. He didn't like the plot, or he didn't like the script. He thought he was a big hotshot producer or director. His ego was taking over" (46).

During the production of *Good Times,* in December 1966, Sonny fired Charlie Greene and Brian Stone and signed a contract with Joe De Carlo. Joe had worked with Sonny & Cher as part of Greene and Stone's management company, but when he announced to Sonny that he was parting with Greene and Stone, Sonny decided to drop them as well and go with De Carlo.

On January 1, 1967, Sonny & Cher became the first pop group to ride on a float in the annual New Year's Day Rose Bowl Parade, in Pasadena, California. And on March 17, 1967, Sonny & Cher began a ten-day concert tour on the East Coast of the United States.

In March of 1967, ATCO Records released the Sonny & Cher album *In Case You're in Love.* Following the formula of their previous two LPs, the duo covered several of the current day's hits, including the Mindbenders' "Groovy Kind of Love," Tim Hardin's "Misty Roses," Ben E. King's "Stand by Me," Gale Garnett's "We'll Sing in the Sunshine," and

Bob Lind's "Cheryl's Goin' Home." Two of the best cuts were Sonny's "Love Don't Come," an exotic and moody song with excellent acoustic guitars, and Sonny's solo on the impassioned ballad "Cheryl's Goin' Home." The album's major backfire was a silly comedy routine penned by Sonny and set to ragtime music, called "Podunk."

Not to be outdone by his mate, Sonny—the pop world's new Pygmalion—not only had the hit "Laugh at Me," which appeared on the Sonny & Cher LP *The Wondrous World of Sonny & Cher,* but also released his first and only solo album in 1967, entitled *Inner Views.* The highlight of this collector's item LP is a Bono composition, the psychedelic-era ballad "Pammie's on a Bummer," which is about a bad "acid" drug trip.

Right after "The Beat Goes On" hit the Top 10, the duo seemed to do an about-face in musical direction. Sonny's conservative views, and his miscalculations with the music he was choosing for the duo and for Cher's solo records, were beginning to color the public's perception of them. The year 1967 was known as "the summer of love," and everyone from the Beatles to the Monkees was experimenting with drugs in their songs (the Beatles' "Lucy in the Sky with Diamonds," the Monkees' "Salesman"), and in their personal lives. *In Case You're in Love* failed to climb to the Top 40 album charts, peaking in America at Number 45.

The sound and fashion of America—and the rest of the world—was changing. The Beatles album *Sgt. Pepper's Lonely Hearts Club Band* represented a whole new sound of rock and roll, and suddenly Sonny's cute autobiographical tunes about him and Cher, and Cher's renditions of Bob Dylan songs, were failing to capture an audience. Furthermore, their calling card, their once outlandish way of dressing, was very quickly becoming less and less radical. Everyone was starting to wear bell-bottoms and other wild and colorful clothes. Now they had to compete with Sgt. Pepper jackets, the Supremes in beaded gowns with butterfly wings, Mama Cass in muumuus and knee-high go-go boots, and a whole new wave of hippies from San Francisco wearing tie-dyed clothes and sporting flowers in their hair.

Instead of just ignoring whatever aspect of the current trends he didn't like or approve of, Sonny chose not only to make his feelings known, but to make a public statement about it as well. Between 1967 and 1969, he began making one managerial mistake after another. Before the decade was up, he would in effect bankrupt the duo, and lose both Cher's solo record deal and the group's as well.

A huge career miscalculation on Sonny's part came when he and Cher appeared in an antimarijuana film that was distributed to high schools by the federal government. This was the same era when young Americans were getting into the drug scene, and the last thing they wanted to see were rock and rollers preaching against pot. All of a sudden Sonny & Cher represented the social values of the old guard. The film was not only ill-timed in its release, it made Sonny & Cher come across like their fans' parents. Talk about a bad career move!

According to Sonny, "The whole sound and style of music began to come out of the drug culture. We didn't want to get into that, so it left us" (17). "The establishment, which didn't go to concerts applauded us. The kids, who did go to concerts, thought we were stupid," said Cher (17). Sonny was later to admit, "We announced publicly that we were against drugs. That just about finished us off—our record sales really suffered. The funny thing is that it would have been so easy to fake it. People think I'm stoned all the time anyway" (47).

One of Sonny's biggest backfiring mistakes was the song "Plastic Man," which the duo recorded and then debuted on TV's *The Smothers Brothers Comedy Hour* on May 21, 1967. "Plastic Man" was about a drug pusher trying to "recruit" others to use drugs, and the slant of the song was decidedly antidrug in sentiment. In addition, Sonny & Cher were heard on the radio making public service announcements encouraging kids to stay in school. This was pretty ironic coming from twenty-year-old Cher, who was a high school dropout herself.

Into this changing marketplace, in April of 1967, Sonny & Cher released *Good Times*. They had a huge premiere for the film in Austin, Texas. Sonny & Cher were flown in on a chartered plane, they participated in a gala parade through the streets of Austin, and, according to Cher, the film did well in that town. However, in the rest of the world it was less than a hit.

The film *Good Times* runs 91 minutes and is about Sonny and Cher fantasizing about the roles they would like to play in the movies. Within the plot of their cinematic fantasies they appear as (A) themselves, (B) a sheriff and a dance hall girl in an 1800s western town (Irving Ringo and Nellie), (C) a hippie-esque Tarzan and Jane (Jungle Morry and Zora), and (D) a gangster and his gun moll (Johnny Pizzicato and Samantha). They got to sing, dance, ride an elephant; and Sonny got to write all the songs used in the film. To give the film additional star power, they hired respected actor George Sanders to play the sleazy movie producer who was the film's villain. It seemed like a brilliant idea on paper; however, when it was released in 1967 it failed to make the huge splash that Sonny had anticipated. Fortunately, he had pre-sold television rights to the film and made back all of the production costs up front. The song "It's the Little Things" was released as a single that hit Number 50 on the *Billboard* magazine charts, and "Beautiful Story" made it to Number 53. The soundtrack album brought in extra money as well. So, through *Good Times,* Sonny and Cher found themselves with a movie credit to their name and money in their pocket. Mission accomplished.

Good Times was no incredible work of art, but it was a fun, silly, rock movie, and it received several good reviews. At the time, the *New York Times* called it a "colorful, sprightly bit of good-humored silliness" (48). Leonard Maltin's *1998 Movie & Video Guide* says, "Back when the singing duo was considered kooky, they made this enjoyable little film" (49).

As silly as the plot is, from the vantage point of the 2000s, viewing *Good Times* is like looking at a 1960s time capsule. During the opening credits, actual footage of Sonny & Cher arriving and performing at the Hollywood Bowl is used. There are some very cute segments showing Cher designing elaborate bell-bottom pantsuit fantasies with colored pencils and markers. Much of the footage, especially on the musical numbers, is really a precursor to music videos, similar to the ones that the Monkees were making famous every week on NBC-TV. There is a nice segment of Cher wandering through the California canyons in her bell-bottoms. There is also a quick glimpse of Sonny in the kitchen of their home, with a gallon can of imported Italian olive oil, obviously cooking up some specialty. The movie, in its own innocent way, is a filmed preview of things to come for Sonny & Cher: Cher as a film actress and Sonny as a future restaurateur. There is also an amusing segment of Cher as a torch singer in a beaded gown and a blonde wig. Little did she know at the time, but in the 1970s she was going to become famous for wearing over a million dollars worth of beaded gowns on national television.

However, while some of Sonny & Cher's material was contemporary and cutting edge in 1967, some of it was embarrassingly silly. Although they were huge rock and roll stars, Sonny kept introducing vaudevillian elements onto their albums. Their debut album, *Look at Us,* contains the silly bit of nonsense called "Sing C'est La Vie," on which the duo sounds as if they are doing a circus skit on a TV variety show. *In Case You're in Love* featured a cut called "Podunk," which found Sonny & Cher setting up one-liner jokes for each other like a vaudevillian comedian and his foil.

This bit of silliness was accompanied by bawdy ragtime music, which was very nearly the epitome of non-psychedelic.

Although *Good Times* had been a bomb, Sonny & Cher found that it didn't hurt their ability to continue to do concert tours. It was also during 1967 that Cher announced that she was pregnant. Again the pair began to make plans for their upcoming parenthood. They were preparing for a weekend gig in Minneapolis, when Cher suddenly complained about stomach pains. As in her previous pregnancy, she suffered a miscarriage. With Cher in the hospital, Sonny attempted to back out of the Minneapolis engagement, but was informed that either he perform alone or be sued by the concert promoter. Backed into a corner, Sonny obligingly flew to Minneapolis with his friend and road manager Denis Pregnolato, and for the first time performed as Sonny *without* Cher.

In September of 1967, Cher's version of the Joe Tex song "Hey Joe" stalled at Number 94 on the *Billboard* charts. In October, Sonny & Cher's greatest-hits album, *The Best of Sonny & Cher,* was released the same month that they made a guest appearance on the hit television series *The Man from U.N.C.L.E.,* which starred Robert Vaughan and David McCallum. Fortunately, *The Best of Sonny & Cher* was something of a hit for the duo, making it to Number 26 on the American album chart in *Billboard* magazine.

The single-disk *The Best of Sonny & Cher* album featured a montage of photos of the duo on the cover, with a colorful baroque pattern of designs framing them. The album featured a dozen of the duo's biggest hits, teaming Top 10 hit "I Got You Babe," "Laugh at Me," "Little Man," and "The Beat Goes On" with their recent singles like "It's the Little Things" and "Living for You." Conspicuously missing from the set was their other Top 10 hit, "Baby Don't Go," which had been on Reprise Records.

To promote their greatest-hits album, Sonny & Cher flew to New York City in November. Their stay in town encompassed Thanksgiving day. When Ahmet Ertegun, the president of Atlantic/ATCO Records, asked the pair what their plans were for the holiday, Sonny told him that they just planned to have a quiet dinner in their hotel room. Ahmet wouldn't hear of such a thing, so he insisted that they join him in his East Side brownstone, where he would be serving dinner for several of his elite friends. According to Sonny, when they arrived there, they were instantly aware that they were out of their league. The dinner guests also included Andy Warhol, actress Viva, filmmaker Joel Schumacher, and

Vogue magazine's flamboyant editor Diana Vreeland. Drinks, cocaine, marijuana, and all sorts of intoxicants were consumed by the guests—except for Sonny and Cher. "Cher and I sat in the corner of a sofa like two aliens," Sonny recalled. "It was eerie, watching everybody get loaded and loony" (35).

After salads and appetizers were served, the turkey was finally brought out. After everyone commented on the fabulous turkey, one young woman stood up as though she was going to say something, and instead projectile-vomited all over the turkey. Sonny and Cher excused themselves and left the brownstone. As they had originally planned, they returned to their hotel and ordered room service.

Cher's next solo single, "You Better Sit Down Kids," became a huge Top 10 hit for her, peaking at Number 9 in America in December of 1967. Another dramatic ballad about the breakup of a relationship, "You Better Sit Down Kids" is sung by a father leaving his children in a marital split. It didn't matter that Cher was a young girl singing this song; she turned it into a soap-opera storytelling, at which she vocally excelled.

In December, Sonny & Cher released their last hit as recording artists for ATCO: "Good Combination." Although "The Beat Goes On" had been a huge hit for them in February, in the United States and the United Kingdom, their five subsequent singles had all bombed. Not one of them cracked the Top 40 on either side of the Atlantic. "Good Combination" peaked at Number 56 in the United States alone. Their presence on the British charts was even more disappointing.

In retrospect, none of the five subsequent songs Sonny & Cher released in 1967 on ATCO were well suited to the marketplace. Not one of them was a worthy follow-up to "The Beat Goes On." That song had been so "hip" and socially conscious. "Beautiful Story," "Plastic Man," and "Good Combination" were all out of the silly vaudevillian/lounge act mode that Sonny's material increasingly veered toward. "Beautiful Story" was a silly pastiche of a song, "Plastic Man" opened with something that sounded like a Salvation Army street band—complete with tuba—and "Good Combination" sounded like the theme song to a 1960s TV show. The best song of the batch, "It's the Little Things," sadly got lost in the shuffle and never became the hit it deserved to be.

All of a sudden, after three years on top and five albums, Sonny & Cher put their recording career on hold. Although the two were continuing to tour as Sonny & Cher, Sonny's focus turned to his new passion, turning Cher into a recording and movie star.

Once considered hip rock and rollers, in December 1967, Sonny & Cher opened their nightclub act at the cabaret at the Eden Roc Hotel in Miami Beach, Florida. This was to be a somewhat oddly prophetic booking for them. Little did they suspect at the time, but the duo was destined to begin the decade of the 1970s as a "lounge act," far from the rock realm and a million miles away from the hit record charts.

The album containing "You Better Sit Down Kids," 1968's *With Love, Cher,* was Cher's fourth solo LP for Imperial. Buoyed by her second Top 10 solo hit, the album reached Number 47 in America. It included her controversial classics "You Better Sit Down Kids" and "Mama (When My Dollies Have Babies)," which set a pattern for her biggest 1970s hits. She excelled at songs that were little soap-opera stories set to rock music. These were truly the precursors to her later hits "Gypsys, Tramps and Thieves," "Half Breed," and "Dark Lady." *With Love, Cher* also included Phil Ochs's "There but for Fortune," Sonny's "But I Can't Love You More," and—naturally—Bob Dylan's "The Times They Are A-Changin'." Many of rock stylists were discovering the classic songs of Richard Rodgers & Lorenz Hart during this era, including the Mamas & the Papas, Bobby Darin, and the Supremes. Not one to miss a musical wave, on this album Cher covered the songwriting team's "Sing for Your Supper."

Cher quickly followed it up with her second solo album of 1968, *Backstage*. The cover of the album depicted Cher looking at her reflection in a dressing-room mirror, as though pensively psyching herself up for a performance. She is made up in her most Cleopatra-like fashion, with her distinctive dark bangs and shoulder-length straight hair. Musically, she ran the gamut of current songs that were hot at the time. On it she covered the Moody Blues hit "Go Now," Tim Hardin's "Reason to Believe," Bacharach and David's "A House Is Not a Home," the Lovin' Spoonful's "Do You Believe in Magic," Miriam Makeba's exotic African-rhythmed "The Click Song," and naturally a Bob Dylan tune, "Masters of War."

The album, which features some of Cher's strongest 1960s singing, failed to produce any hit singles and never made the charts. She stretched out into a diverse number of musical directions. On "Carnival," Cher is cast in a Brazilian jazz setting, and she delivers a wonderful string-laden rendition of Burt Bacharach and Hal David's "A House Is Not a Home." Especially jarring was Dylan's scaldingly bitter antiwar protest song, "Masters of War." In the song Cher denounces the bureaucracy of war. To hear Cher sing "I hope that you die" to warmongers on this Dylan cut one minute, and then jump into the Lovin' Spoonful's lilting song of love, "Do You Believe in Magic," the next comes across as a bizarre musical transition to say the least.

Much of 1968 was spent on the preproduction and production of the film *Chastity*. Against the advice of everyone he asked, Sonny decided to finance the film himself, which turned out to be a huge mistake. Sonny and Cher went to New York City that year to see what they could do to help raise the funds necessary to finance this project. While there, they checked into the St. Regis Hotel and planned meetings with Francis Ford Coppola and William Friedkin. In residence at that hotel was surreal artist Salvador Dali. When Dali ran into the oddly dressed singing duo in the hallway, he invited them up to his suite for dinner. Sensing that they were making a potentially helpful contact for their film project, they accepted. However, Dali had other things in mind for them.

When they arrived at Dali's suite, they were dismayed to find women lounging in see-through blouses and openly gay men being affectionate with each other. Sonny surmised that they had been invited up for some sort of kinky sex scene, which in no way interested them. After an hour of nonsensical talk with the famous painter, finally the party got ready to leave for the restaurant next door to the hotel. However, in the middle of the evening, Dali excused himself and left, never to return. If Dali thought that he was going to get involved in some sort of a sex scene with Sonny AND Cher, he was sadly mistaken. In spite of their revolutionary unisex clothes, Sonny and Cher were quite "square" when it came to sex and drugs.

Ultimately unable to find anyone to invest money in the movie folly that they wanted to produce, Sonny took the couple's savings account, and even hocked their furniture, to raise the funds. *Chastity* was filmed in Scottsdale, Arizona, in 1968, and proved to be an exhausting ordeal. They hired director Allesio de Paola and a leading man by the name of Steve Whittaker. During filming, Sonny found that Cher was getting just a little too close to Whittaker and suspected that they were having an affair. Although he didn't corner her and demand her to stop, he did emphasize that their entire career was pivoting on the success or failure of this film, and that he loved her very much. After that she and Steve cooled it. During the time their movie was filming, one night Sonny and Cher made love and woke up the next morning, convinced that Cher had conceived. They were thrilled to find out that they were correct and determined that Cher would not miscarry this time.

Throughout much of 1968, it seemed that Sonny & Cher were scrambling not to lose touch with the young audience that had made them stars in the first place. In June of that year, Sonny & Cher were among the stars of the "Soul Together" concert at Madison Square Garden in New York City. Their costars included Sam & Dave, Aretha Franklin, Joe Tex, King Curtis, and the Rascals.

On August 4, 1968, Sonny & Cher were one of the top acts headlining the Newport Pop Festival at Costa Mesa, California. They appeared alongside Canned Heat, Steppenwolf, the Grateful Dead, the Byrds, and Jefferson Airplane. This was the antithesis of what they were really all about as a duo. Those other five acts represented the height of the drug culture Sonny Bono claimed to abhor. This was really the opposite of what their personal life together was all about.

By the end of 1968, Sonny and Cher weren't hanging out with the Rolling Stones, Joni Mitchell, or Crosby, Stills, Nash, and Young. They were hanging out with the old guard of Hollywood, like Lucille Ball, Johnny Carson, Mitzi Gaynor, and Rosalind Russell. On the night of the November 1968 presidential election, Cher and Sonny were invited over to comedian Jack Benny's house to watch the election coverage with him and his elite guests. Apparently there was a difference of opinion between the guests when Richard Nixon gave his acceptance speech that night on television. Cher recalls that when Lucille Ball made comically disparaging remarks at the television screen while Nixon spoke on and on, she aggravated *Tonight Show* host Carson. Cher, Rosalind Russell, and Lucy were reprimanded and sent to the den since they couldn't stop giggling and making rude jokes about Nixon. Such social evenings were indicative of how square and out of touch Sonny and Cher's life really was. Here they were trying to remain "hip" and in-touch with the young record buyers who had made them stars, yet they were ensconced in the establishment of old Hollywood.

As Cher was to put it in her 1998 book, *The First Time,* "By 1968, Sonny and I had fallen off the charts. . . . Son's straight-ahead, upbeat music started to sound simplistic and corny. . . . Son and I became so old-fashioned so quickly" (25). According to her, they went from being hip and in to becoming part of the "Geritol" geriatric vitamin set—seemingly overnight.

On March 4, 1969, Cher gave birth to a daughter, whom she and Sonny named Chastity, after the movie they had just completed. Chastity made her debut to the world at Cedars of Lebanon Hospital in Los Angeles, California. The birth of their daughter was a very happy event for the couple. Unfortunately, their film of the same name was a huge failure.

Although *Good Times* was no *Gone with the Wind*, the experience somewhat went to Bono's head. By investing everything in the film *Chastity*, Sonny surmised that Cher would surely become a major movie star and he would become a dynamic force in the film business. Unfortunately, the plan backfired, and they found themselves in hock right up to their ears.

The 1969 release of the film was meant to bring Sonny & Cher back to their young audience. The film was all about a young girl who runs away from home to discover the world and, more importantly, herself. As Chastity, the character in the film, Cher hitchhikes from one soul-searching experience to another, finally ending up in a whorehouse having a lesbian affair with the madam of the brothel. According to Sonny, the film was about "the increase in frigidity and the increase in lesbianism . . . the lack of manhood. The independence women have acquired but don't necessarily want. So many young girls are just spinning their wheels" (13).

Their manager at the time, Joe De Carlo, claimed that

> It was a brilliant movie. But, Sonny wouldn't let anyone finance it, because he didn't want any advice from anyone. And you know you should never put your own money into anything. Sonny is a creative guy, but he has a tremendous ego. He thought the picture would make Cher a great movie star and make them a ton of money (13).

Aside from the film, Sonny & Cher were paying for the thirty-one-room house they had purchased, which was well over their means—especially if anything happened to compromise their income. It was located on St. Cloud Drive in Bel Air and had been sold to them by Tony Curtis for $250,000. According to Sonny, it was purchased on a whim: "Cher would pine for that house. She'd say, 'God Son, I want to live there'" (17). So he bought it for her. In other words, they were really counting on the film *Chastity* becoming a huge hit.

As Cher tells the story,

> Sonny decided he wanted to make this movie, *Chastity*. He wrote it, and it was one of the best scripts I've ever read—especially compared with all the scripts I'm seeing now, which are mostly shit. But he shouldn't have had me do it. Because it was me, his wife—and he's very Italian—he just kept changing it to make things less rough for me. Basically, I wasn't ready. So he spent a whole year and all of our bread on this movie. And then I got pregnant in the middle of it and I couldn't work during the pregnancy.

So, when Chastity was born, we owed the government, I don't know, something like $190,000 (18).

The reviews were mixed. Just about everyone hated the movie, but only some of the critics hated Cher's acting. According to the *New York Post*, "Nothing happens. . . . the performances are devoid of acting presence. Cher is such a non-actress that her performance [does] work, or at least it is inoffensive" (50). Said William Wolf of *Cue* magazine, "Cher has a marvelous quality that often makes you forget the lines you are hearing. Her manner can be described as a combination of tough, disinterested, unhappy, self-critical, and deadpan, offset by sudden jaunty movements of her flexible body" (51).

Sonny and Cher reportedly lost $500,000 of their own money, and ended up owing the government $270,000 in tax debt. "I fought him all the way," claimed Cher of her husband's filmed folly. While her opinion of *Good Times* was "I didn't want to do it, and I was terrible in it," her opinion of *Chastity* was "That was terrible, too. But I got some good notices" (52).

Cher released a single from the movie *Chastity*, which was written by Elyse Weinberg and produced by Sonny. The song was called "Chastity's Song (Band of Thieves)" and it was also a huge flop. Sonny & Cher were dropped from ATCO Records, and Cher was dropped from Imperial Records. However, ATCO was willing to sign Cher for a solo album, but only if Sonny wasn't producing. In the eyes of the record industry, "Chastity's Song" and the duo's recent string of misfires proved that Bono was totally out of touch with the record-buying market and was a bad judge of what would and would not sell to teenagers.

A heavyweight trio of the best producers from Atlantic/ATCO Records took the helm of Cher's 1969 album *3614 Jackson Highway*. The album title was the address of the famous Muscle Shoals Sound Studio in Muscle Shoals, Alabama, where it was recorded. The producers— Jerry Wexler, Tom Dowd, and Arif Mardin—were all known for their hit-making successes with Aretha Franklin and a host of other Atlantic recording artists. The songs that they chose for Cher should have made this album a rock and roll classic. The album included Stephen Stills's "For What It's Worth," which was a hit for the Buffalo Springfield; "(Sittin' On) the Dock of the Bay," which was a huge smash for Otis Redding; and "Do Right Woman, Do Right Man," which was an Aretha Franklin classic. Just for good luck, they even threw in three different Bob Dylan songs, including "Tonight I'll Be Staying Here with You," "I Threw It All Away," and the recent Dylan hit, "Lay Baby Lay" (originally "Lay Lady Lay"). Compared to the Spector-esque sound of her Bono-produced 1960s solo albums, the sound here seemed very flat.

Jerry Wexler was later to say of Cher's talent, "I don't think Cher has a conscious, sophisticated, head appreciation of music. She's not formal or academic. Just flows, you know? No sense of propulsion, it's a sublimation of personality and suppression of the personal musical signature in favor of complete surrender to music" (33).

Unfortunately, *3614 Jackson Highway* was classified as an instant "bomb." It sold few copies, and only made it to Number 160 on the album charts in America. The music and arrangements are very stripped down and low-keyed. While trying to emphasize her hit-making track record as a hippie chick–Dylan interpreter, the producers also removed her pop sparkle.

The liner notes to the album were written by Cher in her own handwriting. She penned these sage words of wisdom to her fans:

> I want to write something that when you read it you'll say "Yeh [sic] that's really groovy," but all I can tell you is what's in my heart, and if you can dig it then I'm happy and if you can't then I'm sorry. Music sets me free; it makes me feel all the things of life. Sometimes when I hear a groovy song it makes me want to get in my car and just drive and sing at the top of my lungs, other times when I hear a song it makes me cry. I don't know if I'm sad or happy but it really doesn't matter. Music can take you away from the bad and bring you closer to the good in life, I really hope the music in this album brings you closer. Peace. (53)

It was 1969, the year of Woodstock, and this was the height of Cher's hippie era. *3614 Jackson Highway* is a fascinating time capsule of an album, highlighted by a soulful rendition of "Cry Like a Baby," an understated version of "(Sittin' On) the Dock of the Bay," and a fascinating version of the protest anthem "For What It's Worth."

According to their recording contract with ATCO Records, Sonny & Cher and/or Cher owed the company more recordings. Sonny was reportedly so unhappy with the *3614 Jackson Highway* album that he simply refused to turn any more recordings over to Atlantic/ATCO. What resulted was a huge stalemate between Bono and ATCO. It was Sonny's plan to just hold on until the contract ran out, and then he would be free to renegotiate with another label when the right time came.

There were only three Sonny & Cher original studio albums released in the 1960s, plus the soundtrack album to *Good Times* and *The Best of Sonny & Cher.* There was certainly a formula to them. Naturally they would be heavily comprised of anywhere between three and six Sonny Bono originals. And the majority of the rest of the cuts were "cover" versions of several of the hits of the day, including "Unchained Melody," "Then He Kissed Me," "500 Miles," "You Really Got a Hold on Me," "Tell Him," "Bring It on Home to Me," "Misty Roses," "We'll Sing in the Sunshine," "Groovy Kind of Love," and "Stand by Me." The soundtrack to *Good Times* was entirely comprised of Sonny Bono originals, including two new versions of their biggest hit, "I Got You Babe." It also featured the fittingly Phil Spector–influenced love ballad "It's the Little Things."

In the 1990s Atlantic/ATCO released a compact disc called *The Beat Goes On: The Best of Sonny & Cher,* which united the reprise single "Baby Don't Go" with the rest of the group's 1960s catalog. With twenty-one cuts on one disc, this is the best single-disc retrospective on the 1960s Sonny & Cher. In 1998, Sundazed Records in America released all three of the Sonny & Cher solo albums on compact discs, each including three bonus cuts. *Look at Us* includes two cuts from the *Good Times* soundtrack ("It's the Little Things" and "Don't Talk to Strangers"), plus "Hello," which is a studio dialogue from Sonny & Cher that was included as the "B" side to the 1965 single "But You're Mine." *The Wondrous World of Sonny & Cher* includes Sonny's song "The Revolution Kind," 1966 non-album hit "Have I Stayed Too Long," and a never-before released gem, "Crying Time." *In Case You're in Love* includes the three final unsuccessful non-soundtrack ATCO singles: "Beautiful Story," "Good Combination," and "Plastic Man."

Meanwhile, Cher recorded six solo albums and a greatest-hits collection entitled *Cher's Golden Greats* in the 1960s, and she placed songs on record charts in England and in America. With the exception of *3614 Jackson Highway,* all of the songs on the first six albums were produced by Sonny Bono, who was also responsible for writing nine of those songs.

As was to be a pattern throughout her solo recording career, Cher's and Sonny & Cher's strongest markets would be the United States and England. From the 1960s through the 1990s, those two countries would continue to differ from time to time as to which of her songs would become hits. In the 1960s, the beautifully dramatic "Magic in the Air" and her version of "Sunny" were hits only in the United Kingdom, while "Where Do You Go," "Alfie," "Behind the Door" and "You Better Sit Down Kids" were strictly United States phenomena.

For Sonny & Cher, the year 1969 had brought about big changes in their lives and in their careers. For the sake of the birth of their child, they finally—secretly—got married. It was after Chastity was born. Sonny had their attorney and their friend Denis Pregnolato be their witnesses. They were officially, legally married in their Bel Air home. However, this time around, the ceremony was not held in the bathroom.

According to Sonny, there were no emotional fireworks, no fanfare, no party, just a simple ceremony. "Even if it wasn't emotional, the piece of paper was significant," Sonny was later to proclaim (35). Now they were really Mr. and Mrs. Salvatore Bono. Once Chastity was born, their focus as a couple wasn't just a career move, now they were a family—a family that was seriously in debt.

During this period of time, even though their musical career was in a slump, they were still notable stars. The majority of their fans had no idea about their tax debt and money problems. Cher continued to be a hit with fashion magazines during this era. She recalls,

> I went away to do a layout for *Vogue* for two weeks in Page, Arizona, and it was the most beautiful pictures you've ever seen. Georgio di Sant'Angelo did all the clothes, but you couldn't buy them. He made them just for this shoot. It was the best session I ever did by far. You've never seen anything like it, ever, ever, ever. Ara Gallant did all the hair and make-up. I had braids down to the floor, and he painted my face. It was all Indian, on horseback and down under rocks, in this place where they shot [the film] *Planet of the Apes.* Georgio did the most beautiful clothes I've ever seen. Copies and extensions of real American Indian clothes. He just took it and went with it. Unbelievable. I was 23 (39).

As the decade of the 1960s came to an end, all was not well in the Bel Air dream home of Sonny and Cher. Both as a duo and recording solo, they had sold over forty million records. However, their once hip, hot, and exciting career was suddenly comatose. They tried desperately to sell the mansion they had purchased from Tony Curtis, but found the market for such huge homes in Los Angles to be "flat" at that time. Since Sonny had hocked most of their furniture to finance *Chastity*, they were living in a huge, opulent, empty mansion.

In Cher's own words, "It was strange. The hippies thought we were square; the squares thought we were hippies. Sonny & Cher were down the toilet" (13). Always a drama queen, Cher insisted on having the last word, and this time around, she was 100 percent correct.

THE SONNY & CHER COMEDY HOUR

The saga of how Sonny and Cher pulled themselves out of the doldrums
of debt is as fascinating as their initial rise to fame. With their recording
contract with ATCO due to lapse, and no movie career, they put together
a nightclub act and hit the road for middle America. However, this was
not a rock and roll concert tour. The venture was clearly aimed at the parents of the kids who had initially been buying their records.

Their nightclub-act phase began with a month-long engagement at the
Frontier Hotel in Las Vegas, starting in July of 1969. They performed two
shows a night as the opening act for Pat Boone. Sonny recalled in his
autobiography that Cher absolutely hated it. Still a victim of severe stage
fright, she was totally freaked out by the fact that she could look right into
the audience members' eyes from her spot up on stage. Sonny told her
just to talk to him and pretend that the audience wasn't there.

Sonny wore a tuxedo, and Cher was dressed in smart-looking pantsuits
or dresses. They were attired as adults this time around, with Cher's new
high-fashioned bell-bottoms as the only echo of their former incarnation.
In their new nightclub act they sang several of their hit songs, but each
was given either an up-tempo or slowed-down arrangement. These new
Las Vegas–styled musical arrangements could never have been confused
with the rock and roll sound of the old Sonny & Cher, nor the folk/rock
flavor of Cher's solo records. Even their new version of "The Beat Goes
On" lost all of its youthful bite, so that it sounded more like something
that Mel Torme might perform with Rosemary Clooney. Their act also

included such staid standards as "Danny Boy" and Beatles tunes like "Hey Jude" and "Got to Get You into My Life." If they alienated the younger market with their antidrug preaching, they were determined to shift gears and appeal to the over-thirty-five crowd.

One of the things that evolved in their nightclub act was a biting sort of onstage bantering back and forth between them. Sonny would play comic "straight man" to Cher's wisecracks, in which she would insult his songs, his lovemaking, his mother, and his singing. Their ad-libbing routines somehow worked well onstage, and they developed quite a sense of comic timing.

According to Cher,

We went on the road and played nightclubs. At first, we died. Then we started getting off on the band, just getting into a little rapping, and then we noticed that people were beginning to laugh so we just started working on it. We never wrote anything down. If something worked, we'd add it, and if it didn't, we'd chuck it out. My sense of humor began cutting a little bit, with him [Sonny], the band, the audience, the hecklers. People would laugh and Sonny would say, "We'll keep it." It was great. That part of my personality had been stifled for so long it was wonderful to use it onstage. I was getting myself together, getting out my frustrations. The act worked and we started building a following on the club circuit (18).

They booked themselves onto the Fairmont Hotel circuit, and many of the engagements were several weeks long. One of the first ones that they did on the road was the Elmwood Casino, in Windsor, Ontario, across the river from Detroit. Cher recalls staying at a seedy hotel across the street from the casino, daily wondering what the hell they were doing there, and how the hell they were going to get out of there. They took whatever bookings that they could get, just to keep paying the bills. A month in Dallas, a month in New Orleans; a booking at the Ionia, Michigan County Fair; slowly but surely they began to get into the rhythm of doing a nightclub act no matter where they were booked. Along the way, Cher began to develop a snappy quick-on-her-feet way of ad-libbing with drunks, hecklers, the band, Sonny, or anyone else who shouted up to her onstage. It was a long haul back to the top of the entertainment business. Cher was to call this particular phase of their career "the nightclub tour from Hell." In looking back on this era, she notes that Sonny was the "charming buffoon," while she played the "glamorous bitch" (25).

In June of 1970, Sonny & Cher opened their new act at the ritzy

Empire Room of the Waldorf-Astoria Hotel, the same building where they had performed for Jackie Kennedy years before. Somehow their comedy routines worked, and their act appealed to an adult audience. All of their months on the road had polished their new act. Said Cher of the abusive put-downs she aimed at Sonny, "At first Sonny didn't like it much. He'd say, 'Cher, you've got a smart mouth!' But it worked" (13). And that was the bottom line. The audiences liked them, and they were drawing crowds. Although their financial situation looked bleak to them, the name of "Sonny & Cher" still sold tickets, and they still did have devoted fans.

Sonny attempted to retaliate comically on stage, but it was Cher who would always come out ahead in their mock battles. He would explain mid-act, "Look folks, now don't . . . don't worry about Cher's smarting off like that, 'cause she's . . . 'cause when she gets out of hand, I take care of her, I give her, you know, a couple belts and that . . . that straightens her right out, you know. So don't worry." He'd turn and look at Cher, who was standing on the stage next to him, and continue, "In fact, I'm really surprised that you're still popping off. Didn't you get enough last night?" Dead silence.

"I didn't get ANY last night," she would deliver deadpan, and the audience would crack up at the sexual innuendo. She would look back at Sonny and ask, "I don't know if you've got a magic act, or what? Now you see it now you don't" (54). Bang, bang, she shot him down.

By now the pair had developed comically cartoonish versions of their own public and private personas, and they were projecting their creations onstage. They came across as warm and friendly and glamorous, and they appealed to audiences of all sorts.

David Hungate, who played guitar with Sonny & Cher on the road recalls, "They hit on a kind of Louis Prima and Keely Smith routine for their live act. Cher, like Keely, was the quiet, sarcastic one, and Sonny was the funny Italian guy. They were warm and cuddly, which I think was part of their appeal—there was a desire out there to repair the rift that had developed between the freaks and the straight people" (55).

Sonny & Cher's comic arguing and songs made an odd rock and roll hybrid of an act, lying somewhere in between *The Bickersons* (Don Ameche and Frances Langford's radio show), and Louis Prima and Keely Smith's famous Las Vegas act. Their new tuxedo-and-dress look also proved to be a huge hit with middle-of-the-road audiences. Based on their growing new success, Merv Griffin signed them to appear as guest hosts on his television show for one week in 1971. Sonny & Cher's stint on *The Merv Griffin Show* was seen by CBS-TV programming director Fred Silverman. He liked their appealing blend of onstage repartee and songs, and he offered them their own six-episode, one-hour summer replacement television show on his network. They jumped at the opportunity, and *The Sonny & Cher Comedy Hour* was born.

Although Sonny & Cher had been quite successful over the past six years in show business, they were not the most sophisticated nor the sleekest performers in the world, so CBS hired a crew to clean up and glamorize everything about the duo. A battery of hair, makeup, and wardrobe people descended on Sonny & Cher and proceeded to add the kind of polish necessary to turn the 1960s swinging hippies–married couple into a glamorous and dazzling pair. Both Sonny and Cher avidly ate up the advice that was given them, and the transformation from the nonconformist duo that starred in *Good Times* to the sexy and appealing pair who hosted *The Sonny & Cher Comedy Hour* was quite dramatic.

Three key people were hired by CBS to immediately recreate Cher by utilizing her natural beauty and accentuating her features, figure, and beautiful long black hair. Bob Mackie was brought in to design a new wardrobe for her, and so began a whole new era of costume glamour unlike anything the world of television had ever witnessed before. Minnie Smith, manicurist to the stars, was enlisted to turn Cher's hands into sculptured works or art, via porcelain "wrapped" fingernails and exotic multicolored, hand-painted polish. Celebrity skin care and makeup specialist Daniel Eastman was hired to clear up Cher's troubled complexion and create a whole new makeup to transform Cher into a gorgeous television star. Up until that point, Cher had always applied all of her makeup herself and had no idea what was cosmetically possible.

According to Eastman, when Cher came to CBS and began filming her first episodes of *The Sonny & Cher Comedy Hour*, she was trying to conceal blemished skin by wearing white base under her makeup. Once she got under the hot lights of the television studio, the covering makeup turned translucent, and the white base undercoat that showed through accentuated her uneven complexion. Eastman stopped the on-camera action, and redid her makeup before they continued filming.

There were three of us basically who were responsible for changing her fur-vest and bangs image into that vamp character you saw on television. It was myself, and Bob Mackie, and Minnie Smith who did her outrageous

porcelain fingernails. You can put the most glamorous, most revealing costumes on her. You can put makeup on her and make her look glorious and
beautiful, but she couldn't walk across the stage in high heels! It was interesting that someone had to show her how to walk in high heels! She was
not accustomed to them. Here she was, looking like a duck waddling back
and forth. It was so funny, we were all laughing and encouraging her (56).

According to Eastman, "When I helped her with her skin care and her
makeup in the early days of *The Sonny & Cher Comedy Hour,* I found
her to be the most open, outspoken, high-camp, and vampy lady I have
ever met. And she says whatever's on her mind. She's one of those 'givers'
in life, whereas a lot of people in this business are 'takers' " (56).
    One of Eastman's real challenges came when he set out to end Cher's
erupting skin problems.

She has a chronic problem. I think it was a combination of stress, nerves,
and her eating habits. I had to go behind her like a little "reminder" to
encourage her to drink plenty of fresh water every day, and to eat natural
snacks, as opposed to the hamburgers and French fries and pizza that she
likes so much. The heavy TV makeup certainly compounded the problem,
because she would be in makeup sometimes for hours on end in the studio. It took a lot of effort from a lot of professional people to package her
and give her that "look" that she took and adapted so well, and even
expounded upon in later years (56).

At the same time, Eastman observed, "Sonny was the aggressive moving force. He was like a father figure, and he would constantly look over
her and make sure she was doing what she was supposed to be doing" (56).
    The Sonny & Cher Comedy Hour was created and filmed at the CBS-
owned "Television City" near Farmers' Market on Fairfax, in Hollywood.
Several of other CBS prime-time productions were produced in that
same building. During this same era, Bart Andrews was one of the staff
writers on *The Carol Burnett Show* in the Television City complex. He
recalls that when Sonny and Cher arrived at CBS in 1971, everyone was
watching them avidly, trying to figure out what on earth they were going
to do on network television. Andrews shared an office with another writer
on the second floor at the Television City complex.

Next door to, and adjoining our office was this new team that CBS had
hired to headline a variety show. A girl in fur jackets and a guy with bangs
came in. They had a couple of hit records, but no one could ever remem-

ber what they were. They just didn't seem to fit in at CBS, and summer replacement shows are usually done very quickly.

They arrived, and a way was made for them for an office, and they moved in and got themselves together. . . . Not a day would go by without giant fights breaking out between the two of them . . . marital arguments in the office, always behind closed doors. But they never worried if anybody could hear them. There was always some tumult, and he [Sonny] always came out the winner. He was very, very domineering. Even beyond fighting with her, he was domineering in terms of telling her what to do (57).

Andrews also observed with utter amazement the transformation that took place during the six weeks that Sonny & Cher were at CBS.

In the course of that summer, Cher blossomed before your eyes, into somebody with a great deal of self-confidence. It was amazing to see. She was a shy person when she arrived. She was just not sure of herself. But by the end of the summer, she was like a different person. The show had done well, and that always helps somebody's ego and feeling of worth. They arrived this crazy-looking couple with those stupid outfits on, and they left in a short time like different people. Their whole lives had turned around based on that one summer show (57).

The Sonny & Cher Comedy Hour—the summer replacement series— had its debut on Sunday, August 1, 1971, and it was an immediate hit. The pair sang and danced, bantered back and forth like they did in their nightclub act, performed in comedy skits, and played host to Jimmy Durante. Somehow it all worked. According to the *New York Post*, "Quite the most delightful new program on the summer screen is the Sonny & Cher comedy-song hour. After seven profitable years on the record market, the vocal duo might just make it on TV" (58). Indeed, they did. The summer replacement show was so good, fresh, and entertaining that CBS brought back *The Sonny & Cher Comedy Hour* as a midseason prime-time replacement, beginning on Monday, December 27, 1971, at 10:00 p.m.

The show's producers were Allan Blye and Chris Bearde, and all of the writers had previously worked together on *The Smothers Brothers Comedy Hour* two years before. Tommy Smothers once commented that he turned on the TV in the early 1970s, and there was the show he had once done with his brother, but now it starred Sonny & Cher! Among the writers on the show was an aspiring comedian and actor who would later make his mark in the movies and on TV. His name was Steve Martin.

The hour-long show was a mixture of musical numbers and comedy skits. Many of the most successful skits were repeated throughout the run of the show. Among the most popular ones were "Sonny's Pizza Parlor," in which Cher played the sexy waitress, Rosa. There was Laverne, the tacky, raspy-voiced laundromat denizen, whom Cher portrayed with comic flair. And there was a musical comedy segment called "Vamps," in which Sonny and Cher would introduce several seductive female characters—all played by Cher—and salute them in song. Each show would begin and end with their now-famous husband and wife dialogues, in which Cher would routinely berate Sonny for his height, his big nose, and his sexual ineptness. And then, there was Cher's elaborate wardrobe of sequined and/or beaded gowns, all designed by Bob Mackie.

Although the couple's reputation and career were mainly based on their 1960s rock and roll image, *The Sonny & Cher Comedy Hour* featured guests who were incredibly middle-of-the-road. Their very conservative list of guests included Ronald Reagan, Bob Hope, Kate Smith, Jerry Lewis, Dinah Shore, Jim Nabors, Danny Thomas, George Burns, William Conrad, and Phyllis Diller. Not exactly a youth-oriented list by any means! Looking at a roster of their guest stars, it is obvious that CBS-TV also insisted that many television stars of its other series (*M*A*S*H*, *All in the Family*, *The Carol Burnett Show*) be frequently featured. From those three shows alone came McLean Stevenson, Jean Stapleton, Carroll O'Connor, Carol Burnett, and Lyle Waggoner. Even CBS-TV canine star Lassie was one of their guest stars. Any celebrities who were truly contemporary came in the form of musical guests like the Supremes, Rita Coolidge, the Temptations, the Jackson Five, Marilyn McCoo & Billy Davis Jr., and Tina Turner.

Meanwhile, there was also the issue of getting their recording career back on track. Johnny Musso was the head of Atlantic Records' West Coast office while Sonny & Cher were stars on the label. According to him, "Everybody thought their career was over, musically. They were playing the circuit of Fairmont Hotels across the country and had a bunch of club dates, but Sonny was so upset with ATCO that he wouldn't record for them" (55).

When Musso was an offered a job heading the Kapp Records division of Decca Records, he decided that he wanted the duo on his label.

I offered to bring Sonny & Cher to Kapp with me. They were going to sign for no advance—Sonny just wanted to have a record out. Then RCA offered them $50,000, which I matched. That's when everybody at Decca thought I was really nuts—Sonny & Cher hadn't had a hit in years. People saw their house in Bel Air with the elevator and the Rolls Royce parked in the drive-way and thought they were successful, even though their refrigerator didn't have any food in it. Later, Sonny and I would laugh about that (55).

Since Sonny was responsible for creating the Sonny & Cher act to begin with, and was famous for writing, producing, and orchestrating their initial success on the record charts, it seemed like a natural choice to have him resume doing exactly that at Kapp Records. Sonny felt that it would be very cutting edge to have Cher's first solo single on Kapp be something poignant and very topical, so he wrote a song for her called "Classified 1A." The song was about a soldier being killed in Vietnam, with Cher singing from the point of view of the soldier bleeding to death. The song was maudlin, dreary, depressing, and absolutely uncommercial. Released as Cher's first Kapp single on March 24, 1971, it went beyond being a "bomb": radio station programmers literally refused to play it, and it died a quicker death than the soldier depicted within it. In Eng-land, the other side of the single, a tepid Sonny-composed ballad called "Put It on Me," was earmarked as the "A" side. Unfortunately, it was also a musical chart failure.

Sonny's first attempts at reviving the recording career of Sonny & Cher were equally as disastrous. On May 31, 1971, Kapp Records released its first single by the duo. On one side was the Paul Anka com-position "Real People," backed with Sonny's composition "Somebody." Actually, both of those songs were beautifully written and sung; however, this time around, the undoing of them was based on the fact that they didn't fit what was hot at the time on the record charts. "Real People" sounded like something from the Burt Bacharach/Hal David songbook, with a beautiful horn section in the middle of it. "Somebody" had a bet-ter chance of capturing an audience; however, it wasn't dramatic enough to get added to any radio station play lists.

Denis Pregnolato, who worked as a manager for Sonny & Cher in the 1970s and was a close personal friend of Sonny's, recalls, "When they put Cher's 'Classified 1A' out, nobody would play it because it's about a guy dying in Vietnam. I remember that Johnny Musso was very nervous, because he'd just signed them, and this was what Sonny was coming up with" (55).

Since *The Sonny & Cher Comedy Hour* was in the works, Kapp Records was in a big rush to get an album out on the marketplace.

Because the duo had started filming the television summer replacement series, and were still performing at nightclubs regularly, there wasn't time to plan and record an album. According to Johnny Musso, "So, I had them record live at the Century Plaza Hotel in Los Angeles, where they'd already been scheduled to play. Ahmet Ertegun was kind enough to give us permission to record several of their old hits, and the album went Gold instantly" (55).

The album, *Sonny & Cher Live,* was released on September 3, 1971. On the cover of the album was a photograph of the duo amidst their act. Sonny was dressed in a tuxedo, bow tie, and ruffled shirt. Cher was wearing a black mesh top, holding a microphone in her right hand. With her arm bent at the elbow, she is seen dangling her left hand, which is bent at the wrist as though she was displaying her manicure. This was to become the classic Cher singing pose, one she instantly became identified with in the 1970s.

Sonny & Cher Live only contained four songs that had been hits for the duo: "What Now My Love," "The Beat Goes On," "I Got You Babe," and Sonny's solo "Laugh at Me." They also performed three Beatles' songs ("Got to Get You into My Life," "Hey Jude," and "Something"), some contemporary ballads ("Once in a Lifetime," "Someday (You'll Want Me to Want You)," and "More Today Than Yesterday") and the Irish standard "Danny Boy." The recording also included some of the duo's emerging comedy bits in between songs. Denis Pregnolato is credited as the album's producer.

As part of his monologue to introduce "Laugh at Me," Sonny would stand in the spotlight alone and say to the audience,

> Seven years ago I had my hair about this long. At that time there were no Beatles, and there were no . . . there was nothing then, and people didn't know how to react. I mean they thought that was very strange. When you had your hair this long people just . . . I wasn't into anything revolutionary or anything like that, actually I couldn't afford a haircut, and so. . . . [crowd laughs] To people then it, really, it was very strange back then. I'd walk down the street minding my own business, and people would look at you and somebody would say "Faggot!" BOOM! [another big laugh from the audience] (54).

As odd of a novelty song as "Laugh at Me" was, Sonny warmly performed it in a heartfelt fashion. Suddenly this song sounded like it meant so much more to him than it had in the 1960s when he wrote it. Back then he was singing the song so that people would stop pointing at him and laughing. In 1971, when *Sonny & Cher Live* was recorded, Sonny was singing with determination, as though it was now a vow that he would somehow pull Sonny & Cher out of the financial mess they had gotten themselves into.

Not only did the *Sonny & Cher Live* album sell over 500,000 copies, it made it to Number 35 on the American album chart. Musso recalls, "It wasn't very well recorded, and we cut it all in one night, but it was a real fast Gold album. Our first pressing was 25,000 copies, which were sold out immediately. The name of Sonny & Cher was still magic, and the success of that album really opened the eyes of the people at MCA [Kapp and Decca's parent company]" (55).

Johnny Musso decided that an outside producer had to be brought in to record Cher solo and Sonny & Cher. Something had to be done to jumpstart both acts' once-golden recording careers. The man he chose was Tommy "Snuff" Garrett, who just happened to live next door to Sonny & Cher in Bel Air. Garrett remembers, "They were on real hard times while I was redoing my house in Bel Air. Johnny [Musso] had signed them and they were looking for a producer. I said to myself, 'I can get a hit on her.' The first song I cut on Cher was 'Gypsys, Tramps and Thieves' " (55).

Cher was about to get a huge hit that was tailor-made just for her. Bob Stone was a writer who had his songs covered by pop artists like Bobby Sherman, the American Breed, and Shades of Blue at the time.

> Snuff Garrett told me that he'd gotten back in the business, and mentioned Cher. He was looking for something between "Bang Bang" and "Son of a Preacher Man" [a Dusty Springfield hit]. I ran home and listened to everything she'd done, and what I liked the best was done in minor keys. She's [half] Armenian, and has an ethnic quality; her voice is deep and dark and heavy. Before long I had a verse and mock chorus "Gypsys and White Trash." They liked it, but I told them I could do better. Within a few days, they were recording "Gypsys, Tramps and Thieves" (55).

"Gypsys, Tramps and Thieves" was so dramatic and ear-catching that it was exactly the song for Cher to kick right over the goalpost with her sound, delivery, and perfect timing. It was absolutely irresistible, and it proved that Snuff Garrett knew more about Cher's voice and her persona as a singer than Sonny did. The way Cher sings on the four albums she did with Garrett during her Kapp/MCA days in the early 1970s is representative of one of the most successful eras of her entire recording career. In the 1960s on Imperial Records, even on songs with a strong musical stance—like "Bang Bang" and "You Better Sit Down Kids"—Cher's vocals sound comparatively light and tentative. On every cut on the 1971 album *Cher* she is commanding, exotic, and immediately ear-catching.

Another song on *Cher*, "The Way of Love," had been a hit in 1965 for British singer Kathy Kirby. A dramatic and sweeping ballad, Snuff thought it was just right for Cher—and he was right. "I tried to fit the songs to her. I never thought of Cher as a singer; she was a stylist, which is quite different. I'll take a stylist every time—when you turn on the radio and hear that voice, you know it's Cher" (55).

The *Cher* album also included her interpretations of contemporary hits like James Taylor's "Fire & Rain" and the Hollies' "He Ain't Heavy, He's My Brother." The selection of these two songs represents part of a continuation of her career-long ability to take songs by male folk/rock singers or groups, record her own interpretive versions, and make the songs seem as if they were written for her. Now that she had already recorded ten different Bob Dylan songs in the 1960s, it was time to explore some other male rocker songbooks in the 1970s. During her years at Kapp/MCA Records, Cher was also to borrow from the song-books of Three Dog Night, the Beatles, the Bee Gees, Seals & Crofts, and Leon Russell.

For the rest of the *Cher* album Garrett chose songs that echoed her ability to excel at songs that dealt with drama and crumbling relation-ships: "I Hate to Sleep Alone," "I'm in the Middle," and the controver-sial "He'll Never Know," which was about a woman who neglected to tell her husband that their son was not fathered by him.

"Gypsys, Tramps and Thieves" was an instant hit, literally shooting up to Number 1 on the American music charts and up to Number 4 in Eng-land. The week of November 19, 1971, the Record Industry Association of America (RIAA) certified the single version of "Gypsys, Tramps and Thieves" Gold, for over a million copies sold in America (joining "Bang Bang" as her second solo million-seller). The song was so popular that eventually the record company reissued the *Cher* album under the title *Gypsys, Tramps and Thieves*. When "The Way of Love" was released as her follow-up single, it sped up the charts into the Top 10, logging in at Number 7 in the United States. The *Cher* album made it to Number 16 on the American album chart, and during the week of April 13, 1972, it was certified Gold by the RIAA.

It was Johnny Musso's goal to repeat the success that he had bringing back Cher's recording career with Sonny & Cher. He again assigned this task to Snuff Garrett. Musso had in mind a song called "All I Ever Need Is You," which had been recorded by Ray Charles. It had been written by a man named Eddie Reeves, with Jimmy Holiday. Reeves had mentioned to Musso that he had been thinking of recording it himself, as he was a recording artist as well.

> I ran into Johnny Musso before a session, and he asked if I was going to do "All I Ever Need Is You." When I told him that I wasn't—I didn't like the song that much—he had me send him a copy of the Ray Charles album. Sonny & Cher had just exploded with their television show, "Gypsys, Tramps and Thieves" was Number One for Cher, and they were looking for a comeback single for Sonny & Cher. Whatever they picked would have gotten a lot of attention (55).

Johnny Musso says, "I played Sonny the song one afternoon, that night we recorded it, and the next day we had an acetate copy to [radio station] KHJ. Within 24 hours from the time I played it for Snuffy, it was on the air. It became the theme song for Sonny & Cher's TV Show" (55).

The single of "All I Ever Need Is You" became an instant hit for the duo, making it up to Number 7 in America and Number 8 in the United Kingdom. Sonny & Cher were officially back on top! The follow-up single, "A Cowboy's Work Is Never Done," repeated the success, making it to Number 8 in the United States. The resulting Sonny & Cher album on Kapp Records, *All I Ever Need Is You,* was released in early 1972. Thanks to Snuff Garrett's production skills, and his instinctive ability to pick hit singles, the project was a huge success, literally bringing Sonny & Cher's recording career back from the grave.

The *All I Ever Need Is You* album also included the duo's version of "More Today Than Yesterday," "United We Stand," and the Fortunes' "Here Comes That Rainy Day Feeling." To keep Sonny happy, the album also contained three of his compositions: "A Cowboy's Work Is Never Done," the previously recorded "Somebody," and a Sonny solo version of the song "You Better Sit Down Kids." "A Cowboy's Work Is Never Done," which was a cute novelty number, was coproduced by Sonny and Snuff Garrett.

All I Ever Need Is You made it to Number 14 in America and was certified Gold by the RIAA, becoming the duo's second Gold album, in May of 1972. Two months later, *Sonny & Cher Live* was certified Gold as well, bringing their total to three albums certified for over 500,000 copies sold in America.

Barry Rudolph worked as second engineer with recording engineer Lenny Capps.

> On Sonny & Cher sessions, it was Snuff and Sonny working together but separately. Snuff was running the show, and Sonny was being Sonny— running around, joking with the musicians, and helping Cher with her phrasing on the vocals. When she was doing the vocals, they wouldn't let anyone watch, she was pretty self-conscious. Sonny had a pretty good ear; if something didn't sound right he would notice. It was more a matter of him not liking something musically than picking out specific mistakes— more of an overview. And on his own sessions. Sonny was trying to be Phil Spector, acting as master of ceremonies (55).

After the show was on the air for eight weeks, a knock came on the front door of Sonny and Cher's Bel Air home. It was their favorite house sales- man, Tony Curtis. He announced to them that the Holmby Hills house he owned, which they had visited and which Cher loved, was for sale. The Holmby Hills house was absolutely huge and way too big for a family of three. It had fifty-four rooms and 30,000 square feet of space. But Sonny knew how much Cher loved that house, so they bought it, for $750,000. According to Sonny, "The mansion was the pinnacle of [Cher's] Cinderella fantasy" (35). Bono claimed that it only took Cher three days to furnish it. The house was also perfect for entertaining. According to Sonny, "Our home always [was] full of friends. Most of them—except Bob Mitchum, Steve McQueen and the Monkees—[weren't] in show business" (50). They were later to regret such an extravagance.

The TV show was a huge hit, and Sonny & Cher were in great demand in concert and in nightclubs and casinos. When they weren't taping their television series, they were on tour. On the road with Sonny & Cher was a top-notch band, including drummer Jeff Porcaro, keyboard player David Paich, and bass player David Hungate. After the break-up of Sonny & Cher, that trio would add guitar player Steve Lukather and become known as Toto. Hungate remembers those big, extravagant Sonny & Cher concert tours, when the TV show was hot and the duo was again producing hits.

> Being with Sonny & Cher on the road was much more fun than Toto. We were traveling on Hugh Hefner's jet, complete with Playboy bunnies, we

were well-paid, and got respect. There was an incredible diversity of people at our concerts, ranging from Oral Roberts in Tulsa, to Bob Dylan in Las Vegas, to Karen Silkwood in Oklahoma. It was ironic that Cher later appeared in the *Silkwood* movie. Karen had entered a Cher look-alike contest while in high school. Her boyfriend who was an old friend of mine, was played by Kurt Russell in the movie. We got to meet people like Jack Benny, Edgar Bergen, and Ed Sullivan, all those old-time show business guys (55).

According to Bart Andrews, when Sonny & Cher first came to CBS, everyone thought that Cher was pretty, but one-dimensional, and that Sonny was a jerk who kept sticking his nose into the inner workings of their TV series. However, with success, all of that changed. Says Andrews, "Sonny became very involved in running the show when they came back on the air on a permanent schedule, without a formal production title. But he was very, very interested in the business end of it, because he had apparently structured their career. There were some people who got annoyed, I remember. But he was very well respected by the time that show was over" (57).

Cher's own uniquely exotic physical beauty was enhanced by the growing number of gorgeous handmade beaded gowns that she wore on camera. She wore outrageous and silly costumes for the comedy skits, but when she sang solos and duets with Sonny, she was dressed in beautiful high-fashion clothes. Cher had, and has, a fantastically svelte body, and costume designer Bob Mackie made the most of all her attributes. Cher never had a big bust, but she had a flat stomach, great hips, and nice, exposable legs. After all those years of wearing bell-bottomed pants, her fans had no idea what her legs looked like when they were finally unveiled.

Mackie had a field day, outdoing himself as a designer week after week. Tuning in just to see what wild and outrageous clothes Cher would wear became half the reason for watching the show. Cher's wardrobe was budgeted at $10,000 per show, and they used every cent of it to make certain that she was *the* top mannequin of television land.

"She was more of an innovator than anyone realizes," says Bob Mackie of Cher's importance in the fashion world.

> She had established the look of the sixties bell-bottoms and all—and I just helped her establish a look for the seventies. We started off making her kind of glamorous, and then we went to *really* glamorous. But Cher wore

my clothes like they were a pair of jeans. I know what clothes can do, and I know what they can't do. If someone else had been wearing those gowns, it wouldn't have been the same. No one else has Cher's ease. And no one else has those armpits! Cher has the most beautiful armpits in the world. As much as anything else, I designed for her armpits (37).

With regard to wearing Mackie's fantastic gowns, Cher explains,

The first time I ever worked with him was right after Chastity was born. We did a *Carol Burnett Show.* We worked with him for the summer season of *The Sonny & Cher Comedy Hour,* which was 1971. He was really expensive. We could only afford him to do a few costumes for the show. . . . I think I had two beaded dresses the whole time [during the 1971 summer replacement series]. But he did lots of extra stuff because he was really excited about the glamour. In *The Sonny & Cher [Comedy] Hour* we had lots of clothes for sketches; we had the opening and the closing numbers. We had a concert, and we had my solo spot, so there were plenty of spaces to dress up. . . . The first summer we only did six shows. Once we really started the season we did have to have thousands of dollars, because each one of these gowns was four or five thousand dollars, even in those days. They were all beaded (39).

Then there was Cher's incredibly versatile hair. During this era, she just kept letting her luxurious black hair grow longer and longer, until it was down to her waist. One of her trademark onstage affectations was brushing strands of her long, dark hair out of her eyes or shaking those trademark tresses.

With all of the skits that she was doing, and all of the characters she was playing, her hairstyle would change several times per show as well. So that she didn't damage her own fantastic hair, she would also wear wigs whenever possible. To design and care for all of her wigs, Cher employed a woman who went by the professional name of Renate [Leuschner-Pless]. Says Cher,

We got Renate because there were so many changes in the show and it had to be done so fast, and nobody knew what to do with my real hair. So Renate had this special way of wrapping it when my hair was long, and she could just get it up there. That way I could do like fourteen changes a show. We'd shoot the show in two days, so that was a lot of changes to just whip in and out of. I would always start the show and end the show with my own hair down. I always wore my hair down to begin the show and to end the show (39).

Cher wasn't a conventional beauty. She had a very angular nose and face. She also had a crooked-toothed smile. Her two upper incisor teeth were long and protruded. She had an exotic look that was very real, and natural. This was all before the cosmetic dentistry and cosmetic surgery that she would have performed on her face and body. The Cher whom television audiences fell in love with in the early 1970s looked very different than Cher of the late 1990s.

In 1972, Cher was on the annual "Best Dressed Women" lists. In Bob Mackie's opinion,

> There hasn't been a girl like Cher since Dietrich or Garbo. She's a high-fashion star who appeals to people of all ages. She's a great influence on both adults and teenagers. It's never happened before. She can stand there in the wildest garb and get away with it. It's fun to watch a performer who is so connected with fashion. We never thought of any 'Best Dressed List' possibilities. She has a sense of humor about her clothes as well as a sexy, glamorous feeling. She used to be crazy—but funky. She switched to glamour and now it's taken hold with younger people to be glamorous, well groomed. It's a good influence (59).

In 1972 Bob Mackie observed, "Summer clothes worn this year are what we did for Cher on last season's summer replacement show backless halters, slinky jerseys, et cetera" (13). Suddenly everyone was watching and imitating Cher and her clothes.

There were also several dramatic battles over costumes with the censors. Cher had such a great body that Bob Mackie would push the envelope more and more to reveal flesh here and there. Most controversial was showing her navel on network primetime television. Just ten years before, actress Barbara Eden was forbidden from exposing her belly button in her bare-midriff costume on the TV series *I Dream of Jeannie.*

Cher was constantly battling the censors. She knew she had a great figure, and she wanted to show it off.

> You couldn't do anything [sexual] on television [in the early 1970s]. All the stuff I wanted to do that was just a bit grown-up would be misunderstood by them. The censors were just so ridiculous. One time I did this beautiful solo on the show and they said they were going to make me go and change my outfit. Bob [Mackie] had made me this beautiful kimono, and underneath it was this long slip. It was really pretty, and they said, "No, no, you look like a hooker," and I said, "I'm just standing in front of a window!" So [producer]

Norman Lear was walking outside and I ran out and said, "Norman, come in here and look at this number and tell the censor what you think." I was singing "Sunshine on My Shoulders" by John Denver, and Norman turned to the censor and said, "You must be really sick if you can find anything dirty in that!" So we got to keep it. I was the first person ever to show my belly button on TV. The censors didn't like that at all, but I had already been doing it when they decided they didn't like it. I was already wearing those clothes and people loved those clothes. Women just loved them (39).

Cher found herself addictively swept up in her whole glamorous transformation. "I took it all pretty seriously," she was later to admit. "We all want to be sexy because it makes us valuable. I always wanted to be valuable, and before I became an entertainer, I was just not valuable to people" (13).

She recalled something that photographer Richard Avedon once told her in the 1960s. "He said, 'Sweetheart, you're never going to be on the cover [of *Vogue* magazine], because you're not the "look."'" Well, one day they did put me on the cover—while *The Sonny & Cher Comedy Hour* was on—and it was a huge success. I realized then that you have to make people change their whole idea. You have to convince them" (37). What Cher was doing in turn was convincing herself of her own personal worth.

To give a counterpoint to her glamorous image, Cher and her writing staff came up with a truly tacky recurring character for her to play in skits on the show. Cher called her Laverne. She was a little potbellied in the stomach (thanks to padding on Cher's body), and she wore tiger-skin-patterned clothes that were inappropriately too tight. She wore cats-eye-shaped glasses, and her curly red wig was wrapped in a scarf, as though she was still wearing curlers underneath it. She was also always chewing gum in a most aggravating fashion.

Of the development of this character, Cher explains,

Laverne started when we did a takeoff of [the TV series] *All in the Family* and everyone liked me doing that kind of character, so they wanted me to come up with a woman in a laundromat. Slowly but surely Bob [Mackie] and I came up with the costume. It was my copy of a Lucille Ball hairdo, only we gave her terrible roots. The [exposed and drooping] bra strap was Bob's idea; it was so perfect. The bra strap makes it. But I couldn't come up with the voice. I tried doing it every which way. At the very last minute before we did her live in front of an audience, the prop man gave me some bubble gum—I can't do Laverne without gum in my mouth and Laverne came out. She just had a life of her own (39).

Sonny & Cher became the hip new married couple for the 1970s. For a generation raised on situation comedies with perfect TV families, the newly glamorized Bonos seemed like the perfect couple for the "me" decade. Sponsors liked them, because although they looked hip, they had a squeaky clean and conservative image. In a cover story in the March 18, 1972, issue of *TV Guide* magazine, Sonny announced on behalf of he and Cher, "Our lifestyle has changed a lot. 'Matured' is the word I'd use. When we first hit we were looser, wilder. Now we're more security minded. . . . I think the important thing is to have standards and rules. I want to make sure we display them ourselves and pass them along to our daughter" (47).

Life soon became very hectic for Sonny and Cher. Sonny loved the fast pace that their career was taking, and the idea of guiding the ship. Their television show was renewed for the 1972–73 season, and it aired at 8:00 p.m. on Friday nights from September to December. In December of 1972 it was moved to Wednesday nights from 8:00 to 9:00 p.m. In the 1973–74 season it occupied the 8:00 p.m. Wednesday night slot. When they weren't filming their television show, they were on the road doing their concert and nightclub act around the country.

On May 1, 1972, Kapp Records released the Cher solo single "Living in a House Divided," which reached Number 22 in America. A beautiful ballad about the demise of a marriage, written by Tom Bahler, this set the tone of her latest album, the all-ballad set *Foxy Lady*. More of an adult contemporary album than a pop/rocker like the *Cher* LP, *Foxy Lady* is one of Cher's most focused and beloved albums. All of the songs on the album are moody heartbreakers like "It Might as Well Stay Monday (From Now On)," "Don't Ever Try to Close a Rose," and "Don't Hide Your Love." Cher also covered Leon Russell's "Song for You" and sang a slow, growling version of Three Dog Night's "Never Been to Spain." In September of 1972, *Foxy Lady* peaked at Number 43 on the album charts in America.

In addition, *Foxy Lady* was the only one of Cher's four MCA/Kapp albums with Snuff Garrett to include any songs or any participation from Sonny. He is represented on *Foxy Lady* by his composition "The First Time." Also, he was the coproducer—along with Snuff Garrett—on three of the cuts. One of the songs from this set, "Let Me Down Easy," gives a great preview of the trademark "Cher vibrato" that her 1980s and 1990s recordings are now so famous for. Vocally, this was Cher's new peak performance. Snuff was picking songs for Cher that were challenging and stretching her vocal capacity, and it is especially evident on this album.

In June of 1972, Kapp Records released the next Sonny & Cher single, "When You Say Love." The duo recorded their version of this warm, up-tempo, love song—complete with full background chorus—and took it to Number 32 on the music charts. The bizarre twist to this song was the fact that it was instantly recognizable to anyone in earshot of a radio or television that summer. That was because it was exactly the same song as the concurrent beer commercial being broadcast everywhere that year: "When You Say Bud." While the song was a big hit, that summer everyone kept asking the same musical question "Isn't that Sonny & Cher singing the Budweiser commercial?" Admittedly, it was a strange choice as a Sonny & Cher single, but it somehow sold records—and beer.

Watching Snuff Garrett get all the credit for bringing back Sonny & Cher's recording career started bothering Sonny Bono more and more. Furthermore, Sonny didn't like some of the decisions that Garrett was making for the duo's musical identity. It wasn't long before a rift between them exploded. Sonny couldn't wait to depose Garrett.

Reportedly, Garrett had selected Cher's new single, another story-song, entitled "The Night the Lights Went Out in Georgia." When Sonny heard the song, he hated it. Sonny delighted in getting Snuff thrown out as Cher's record producer. Meanwhile, Garrett was so convinced that "The Night the Lights Went Out in Georgia" was a hit, that he gave the song to television actress Vicki Lawrence. Once again he was right in knowing a hit song when he heard one, and Lawrence's version went straight to Number 1 in America in April of 1973.

Exactly at this time, Kapp Records was no more, as it was absorbed into MCA Records. Sonny seized this opportunity to get Snuff Garrett out of the way and begin producing Cher and Sonny & Cher records by himself.

Reluctantly, MCA gave Sonny the chance to be in control of his and Cher's recording career again. He wanted to produce on his own, but MCA wasn't about to go for that. Sonny was allowed to produce the next Cher album, and the next Sonny & Cher album was to be produced by and/or with his friend Denis Pregnolato. Unfortunately, the resulting albums were complete disasters.

The biggest musical nightmare that Sonny orchestrated was the title cut to the worst Sonny & Cher album, *Mama Was a Rock & Roll Singer, Papa Used to Write All Her Songs.* It was another autobiographical Sonny

Bono composition about his life with Cher. This time around, in the context of the song he bitterly made fun of the title of Cher's previous album, *Foxy Lady*, lyrically claiming she was "vamping" everyone in town and had effectively "messed up the world" of Sonny & Cher. This was clearly a "fuck you" note from Sonny to Cher. The highly unmelodic song was an expensive vanity project that was doomed from the start. According to assistant recording engineer Barry Rudolph,

> We had 52 musicians crammed into every nook and cranny of Larrabee Studios. There were four or five guitar players, a full brass section, two or three percussionists—maybe 25 people in one room, with Cher in a vocal booth. Across the hall, we had four or five Hawaiians playing six-foot sticks. In another room, we had a harp player. In the control room, we had six background singers, live. Paul Beaver was playing the Moog synthesizer. Everything was written out by Michael Rubini, but Sonny kept adding things. It took all those musicians ten minutes to file out of the studio for what was supposed to be a ten-minute break (55).

The song was an overproduced debacle that ran over nine minutes in length. When it was cut down to a single running three minutes and forty-one seconds, it made it onto the music charts and stalled at Number 77. The Sonny & Cher album *Mama Was a Rock & Roll Singer, Papa Used to Write All Her Songs* only made it to Number 132 on the charts, as compared with its predecessor, the duo's *All I Ever Need Is You*, which made it to Number 14 with Snuff Garrett producing.

The strongest songs on the album were the duo's cover versions of Albert Hammond's "It Never Rains in Southern California," the Doobie Brothers' "Listen to the Music," Johnny Nash's "I Can See Clearly Now," and Neil Diamond's "Brother Love's Traveling Salvation Show." The most significant song on the album was written by Bob Stone, who had given Cher "Gypsys, Tramps and Thieves." It was a song called "The Greatest Show on Earth." It was about the breakup of a marriage, with Sonny singing about his wife walking out on him. Never was there a more prophetic or autobiographical song about the Sonny & Cher saga. In time it would become crystal clear just how true it was to be.

After Cher recorded two of the most successful albums of her career—*Cher* and *Foxy Lady*—at Sonny's insistence he was allowed to produce her next album, *Bittersweet White Light*. Tackling eleven "standards" like the ones she was occasionally singing on the television series, Cher warbled her way through "The Man That Got Away," "Am I Blue,"

"How Long Has This Been Going On," "More Than You Know," a sort-of schmaltzy Al Jolson medley, and several other songs from 1918 to 1953. Instead of being a beautiful masterpiece, the resulting album was heavily overproduced. On some of the songs—especially "By Myself"—Cher's singing style is so completely over-the-top that it devours the subtle ballads. This point was to be further driven home two albums later when she recorded a subtle and stunning version of Irving Berlin's "What'll I Do," and beautifully nailed the song.

Bittersweet White Light was a complete "bomb" that self-destructed after reaching Number 160 on the *Billboard* album chart when it was released in 1973. A single of "Am I Blue" was released, but it went nowhere. Bette Midler had just recorded a superior version on her *Divine Miss M* album the previous year. Cher's first MCA album and Sonny & Cher's first MCA album were both huge sales disappointments. An edict came down from the top brass at MCA: Sonny Bono was out as Cher's producer, and Snuff Garrett was reinstated.

Now that Sonny & Cher were huge television stars, their previous record companies jumped at the opportunity to capitalize upon all the publicity that they were generating and all of the current exposure on the radio airwaves that they were receiving. In 1972, United Artists Records, which now had control of Cher's Imperial Records material from the 1960s, released two separate two-record sets *Cher/Superpak* and *Cher/Superpak Volume II*. Each contained twenty-four Cher solos, taking the best of her first five solo albums for Imperial, from 1965's *All I Really Want to Do* to 1968's *Backstage*. In February of 1972, *Cher/Superpak* reached Number 92 on *Billboard's* album chart in America. The following year, ATCO Records got into the act, releasing the 1973 two-record album set *The Two of Us,* featuring twenty-four of the best cuts from the duo's first three albums for that label, from "I Got You Babe" to "The Beat Goes On."

Cher and Sonny & Cher were big news again. Record shops were filled with their releases. By 1973 there were thirteen different Cher albums and ten different Sonny & Cher albums. They were on the covers of magazines, they were appearing in concert year-round, and they were on television screens every week. Not only had they revived their careers to the point of their popularity in the 1960s, they had surpassed it in every way.

In spite of some temporary slippage on the charts with the two Snuff Garrett-less albums, Sonny & Cher's career was going fantastically in

1973. They were in their third season on television, and *The Sonny & Cher Comedy Hour* was still rated in the Top 10. As long as Garrett was producing them, their records were selling, and they were in demand on the nightclub and concert circuit. They had even incorporated their adorable little daughter, Chastity, into their weekly variety show, and they appeared to be America's ideal hip and happy couple. Unfortunately, that was not the case after the cameras stopped rolling. Unbeknownst to Sonny, their marriage was eroding amid all of the high-profile activity.

One of the lyric lines to the song "Mama Was a Rock & Roll Singer Papa Used to Write All Her Songs" found Sonny accusing his "foxy lady" of "going and messing up the world." This *truly* applied to Sonny Bono's ability to pick and produce hits, circa 1972–73. It also applied to Cher's personal frustrations with her new life at the top. It wasn't all a bed of roses—by a long shot. Although no one knew it at the time, the LP was to be the final Sonny & Cher studio album ever to be recorded.

According to Cher,

> The first year we were doing our CBS show, I had had fourteen days off out of 365. The second year, between the show and personal appearances, I didn't have even one day off. I developed all sorts of ailments: stomach trouble, skin rashes—from nerves. I told Sonny I just couldn't take it anymore. He told me that I could—I just had to try, that's all. He was right. I did try, I did make it. I was able to keep up with the work schedules, just like he said—but I was miserable (60).

She further explained, "Even though Sonny always gave me the spotlight on-stage, he had this macho thing about keeping me in the background off-stage. A real pain in the ass. The whole time I was married to Sonny, we hardly ever went anywhere, and I never really knew that many people. I was really isolated" (6).

Her mother, Georgia Holt, recalls,

> I was thrilled by their success. I continued to worry about Cher. Then gradually Sonny came between us. He thought I was too influential in Cher's life. When Chastity was born, I became the happiest grandmother in the United States. When Sonny and Cher were working, Chastity spent a lot of time with me, and I loved every moment of it. She is a sweet, beautiful girl. Sometimes I let Cher know I thought she was working too hard. She was always getting sick and winding up in the hospital. She goes

beyond her endurance and doesn't get enough rest. Once she went on-stage with a 102 degree fever! I was the last one to know that Sonny and Cher weren't getting along. They kept all their unhappiness from me (11).

According to Cher, her life with Sonny had been going downhill for a long time.

> After the baby was born, things started to get different, but not so that he [Sonny] even noticed. I started feeling more like a woman. I carried over half the load, but I knew I never would have been out there if it weren't for him. Otherwise, I might as well have been in a closet someplace in east Guam. But as I started feeling more mature, I got more pissed off about things I wanted that weren't exactly outrageous and he just laid a definite "no" on them. One of the things I originally found so attractive about Sonny was that he really believed women should be taken care of. Even-tually, it got to the point of driving me crazy (18).

Although they had continued to tape their weekly show together, things around the set of *The Sonny & Cher Comedy Hour* were getting too bizarre to handle. The pressure of breaking up with your spouse, and having to work with him week after week, all the while pretending that nothing was wrong, finally proved too much for Cher. According to her, "I remember one night singing 'I Got You Babe' at the end, thinking 'I can't wait until I'm off the show so I can go see my boyfriend at the beach" (61).

Cher felt she was chained to a never-ending treadmill. Remembering the nonstop pace that she was traveling at in 1972 and 1973, Cher said,

> I was growing up and he wasn't catching up. Plus, from the time we began the show until I left him, it was constant work. I went to the hospital two or three times a year—I have anemia and lose weight very easily. And we had a schedule that would break a three hundred pound truck driver. We'd do the show, then weekends and holidays we'd do one-nighters and inter-views and picture sessions (18).

She finally reached the end of her rope.

> If you watched *The Sonny & Cher Comedy Hour,* you assumed I was this wisecracking girl who ran our lives off-stage, 'cause Sonny seemed so meek and easygoing. Hah! In real life he was this Sicilian dictator husband—I could say nothing! We were in the Nielsen [TV ratings] Top Ten, we had

all this money, everybody told me how lucky and happy I was—when actually I weighed 93 pounds. I was constantly sick, could not eat, could not sleep (19).

I shopped all the time, because that was the only way I could get out of the house alone without being supervised. Just shopped my ass off. Then I took up needlepoint—my God, I needlepointed everything. I could have made a needlepoint stove! I was so unhappy. Everyone was having a great time but me. I'd be put in bed after the show, take off my lashes, and just go to sleep. And they'd stay up. And I just thought, Goddamn, I'm 26 [years old], these ten years have gone by so quickly. I just wanted to be a human being, to go and do things (18).

Cher finally reached an impasse one night after a show in Las Vegas in late 1972.

Two decades later Sonny Bono was to claim in his autobiography that their breakup was entirely Cher's doing. According to him, on November 15, 1972, Sonny & Cher were booked to perform two shows at the Flamingo Hotel. They performed their first show to a packed house. In between shows, Cher went back to the couple's suite, while Sonny, Denis Pregnolato, and their guitarist Bill Hamm went over to the Hilton to watch Tina Turner's show. They returned to the Flamingo in time for Sonny & Cher's second sold-out show of the night, which received three standing ovations.

After the show, Sonny and Cher rode the elevator up to their suite, making only small talk along the way. When they got to their suite, Sonny threw his jacket on the bed and began unbuckling his belt. Cher shot him a look that he claimed "was completely foreign to the repertoire I knew so well from ten years of being with her" (35). She then told him that she wanted him to leave the room.

When he asked why, she told him that Bill Hamm was on his way up. Assuming that it was to go over some music with her, he was shocked when she told him that she was in love with Hamm and wanted to sleep with him, and that he would be arriving at the door any second now. When Hamm arrived suddenly, the three of them were frozen in time for several wordless seconds. Sonny recalled looking over at the fully stocked bar of the suite and considering smashing one liquor bottle over Hamm's head and the other one over Cher's. Instead, he left the suite and wordlessly shut the door behind him.

He went downstairs into the casino, and began playing blackjack.

When Hamm's girlfriend tapped him on the shoulder and asked him if he had seen Bill, he poured out the whole story to her. As insane as it seems, he asked if they could go up to her room to discuss the situation. As a matter of just retribution, Sonny and Hamm's girlfriend had sex in her suite, and he spent the night. Around five in the morning, Sonny recalled that Hamm returned to his room, and Sonny left. No fight. No argument. Sonny just said "See ya later" as he left Hamm's room (35).

All day Sunday, Sonny argued with Cher, trying to salvage their marriage. She simply told him that it was too late. They had two shows booked for that night, and before the show, Sonny, Cher, and Bill Hamm met in the dressing room to talk it all out. When Sonny told Denis what was going on, both shows were canceled that night, and Denis made plane reservations for Cher and Bill to fly to San Francisco.

Cher was less forthcoming with details when she later recounted the story of their breakup. In her version of the story she claimed, "One day I thought, 'I'm gonna jump off the top of this building, or I'm gonna leave Sonny. And that night I thought, 'Fuck it, I can't jump off the top of this building. And, I left him. But for me it had come down to a choice, and it took me forever" (62).

What was Sonny's reaction? According to her, " 'He said, 'O.K.,' " and she walked out. However, she explained, "He told me later he thought about throwing me off the balcony" (18).

> It wasn't even an argument. I just left. I said I needed three hundred dollars and I was going to San Francisco, and Sonny gave me the money. I said afterward, "Why did you do that?" Sonny said, "Because you never said anything like that before, so I figured that you must have meant it." I didn't have a black eye. If I had a black eye, everyone would have known about it. In eleven years Sonny never laid a hand on me, which I think is a terrific thing (34).

And so began the liberation of Cher Bono.

DARK LADY

Cher returned to Los Angeles to the couple's massive Holmby Hills home, and she and Sonny proceeded to live separate lives under the same roof, keeping news of their breakup a secret from the public. On December 9, 1972, Sonny & Cher finished filming their TV program's Christmas episode. From the TV viewer's perspective, if looked like just another warm and loving episode of their program. In reality, it was the beginning of the end of *The Sonny & Cher Comedy Hour,* and the end of Sonny & Cher—pop music's perfect couple.

From 1973 to 1974 Sonny & Cher kept performing together in concert and on their television show. The public and their fans were kept in the dark about the unthinkable truth behind the façade of the pop world's sweethearts. While their marriage was completely over, their professional career continued. Sonny & Cher were starting to live the themes of their songs—especially their recent duet about the breakup of a marriage, "The Greatest Show on Earth."

Cher's affair with Bill Hamm only lasted a few months. At that point, she began dating another member of the Sonny & Cher band, keyboard player David Paich.

In an effort to recover Sonny & Cher's suddenly slipping appeal on the album charts, MCA called for another live concert album to be recorded. The resulting album, *Sonny & Cher Live in Las Vegas, Volume 2* was released on October 15, 1973, and did even less well on the charts, only reaching Number 175 in America. It was recorded at the Sahara Hotel in Las Vegas and was produced by Sonny's friend Denis Pregnolato.

A live version of Cher singing the song "Superstar" was released as a Sonny & Cher single, but it failed to chart. Although it was a fantastic song, and Cher did a great job singing it, it was a bad idea as a single. Rita Coolidge had originally made it famous in 1970 on Joe Cocker's *Mad Dogs and Englishmen* album. Bette Midler had just recorded it on her *Divine Miss M* album, and the Carpenters' version had already been a Number 2 hit in 1971.

According to band member David Hungate, "For a whole year, we were operating behind a façade. Sonny had his girlfriend on the road, Cher was seeing whoever she was seeing at the time, and they were appearing on-stage as this all-American couple. Sonny was under a lot of stress, making the comeback and knowing that he could lose it all again overnight" (55).

They also continued living in their mansion together, at least under the same roof. Sonny and his new girlfriend, Connie, would occupy one end of the house, and Cher would come and go at the other end. It was the living embodiment of Cher's hit song "Living in a House Divided."

On September 20, 1973, thirty-one-year-old music industry insider David Geffen threw a star-studded party at his new club, Roxy, on Sunset Boulevard in Los Angeles. Among the celebrities to attend that night, and listen to Neil Young perform, were Carole King, Elton John, Bob Dylan, and Cher. Although Geffen had originally met Cher a decade earlier when she was a background singer of Phil Spector's at Gold Star Records, that particular night sparks flew. Geffen gave Cher his Beverly Hills address and invited her to have dinner there the next night, and she accepted.

Geffen and Cher sat up until late at night pouring out their own personal frustrations to each other. Cher told him how painfully disastrous her marriage to Sonny was—and how they were now holding their relationship together just for the sake of their careers. Geffen was equally as frank and forthcoming with revealing his deepest and darkest personal secrets. Most notably, he confided in her that he couldn't decide whether he was gay or straight. Having been exposed to gay men and women all of her life, Cher was undaunted by this revelation. He also told her that he longed to have a functional relationship with a woman, because he felt that this would make him by far the happiest. According to Cher, they instantly hit it off. Within several days she began a sexual relationship with him, the first functional heterosexual one of his life.

"I'm not alone anymore," Cher recalls thinking to herself once her affair with David Geffen blossomed. "I was the first person to share his bed *and* to share his life. . . . we were really crazy about each other" (63). After that, they were inseparable.

Although Cher was in love with David, and the attention he showered her with, her daughter Chastity was not. "I really didn't like Geffen, because he was the first person Mom dated after my Dad," she was later to say. "Actually, Geffen tells the funniest story. Apparently, I walked in on him in the bathtub when he was naked, and I made some comment about my Dad's dick being bigger than his" (64).

The failure of Cher's all-standards *Bittersweet White Light* album drove home the fact that although it might be fun to watch Cher sing these old songs as costume vignettes on the duo's television variety show, she was no Billie Holiday when it came to singing the blues. What the public loved from Cher—and always has—were sweeping mini-musical dramas set to rock and roll.

Anxious to return Cher to hit-making status, Snuff Garrett was back on the case for her next pair of MCA albums. Snuff worked with a musical arranger named Al Capps. It was Capps, along with a writing partner named Mary Dean, who came up with "Half Breed." Playing up the fact that Cher's mixed heritage includes some Native American roots, the song was tailor-made for her. It included an all-male Indian tribal chant, which sounded reminiscent of Johnny Preston's 1960 hit "Running Bear." However, according to Garrett, the chant on "Half Breed" actually mimicked a Dallas, Texas, jingle for a local Pontiac dealership, not Preston's song.

The song was brilliantly conceived and executed as a Cher story/song about a girl shunned for being half American Indian and half white. The *Half Breed* album cover featured a striking photo of Cher on horseback in the wilderness. The whole project was a smashing success. "Half Breed" zoomed up the charts in America, hitting Number 1 in October 1973. The album went to Number 28 on the *Billboard* chart and was certified Gold.

When Cher debuted "Half Breed" on television, Bob Mackie designed one of his most famous spangled—and controversial—outfits for her to wear. Atop her head she wore a huge white-feathered headdress, decorated with alternating red and yellow feathers, cascading from her head down to her toes. As a top, she wore a 1970s-style backless halter top with sequins and tassels, and from the waist down she wore a long loincloth that reached down to her silver-strapped platform shoes. Not only did her navel show in this bare midriff Native American-inspired outfit, she appeared to be half nude!

According to Cher, at the time, "I remember when I first got that [outfit on] I thought, 'Oh my God, Sonny's going to have a heart attack when I walk out in this!' It looked like I was naked and he was always a little bizarre about that. But he saw me in it, and he was O.K. with it" (39). The "Half Breed" outfit was in fact so hot that Mackie actually produced it in several colors for her.

The other sort of over-the-top story/song that Cher sang on the *Half Breed* album was a song, written for her by John Durrill, called "Carousel Man." It was "Gypsys, Tramps and Thieves" in a carnival setting. The bulk of the rest of the album was made up of several of the current rock ballads of the era, including Paul McCartney & Wings' "My Love," the Bee Gees' "How Can You Mend a Broken Heart," and the Beatles' "Long and Winding Road." Another song was one that had been a hit for Seals & Crofts of "Summer Breeze" fame. It was originally entitled "Ruby Jean & Billie Lee" and was written about the duo's respective wives. Cher took the song and made it more personal to her by turning it into a song for her daughter, entitled "Chastity Sun." It was quite effective, and was one of Cher's favorites from this album.

Another song from the *Half Breed* album, which was perfectly auto-biographical, was the Gloria Sklerov and Harry Lloyd composition, "Two People Clinging to a Thread." It was another song about two people living under the same roof while their relationship had totally eroded. Cher's singing on this song sounds convincingly effective.

In early 1974, Sonny & Cher finished filming their final episodes of *The Sonny & Cher Comedy Hour.* One of the last skits that they taped found Cher portraying the role of Mother Nature and Sonny a seeker of truth and wisdom. "Mother Nature, what is the secret of life?" Sonny asked Cher. Instead of reciting the line she was supposed to say, Cher looked at him and blasted back, "Go fuck yourself" (35). It was getting increasingly difficult for them to even be civil to each other.

Thursday, February 22, 1974, was the final taping day of the last episode of *The Sonny & Cher Comedy Hour.* Afterward, the duo was scheduled to board a plane for Houston, Texas. It was there that they were booked for what would be the final Sonny & Cher concert performance. Prior to leaving the studio, Sonny said to *TV Guide* reporter Rowland Barber, "Our future begins tomorrow, with the rodeo at the

Astrodome. I don't know what Cher's doing, but after that I'm taking a little vacation" (65).

They were scheduled at the Astrodome for two shows, and a local rodeo was going on there at the same time. According to Sonny, they both arrived in separate cars, performed an afternoon and an evening show, and left in separate cars. What Sonny recalls the most was the smell of animal dung wafting up from underneath the temporary stage from which the duo sang to Houston's enthusiastic rodeo fans. According to him, "The whole place smelled like shit. It was an appropriate metaphor for what Cher and I had become, the whole dismal, depressing, distressing situation" (35). At that point, "the love children of a generation" went their separate ways and allowed their lawyers to sweep up the shattered pieces of their private and personal partnership.

On February 20, 1974, Cher had marched into court and filed for divorce from Sonny. Publicly she would claim that being married to him made her feel like she was living a life of servitude under him. From this point on, the adventures of Sonny & Cher shifted from the network TV screen to the covers of magazines like the *Star* and the *National Enquirer*. In the press, the separated duo began to pour out their individual sides of the story. Their millions of fans were in shock.

However, no one was more stunned than Sonny. He couldn't figure out why Cher wanted out of their marriage, let alone their successful business enterprises. When the pieces settled, Sonny was to claim,

I was Cher's foil, her heavy, her boob. But I didn't mind playing straight man because I knew that once our time before the TV cameras was over, and we went home, I was the boss. We cooked and we loved, and we did all the things that a husband and wife do. But you wouldn't know it from the things Cher has said about me. Cher's an ingrate. I made her what she is today. She's never had the decency to set straight all those rotten lies about me—where she said I loafed while she did all the work. Not only are these stories lies, but they've begun to hurt my career. When we began, I used to have to coax Cher to go on stage, because she was frightened (66).

Then came the day when she lowered the boom on me. We had just resigned a three-year contract for our television show and were playing in Las Vegas when Cher came to me one night before the show and whispered, "Sonny, you told me that if anything ever was bothering me that I should tell you, right?" I said, "Right. What's on your mind?" "The truth is," she told me, "that it makes me jumpy to have you around the house. I feel as if I can't be myself. I can't play the radio. I can't listen to records. So you'll move out, O.K." (66).

According to Bono, "I muttered, 'Cher, don't you realize what this will do to our careers? Your career? America will hate you. This will be your Nagasaki. We are the love children of a generation. Don't you realize that every time I push back a strand of your hair, a million fans go out and buy another Sonny & Cher record? We're America's sweethearts' " (13).

What were their alternatives? Could they possibly have split up privately and still gone on as "America's sweethearts" on camera? Admitted Sonny,

> Our separation remained a well-kept secret for a year, throughout which we continued to perform together on television as if nothing had happened. I would have worked that way indefinitely. I was even willing to go along with CBS [TV] exec Fred Silverman's idea to do *The Sonny & Cher Divorce Show,* designed to show that divorced couples need not necessarily hate each other. It was Cher who was unwilling (13).

Ironically, it sounded more like she was leaving her father than leaving her husband. In many ways this was exactly true. Admitted Cher, "We never should have gotten married. Our life together was a good show, but the cast was all wrong. He was playing husband, mother and father. I was Chastity's mother, but I was really the older child. Sonny needs unquestioning adoration from a woman, and I couldn't give that to him" (67).

The last episode of *The Sonny & Cher Comedy Hour* aired on May 29, 1974. It was the show's sixty-fifth episode. While Sonny was living with model Connie Foreman, Cher was very publicly involved with David Geffen and living with him.

When Cher was with Sonny, she was used to having everything done for her. With David Geffen, she grew used to having the same kind of pampering, plus lots of expensive gifts as well. He made certain that her white Porsche Daytona always had a full tank of gasoline and loved squiring her around town. Here was a man who wasn't even certain whether or not he was heterosexual—and all of a sudden he had one of Hollywood's most glamorous and famous women on his arm. They were photographed together at the Grammy Awards, and *Esquire* magazine even wrote a huge article about their affair, called "The Winning of Cher." Anticipating marrying Cher, Geffen purchased a gorgeous Rolls Royce for her, but she didn't like it, so he gave the car to his brother and replaced it with an expensive diamond necklace. On another occasion, he bought her a large diamond ring to bribe her to quit smoking.

The very public breakup of Sonny & Cher was a glitzy real-life soap opera at its best. In a June 1, 1974, cover story in *TV Guide* magazine, the battling Bonos each took the opportunity to state their sides of the story. Proclaimed Cher,

> Sonny was more of a mother to me than my own mother, if you know what I mean. But now I have to break out. And, Sonny's not willing to make the transition with me. He's always been used to Cher's being one way. It's doing this show that's changed me. It was my first chance at really being a 50/50 partner with Sonny. . . . If nothing else ever happened to me, I'd have this high point in my life to look back on (68).

In the same article, Sonny pondered, "Separation sure is different when you're publicly known people. I think it's big of Cher and myself to say, 'Hey, we have some problems.' Of course it affects [the audience]. It affects us on-stage—can't help it. But you saw the taping. There was more warmth than ever before between them and us" (68).

By 1974, Cher had recorded and released twenty-five record albums with and without Sonny, she had made three movies, and she was the star of one of America's most popular Top 10 television shows. However, none of the publicity and notoriety that she had received up to this point could top the media coverage she got when she broke up America's favorite couple and filed for a legal separation. This was just the beginning of the tabloid fireworks between Sonny and Cher, while the divorce proceedings dragged out over the next two years. It was clear that the real-life Sonny & Cher show was far from over.

While David Geffen was a wizard in the record business, he was not especially handsome. At the time, Cher quipped of her new lover, "I traded one short, ugly man for another" (17). Whatever Geffen might have lacked visually in the sex appeal department, he certainly made up for it in the business arena. Already a self-made millionaire in 1974, David had founded and become chairman of Elektra/Asylum Records, where he personally discovered, signed, and nurtured the talents of several singer/songwriters, including Joni Mitchell, Laura Nyro, Carly Simon, Jackson Browne, and Judy Collins. He was not a record producer, but the record business's hot new deal maker. He was also instrumental in shaping Cher's new life post-Sonny. He encouraged her to get her business affairs in order, bolstered her ego and insecurities, attempted to set her life on the right track, and eventually asked her to marry him.

Although Sonny & Cher were through, Cher's solo career kept on chugging along like nothing was wrong. *Half Breed* had been such a hit in 1973 that MCA put her back in the recording studio with Snuff Garrett. This time around, they came up with their most adventurous album together. The 1974 album *Dark Lady* starts out with steam engine propulsion with Alan O'Day's exciting "Train of Thought." It then glides into the medium tempo "I Saw a Man and He Danced with His Wife," a beautiful John Durrill song about love lost.

Snuff Garrett had several different songwriters he liked to work with. One of them was Durrill. He was one of the founding members of the Five Americans ("Western Union," 1967), and he was presently the keyboard player with the Ventures ("Hawaii Five-O" theme, 1969). He was also responsible for what is perhaps Cher's most tailor-made hit, "Dark Lady." Says Durrill, "I had the idea of a woman meeting a fortune teller. I originally had a totally different ending, though. I was in Japan with the Ventures, when I got a note from Snuff 'John: Make sure he kills her.' So I went ahead and rewrote the last verse of 'Dark Lady.' Everybody knew it was a hit the minute they heard Cher's vocal on the playback, though she didn't particularly like it" (55).

Garrett once again proved that he knew a surefire hit when he heard one. "Dark Lady" was exactly that. When it was released in the spring of 1974, it became her third Number 1 hit in America and was so popular that it was also certified Gold for selling over a million copies. It also made it to Number 36 in England. (Oddly enough, it was to be Cher's last single to even chart in England in over ten years.)

Three of the most fun songs on the *Dark Lady* album are "Rescue Me," "What'll I Do," and "Miss Subway of 1952," which are all completely different from one another. Bette Midler at this point had produced two hit albums proving that she could not only sell a sad ballad, but she also excelled at bawdy songs on which she played what used to be known as "a broad." Cher admired Bette, and the song "Miss Subway of 1952" was her tribute to the woman who called herself "the divine Miss M." In fact, Cher ad-libs at the beginning of this Mary F. Cain song with "To my idol the 'Divine,' let's hope this never happens to us." She then proceeds to sing of a disheveled woman cut from the same cloth as her comic creation Laverne.

"Rescue Me" had been a hit in 1965 for Fontella Bass. This was to become the first in a series of great remakes of "girl groups"–style 1960s tunes Cher would record. By the end of the century, the tally of Cher songs using this formula was to include "The Shoop Shoop Song," "Oh No Not My Baby," "Baby I Love You," and "Christmas (Baby Please Come Home)." As on "Rescue Me," Cher sounds like she is genuinely having a fun time singing these songs.

By deciding to record the Irving Berlin song "What'll I Do" Cher proved once and for all that she could sell a classic "standard" song with the best of them. In 1974 the new Mia Farrow and Robert Redford film version of *The Great Gatsby* was all the rage. Music and fashion all went 1920s-style that season, from the photo of Redford in his strawberry ice cream–colored Gatsby suit, to a revived interest in the music of Irving Berlin. An instrumental version of the song "What'll I Do" was used as the theme for the movie, and Cher happily jumped on the Roaring Twenties bandwagon with her own version of it, yielding a classy and beautifully orchestrated recording.

This highly varied album ends with Bob Stone's "Apples Don't Fall Far from the Tree." This was another one of Cher's shady-lady tales told in song. In this one, she lyrically tells of a woman who finally falls in love with a man who has no idea that she once sold herself at a brothel called Ruby's.

For the album cover of *Dark Lady*, Cher enlisted famed fashion photographer Richard Avedon, who had photographed her several times in the past for *Vogue* magazine. The exotic-looking black-and-white photo was a full body shot of Cher, dressed in a sheer black ankle-length gown, holding a black cat like the one she sang about in the album's title song. It was such a striking photograph that *Newsweek* magazine ran it in their regular "Newsmakers" section of the magazine. The cat's hind feet were planted on Cher's exposed right shoulder, and its front feet were on her outstretched palms. According to Cher, "The cat was a superfine feline. It had incredible claws, but they never came out once" (69). From this point onward, the covers of Cher's albums would all be elaborate costume affairs, utilizing some of the hottest photographers in the business.

Released on May 13, 1974, *Dark Lady* was quite successful, yet it only made it to Number 69 on the American album charts. Still, it continued to produce hit after hit for Cher. "Train of Thought" made it to Number 27 in America, followed by "I Saw a Man and He Danced with His Wife" at Number 42. "Rescue Me" was later released as a single, in 1975.

Actress Sally Kirkland became acquainted with Cher during this transitional period in her life.

When I first met her, it was in 1974. I was giving a party for Bobby De Niro
and Al Pacino. It was a party I had given to welcome them both to Hollywood, from New York. Cher came to that, and so did Mama Cass, and
hordes of others. I remember that Bobby was hiding outside the house,
because he was so intimidated. I remember that Cher was thrilled to meet
him. That was when I first met her. She would always come to the parties.
I have to admit, that it was Cher who gave me the courage to dress outrageously. I always liked her, and was always grateful that she was so
uniquely her. I had gotten to watch her on TV for years, and a lot of my
hippie look was copycatted from her. She has an amazing amount of
courage and balls. When she broke up with Sonny, she went down a road
that was not an easy one. For the most part, she has been a single woman
taking on the world as a single woman. I am sure that myself, and many
others have made bold decisions based on the strength we have gotten
from her courage. I could sense it the minute I met her (70).

Cher's current record deal had ended with MCA's 1974 release
Cher/Greatest Hits, which peaked on the charts at Number 152 in
December of that year. As part of Sonny & Cher, her last MCA album
was the *Sonny & Cher/Greatest Hits* album, which included all of their
Kapp/MCA studio-produced hits plus the live nightclub versions of their
signature songs "The Beat Goes On" and "I Got You Babe." It also
marked the first album appearance of their Budweiser beer theme–like
song "When You Say Love." Unlike an effervescent bottle of beer, sales
on this album were decidedly flat. Released on September 3, 1974,
Sonny & Cher/Greatest Hits only made it to Number 146 on the *Billboard* album chart in America.

Thanks to David Geffen's negotiating, Cher signed a new $2.5 million
record deal with Warner Brothers Records. It was also Geffen's idea to
reunite her in the recording studio with Phil Spector. According to Geffen at the time, "Phil Spector was my idol. He was God" (71). Since Cher
had sung on three of Phil Spector's biggest hit productions—"Da Doo
Ron Ron," "You've Lost That Lovin' Feeling," and "Be My Baby,"—it
seemed like a logical step to put Cher back in the studio with him. Spector's manic behavior during this era is equally legendary in the music
business. After he married Ronnie Bennett, the lead singer of the
Ronettes, he had lived holed-up in their Los Angeles mansion, only occasionally venturing out into the light of day. In the 1970s, Ronnie had
escaped Phil's clutches and much like Cher, was trying to find her own
way as a solo singer. Phil's last major project had been remixing some

jumbled-up audio tapes that the Beatles had produced before their *Abbey Road* LP, and they were released as the Fab Four's 1970 farewell album *Let It Be*.

Geffen cut a deal with Warner Brothers Records and Phil Spector to record and release one Cher test single on "Warner/Spector Records." The resulting 1974 single was to be Cher's big "break out" hit on the label. Unfortunately it was a highly noncommercial failure. The "A" side was "A Woman's Story," which was a big dramatic "wall of sound" ballad with an ethereal chorus of voices, sounding as if Cher was delivering a message from heaven above. The "B" side was a slowed-down version of the Ronettes' 1963 smash, "Baby I Love You." Cher's vocal on "A Woman's Story" is really quite strong and forceful; unfortunately, the sound of the song was simply not what was commercial in 1974. The public wanted to hear more trashy story/songs à la "Dark Lady" and "Gypsys, Tramps and Thieves" from Cher. They didn't want eclectic audio artwork from her. To her audience she was a pop star at that time and was not considered to be a serious rock diva. The follow-up Spector-produced single was a duet with Harry Nilsson, entitled "A Love Like Yours." Again, it came and went without much fanfare. Today, original copies of "A Woman's Story" are ultimate collectors' items, second only to copies of "Ringo I Love You" and original 1970s Cher dolls. After "A Woman's Story" and "A Love Like Yours" failed to become hits, Spector was out of the deal.

Still following David Geffen's advice, Cher began work on the first of three solo albums for Warner Brothers. It was their intention that this was the album that was going to make millions of fans around the world take her seriously as a rock star, and not as just a pop singer. At the time Cher announced,

> Last year I started listening to everything I could get my hands on—Stevie Wonder, Elton John, James Taylor and Carly Simon, Joni Mitchell, Bob Dylan, everybody. By listening and singing along I started developing things that I didn't have. I certainly got the instrument to work with. "Gypsys, Tramps and Thieves" and all those songs are million-selling songs. But they are ridiculous because artistically they aren't fulfilling. Money-wise, they're great, but I would like to spend four or five months on an album and do something really fantastic (34).

That album that Cher did take her time with was released in 1975, and it was truly one of—if not THE—best complete album of music that she was to release that entire decade. The album is entitled *Stars,* and it was beautifully crafted by writer-producer Jimmy Webb. Cher herself hand-selected the majority of the cuts on the album, taking mostly non-hit material from several hit albums.

The *Stars* album was to be her breakout serious rock and roll album. The songs that appear on it include compositions from several recording artists who were popular or becoming popular in 1974–75 and were considered serious contemporary songwriters. *Stars* included Eric Clapton's "Bell Bottom Blues," Jackson Browne's "These Days," Little Feat's "Rock & Roll Doctor," Neil Young's "Mr. Soul," Michael Martin Murphy's "Geronimo's Cadillac," and her first recording of the Boudleaux Bryant song "Love Hurts," which had been a hit for the rock group Nazareth. On this particular album, she performed the song as a lovely string-laden ballad. She even delved into reggae on Jimmy Cliff's "The Bigger They Come the Harder They Fall." The album's heart is its final cut, a poignant version of Janis Ian's lament "Stars." The song deals with the loneliness of fame.

The cover of this album was again an eye-popping work of art. This time around it was a close-up portrait of Cher, glamorously made up with tiny Christmas lights around and on her. Long shutter speed photography was employed, and Cher was obviously directed to move ever so slightly to allow the tiny colored lights to imprint arty streaks of color through the photo.

Stars was totally unlike any Cher album that had preceded it. Her vocal work, especially on the title cut, sounds like it was really sung from the heart. Unfortunately, she soon found out that serious contemporary folk/rock ballads weren't what the record-buying public was looking for from the reigning pop princess of TV land. This was stripped-down Cher, the serious songstress, no glitz, no glitter, and no Las Vegas arrangements. No one cared.

The *Stars* album sold almost zero copies and didn't produce a single hit, peaking at Number 153. One of the problems was the fact that new female singers were arriving on the scene—stars like Gloria Gaynor (*Never Can Say Goodbye*, 1975) and Donna Summer (*Love to Love You Baby*, 1975)—emerging with albums full of the latest musical fad to sweep America and Europe. It was fast, danceable, and the exact opposite of the kind of rock ballads that Cher chose to sing on *Stars*. It was called disco. Since its emergence in 1974, disco began to give several of the biggest stars of the early 1970s some serious competition on the record charts. For Cher, this was the beginning of one of her longest slump periods. She continued to release albums, but not to produce hits.

One of the first things that Cher did to mark her liberation from Sonny was to head to a tattoo parlor. According to Cher, "After Sonny and I separated, I got my first tattoo. I thought it would be something different, a statement of freedom. 'Good girls' didn't have tattoos then, no one was doing it" (16).

For her first body "inking," Cher decided upon a tasteful butterfly—flying across her butt cheeks. She claimed that she chose that spot because it was "where no one could see it." Well, that was true, at least until the late 1980s when she cut her costumes up to the point where they were fully exposed. (The best sight of Cher's butterfly-tattooed ass-cheeks is in the centerfold of the British CD *Cher's Greatest Hits 1965–1992*, where they are exposed through fishnet stockings and an immodest thong.)

"The butterfly was more than a symbol of rebellion," proclaimed canvas-like Cher, the tattoo junkie. "It was really the first step of an experiment to start making decisions on my own. I was 27 years old, but I had lived a sheltered life. I'd never gone on an airplane by myself. . . . I'd never been in a bank. I had made so few real decisions that I was bound to be bad at it. I was right. I *was* bad at it" (16).

According to her skin specialist, Daniel Eastman, the tattoos were originally intended to cosmetically hide a nasty sunburn on her *derrière*. Cher had very cleverly concealed a slight sun mishap without anyone being the wiser.

> Now, here's a girl who's [American] Indian and Armenian, and her skin can accept a lot of sun, and she's an avid sun worshiper. Once when we were in Miami, she overdosed on the sun—seriously, she severely burned her butt. As a result of the burn that she received, she had a tattoo tattooed over the damaged scar tissue, so you can't notice it. That's what that clever little tattoo on her tush is for (56).

During this era, circa 1974–75, Cher began making statements about how she longed to branch out as an entertainer. According to her, she wanted desperately to land a movie role, but she found no takers. In spite of all of the sketch comedy work she had done over the past four years, no one took her seriously as an actress. "I'd also like to try a movie, but the parts that they are giving women these days aren't for me," she said at the time. "You have to be Barbra Streisand or Katharine Hepburn. You can't name five women who are getting roles that are more than just stuck in there because there has to be a female in the movie. I'd like to see a female *Butch Cassidy and the Sundance Kid.* Women today have more adventurism than men" (34).

At the time, Mike Nichols was getting ready to film *The Fortune,* and Cher talked her way into an audition. Nichols claimed that she was all wrong for the part, and he turned her down with the explanation, "There are two kinds of girls in the world: the kind you want to fuck, and the kind you don't." The role was for the latter, and Nichols told her that she couldn't believably act the part. "You're going to be sorry, " Cher remembers saying to him in their brief encounter (37). Years later he asked her to costar in *Silkwood,* but in the 1970s no one in Hollywood took Cher seriously as an actress.

On the other hand, no one in Hollywood took Sonny seriously as an actor either—much to his disappointment. "I was up for a part in *Godfather II,*" he explained in 1974. "Well, I missed out on that, and I really wanted it. Now I've just missed a part in *Earthquake.* They decided the character should be a black man. So, I'm still trying. It's the one thing in the world I want most to do—be a movie actor" (65).

In 1974 MCA Records released a final recording by Sonny Bono as a single. It was his own solo version of his Vietnam protest song, "Classified 1A." He produced the cut, which was arranged by his band member David Paich. It didn't work as a single for Cher in 1971, and it certainly didn't work for Sonny as a solo recording artist either. The flip side of the single was a new autobiographical song about his relationship with Cher called "Our Last Show." This dreary destined-to-fail single found bewildered Sonny singing about his shock over what had happened to him and Cher, as singing partners and as husband and wife. (Unavailable for years, both of these songs were released on the 1995 compact disc collection *All I Ever Need—The Kapp/MCA Anthology.*)

There was clearly only one alternative for Sonny solo, and Cher solo, and that was to return to television. No one wanted either of them in the movies, no one asked him to produce records, and no one cared to listen to Cher as a serious vocalist on records. And so the aborted idea of doing *The Sonny & Cher Divorce Show* gave way to two separate new ventures in the 1974–75 TV season, ABC-TV's *The Sonny Comedy Revue* and CBS's *Cher* show.

It was Sonny who made the first move. *The Sonny Comedy Revue* made its television debut on September 22, 1974. The producers utilized

some of the same comedy troupe from *The Sonny & Cher Comedy Hour*,
like Teri Garr (who had yet to become a comedy movie star) and Free-
man King. Art Fisher was again the director (without his former co-
director Jorn Winther), but the sparkle that had made the former show
work was clearly its missing element: Cher. It wasn't that Sonny didn't
try hard enough; he needed Cher as his counterpart. The show lasted an
unlucky thirteen episodes before it was canceled.

Next, Cher came up to bat. Her return to television began with a
Wednesday night prime-time special entitled simply *Cher*. It was followed,
four nights later, on February 16, 1975, by the weekly *Cher* show. The TV
special made a huge splash, with a small fortune spent on costumes alone
and three superstar guests: Flip Wilson, Elton John, and Bette Midler.
Although Wilson was famous for his own early 1970s TV series, Elton and
Bette were rarely seen on network television, and the show was a highly
rated, delicious treat. The first regular show featured guests Tatum
O'Neal, Raquel Welch, and Wayne Rogers of TV's *M*A*S*H*.

The elaborate wardrobe for the *Cher* show was as much a part of the
show as its star. According to designer Bob Mackie at the time,

> Depending on the number of costumes, Cher's clothes bill for her weekly
> show runs between $3,000 and $10,000. And for the special she did with
> Elton John and Bette Midler, the bill hit $30,000. I understand Cher's
> wardrobe is the biggest ever for a weekly TV show. But then, of course,
> her gowns are very much a part of the show—and since she owns the pro-
> duction company, she also owns all the clothes (72).

Cher was very excited about her new television show . . . at first. "The
look is really hot!" she exclaimed before either of her shows aired. "It's
not quiet. It doesn't lay back. It's just hot. It comes out and punches your
brains out" (73). And that was just the set and costumes she was talking
about!

"Everybody I'm having on the show are people I like to see," she
continued.

> I'm tired of seeing the same old guest stars who turn up on every show. I
> think it's important on a variety show to see people you don't ordinarily
> see. As for songs, I'll be doing both old and new songs. I open my special
> with "Let Me Entertain You," and my series with "You're Nobody 'Til
> Somebody Loves You." A lot of ladies in this business can sing rock & roll,

but not old songs, and vice versa. I'm at home with both. I find it easy to
do old songs. I like to do everything (73).

The press on the special and the first regular episode was quite favorable.
According to *Variety*, "A winner . . . more direct focus was on Cher the
singer, skit player, and monologist—not to mention clotheshorse—and she
did well (if not spectacularly) in all roles. . . . there seem enough pluses to
suggest that *Cher* will make it" (74). And, the *Los Angeles Times* exclaimed,
"Three cheers for Cher and her new CBS variety show. . . . Sonny without
Cher was a disaster. Cher without Sonny, on the other hand, could be the
best thing that's happened to weekly television this season" (75).

Newsweek magazine's review, however, was mixed when it pointed
out, "Cher goes back to playing second banana to the show's real star—
a cool, hip, certifiably freaky costume designer named Bob Mackie. Television hasn't shown so much glitter and flash since NBC did a special on
Liberace's closet." The publication's review also pointed out, "Her show-
opening chats with the audience sorely miss the presence of Sonny as a
foil. Either monologues are just not Cher's métier, or she should sue her
writers for nonsupport" (76).

The fact that her show was broadcast at 7:30 p.m., the traditional network "family hour," opposite the long-running G-rated *The Wonderful
World of Disney*, began to pose immediate problems with the show's
censors. First of all, Cher was not allowed to show her belly button under
any circumstances. On *The Sonny & Cher Comedy Hour*, which was
shown an hour later, she was allowed to be humorously suggestive. Cher
recalled, "We had one scene where I was dressed up like Cleopatra and
had on these two brass plates, and I walked up and said, 'How do you like
my gongs?' I meant, it was no such thing as double entendre. I was just
saying, 'How do you like my tits?' Everyone was hysterical" (33). Well, on
the *Cher* show, the censors were not laughing at her antics. Cher found
herself fighting with the network constantly.

One of the major conflicts came on the first regular episode of *Cher*.
According to Cher at that time,

They [the censors] pulled Raquel Welch's number. I'm really pissed off
about that. Raquel and I were becoming really good friends. She is
strange, but I like her. We did this number together. We came out in
dresses and sang a song—no horrible gyrations, no anything. And she did
a solo number, which was really nice. Well, first we got a call that they were
cutting out the duet between the two of us because the program director

said it was too suggestive. Then they said we could keep the duet, but her number had to go. Because she was singing a suggestive song, and she placed her hand—God forbid—on parts of her anatomy! The song was "Feel Like Making Love"—I mean, it was a hit song. George Schlatter, my producer, got back the duet but couldn't save Raquel's solo. When she found out about it, God, she just freaked, because she'd worked so hard on it. I don't blame her; I would have been really pissed off, too. So she called the network and got some guy who didn't even have the guts to tell her that it was their idea—he told her it was mine. Then she called me, and she was furious. She read me up one side and down another. And I said, "Raquel, I swear to God on my daughter's life, I had nothing to do with it!"—and she hung up on me (18).

"Before," explained Cher, "Sonny made the decisions. He sat in with the producers and writers. He decided what I would do and I went along with it. Now I decide" (75). Suddenly, Cher was in the hot seat. When things went right she got the credit, and—as with the Raquel Welch episode—when things went wrong, she got the blame.

The spotlight was firmly focused on Cher now, both on the network and in the limelight of her personal life as well. Although she had left Sonny, there was a third person to consider before the divorce of the decade got underway, their daughter. Sonny wanted to divide little Chastity's time evenly between the two of them, but they soon found themselves in a heated battle over child custody.

Cher's stance on the subject was

Chastity is probably the most loved and best behaved child in the world, and she's very affectionate. She's got drums and she's got guitars—all that kind of stuff. She thinks it's fun and she's got a good sense of timing, good pitch and rhythm. Sonny would like to have her for half the time, but I think she's too young. He's a good father, but I don't feel she should be split in half. He disagrees, and we're going to have a big argument. But there are some things I just can't be pushed into doing (34).

According to Sonny,

There was a while back when Cher and David Geffen were together that they tried to put that "weekends only" visitation nonsense on me. I would like to believe David was the one who was difficult about it. Those kinds of rigid rules can't apply in our business. I was doing my TV show then and working on weekends. So I went to court and had my say and things loosened up considerably. When Geffen was gone, Cher couldn't have been nicer. I see Chas often and keep her for several days at a time, and there is no longer any problem (77).

To further aggravate Cher, Sonny took a guest-starring role in a television show that was on ABC-TV at the exact time that her show was being broadcast on CBS. In this way, many of the real Sonny & Cher fans would be torn and might skip Cher's weekly variety series just to see if Sonny could act without her. Cher was fuming. "He appeared as a guest star on *Six Million Dollar Man* earlier this season," she complained. "The show is opposite me, and I'm quite sure he knew it would hurt me. That is perhaps the only reason he did it. At the time, I told myself I didn't care what he did. And I didn't give the slightest thought to his career, because I honestly didn't care what happened to him" (78).

Sonny was aggravating Cher. The CBS censors were constantly on her tail, disapproving of this or that. David Geffen, whom she nicknamed "Mr. Beige," kept bugging her to marry him. Raquel Welch was pissed off at her. And to top it all off, just as her solo television series was getting off the ground, Cher attended a party in Los Angeles and, with no conscious effort, found herself embroiled in a huge drug scandal that resulted in someone's death. The cover of the *New York Daily News* from February 21, 1975, carried a photo of Cher and a huge headline that read "Hunted in Death of Rock Star. . . 2nd Drug Victim Saved by Cher." It had all begun the previous fall.

Millionaire stockbroker Ken Moss threw an impromptu party in his Hollywood Hills mansion, following a performance by the Average White Band at the club the Troubadour. Cher had been in the audience that night and was invited over to the Moss mansion. When she got there, someone produced a bottle of white powder, which everyone thought was cocaine. It turned out to be a combination of morphine and heroin. Several people inhaled some of the powder, expecting a coke buzz, and instead of buzzing began passing out. The drummer for the Average White Band, Robbie McIntosh, was taken back to his room at the Howard Johnson motel in North Hollywood to sleep it off. He died nine hours later. Another member of the band, bass player Alan Gorrie, became ill, and Cher came to the rescue. She called her doctor, actually her gynecologist, who advised her to keep him conscious by walking him around, and to induce vomiting. She did as she was told, and she saved his life. Of course the newspaper headlines made a big scandal about the ordeal. Cher was not found doing anything illegal, it was just that she was at the party, and once the grand jury hearing became public, it was her name that made the headlines. The *National Star* published a story in its October 13, 1974, issue entitled "Cher Saves Guest at Drug Death Party." Somehow, no matter what she did, or where she went in the late 1970s, Cher was constantly making headlines.

Cher's solo TV show was already getting to be a drag in early 1975. Everything had been so simple when Sonny had been there by her side; now the whole event was becoming a huge hassle. She came up with a solution. She wanted to ask Sonny to appear on her show semiregularly. "It was me. My idea," explained Cher.

I made the decision after I'd done four *Cher* shows. Nothing to do with the ratings. Doing a show alone was more than I could handle. I had to be into everything, from helping on scripts to picking the music. And they had me doing a monologue. That's not like me, to be out there alone making the jokes. I have fun working. Well, I wasn't having any fun (79).

Anyone who knows me knows I'm great at shooting off my mouth, and I impulsively announced that I wanted to have Sonny on one of my shows this year. After I said it, we asked Sonny to be on one show, telling that top pay was $7,500. His agent replied that he would do six shows at $12,500 per show, but only after I settled his lawsuit against me. First, I told him our show's budget couldn't afford him. Then I got to the suit (80).

She could afford a $30,000 wardrobe budget, but she couldn't afford an extra $5,000 for Sonny?

She explained, "I always [in the past] signed everything Sonny told me to sign," not realizing the can of worms that she had inadvertently opened.

While I was married to him, Sonny had signed me to a contract with a company he set up called Cher Enterprises. I signed the contract, but I really didn't know what I was signing—I always thought Sonny and I were partners. According to this contract, I was supposed to receive a salary from Cher Enterprises, but I never knew that because I never got a salary check. I don't mean to imply that Sonny never gave me money—he gave me anything I wanted. I shopped like a madwoman. I had a charge card for everything. When I was bored or bugged, Sonny used to say, "Run along, Cher, and buy something." I never wrote checks because I didn't know how to write a check. Besides, my checks wouldn't have been any good anyway—they all had to be countersigned by Sonny or the business manager (80).

According to Cher, "Sonny and our attorney seemed to own the company, and I was just an employee. It even said that I was allowed two weeks paid vacation! So they're suing for $700,000 in gigs I didn't perform. I'm suing for half the company" (10).

The whole mess was finally cleared up after several months of suits and countersuits. With David Geffen's encouragement, on July 9, 1975, Cher marched into Santa Monica Superior Court and filed for divorce from Sonny. After they had ironed out all their financial difficulties, Sonny agreed to appear occasionally on the *Cher* show at a fixed rate of $7,500 per episode.

Since Cher was now free to marry "Mr. Beige," Geffen persisted with his proposals. Cher was really enjoying her freedom from Sonny, and she turned down David's proposal. "He reminded me too much of Sonny," Cher later admitted. "He wanted to get married and I didn't. He was ready and I wasn't. I'd been and he hadn't. It was a pay or play deal" (18).

Now, from a post-1990s perspective, it was perhaps for the best. Although David was to continue to be a strong Cher ally, especially in the mid-1980s, in 1992 he finally publicly "came out," revealing that he was gay. Although she was still seeing David when she met her second husband, it too wasn't a path that she had expected to walk down.

"It was a full moon," said Cher, precluding the whole saga of how she got involved with rock star Gregg Allman. It happened during one night of club hopping in 1975, and she was in a strange mood.

> I always get in trouble with a full moon. I met him at the Troubadour. He was playing with Etta James, and I was a fan of hers. I didn't really know anything about the Allman Brothers. I was quickly educated, though. Anyway, we went—David Geffen, and me and my sister, a whole bunch of us. I'd been going with Dave, but by then he and I were kind of broken up. And this chick came up to me and said, "Gregg would like to meet you." I said, "Fine." He came up and grumbled a couple of unintelligible words. He talks way down in his throat, low, growly, and sexy (18).

Allman distinctly remembers his impression of Cher the first time he laid eyes on her. "I looked at Cher and she looked like an Egyptian idol. And she stuck out her hand and her fingernails were about three inches long. Boy, was I hot to trot! David Geffen was sitting next to her and I didn't even see him. I didn't see Tatum, I didn't see Georganne, I didn't see Paulette. I just saw her" (81).

That evening Cher excused herself from David Geffen and the rest of her party under the guise of going to the ladies room. She was actually going backstage to see Gregg. When she returned to her table and all of her friends, she found Geffen in a snit. "What was that about?" he demanded to know.

Always painfully blunt about her business, Cher told him that she had gone to visit Allman. After the show was over, Cher, Geffen, Tatum O'Neal, and the rest of the party went to the Beverly Hills Hotel, where David had taken up residence in Bungalow Twelve. When they arrived there Geffen went into a jealous tantrum over Cher's blatant flirtation with Allman.

"If you see me walking down the street," he yelled at her, "you better cross over to the other side. And I want all my presents back."

"You know, you can have some, but there are certain ones I'm not giving back," she snapped back.

"I'll sue you," he shouted threateningly.

"Go ahead," Cher dared him (63). That was to be the last conversation they were to have for quite some time.

After meeting Cher at the Troubadour, Gregg called her and asked her out on a date. She accepted.

He took me to Dino's, where it's really dark, and [he] started to suck my fingers. I thought, "Wait a minute; back up." I said, "Why are you doing this?" Next he asked me to go with him while he met some guy, but first he wanted to change his clothes, which he did every ten minutes. So we split, and a while later he started to kiss me. I just ran out the door. I told him not to bother to show me the way.

Next night, he called me and asked me out. I said, "I don't like you and you don't like me. I had a horrible time last night and why are you calling?" He said, "Maybe we could have a good time tonight." So we went out. We danced and then, while we were driving down the street, he was telling me something I didn't care about, so I said, "You know what? I hate fuckin' small talk. You are boring the shit out of me and I've got nothing to say to you. I know that you must be interesting and I am, too, so what gives?" I said we should really talk. He started to laugh, and I mean very slowly, like two-months slowly. Pulling words out of Gregg Allman is like . . . forget it. Finally things started to get a little bit more mellow when he found out that I was a person—that a chick was not a dummy. For him up 'til then, they'd had only two uses: Make the bed, and make it *in* the bed. That's it (18).

Manager/producer Loree Rodkin was with Cher and Gregg on one of their earliest dates, a dinner at the very "in" Chinese restaurant Mr. Chow. According to Rodkin, "Cher has this little-girl quality. Gregg passed out over a plate of Chinese food, and she said, 'Oh Loree, isn't this sweet, he's so tired.' And I said, 'Cher, he's a junkie' " (22). Cher had never been with a drug addict, so she was naive about all of the warning signs. She seemed to have simply chalked up the strange behavior to Gregg's party-all-night lifestyle. Cher claimed that among Allman's attributes was the fact that he always conducted himself like a perfect Southern gentleman. According to her, "One thing about him, he had beautiful manners. He never swore. Ever. He called me Miss Gutter Mouth" (61).

On June 30, 1975, five days after Sonny and Cher's divorce became final, Cher married Gregg Allman. She was deeply in love with him, and she thought that she really knew him quite well. What she still didn't realize, however, was the fact that he didn't just dabble in drugs—he was a major-league heroin addict.

Nine days after their Las Vegas wedding, Cher filed for divorce from Allman. She remembers, "When I called him to tell him I was filing for divorce, he was so high he didn't even understand me. He said, 'O.K., I gotta go rehearse.' Three days later, when he came down to Earth and understood, he immediately flew to Buffalo to a husband-wife psychiatric team that specialized in treating drug addicts."

"In the midst of all this," Cher explains,

I had to go to the hospital and have some polyps removed. When I got out of the hospital, Gregg's doctor called me from Buffalo. He said that Gregg was really trying to help himself. The doctor told me that in all the years he'd been a doctor, he had never seen a man try as hard as Gregg was trying to beat drugs. "If you have no love for this man and want to dump him," the doctor said, "that's one thing. But if you love him, you should come. It could be a turning point for him." I knew I should go, but in a crisis I reverted to type—I called Sonny and asked him if he could come over and discuss something important. He came right over. I told him the whole story, and he said, "Cher, if you love him, go to Buffalo, what have you got to lose? If the guy is really honest and wants to get free, maybe you can help him. If he doesn't make it, you will have tried. If you don't go, you'll always wonder what would have happened if you had gone." That was really terrific advice. Something else was terrific—that was the last time I needed Sonny (80).

Sonny in the meantime was dating a new girl, a model named Susie Coelho. Cher thought she was very nice, and it looked like Sonny and Cher had finally made peace with each other and their illustrious past. However, another person from the past reappeared in 1975—Cher's problematic father. This time around he was suing her for $4 million for referring to him in the press as "a compulsive gambler and a heroin addict." A cash settlement out of court cooled out Sarkisian once again. Cher claimed at the time, "Whatever he's doing, it's probably illegal" (82).

However, Cher's heroin-addict blues were far from over. Allman may have temporarily cleaned up his act, but Cher was in for more heartaches from his addiction. "Marrying Gregory was one giant mistake," Cher was later to admit. She remembers one occasion after Gregg had supposedly dried out.

> There were some people over at the house in the den. I had this gorgeous coffee table, antique painted glass set in lovely old wood—and these people were doing lines of coke off my fucking coffee table! I was so pissed off! "Don't you guys have any respect for anything? Get that stuff off my table and don't do it in my house!" I will not deal with people on drugs, 'cause when they're junkies, they're not people anymore (19).

Although she had filed for divorce from Allman, she changed her mind, and thought that she could help dry him out.

In the interim, the Allman Brothers band broke up, and the band's fans blamed Cher. According to her, "Well, I really had nothing to do with breaking up the band. I really had to do with straightening out Gregory and if that broke up the band, then I'm glad. I would do it again at a moment's notice because I think that saving Gregory is much more important than saving the Allman Brothers" (83).

Meanwhile, back in television land, during its run in 1975, the *Cher* show certainly had its share of interesting cutting-edge guest stars, like David Bowie and sexy soul trio LaBelle. On November 8, 1975, David Bowie made his American network TV debut on her show, singing his latest hit, "Fame," and dueting with Cher.

LaBelle had just scored a huge Number 1 hit with the song "Lady Marmalade." One of the hottest songs from this era, it contained the French chorus lyrics, "*voulez-vous coucher avec moi ce soir.*" Most Americans had no clue that the phrase, interpreted into English, meant "do you want to sleep with me tonight?"

To top off the controversy, the trio of singers who made up LaBelle—Patti LaBelle, Nona Hendryx, and Sarah Dash—were in their "silver phase." Each of the ladies wore huge silver earrings, silver jewelry, and silver costumes that looked like something designed for a futuristic outer space film. Sarah's trademark costume was perhaps the most controversial, as her top consisted of two sterling silver cups identical to the shape of her breasts, held in place in an invisible fashion. Cher knew instantly that she was going to have a ball matching their outrageous outfits and singing with the trio.

Sarah Dash recalls,

> I met Cher at her show. We had a three or four day rehearsal, and Redd Foxx was on the show with us. He was doing the comedy part, and we were the music act. We clicked right away. She is such a gracious person, and very smart. In fact, when we met her, she and Sonny had just split, and she was working to pay him for her divorce. She wasn't shy about saying anything about it, she was very candid. We were wild, and she was still having a great time, a real great time. In fact, when we went to California, I got bored and I shaved my eyebrows off. Everyone was saying, "Your skin looks so smooth—from the hairline to the chin." And, nobody really realized what had happened. So, finally I said, "Cher, I shaved my eyebrows off." She said, *"That's* what I've been looking at. I didn't know what was different, but I knew it was something!" Then, we were having discussions about shopping—who could out-shop who. I said to Cher, "I bet I can out-shop you." And she said, "No you can't!" We talked about how we went to the same stores at that time (84).

LaBelle not only sang their huge hit, "Lady Marmalade," on the show, but they also had a duet with Cher. Both Cher and Bob Mackie had a great time coming up with the right silver-and-feathers costume for her to wear for her number with LaBelle. According to Sarah Dash, "Bob Mackie was there, and he examined our clothes. He looked at them and thought they were well-made. And, he didn't do bad for her, with that 'look.' Because at that time, Cher sang with all of her music acts" (84).

However, for LaBelle to sing "Lady Marmalade" and wear their trademark silver costumes, they had to make some concessions for the network censors. "I remember too, that there was a censor there, because they wanted to spray my silver bra with some duller, and I went ballistic," explained Sarah.

I said, "No, this is sterling silver, you can't do that." Then Cher said, "No! You've gotta show them." Bob Mackie came out and pinned my cape to the top of my bra, so you could see it just barely so, but not expose the way I had it. Cher said, "No, you can't do that, that's her 'look.' " That was great. I loved the way she stood up for it. And then they were wondering whether we could say *"Vous les vous coucher avec moi se soir"* on national TV, when no one knew what the French meant. But, the censors were there. It was funny—they were censoring everything. They made us say *"danse"* on her show *"Vous les vous DANSE avec moi?"* instead of "sleep." Cher wasn't too happy about that, but she was really gracious. So that was fun. She was really great to work with. And, after our number, she was so out of breath she was holding her chest. We thought that was so funny. When we were done, she said, "You wore me out" (84).

Dash was also impressed with the way Cher was raising her daughter. "Cher was so gracious, and Chastity at that time was maybe like six or seven years old," Sarah explained.

And, what I loved about the way Cher raised her if you offered Chastity a piece of candy, Chastity would say, "Mom, is it O.K.?" And Cher would say, "Yes." I thought that was so cool being in show business, and being so conscientious about how you raised your children. I just felt that Chastity was one of the more gracious entertainment children—show biz kids. And, she had such class at that age (84).

In addition to having different musical guests on her television show during this era, Cher remained friendly with several of her costars off the set as well—swapping shopping tips and manicurists. According to Sarah Dash,

She came backstage one time after one of our shows. She had these nail people come to me, and she was kinda upset that they had been over-charging the people she had been sending them to as clients. So, we both had the dark nails. I have a picture, in fact, of us sitting backstage with Cher. She and I both had the long, dark nails, because we were into the nails, because that was when the long manicured nails were beginning to happen, and dark was "it" (84).

Cher's solo show continued at a clipping pace during the fall of 1975 and ran until January 4, 1976. Cher had invited Sonny to be a guest on several episodes of her *Cher* show, and they were getting along marvelously, both on the set and off. And, more important, their old comic chemistry was working on camera. They decided that they were working so well together that they might as well regroup and do their old show again. Hence, February 1, 1976, marked the debut of the new version of *The Sonny & Cher Comedy Hour*, entitled *The Sonny & Cher Show*, as though the name change could possibly spare anyone any further confusion.

Cher said in a 1976 *TV Guide* magazine cover story, "It was me, my idea. Doing a show alone was more than I could handle" (85). According to Sonny, in the same publication, he was flabbergasted by Cher's offer, especially after their bitter divorce from each other. "I said, 'As long as I know you, Cher, I will never cease to be amazed by you.' Then I said, 'Well, why not?' Doing a show together made a lot of sense. . . . I knew the terrible demands on Cher. Now she's back where she belongs" (85).

Speaking of confusion, here was Sonny Bono and his ex-wife Cher Sarkisian Bono Allman starring in a comedy program once a week as if their divorce and all the lawsuits had never happened. Then, to top it all off, Cher discovered that she was pregnant with Gregg's baby. How would the American public deal with all this nonsense? Well, needless to say, had it been anyone other than Cher, she might have ended up tarred and feathered by an angry mob instead of bugle-beaded and feathered by Bob Mackie.

Not only had Cher appeared in a leaves-nothing-to-the-imagination outfit on the cover of *Time* magazine—March 17, 1975—but by now the real-life "Sonny & Cher & Gregg Show" was now a permanent running feature on the cover of all of the weekly tabloid newspapers. Twenty some years before, Ingrid Bergman had been run out of Hollywood on a rail for having a baby out of wedlock, and now here was Cher starring on American network television with ex-husband Sonny while pregnant by her drug-addict rock-star husband. This was definitely a "first"; Cher was undisputedly the high priestess of the 1970s "me" generation.

While all of this was happening in Cher's career, Gregg Allman was busy screwing up not only his own life, but the lives of several people around him. Since Allman and his record label, Capricorn Records, were both from the state of Georgia, when Jimmy Carter was running for president of the United States, Allman enlisted lots of state supporters.

In fact, the night that Carter took office, Cher and Gregg Allman were among the new First Family's first dinner guests in the White House. As Cher was to explain, "Gregory was from Georgia, and we supported him, so after the inauguration we were sort of just looking around the White

Even as a teenager, Cher was destined to become someone special. As she has proclaimed: "This is my life—and I get to do everything I want to do. I don't really care what anybody thinks." (*AP/Wide World Photos*)

Sonny & Cher not only made million-selling music together, they also made fashion statements wherever they went. Occasionally it got them thrown out of the posh hotels in which they were staying. December 7, 1965, Cher and Sonny boarding a plane for Hawaii for a scheduled concert date. (*AP/Wide World Photos*)

At first Cher was painfully shy. The first time she was to record a solo song, she insisted that Sonny be in the studio singing along with her. And so was born the duo of Sonny & Cher. (*MJB Photo Archives*)

Eleven years older than Cher, Sonny Bono was not only her songwriter, singing partner, producer, and boyfriend, he was also her mentor and the father figure she felt had been missing in her life. (AP/*Wide World Photos*)

Sonny & Cher were known in the 1960s as the rock and roll world's hip and hot married couple—or so the public thought. Although they claimed to be husband and wife, in reality they were not married until the end of the decade. (*MJB Photo Archives*)

Cher and Sonny singing from a balcony on a 1966 Danny Thomas TV special. (*AP/Wide World Photos*)

The very first Cher albums found her cast as a folksinger, covering the songs of Bob Dylan, Jackie DeShannon, the Byrds, and Pete Seeger. (*AP/Wide World Photos*)

Sonny & Cher made a high-profile appearance at a Sunset Strip protest demonstration in Los Angeles on December 11, 1966. As part of a crowd of 500, they protested an enforced curfew. (*AP/Wide World Photos*)

Cher loved designing her own bell-bottomed pants outfits, which were sewn together by a pair of seamstress friends. Sonny often sported a matching ensemble. (*AP/Wide World Photos*)

Although she had an innocent look about her, young Cher admits that she swore like a truck driver as a teenager. According to her, "I was Sadie Thompson on the outside. But still a secret, heavenly star on the inside." (*AP/Wide World Photos*)

Sightseeing during a promotional tour in Hamburg, Germany. Sonny & Cher were as big in Europe as they were in America. (*AP/Wide World Photos*)

With hit songs like "Bang Bang (My Baby Shot Me Down)" in 1966 and "You Better Sit Down Kids" in 1967, Cher's solo recording career was established alongside that of Sonny & Cher. (*AP/Wide World Photos*)

Their unique way of dressing, as well as musical appearances on mainstream television shows like *The Hollywood Palace* and a guest-starring gig on *The Man from U.N.C.L.E.*, made Sonny & Cher instantly recognizable stars. (*AP/Wide World Photos*)

Sonny & Cher were so popular in the mid-1960s, an attempt at movie stardom was inevitable. The film *Good Times* gave them the showcase to act out all of their cinematic fantasies. (*AP/Wide World Photos*)

In the "Western fantasy" segment of *Good Times,* Sonny played a hippie-like sheriff, and Cher was a dancehall singer in a saloon. (*Anchor Bay Films/MJB Photo Archives*)

In *Good Times* the duo also portrayed a hippie-like Tarzan and Jane—known as "Jungle Morry" and "Zora." (*Anchor Bay Films/MJB Photo Archives*)

In the 1970s, the duo went from rock stars to television stars. Cher as her outlandish gum-chewing "Laverne" character, flanked by John Davidson and Sonny. (*AP/Wide World Photos*)

In addition to their hit television show in the early 1970s, Sonny & Cher were also a huge Las Vegas headline act. (*AP/Wide World Photos*)

Cher as Mother Goose on *The Sonny & Cher Comedy Hour*. (*AP/Wide World Photos*)

The duo's weekly television program and 1970s hits, including "All I Ever Need Is You," gave the public the illusion that they had an ideal marriage. In real life, Sonny had a live-in girlfriend, and Cher was dating one of the duo's band members, David Paich. (*AP/Wide World Photos*)

Cher in a swashbuckling outfit to promote her single "Pirate." (*Harry Langdon/Warner Brothers Records/MJB Photo Archives*)

Cher's solo recording career was hotter than ever as she racked up three Number 1 singles: "Gypsies, Tramps, & Thieves," "Half Breed," and "Dark Lady." In her "Half Breed" phase, Cher brought Native American fashion to a new height. (*MCA Records/MJB Photo Archives*)

Thanks to her model-thin body and the help of master costume designer Bob Mackie, Cher took television costuming to outrageous new heights. (*MJB Photo Archives*)

Elton John, Cher, Flip Wilson, and Bette Midler on the debut one-hour special episode of TV's *The Cher Show* in 1975. (*AP/Wide World Photos*)

The lives of Sonny and Cher became the number one real-life soap opera of the 1970s. Not long after their official divorce, Sonny married Susie Coehlo (left), while Cher wed drug-addicted rocker Gregg Allman. Susie, Sonny, and Cher at the opening of Bono's restaurant in Los Angeles. (*AP/Wide World Photos*)

Cher leaving Santa Monica Superior Court, having just filed for divorce from Sonny Bono. A year later she came back to the same courthouse to divorce Gregg Allman. (*AP/Wide World Photos*)

A reconciled Cher and Gregg Allman in 1976 celebrating the birth of their son, Elijah Blue Allman. Still entangled in this rocky marriage, Cher was simultaneously starring opposite her ex-husband Bono on their second series together, *The Sonny & Cher Show*. (*AP/Wide World Photos*)

Cher with her son Elijah Blue Allman and her daughter Chastity Bono at London's Heathrow Airport. Cher was amid the short European concert tour to promote 1977's *Allman & Woman* album. (*AP/Wide World Photos*)

By the end of the 1970s, Cher was ready for a new era of her turbulent life. She divorced Gregg and legally shortened her name from Cherilyn Sarkisian LaPiere Bono Allman to "Cher." (*Harry Langdon/Casablanca Records/MJB Photo Archives*)

On her 1979 television special, *Cher . . . And Other Fantasies*, the diva donned roller skates to do a take-off on the ballet film *The Red Shoes*, which she entitled "The Red Skates." (*AP/Wide World Photos*)

Cher at her highly publicized roller disco party in Brooklyn in 1979. The top she is wearing looked opaque to the naked eye, but once she removed the jacket, and photographers' flashbulbs hit it, it appeared transparent. (*Waring Abbot/ Casablanca Records/MJB Photo Archives*)

Cher was undoubtedly the most written-about, most talked-about, and most photographed celebrity of the 1970s. During that decade she was the star of three separate network television series and had three million-selling Number 1 singles and two divorces. (*Harry Langdon/Casablanca Records/MJB Photo Archives*)

House when 'Miz' Lillian [Carter's mother] stuck her head out from around the corner and asked us to stay for dinner" (8). Not long after being publicly photographed cavorting around with Allman and Cher, President Carter found Gregg's resurfacing drug dependencies an embarrassment. Especially when Allman was hauled into court to testify before a grand jury about his heroin and cocaine addiction.

Gregg had a long history of family trauma, and he used drugs as an escape. When he was a young boy, his father was murdered by a hitch-hiker whom he had picked up along the roadside. This was just the first of the tragedies of his life. It was his older brother Duane who first found fame in the music world, having been a session guitarist on several records by Aretha Franklin and Wilson Pickett. According to Gregg, "[In 1969] my life didn't have any point. I said, 'the hell with it.' Then I got a call from Duane that he had put a band together—two drums, bass and two guitars. He said, 'Man, we need you to wrap it up" (86). And so, the Allman Brothers band was born.

The group went on to record five Gold and three Platinum albums Their most notable chart single was the Top 10 hit "Ramblin' Man" in 1973. Ironically, it had hit Number 2 on the *Billboard* charts, while at Number 1 was Cher's own "Half Breed." However, the group seemed plagued by one misfortune after another. In 1971 Duane was killed in a motorcycle accident. A year later the group's bass player, Berry Oakley, was also killed in a motorcycle accident. Gregg began to hate his life, and drugs seemed like a logical escape.

"There are cats out there who are gonna hit on anybody with a guitar strapped around his arm. The guy [dealer] says, 'Hey, baby, you wanna buy? Just poke some of this into your arm, or up your nose, or anywhere, and it'll feel better.' " Recalls Gregg, "It was like a cat in my body. His air is used up, and his claws are out, and he's running around inside trying to get out. Then bam! The old spike [syringe] goes in and you can almost see the cat go to sleep at the bottom of your foot. But you know he'll wake up and try to get out again" (86). Unfortunately, Gregg couldn't seem to get that cat out of his veins. When he gave up drugs, he turned to booze. It was a vicious cycle, but there was Cher, the sequined queen of TV land, standing by his side time and time again, trying to straighten him out. After her first attempt to dry out Allman, Cher announced to *Time* magazine, "I laid down the law on drugs, and it's been wonderful to see Gregg's eyes clear" (17). Unhappily for Cher, Gregg's lucid moments were always short-lived.

Cher and Gregg's strained relationship was doomed from the very start. As soon as she started dating him, his ex-girlfriend, James Arness's daughter Jenny, committed suicide over the demise of her affair with Allman. She left behind a twenty-three-page suicide letter, five of the pages devoted to Gregg.

One of the real turning points in Cher and Gregg's relationship came in 1977 when Gregg testified in court against his road manager, Scooter Herring. Herring was arrested for supplying Gregg with half a gram of coke a day. Even though the federal judge trying the case claimed that the person who ought to be prosecuted was Mr. Allman, Gregg was granted immunity if he would corroborate the charges against Herring. "Man, it was heavy in there," recalls Allman of the court hearing. "If I had refused to say anything, they were going to make me do a couple of years" (13). Several people branded Gregg a "stool pigeon" for saving his own skin by putting Herring behind bars. Commented Allman,

> Scooter was my best friend, and he probably still is. And I would like to say that the bottom line of this whole thing is that he got a sentence of 75 years for conspiracy to sell cocaine, which is a pretty goddamn bullshit sentence if you ask me. . . . He's alive and well and walking on the streets today. He never went [to prison], he appealed it. He'll probably appeal it for the rest of his life. If they think I sold him down the river, anybody who thinks that is full of shit (81).

While she was married to Greg, Cher received a surprise phone call from David Geffen. He had called to make amends with her as friends. Cher dumping him several months ago had been devastating for him. It wasn't until he took the 1970s fad course EST (Erhard Seminar Training) that he was able to get over his depression. "Everything is fine. I still love you," he proclaimed to her, "but we don't have to be together. Everything is great, and we can be friends."

After she told him that she was happy for him, he changed the subject to the diamond necklace and diamond ring that he had given to her when they were together. "I still want my jewelry back," he said in a demanding tone. Cher was equally firm with him when she replied, "Dave, go fuck yourself. I'm not doing it" (63).

In the summer of 1976, Cher gave birth to a son, whom she named Elijah Blue Allman. She later admitted that she should have just had Elijah out of wedlock. It would have saved her a lot of headaches with Allman. "I just wish I hadn't married Gregory to get Elijah," she explained.

"I wish I were the kind of person who could just do it on the run, a one-nighter, not have to live with the guy! When you're not used to making decisions, you don't do it well" (19). Gregg Allman claimed, "I'd like her to be pregnant all the time. She's so happy then. Our astrologer told us we should have five kids anyway" (87).

Cher may have been hopelessly in love with Allman, but her daughter, Chastity—who was only seven years old at the time—could see right through him. "Gregg was a complete fuck-up," recalled Chastity, years later.

> He was the kind of guy who would say, "Oh, we're gonna do this great thing," and then not show up. . . . My worst memory of Gregg is when he picked me up from school one day. I guess he was drunk, and he couldn't find his way back to Malibu. We got lost, and finally this guy said, "I'm going that way, follow me." We followed him, and we ended up at this bar where Gregg got more drunk and picked up girls. We ended up getting home at around 11:00 or 12:00 at night. My mother was totally freaked because we were supposed to be back by 4:00. He was a big disappointment for a kid, because he would just let you down every time (64).

Following all of this activity, the public was getting weary of the whole triangle of Cher-and-Sonny-and-Gregg. Cher was running out of the will to keep this bizarre juggling act together. She had to be lovely and charming on network TV while she was busy monitoring Gregg's substance abuse at home. "Our whole world was shot to ratshit. I ought to write a soap opera," she complained at the time (88). She certainly was qualified for that task. In the mid-1970s, only TV's *Mary Hartman, Mary Hartman* had more plot twists.

While *The Sonny & Cher Show* was still running, Cher remained candid about Sonny. In February of 1977 she was quoted in a *Long Island* magazine interview discussing Bono's "male chauvinism." When asked if he had changed since their divorce, Cher explained,

> He's changed outwardly in a lot of ways. He was such a pig before. "Male chauvinist" hardly describes it at all. Now I think he's gotten a lot more open to just seeing people as people, not men as intelligent, and women as unintelligent, but just being open to accept people as they come. . . . When I left him I didn't know shit. I mean, I didn't know anything. All my opinions were Sonny's, all my ideas had so much of his influence. I mean, I could have lived and died and never lived (83).

The Sonny & Cher Show ran out of steam on March 18, 1977, when the last original episode was broadcast. The show continued in reruns until August 29, 1977. During this period, Cher released two solo albums for Warner Brothers Records that were serious sales "bombs." *I'd Rather Believe in You* (1976) was produced by Steve Barri and Michael Omartian. On it she tried an assortment of pop ballads and some interesting cover tunes. The best cuts on the album included Barry Manilow's "Early Morning Strangers," Eddie Floyd and Steve Cropper's "Knock on Wood," and a cover of the early 1970s hit "It's a Cryin' Shame." The one single released from the album was Cher's version of the song "Long Distance Love Affair."

Not even the striking black-and-white photo by Norman Seeff of Cher in skin-tight blue jeans, with her long dark hair alluringly blowing in the breeze of a wind machine, could seduce record buyers. *I'd Rather Believe in You* remains a little-known gem amidst Cher's growing catalog of recordings. It never made the charts.

Her 1977 follow-up album, *Cherished*, wisely reunited her with the man who was responsible for her biggest hits, Snuff Garrett. The album included some great new material, most notably Peter Allen's "She Loves to Hear the Music." And John Durrill, who given her "Dark Lady," "Dixie Girl," "Carousel Man," and "I Saw a Man and He Danced with His Wife" in the past, contributed three songs to this album: "Thunderstorm," "Dixie," and "Love the Devil Out of Ya." Al Capps, who gave her "Half Breed," contributed another Native American–themed song for this LP, "War Paint and Soft Feathers," which was one of the album's singles. The other one, which was out of Cher's story/song mold, was the sea-faring song "Pirate." Even a reunion with Garrett, Durrill, and Capps didn't work for her. Although they did their best to copy the formula that had worked so well at Kapp/MCA at the beginning of the decade, the public wasn't buying.

During the summer of 1977, gossip columnists were reporting that both Gregg Allman and Cher Sarkisian La Piere Bono Allman were hospitalized on the East Coast. Gregg was in a Connecticut rehabilitation clinic, Silver Hill Hospital, and Cher had checked herself into New York City's Doctors Hospital. According to the September 2, 1977, issue of the *New York Post*, "That heavily bandaged figure leaving Doctor's Hospital on the Upper East Side this morning was Cher. She has just spent two weeks having breasts, chin and cheeks lifted. Cher headed out to West Hampton, where she'll recuperate for the next month" (89). *People* magazine referred to the work she had done as being "on-the-sly" (90). But with Cher, few things remained a secret for long.

Cher came up with a great idea that was going to help her disintegrating marriage and revitalize her record career all in one fell swoop. She and Gregg were going to record an album together. To top it all off, the names "Gregg" and "Cher" were not to appear on the cover, or for that matter, anywhere on the album sleeve. Instead, the LP was released as *Two the Hard Way* by "Allman & Woman." Even Warner Brothers Records was embarrassed, but obligingly released it without any fanfare. Everyone argued with Cher over her decision to even get involved in the project. She remembers, "My publicist said I couldn't possibly make a record without my name on it, so I fired the publicist" (91).

Theoretically, *Two the Hard Way* could have reached two diverse audiences, Gregg's rock fans, who had never bought a Cher album, and Cher's cult, who would never think of purchasing a Gregg Allman record. Unfortunately, no one wanted to have anything to do with the album, and it never made the record charts. Oddly enough, one of the songs that Cher and Gregg chose to perform on the album was the Smokey Robinson & the Miracles song "You Really Got a Hold on Me." Sonny & Cher had recorded the exact same song on their first album together. The first line of the song is "I don't like you, but I love you." Odd that she would record that song with both men she obviously loved, but eventually professed not to like.

Reportedly, Cher and Gregg spent $100,000 of their own money to promote the album on their own, since Warner Brothers refused to spend a cent on it. The pair went off on a European promotional tour to launch *Two the Hard Way*, but the album, the marriage, and their whole union ultimately proved to be one huge mistake heaped upon another.

On November 6, 1977, the controversial duo of Allman & Woman left America for Europe, where they planned to do a twenty-nine-day concert tour to break in their act. Allman remembers that the audiences who came to see them were quite bizarre to say the least. Cher's crowd wanted to see the sequined television star, and Gregg's audience came to hear some beer-drinking, drug-influenced rock and roll. According to Gregg, "She had the people in the upper-age bracket, who came wearing corsages, with eight-to-eleven-year-old children. Then there were the Allman Brothers people, the backpackers. Her audience would never think of yelling out to people on-stage. But mine was always giving a lot of hell, calling out songs. It got to her" (91).

That's not all that got to her. Although he had just "dried out" from drug use for Cher, along the European trip, Gregg began to drink. "I just slipped once," he claimed, but at this point, "once" was the straw that broke the camel's back (91). On December 3, Cher pulled plug on the tour, told Gregg goodbye, and flew home.

When Gregg came back to the house that he and Cher shared, he found an armed guard waiting at the gate to greet him.

> I came back home, got out of the limousine, and there was this guy with two .357 Magnums on his side. I jumped out of the car real quick and I said, "Hey, is somebody bothering our babies, somebody break in or something?" He said, "No." And I said, " 'Why the hell are you here? Push the button on the gate and let me in." He said, "I'm sorry, I can't do that." I asked him "Why not?" and he said, "I'm here to keep you out." And I said, "Well, what about if I just jump over this goddamn gate and strangle your ass?" He said, "Well, Mr. Allman, I'll have to shoot you." What could I do, you know? The secretary came out and gave me a key to my Corvette. I took two cents out of my pocket, flipped them to her, got in the car, and just blazed out of there. They told me my clothes were at the Holiday Inn, which is the grimiest place in the world (81).

And so ended the Gregg and Cher show.

People couldn't understand why Cher ever married Allman. "I just didn't know then about drug personalities. He'd say, 'I'm going to get a pack of cigarettes,' and I'd see him four days later," she commented. "There were a couple of times when he was straight, and then he was lovely" (62). For that matter, her public couldn't figure out why she left Sonny in the first place. "People ask me if I left Sonny for another man," she said. "I tell them, 'No. I left him for a woman—ME' " (17). She later described her relationship with Allman in this fashion: "Being married to Gregg was like going to Disneyland on acid. You knew you had a good time, but you just couldn't remember what you did" (92).

In the middle of all this activity, the year 1977 had also seen the debut of the Sonny & Cher dolls. Barbie dolls had been a hit since the 1960s, but Barbie never had a wardrobe like Cher, so the Mego Corporation, a toy manufacturer, jumped at the opportunity when Cher gave her approval. According to Frederick Pierce, head of the doll division of Mego, "We wanted to give Cher [the doll] a friend, so we thought we should make an Elton John doll. So we thought about a Gregg Allman doll—but kids don't even know who he was. They don't even know that Cher and Sonny aren't still married" (93). Hence the Sonny & Cher dolls debuted in toy stores across the country, complete with Bob Mackie–designed wardrobes.

The Cher Doll had a wardrobe right out of *The Sonny & Cher Comedy Hour*, complete with Cher's "Half Breed" spangled loin-cloth and sequins costume ("Indian Squaw"), the feathered number she wore on the cover of *Time* magazine ("La Plume"), and a "Dark Lady" outfit ("Fortune Teller"). The Sonny Doll had his own varied wardrobe as well: trench coat and suit ("Private Eye"), silver *lamé* ("Space Prince"), and "Dark Lady"–inspired ("Gypsy King"). It was probably a good thing they didn't create a Gregg Allman doll, or it would have had to include drug paraphernalia. And if they had gone through with an Elton John doll, it would just want to borrow all of the Cher Doll's flashiest outfits!

In addition to the fashion figure doll, Mego also created a "Cher Makeup Center" for little girls, complete with a one-third life-size plastic bust of Cher, ready for budding Max Factors. The cover of the box for the Cher Makeup Center boasted that it included "Cher's vinyl signature bag, compact with four makeup colors and lip brush, eyeliner, adhesive, powder puff and sponge, six rollers, two barrettes, hairbrush and comb, bobby pins, two braided ribbons, and two elastic hair ties." As 1978 dawned, it was time for the pop diva to take inventory. In the past year Cher had left prime-time television, recorded two dismal albums, lifted her bust and her cheeks, dropped her second husband, and become a doll. It was now time for her to move on to greener pastures.

On April 3, 1978, ABC-TV broadcast Cher's new one-hour special, appropriately titled *Cher . . . Special.* Her guests this time around were Dolly Parton and Rod Stewart. In one of the skits, Cher performed all of the roles in her version of *West Side Story*.

> I remember my mother bringing the album of *West Side Story* to me after a trip to New York. I decided when I was grown up, I'd play every part. So in the musical number using a medley from the Broadway musical, I sing all the roles Tony, Maria, Anita, and Bernardo. I'm even all the Jets in the "Prologue" and "Jet Song." We'll do several songs, including "Maria," "Tonight," "I Have a Love," and "Somewhere" (94).

In another segment, Cher and Dolly were seen discussing each other's lives and careers. When the subject of Cher's divorce came up, Cher sang "I'm Back in the Saddle Again." Dolly promptly warned her, "Toot Toot Tootsie Don't Cry."

Cher clearly wasn't sitting at home crying. She had had it with her boyfriends, and now she was busy hanging out with the girls. One of her closest friends at the time was Diana Ross. "If I ever needed Diana, I could call her anytime," proclaimed Cher, who also admitted,

> My best friend now is Kate Jackson. We met about three months ago [January 1978] on a cerebral palsy telethon and hit it off right away. We discovered we're very much alike. Since I didn't have a boyfriend at the time, we started going to movies together, played racquetball, and palled around. It's fine. Nobody bothers us because we both have to be up early, we can adjust our hours. It was nice for me, because I didn't have any real friends and I didn't want to be going out just to go out. I didn't want to be hung up on going out with guys, but then I don't particularly like sitting home, so it was nice the two of us could go anyplace together and nobody would hassle us. I like Kate—she's really special (94).

Cher was now looking for new horizons for her career, and for her personal life. In 1978 she was toying with the idea of developing her own movie project. According to her at the time, "Kate Jackson and I have written a project. Chastity, Kate, and I had been spending the weekend at Jane Fonda's and we were coming back in my Jeep when I had the idea of an updated *Route 66*—two women driving around and getting into different situations" (95).

Several new situations loomed in Cher's future, including a new boyfriend, a hot new record deal, and a Broadway show. According to Cher, she was bored with her life, and she was really looking for a change. When she cut off her famous waist-length hair, which had long been the trademark of Cher of 1970s television, her fans were in shock. However, unlike Samson, when Cher had her luxurious locks shorn off, she emerged even stronger than before!

7

DISCO DIVA TO BROADWAY BABY

Just as she had resurrected herself in the past, by 1979 Cher had created a whole new life for herself. It was as though the Sonny and Gregg episodes never happened at all. She made a drastic move by legally removing all of her previous surnames, and now she was officially known by one name only: "Cher." She had a new boyfriend, a new certified Gold album, a new Number 1 hit single, a new $5-million house in California, a new network television special, and a whole new outlook on life.

"I'm getting ready for a fresh start in the New Year," she announced as 1978 came to a close. "I've made mistakes because I've never played it safe, but I give myself credit because I do go on trying for a good life. I'm very happy though, now, getting ready for the New Year ahead. I think it'll be marvelous with everything happening for me" (96).

Just as she had cut off her hair the year before, she began the new year by shearing off all her last names. She explained at that time, "With these final papers in order, I'll no longer be Mrs. Bono, Mrs. Allman, or Mrs. Anybody. I don't even have the title Miss Sarkisian, because I don't want a last name. I'm going to petition the court so I can be legally known by the one name of 'Cher' " (96). And so she did, effectively removing all traces of the men in her past—Sonny, Gregg, her father, and her stepfather.

The new man in her life continued her reputation for the unexpected and bizarre. He was Gene Simmons, the lead singer of the rock group KISS. Simmons and his three partners in the band were—and still are—as famous for their outrageous black-and-white Kabuki-like facial makeup onstage as they were for their multimillion-selling rock and roll albums. They refused to be photographed without their trademark makeup, and their public had no idea what they looked like without it. Simmons, who is also the group's guitarist, was renowned for his in-concert special effects. Two of his signature routines were breathing fire out of his mouth and drooling flame-red stage blood off of his exceedingly long tongue. In a decade that is now famous for the emergence of costumed theatrical rock acts—like Alice Cooper, Elton John, and David Bowie—the group KISS excelled.

Cher had met Gene at a party that Casablanca Records threw in 1978. She had just dumped Gregg Allman and was once again free to come and go as she pleased. As she explained it, "I went to a Casablanca party, and someone said that Gene Simmons was there, and I said, 'Oh God, I'd love to meet her. I've seen all her movies.' Everyone just got hysterical" (6). Cher had thought that she was going to meet actress Jean Simmons (*Great Expectations* 1946, *Hamlet* 1948, *Spartacus* 1960). Boy, was she in for a surprise.

According to Gene,

> We pretty much disliked each other on first sight. We talked until five in the morning and never even held hands. Then I had to go to New York and I thought I'd forgotten all about it—after all, one girl is just as flyaway as the next. On the plane I found the stewardess coming on really strong to me. Normally, I would have done something about it. Instead I found myself thinking about this skinny girl with strange teeth and a big nose. We're taking it one step at a time. It's weird for me because until I met her, I was just like your everyday rock musician. I've slept with anything that quivered (97).

"There's a new strength to my life and a peace," proclaimed Cher at the time.

> Gene has made some of that possible, because he's not just a musician behind a mask. He's an intelligent man who doesn't smoke or drink, so I can't be accused all this time of being involved with somebody off-the-wall. I really do love him. I'm not seeing anybody else—but at the moment we don't want to live with each other full-time. I want to live by myself for a while, because right now my career must come first (96).

Gene was of the perfect disposition for Cher—especially after the Gregg Allman nightmare. According to Cher, "Gene takes Chastity to the movies and they get in food fights. He's teaching Elijah to swim. When he had time off and I wasn't home, he came to be with them. It's hard to find someone who likes your kids as much as you do—especially when they didn't have anything to do with it" (98). For Cher, Simmons was everything that Allman was not.

The whole KISS connection reached the status of a "family affair" when Cher's sister, Georganne La Piere began dating another member of the group, Paul Stanley. Georganne had gone on to an acting career, and in the early 1970s she originated the role of Heather on the afternoon soap opera *General Hospital.*

When Fred A. Bernstein interviewed Gene Simmons's mother, Florence, for his book *The Jewish Mother's Hall of Fame,* Mrs. Simmons told him that Cher once came out to her home on Long Island for a Passover seder. According to Florence, Cher spent three hours standing at the dinner table during the holiday meal. The reason that she couldn't sit down was that she had just had her tattooed butt surgically lifted!

In 1978, the four members of KISS, based on their strong popularity, each released simultaneous solo albums, *Gene Simmons, Paul Stanley, Ace Frehley,* and *Peter Criss.* Gene invited Cher to sing on his self-titled album, and she is heard on it, singing on the song "Living in Sin." The song is a musical ego trip, with Gene singing about picking up one of his young teenage female groupies and "living in sin at the Holiday Inn." Cher can be heard on the record singing background vocals, and in the middle of the song, she is the voice of the groupie who phones Simmons's hotel room and gushes accolades to him.

In January 1979, Cher and Sonny reunited for a special appearance on *The Mike Douglas Show,* but it was Cher's relationship with Gene Simmons that was keeping her warm throughout the rest of the year. Said Cher at the time, "I don't think that Gene's particularly attractive. I just like him. He's very loving and he gives me a lot of support. He's excited about what I do. He's glad I don't really *need* him, but rather *want* to be with him. He's perfect. I couldn't ask for anyone better" (99).

Through working on Gene's album, which was released by Casablanca Records, Cher met the president of the record label, Neil Bogart. Since Cher's Warner Brothers contract had lapsed, she was shopping for a record deal, and she accepted an offer from Bogart and began work on a new album. The album, which was released in February 1979, was entitled *Take Me Home,* and the cover of it is still one of the most famous and most outrageous photographs ever taken of Cher.

In the photo, she is wearing a gold-plated bikini made of metal and a wing-like headpiece that made her resemble a 24-karat Viking goddess out of some erotic Valkyrie fantasy. Cher was a vision in gold, and skin. Although she had a gold *lamé* cape draped over her back, more of her flesh was exposed than covered. Even the breastplates had cut-out holes in them. The photo, taken by Barry Levine, is one of the most outlandishly stunning photographs ever to grace an album cover, before or since. Cher's body was in excellent shape, and she made the most of it for this session. Also contained on the album is a standing shot of Cher in her gilded Viking warrior get-up, which showed off the costume's low, plunging, winged bikini bottom, with wings that fly outward several inches past her hip, and a matching gold scabbard strapped to her hip.

The year 1979 is remembered for being the height of the disco craze in America, Europe, and Japan. Ever since Cher had boogied at the 1977 opening of Studio 54, America had been listening to the hot synthesized dance beat of disco. The Village People, Donna Summer, K.C. & the Sunshine Band, Grace Jones, Sister Sledge, Chic, Gloria Gaynor, and Tavares all had careers that were made on the dance floors. Those established performers who were adaptable enough to "go disco" with their music also scored hot disco hits as well. On this list were Rod Stewart ("Da Ya Think I'm Sexy"), the Bee Gees ("Staying Alive"), Blondie ("Heart of Glass"), the Supremes ("I'm Gonna Let My Heart Do the Walking"), Diana Ross ("Love Hangover"), Sarah Dash ("Sinner Man"), Mary Wilson ("Red Hot"), Bonnie Pointer ("Heaven Must Have Sent You"), and Martha Reeves ("Skating in the Street") all had chart hits during this era by adopting a disco beat. Why shouldn't Cher join in on the craze?

Casablanca was the home of the Village People, Donna Summer, the Ritchie Family, and Pattie Brooks. Neil Bogart knew how to sell disco records to the public like nobody's business. According to Cher, "When I went to Casablanca what I really wanted to do was rock & roll. Neil Bogart said that wasn't my strongest thing 'Do this first [disco], and let me try to get you back into the music scene' " (100).

Said Bogart at the time, "Cher is a fascinating woman with much more depth than she is usually given credit for. Her gifts are unique and I think, in the past, she only scratched the surface on the talent she has, I look forward to a long and rewarding relationship with her here at Casablanca" (13). He proved to be a man of his word.

Bogart put Cher in the studio with Bob Esty. Two additional cuts were produced by Barry Manilow's co-producer Ron Dante. Esty was fresh from his successes working with Donna Summer and Barbra Streisand when he was asked to produce Cher's *Take Me Home* album. He produced Streisand's song "Main Event," and he had worked on Summer's *Once Upon a Time* album and the biggest song of her career, "Last Dance." Bob and his writing partner, Michele Aller, were signed to Casablanca Records as a singing/songwriting team, patterned after Ashford & Simpson.

Speaking of the evolution of working with Cher, Esty explained,

> I had just done "Last Dance" with Donna Summer, had cowritten it, and arranged it and produced it, and later that year signed with Casablanca Records. They had just signed Cher to the label, and the president of the label, Neil Bogart, wanted to break her back into the recording business, because she'd been having a rough time. Her variety show had been canceled, she had divorced Sonny, so it was not a real good time for her. Neil Bogart had lived next door to her in Malibu, and Barbra Streisand lived right there too with Jon Peters. Neil said to me, that Ron Dante had produced an album for Cher with Charles Koppelman as executive producer. I think it was a thing where he had signed her, and according to Neil, he heard the album, and it didn't hit him as anything but just what she had done with the other three [Warner Brothers] albums a combination of all kinds of songs—some standards, rock—just a typical Cher album at the time. Neil wanted her to fit the Casablanca image. Now, the Casablanca image was either disco, or KISS. So, he wanted her to have a hit like "Last Dance." So Michele and I were asked to write a song in the style of "Last Dance," which she could sing. At the time—like everyone else—I was thinking "Cher? Disco?" (101).

The first song that they worked on was "Take Me Home." However, it didn't go very smoothly at first. "I played 'Take Me Home' for Cher, and she said she liked it," Esty explained.

> I think she would have liked anything at this point. It was exactly what Neil Bogart wanted. So, we went in and tracked the record, and I sang the "guide" vocal, and I have a high enough voice so that I could do it. So we attempted a vocal with her, and she was having trouble, because it was a style of music she wasn't used to, and I think she thought it was long with too many sections. And, I was trying to work with her on her approach to the song. I don't know this for sure, but I got the feeling that nobody except Sonny had ever asked her to do one of her vocals over again, or try singing it another way. And I think she was a little bit put off by it. I now

know she's insecure, but I didn't know that at the time. And I think she felt a little bit intimidated and unsure. So, she asked Charles Koppelman to come in and sit with her while she did the vocals, and not me. That made me feel kinda weird. But, I figured, "Whatever she wants." She went in and did the vocals, and she still couldn't get them. Then it was decided that it was too high, so we brought it down another key, and retracked the whole thing again. I worked with her on the vocal, and by working on it I got what I thought was a rapport. I thought that everything was fine, but then I noticed that she would come into the studio and she'd sit in a corner and just put her head down, like not wanting to be involved at all. Then I would tell her that it was time for her to go in and sing, and she would go out and sing her heart out. It was very strange (101).

Finally, Aller and Esty, writing tunes for the album, and Esty producing, reached a better working relationship with Cher. "We recorded the other songs for the album, and she did a great job singing them," recalls Esty. "She was a real trouper. She just did it until it was right, and I think that she did some of her best vocals ever on that album" (101).

Esty found that of all the songs on the album, "Git Down (Guitar Groupie)" was the one that best fit her personality. "Cher is a groupie in many ways," he explained.

She loves musicians, and finds them attractive in many ways. She finds them sexually attractive, although they may not be physically attractive. She finds them "hot," especially bass players, guitar players. So, Michele and I had written this song about a girl we both knew, and we just adapted it to Cher. We added lyrics about her. That was the first song that we tailored to her as a person. That was probably the only song on the album that she liked, really, except her own song she wrote about Gregg. Then the album was released, and "Take Me Home" was a hit. The best thing about her, is when she puts on "Cher"—as anybody who is a real star knows how to do—she becomes bigger than life. She's so charismatic, she was a big hit at the *Billboard* Disco Convention. It was a great moment for me (101).

The resulting *Take Me Home* album instantly put Cher back on top. It sold over 500,000 copies in the United States, and was certified Gold. For Cher, it was one of her biggest solo albums, and it made it to Number 25 in *Billboard* magazine. The title cut, "Take Me Home," sold a million copies, was certified Gold, went to Number 8 on the pop charts in America, and to Number 1 on the disco chart. All of a sudden Cher was back on the record scene in a big way, with one of her most popular and sexy singing performances. The song was also a hysterical come-on line, a perfect anthem for "the Sexual Revolution" of the 1970s. "Take Me Home" was a danceable invitation to be picked up for a sexual affair, and who better to be singing such a song than rock and roll's favorite vamp with one name, Cher.

Cher had not had a Number 1 single of any sort since 1974's "Dark Lady." She had spent the intervening five years starring on the covers of all the tabloid magazines in the grocery stores. Cher laughed at the critics who scoffed at her doing disco, by quipping, "You can't dance to the *National Enquirer*" (13).

Take Me Home was a different kind of an album for Cher, both in the way it was structured and in the music it contained. After the 6-minute, 47-second title cut, Cher chose a mixed bag of songs to record on this album, which was to have the distinction of being the third Gold album of her solo recording career. In addition to "Take Me Home," three of the other cuts on the album were composed by producer Bob Esty and his writing partner Michele Aller: "Wasn't It Good," "Say the Word," and "Git Down (Guitar Groupie)."

The song "Wasn't It Good," which directly followed "Take Me Home" on the album, finds Cher asking her sex partner if he enjoyed being "done" by her. If "Take Me Home" is the courtship dance pick-up number, then "Wasn't It Good" was obviously the après sex, cigarette smoking, afterglow number, set to the same danceable beat. The third cut on the album, "Say the Word," seems to continue the story of the star-crossed disco lovers, with Cher looking for some commitment and devotion from her partner. All of the songs on this well-produced disco-tinged album deal with relationships on one level or another. On Peppy Castro's "Happy Was the Day We Met," Cher sings of a love affair, while synthesizer bursts audibly mimic emotional fireworks in this dance floor affair.

In this way, on the original vinyl configuration of this album, *Take Me Home* devoted the entirety of side one to disco-paced songs. Side two contained five cuts, offering a mixed bag of rock songs and more personalized ballads. Aller and Esty's "Git Down (Guitar Groupie)" managed to mix rock guitar work with disco-styled flourishes. Cher got to use her vibrato-filled, torch song ballad-singing voice on Richard T. Bear's "Pain in My Heart (Love and Pain)" (produced by Ron Dante). Tom Snow's "Let This Be a Lesson to You" gave Cher an anthem-like, background chorus-filled song to proudly rave.

The two ballads that closed side two were among Cher's favorite cuts. The song "It's Too Late to Love Me Now" was a composition (by Rory Bourke, Gene Dobbins, and Jay Wilson) that Dolly Parton gave her to sing, and the song "My Song (Too Far Gone)" represented the first time that Cher had recorded a song she wrote. Composed with Mark Hudson of the group the Hudson Brothers ("Rendezvous"), "Too Far Gone" was a message song to Gregg Allman. It contained the lyrics "he'll never really know his son." Cher had been making quite a few public statements during this era about the fact that Elijah Blue Allman rarely ever received so much as a phone call from his estranged father.

On March 1, 1979, I had my first in-person interview with Cher, at her suite in the Pierre Hotel in New York City. She was very excited about discussing all of her creative projects and career aspirations. She was especially enthusiastic when she talked about her *Take Me Home* album, which marked her return to the hit lists and the cutting edge in popular music.

"I like this album," said Cher that day.

> I don't ever listen to my own albums, but there are a couple of cuts on this album that I really like. I must say that I like the second side more than I like the first side. It's a little bit more my kind of music to listen to when I'm working. But, I don't know; it's strange I never thought that I would want to do disco. I don't really know why I had that feeling in my mind. I guess that it's the kind of disco that [she thought for a moment] I didn't want to be the kind of disco artist that "Anybody could do the song." You know just the same beat over and over again. I think that "Take Me Home" is a really good song—it *just happens* to be a disco song. I love disco to dance to. I just never thought that I would be accepted by that audience. I guess that I thought that, more than anything else. I like it, and I like being able to do it, and I guess that I was afraid that if I did it [she paused to think] First of all I wasn't sure that I could do it and sing it right, 'cause I just felt that my style or whatever, it's so "me." I mean, you can't hear one of my records and not know that it's me, you know. And, you either like it, or you don't like it. And I thought "I wonder if I'll be able to fit into this kind of pattern." But he [Bob Esty] wrote the song for me, and it just seemed to be real terrific. It was a good experience, 'cause I was real nervous, and Bob was real terrific in the studio, and I like all the songs really (1).

She reported that she was already making plans for her next Casablanca album. "We've got some great ideas for disco. I'm really excited about it" (1).

When I said to her, "You really have rock and roll roots don't you?" she replied,

Yeah! I just can't get it out of my blood. I love it—I love rock and roll! I'm crazy about it. I even think of disco as rock and roll. I just think of it as all rock and roll somehow. It's just "today" music, or "my" music, or something. I love it. I love the Doobie Brothers, but I love Gloria Gaynor too. She's amazing. I mean, "Never Can Say Goodbye" was one of the best songs I've ever heard. There are songs that just transcend. They're just incredible songs. People who keep saying, "There's no such thing as disco". . . it's like saying, "The world is flat!" It's here. . . . people should really know it. It's terrific! It's great music to dance to. I think that danceable music is what tells everybody what's "in" (1).

Cher told me that she was especially proud of "My Song," which she wrote. "It's the first one that I decided to record," she announced. "I've been writing a lot lately. Usually I just write them and throw them away, and sometimes I just write them and stash them but I'm kind of more into writing them and recording them" (1).

When I interviewed Cher that day, there was a third person in the room, her current boyfriend, Gene Simmons from the rock group KISS. When I suggested to them both that they should record a whole album together, they both said at once, "No!" Then Gene replied, "Both of our fans would kill each other. There'd be civil wars" (1).

Take Me Home instantly put Cher back in the forefront of the recording business. Instead of attempting to recapture the formula of her early 1970s work with Snuff Garrett, Cher found herself perfectly riding the disco wave that was sweeping the world in 1979, and excelling at it. When the single and album were released, Casablanca Records was determined to go all out to promote it. At the time, *Billboard* magazine was an active force in promoting disco records, and they were hosting annual disco conventions, in which disco DJs from all over the country and the world converged on New York City to hear all the latest records, and virtually party their brains out for a solid week. On February 26, 1979, Casablanca threw a huge party at a roller skating disco that commenced around midnight. Word soon leaked out that Cher was to be the special guest hostess, and it was *the* hottest ticket in town, especially since it was a private party.

Barbara Shelley was the head of the publicity department at Casablanca when this event was held. It was her job to get every photographer in town there to shoot pictures of Cher. No problem; everyone in Manhattan for the disco convention was fighting over tickets to the event. However, the next day it was Barbara's job to try and stop the newspapers from publishing the photos they had taken of Cher. She distinctly recalls,

> It was the Billboard Disco Forum, and Casablanca was throwing a lot of parties that year. Roller skating was "in," it was really happening then. It was the rage, everybody was going roller skating, and roller rinks were popping up in New York City faster than singles bars. What we decided to do was to rent the Empire Roller Disco in Brooklyn, and we bused in several hundred people from Manhattan. I remember the party cost $20,000. We had a buffet dinner and all kinds of shenanigans going on. There were clowns, there were people dressed up to look like movie stars, and there were photographers galore. Cher is the kind of person who photographers love to shoot, because she's so gorgeous, so every photographer in New York City was there (102).

> The thing that was most memorable about the evening was the fact that Cher was wearing this fabulous roller skating outfit of black spandex pants, white roller skates, and this real glittery tiny top that looked like a skintight shirt that was sequined and reflected the colored lights every time she went around the rink. She had three bodyguards skating on either side of her; she didn't skate alone. The funniest thing about the whole evening was that the shirt that Cher was wearing didn't just reflect the light, it absorbed the light. When the photographer's flashbulbs hit the shirt, the light was absorbed by the cloth of her shirt, and in the photos it looked like [bra-less] Cher was wearing a totally see-through blouse. In the photos the next day, it looked like Cher was virtually topless, and just wearing black spandex pants! So, our job in [Casablanca's] publicity [department] was to attempt to recapture all of those photographs before they appeared in print . . . which was next to impossible. That was one of the funniest things that has ever happened to me in over ten years as a publicist (102).

While Cher was in New York City, she spent part of her time looking for an apartment she and Gene Simmons could purchase. Unfortunately, co-op apartments in Manhattan cannot be purchased without the prospective buyer being screened by the other residents. It seemed that no one wanted Cher moving into their building. Even the Upper West Side fortress known as the Dakota turned her down. "They're sorry they admitted John [Lennon] and Yoko [Ono]!" Cher told me during our interview, of the residents' board of the Dakota and their refusal to sell to her.

I don't know what they think I'm going to do there, but they're not so crazy to have entertainers. When the lady was showing us [she and Gene Simmons] apartments, she said, "Well, there's some apartments that I can't show you because Gene is Jewish, and there are some apartments that I can't show you because you're an entertainer." So, I was telling Diana [Ross], "Well, Jesus Christ, Diana! This is ridiculous." She said, "What about me? I'm black, I'm an entertainer, and my husband [Bob Ellis] is Jewish!"—this was at a time when she and Bob were still together (1).

She really had her sights on moving to New York City at the time. Comparing it to Los Angeles, she told me,

There's nothing—there's no place to dance in L.A. L.A. is the vast wasteland for anything like that. L.A. rolls up at 11:00 p.m. People aren't geared to nightlife out there. I like New York a lot. It's a place that I've always enjoyed coming to. There's so much to do here. When you walk down the street, and you walk out of the door, and everything is right there. It's not like Los Angeles where you really have to make plans to do something. I like Los Angeles, I mean I would never give up my house there because it's a kind of a life that I can also feel comfortable with, I've lived there my whole life, and there's something about it that I enjoy, but I also enjoy New York. I have those two kinds of personalities really lazy and laid back, and also with a lot of energy and loving to do stuff. And, I like plays, and you guys get all of the movies here first (1).

Cher's long-standing battles with the network censors also marred the television special she had just taped—*Cher . . . And Other Fantasies.*

The censors have always been on top of me to make sure that I didn't show anything, but somehow when they're busy worrying about showing something, we stick something [suggestive] in with a line in something. There are so many strange opinions on television, because on one end you have this faction that's trying to get sex off the air, and on the other end you've got everybody in America who wants to see tits and ass and violence. *Charlie's Angels* is the biggest [TV] show, and it's not because anybody there studied with Dame Edith Anderson or Evans. It's because they look good. . . . they look *real good.* I see Cheryl Ladd's tits every time I turn them on (1).

With regard to her own battles, Cher admitted,

I don't scrub so easily anymore. I just don't, or I just won't. I said, "I'll deliver you guys the show, and if you don't like it, you can put it anyplace you want to, but you can't say, 'Make a show for eight o'clock,' you have to make a show." It shouldn't be up to the artist to fit the network's time that they're going to show the show. They should just say, "Make the best show that you can," and put it whereever they can (1).

One of the projects that Cher told me about in 1979 was her entry into major motion pictures. She had purchased the rights to a 1945 film entitled *The Enchanted Cottage,* and she was attempting to produce it and star in it. In the plot, Robert Young and Dorothy McGuire are misfits who met with circumstances that made them both unattractive to others. Young was a World War II pilot who had been in a accident that scarred his face permanently, and McGuire's character was always considered ugly. However, when they were in one particular cottage in the woods, in their eyes each appeared to be flawlessly attractive to the other.
"It's hard to explain this film," she told me.

It's a remake of an old film called *The Enchanted Cottage,* only it's really modern. It's a great film, and we're going to do it real modern. I play the Robert Young part, actually. Instead of being a pilot, I'm a singer in a band like Heart, and it's the same idea of the old one, just modernized so that it fits into what would be really upsetting to them today if something happened to them. I own the film, I bought the rights to the original about three years ago, and I'm going to do it at Universal. It's a musical film like *Saturday Night Fever* was a musical film, or *A Star Is Born.* It's not the old kind of musical, but it's a movie with music segments. It's a real good vehicle for presenting that story (1).

She introspectively added, "I know for myself, if something happened to my face, or something happened that would change me physically, my career and my life would be pretty much down the tubes" (1).
Naturally, Cher had her own distinctive ideas as to how to shape it around her own image, for what would have been her entry into major motion pictures. "We're going to do it different," she promised.

The cottage is not like a cottage, it's a place. We're going to do it in Colorado. It has something to do with a [recording] studio like Caribou. As a matter of fact, the guy said that we could use Caribou, he was really excited that we would do it. And it will have something to do with a part of this place that was built over a [sacred] place, or somehow, to get the enchantment part in. Because in the end of it, if you'll remember, Mildred Natwick said, "The enchantment—there's nothing in the cottage; it's in you guys." So, that's the most important thing to show. I love it. I've seen it everytime—I've seen it a million times. And, there's some parts that I laugh at. Mildred Natwick, I always laugh at her, because she's right-on-the-money. But there's still something about the film, that you've really got some feeling. I've got a terrific writer the girl who wrote *Coming Home* is writing the screenplay (1).

At the time, Cher was considering being the executive producer of the film. Among the male stars she was thinking about costarring with were Gary Busey and Jon Voight.

She was also already considering doing a play on Broadway. "Yes, I would love to do it," she exclaimed.

It would have to be the right show, because I think to really do that kind of work every single day, it's got to be something that's really right for you. You can't just like screw around. It's not like doing television, where "I'll do it once, if I don't like it, it's fine." I was talking to Elliott Gould about that, because he's thinking about doing another show, and I would really like to do it. I would like to do something like *Hair* in the seventies, you know, something really contemporary, with lots of singing and dancing— and BIG! I don't know if that would be a good idea but it's something that I'd like to do. I would like to do that. Something with a lot of Bob Seger music in it (1).

With regard to her children, nine-year-old Chastity and two-and-a-half-year-old Elijah, Cher claimed that they each listened to tapes on portable players. Speaking of Elijah, she said, "He listens to KISS tapes on his way to school. Chas listens to Richard Pryor on the way to school, and Steve Martin, and KISS tapes. They get a lot of input. . . . they get a lot of *extra* input, and I guess that it's up to them to decide how it's going to affect them" (1).

On March 7, 1979, the NBC-TV special, *Cher . . . And Other Fantasies* was broadcast. Her guest stars included Lucille Ball, Shelley Winters, Elliot Gould, and Andy Kaufman. In the opening segment, Cher is seen in about twenty-five costumes, beginning with nothing on but a long wig, as Eve in the Garden of Eden, while she sings, "T'ain't Nobody's Business If I Do." The *New York Daily News* described it as "slightly gaudy, but amusing." The *New York Times* spoke of the splendor of the sets and costumes, pointing out, "Cher seems more than ever like a figure in a Byzantine court ceremonial . . . her gorgeous robes, the unchanging expression on those marmoreal features, the seeming sightlessness of those almond eyes, the cool, uninflected voice, an essential androgyny, all suggest nothing so much as a figure from an icon or mosaic brought not fully to life" (103).

In 1979, Cher was amid the construction of a new house in Los Angeles, which was destined to eat up much of her available cash. Located eight minutes from Beverly Hills, the house has a totally Egyptian motif. Constructed of columns with a papyrus design and a sandstone wash, it has an atrium in the middle, with a sliding roof covering it. Said Cher of her sudden ancient-Egypt fixation, "I'm crazy about that part of the world. I even loved [the film] *Death on the Nile,* because it showed Egypt. You could say the house was strongly influenced by Zeffirelli's [film] *Jesus of Nazareth.* The architect and I got lots of ideas from the souvenir book that went out with the film" (104).

She further explained, "My architect is amazing. He and I spent a lot of time working together on the house. He's really talented and highly respected. I've been reading about Egyptian architecture for the past two years. In the middle of the house there's a two-story atrium and the roof will slide away so it becomes open air" (95). The house ended up going massively over budget, sapping most of Cher's available cash, and it wasn't too long before she was unsuccessfully attempting to sell it to recoup her investment.

Cher also delighted in telling people that her two best buddies were singing stars who hated each other. "I know it's difficult for a lot of women, but I think I'm really easy to get along with," she explained.

I know that must sound awful, but I know that I get along with Diana [Ross], and I get along with Bette [Midler], but I also know that Diana and Bette don't get along. They're not friends because they probably never made the effort. I mean, for a long time I didn't like Diana, and I didn't even know her. But when I was going out with David Geffen, who was friends with Diana's ex, Bob Ellis, I met Diana and just loved her. And I met Bette when I saw her perform at the Troubadour. I bought her a pair of shoes that she wanted but couldn't get because she was leaving town and that's how we became friends (6).

When Cher took her new concert stage show to Caesar's Palace in Las Vegas and to the Universal Amphitheater in Los Angeles that summer, the program was filled with costume changes and conceptual staging. During one of her offstage costume changes, the transition was bridged by female impersonators dressed as Bette Midler and Diana Ross, to poke fun at her friendships with the two totally different women. Cher once announced onstage her rule of thumb for live performances, "Never be in one dress longer than eight minutes" (105). She lived up to her promise consistently. Critics continually blasted Cher's "style" over "substance" onstage, but everyone was always dying to see what in God's name she was going to wear next in her shows.

She once confessed in the *Los Angeles Herald Examiner,*

You know, to this day, when I'm feeling nervous, I get this sensation that I'm the Dinah Shore of rock. I really love Dinah, but let's face it, she can't do anything. She's just Dinah. And I think sometimes that I'm just like that. I don't have a spectacular voice. I'm not that attractive. I don't stand out at anything. But sometimes, just being famous is enough (20).

In her case, just being Cher is enough. However, she longed for more.

Randy Jones, the original cowboy from the group the Village People, met Cher for the first time during this era. "Village People were on Casablanca Records, and Cher was as well," he recalled.

She already released *Take Me Home,* the album, produced by Bob Esty. We were in Miami, and we were at the NARM (National Association of Record Merchandisers) convention, where labels take their acts to perform, or show the acts off to the people who are buying the records—Sam Goody's, K-Mart, Wal-Mart—all those people. She performed, did her number, we did a song or two. Afterward, I enjoyed a very nice limousine ride with her, and Neil Bogart, and Joyce Bogart—who was Donna Summer's manager. I must have been like a kid, with my eyes wide open. I was sitting in a limousine, across from the president of my record company, across from the manager of Donna Summer, and sitting beside Cher. I used to lay on the carpet in front of the television in my parents' living room in the sixties, watching her as a star. And here we were, buzzing down the freeway, and just talking like regular people. It was really a wonderful experience. Initially, I was totally starstruck earlier in the evening, and upon meeting her as a labelmate—I was kind of awestruck. But, what I think impressed me the most, being in the close confines of a limousine hurdling down the highway at 65 miles an hour, was that she was very normal. I remember her mentioning something about one of her kids, because Neil and Joyce had two or three children at that point. They were all commiserating about having children. One of her comments was made in the voice of her character, "Laverne," about however she dealt with the problem. I was impressed that she just let me see her as a person, and not that Barbie doll from television. She was just a mother talking about her children. We aren't that different in age. What impressed me physically about her, was her size. She's so small. Like Marie Osmond, even her hands are tiny. Cher and Marie have big heads, but they are tiny people. She seemed so little and delicate in person. That evening, it wasn't like she was Cher, being "Cher," so much as she was just being Cherilyn (106).

Now that she was a disco star, Cher crossed paths with the members of the Village People quite a bit in 1979. Randy Jones explained,

The next time I saw her, she was over at the Casablanca offices, and I ran into her. We just exchanged words, and she mentioned that she was going to be recording in the studio, and she just offhandedly said, "You should come by." And, I have found out since then, that she is not always the most open person about her recording, so, for her to say that, was something. So, I went over there and visited her. She wasn't actually singing when I arrived there, but they were mixing the tracks. I sat with her for a half hour to 45 minutes. Bob Esty was producing. That was the second album she was doing for Casablanca, *Prisoner.* I remember her making faces while she was listening to stuff. Everyone becomes more accustomed to hearing their voice, and is pleased with it, as time goes by, but she was wincing at some of the things she heard that day. I got the impression that she was singing on that album, in a way she had never sung before. I don't know if that was a good thing, or a bad thing, but she was recording in a different musical direction on that album (106).

Randy and Cher even became friendly enough to the point where they exchanged gifts with each other.

There was a shop called Machismo on Melrose Avenue at that time, which had all kinds of great gifts. They had half life-size figures that were like dolls, but they were soft-bodied dolls they made of like Marilyn Monroe, W. C. Fields, and Mae West. But, they would custom make them for you. So, I went there and I met the guy and asked if he could make two of them to look like the Laverne character, that Cher did on her show. I kept one, and I sent her one at the closing of her show in Las Vegas. It was half life-size, but for her, that was small! It had the tight pants and the headwrap, and the glasses, and the beads. When we did four or five nights at the Greek Theater [in Los Angeles], she had sent to me—for opening night— a pair of lycra pants, that were studded with rhinestones. So, when you wore them on stage, you just spattered light everywhere like a mirrored ball. She told me that they had belonged to Gene Simmons. On our opening night, I wore them with cowboy boots, and my guns. When I came out on stage in them, I could see the other guys in the group seething with jealousy. I looked like a dancing mirrored ball—thanks to Cher (106).

While Cher was busy touring in concert that summer, her next single was on the airwaves, further capitalizing on her *Take Me Home* comeback album. The song "Wasn't It Good" made it to Number 49 on the pop chart in *Billboard* magazine in America.

In the autumn of 1979, Cher released her second album on Casablanca, *Prisoner.* Her first single off of the album was a song called "Hell on Wheels," which was an ode to her roller skating passion. One of the most memorable songs on the album is a cut called "Shoppin'." Talk about autobiographical—she even pokes fun at that initial shopping spree she had in the 1960s when she bought the three Rudi Gernrich outfits she never wore, ad-libbing, "Miss, how many colors do you have?" If you listen closely to the background tracks on this amusing cut, you can hear Cher poking fun at male genitalia, as though it was actually sex she was shopping for. "It's all pink and wrinkled," she says as though to a sales clerk, directly followed by the comment "What a darling little bag." One thing that you have to admit about Cher, when it comes to being outspoken, she certainly has "balls!"

On the cover of the *Prisoner* album we see a stark-naked Cher, covered in only a long black wig and metal chains that bind her to an ancient marble column. Was Cher beginning to feel like a prisoner of her image? According to her, this photo was not warmly received by women, many of whom found it demeaning to their sex. "I got into so much trouble because of this album cover. I had so many women's groups mad at me. They were pissed off. 'What did this mean, that I was chained up to the pillar?' I don't know, what do you think it means?" Cher asked (39).

Of the eight cuts on this album, six were specifically written for her and about her. The album opens with the pop/rock title cut, "Prisoner," which was written by her former boyfriend and Toto member David Paich, along with David Williams. Another of the highlights on the album, was Cynthia Weil and Tom Snow's "Holdin' Out for Love," a medium-paced rhythmic ballad about looking for a true love, instead of picking up dates at the disco.

Four of the songs on *Prisoner* were penned by Michele Aller and Bob Esty. "Shoppin'" was about Cher's favorite hobby; "Hell on Wheels"

highlighted her then-current favorite sport—roller skating; "Holy
Smoke" pokes fun at the state of world circa 1979; and "Outrageous" is
truly a Cher theme song if ever there was one. On it she sings about wearing whatever she wants and putting on a flashy stage show. Writing with
another collaborator, Michael Brooks, Bob Esty provided Cher with
"Mirror Image," which makes jokes about the Cher everyone reads about
in the press.

Bob Esty explained of the project that became the *Prisoner* album,

> Meanwhile, I was working on her second [Casablanca] album, which was
> originally entitled *Mirror Image,* and it was going to be all songs about her.
> "Hell on Wheels" was about her roller skating. "Shoppin' " was about her
> shopping fetish. "Holy Smoke" was about the gas crisis which was going
> on. She had a Ferrari and a Jeep, and we just pictured her at the gas pump,
> complaining. And then we wrote "Outrageous," because of the fact that
> she is two different people. When she is herself, she is kinda like a rock &
> roller biker babe, and yet when she puts on her show she is all glamour
> and glitz. And then "Mirror Image" was a song about what it's like to have
> your face in the tabloids every day of your life, surrounded by publicity,
> and wondering if people really believe all the crazy stories or not—and
> sometimes wondering if you believe it yourself. We had a concept the front
> of the album would be Cher in her public persona in a beautiful outfit—
> on her bed, or whatever it would be—looking sexy and fabulous. And, then
> the back cover would be the mirror image, her looking frustrated and sur-
> rounded by all this tabloid publicity spread out on her bed (101).

Although the projected *Mirror Image* was intended as a concept album,
it ended up evolving into *Prisoner.* "What happened was, she never liked
the style of music she was asked to do—dance music," said Esty.

> She loves rock & roll. So, she asked the members of Toto to write her a
> song, and they wrote her a song called "Prisoner." You have to understand,
> David Paich and some of the other members of Toto were her band on the
> road. She was in heaven when they came into the studio and did their
> track, of a song I don't think they spent much time writing to tell you the
> truth—it's kind of a one line song. But, she loved it, and that was what was
> important. She brought in the song "Boys & Girls," which she liked, so we
> did it. And of course she went to [photographer] Harry Langdon, who did
> the *Prisoner* photos with the chains, and the whole thing—gorgeous pho-
> tos, beautiful shots. But, then the original concept of the album was not
> there anymore (101).

Unfortunately, Cher's *Prisoner* album did not become the huge success that *Take Me Home* was. "Hell on Wheels" only made it to Number 59 on the *Billboard* Hot 100 chart. An almost-overlooked album at the time of its release, *Prisoner* is one of the most fun albums Cher has recorded. In the 1990s both *Take Me Home* and *Prisoner* were combined on seventeen-cut compilation CDs—first as a German import on Spectrum Records in 1990, and then as the American release entitled *Cher: The Casablanca Years* on Casablanca Records in 1996.

Although Bob Esty was one of the people who were largely responsible for Cher's 1979 "comeback," they didn't remain close friends. However, his writing partner, Michele Aller, was to become one of Cher's background singers in her concert tours in the 1980s. According to Esty, "I've always felt an kind of aloofness from Cher. Although she once had me over to her house to maybe give Chastity some vocal lessons. I got the feeling, even then, that Chastity wasn't interested in becoming a singer" (101).

While she was still very much into her disco mode at Casablanca Records, Cher was one of the label's stars to be featured on the soundtrack album from the movie *Foxes*. A 1980 teenage coming-of-age film, set in the disco era, *Foxes* starred Jodie Foster, Cherie Currie (of the Runaways), Randy Quaid, Laura Dern, and Sally Kellerman.

Giorgio Moroder, who was most famous for turning Donna Summer into a star, produced a two-record set of dance tunes for the *Foxes* soundtrack. The album also included Summer's hit "On the Radio," Janis Ian's "Fly Too High," and Angel's disco-rocking "20th Century Foxes." Cher's song on the album, "Bad Love," is especially notable as it was written by Cher and Moroder. It is Cher's only recorded disco composition as a writer. She sounds game and bouncy on this rarely heard cut. While Moroder's music on "Bad Love" sounds like a cross between Cheryl Lynn's "Star Love" and Donna Summer's "Bad Girls," it is a prime Cher cut, circa Studio 54.

With the start of the new decade, Cher was ready for a whole new persona. Her romance with Gene Simmons came to an end, and her pal Diana Ross began dating him, reportedly with Cher's full approval. Cher had a new obsession to occupy her time, rock and roll guitarist Les Dudek. Her fascination with Dudek extended beyond the physical, as she struck upon the idea that what she really wanted to do was to start her own rock and roll band. According to her, "I've always wanted to sing with a rock band even when Sonny and I first started out" (6). Well, she was about to have her chance.

A small item in *People* magazine announced that Cher had formed her own rock band, but no one was talking about its name, or anything about it. "Expect something weird and wonderful," the magazine predicted (107). In August 1980, Daryl Hall & John Oates, the rock duo, had booked several concert dates on the East Coast, including gigs at the Garden State Arts Center in Holmdel, New Jersey; at the Dr. Pepper Music Festival in Central Park in New York City; and in Bethlehem and Pittsburgh, Pennsylvania. On the bill with Hall & Oates was an opening act calling themselves Black Rose. No one had any idea that Black Rose was in reality Cher, Les Dudek, and their new rock band.

No announcements were made before the show, or from the stage during the band's performance. Cher and Les wanted to break in the act as a totally unknown band and see what happened. It wasn't long before word leaked out that the girl screaming high-decibel rock and roll up onstage was actually one of the most famous women in the world—Cher.

A lot of things happened at the dawn of the 1980s. The music industry suddenly changed focus. Disco was out, and stripped down, early 1960s-style rock and roll was "in." Suddenly, even the word "disco" was out. It already sounded *sooo* 1970s, and so outdated. It began to go underground, and it was now to be called—even by *Billboard* magazine—"dance" music. Several popular 1970s acts suddenly abandoned synthesizers and strings to adopt the sound of "punk" rock.

The high priestess of California pop/rock, Linda Ronstadt led the pack with her Platinum 1980 album *Mad Love*. Carly Simon went for harder rock on her 1980 album *Come Upstairs*. This was also the year that Pat Benetar hit it big with "Heartbreaker." This all opened the door for the Go-Go's in 1981. Then in 1982, Bonnie Raitt followed suit with her album *Green Light*. It was an era for girls who rocked. In other words, this was the perfect time for Cher to be taken seriously as a "rock" star.

Cher's new album, also entitled *Black Rose,* was released by Casablanca Records with no fanfare whatsoever. The cover had nothing on it but an illustration of a woman's high-heeled foot, bearing the tattoo of a black rose and wearing a menacing pair of spiked ankle bracelets. On the back of the album cover is a photo of the band, free of any identifying names of the people in the photo. The inner sleeve simply states among the album credits "Vocals: Cher."

After her identity leaked out to the press, Cher granted several interviews to explain her latest project. In each instance she stressed her commitment to the band, and downplayed her role in it. "I just decided I wanted to become part of a real rock & roll band," she stated at the time. "Black Rose isn't 'MY' band. I'm just the group's singer—it's as simple as that. I know that a lot of people think that it's pretty bizarre that I've joined a band like this, but it's something that I've been wanting to do for a long time" (108).

> Obviously a lot of people are going to wonder why I want to give up the Vegas routine and join a rock band. I know that I still have a particular image, and that's not going to change overnight. TV and Vegas are still a part of my life, but they had become very repetitious and boring for me. I just wanted to have a little more fun as a performer, and rock & roll gives me that opportunity. It's a very free-flowing and unpredictable medium, and that's what makes it so much fun (108).

Obviously, unpredictability is one of Cher's finer points.

> I don't want people to get the idea that I'm in Black Rose as a one-shot deal. I'm committed to this band as an ongoing venture. I'm not saying that I'm not going to play Vegas or appear on TV anymore, I mean those things are still an important part of my life, but Black Rose is also going to remain an important part of me. We have some incredible people in the group. I think Les is one of the best guitarists around, and Mike Finnegan, who's our keyboard player, and Rocket [Ron Ritchotte, guitarist], are really incredible on stage. In this band we're all sharing equal footing, which is something I really like. I think that if people will just open up and give us a chance, we can convince even the true skeptics that we can rock & roll with the best of 'em (108).

However, the album never even made it onto the record charts, and the critics ate her alive. "The critics panned us, and they didn't attack the record they attacked me! It was like, 'How dare Cher sing rock & roll' " (37).

When they were all in Los Angeles, Cher and the members of Black Rose wandered into a new wave club to catch a couple of the bands that were performing. Cher immediately felt that the audience there that night was amazed that the former star of the G-rated *Sonny & Cher Comedy Hour* would bop into a punk club and not expect to get heckled. She told *Rolling Stone* magazine, "They didn't appreciate me being there at all. I was just in the audience and somebody said, 'Hey Cher, where's Sonny?' It really pissed me off, so I told him, 'He's at home, fucking your mother' " (100). Touché Cher!

From the very first drum and guitar downbeat, it is very clear that the *Black Rose* album is a very different musical affair for Cher. With all-male background singers, exciting guitar work, and multilayered keyboards, the song "Never Should've Started" kicks off this raucously energetic eight-cut excursion into Cher the rock and roll singer. One way to describe the *Black Rose* album would be to say that this is what Cher would sound like if she were fronting the group Heart. Her vocal power and ass-kicking attitude throughout make this album unlike any other Cher LP—before or since.

Perhaps the fact that it was not originally marketed as a "Cher" album allowed her to really let loose and swear and scream and shout with the abandonment of a banshee in heat. On the song "Julie," Cher sings about a rival for her boyfriend's affections. She ad-libs threats toward Julie, calling her a "liar and a bitch." On the song "We'll All Fly Home," she sings of a "lonely fucking stranger" standing out in the cold. On "88 Degrees," Cher ponders her own fame and the temperature, complaining, "Shit, it's 88 degrees!" Cher was no longer the innocent teenager who had once recorded "Baby Don't Go," nor the G-rated TV show hostess. She was now the lead singer of her own hard-rocking 1980s band, and she was ready to let loose. Always one to worry about the shape and sound of her singing voice, on a couple of the songs on the *Black Rose* album, Cher sings several of the lyrics—especially "We'll All Fly Home"—sounding like she'd had several belts of whiskey, a pack of cigarettes, and attended an all-night party before heading off to the recording studio. This is the one and only "punk rock" Cher album, and it is a unique original.

Cher has always been one to take pride in remaining on good terms with her ex-boyfriends. For two of the *Black Rose* cuts she turned to a pair of her ex's: David Paich for "Never Should've Started" and Bernie Taupin for "Julie." Concurrent boyfriend Les Dudek wrote the cut "You Know It," which he sings as a duet with Cher.

Cher had great hopes for Black Rose. At the time she proclaimed,

> I'm very pleased with the album. And I must admit, I don't think my voice has ever sounded better. My voice has always been very strong. In fact I always thought it might be a little too brash for the type of material I did. Now though, I need every bit of volume I can get just to be heard over the music that the guys put out. I've always been more used to having an orchestra there to help me along. In rock & roll it's just every man for himself (108).

When it was originally released in 1980, the group's self-titled album was a sales disaster. Since the cover didn't have Cher's photo or name on it, many of her fans had no idea that she had a new album in the stores. Largely forgotten for two decades, in 1999 this eight-song LP was released as a compact disc entitled *Cher: Black Rose* by Spectrum Records in Germany. It remains a fascinating time capsule of an album in Cher's highly varied recording career. At the time she longed to be taken seriously as a rock and roll songstress, and the group and the album *Black Rose* provides audible evidence of her 1980s musical evolution.

Black Rose marked the fourth time she had teamed with her current lover to produce music. First there was Sonny & Cher, then Allman & Woman, then her duet with Gene Simmons on his solo album, and now she was the lead singer of Les Dudek's band Black Rose.

According to Cher at the time, "Les is the person I've had more fun with than anybody I ever knew. He has a wonderful sense of humor. He's really carefree and not very materialistic at all. We just have a good time doing nothing—riding motorcycles and doing nothing" (109).

By 1981, that's precisely what Black Rose was doing, nothing. That was not the Cher that the public wanted to pay money to see. Black Rose promptly disbanded, and when Les Dudek wanted to get married to Cher, she got cold feet, and her fascination with their relationship fizzled. By June she was back on the concert road, earning money to pay for her Egyptian house, which had eaten up three times more money than it had initially been estimated to cost to construct.

Sighed a resigned Cher, "Las Vegas is my gig. That's how I pay my rent and my kids' school. It's not my favorite thing to do. It's like a play; there are lines, and it's the same every night. It's not like walking onstage with a band, where I can wear what I want and say what I want" (100). She decided that if she felt that way about it, she might as well be doing theater on the legitimate stage.

Before she moved on with her career, however, she tackled the press, and specifically questioned the rights of the press to print stories about "public figures" without specific consent. Cher sued two magazines for $30 million in damages and won her case. In subsequent appeals on the part of the publications, she lost half of the case, strengthening the rights of the press as defined under the First Amendment of the Constitution of the United States.

In April of 1980, Cher consented to grant an interview with freelance writer Fred Robbins, to appear in *Us* magazine. When the writer chose to concentrate his line of questioning on Cher's personal life, instead of the group Black Rose, which is what she wanted to talk about, she complained to *Us.* The magazine decided not to publish the story, and Robbins was paid a "kill" fee for nonpublication. This left Robbins free to sell his story to whomever he chose. He subsequently sold the interview to two magazines, *The Star* and *Forum.* Since there was no overlapping of the two publication's audiences, both publications advertised their stories as being "exclusive" interviews. Cher based her $30-million suit on the fact that she would never grant interviews to either of those publications. Cher did not at any time contest the contents of either article as being either "libelous" or in any way "untrue."

In the first round, a federal judge ruled in Cher's favor, based solely on the exclusivity claims in the headlines that were used to advertise both magazines' articles. She was to be awarded $750,000 in damages. In later appeals, the Supreme Court upheld the previous decision for *Forum* to pay $269,117 in damages for advertising their interview in a way that would suggest that Cher was a regular reader of the sexually based publication. *The Star,* however, won its appeal against the previous decision that they should pay Cher damages for advertising their "exclusive series," because it was in fact a series that was exclusive to that publication.

According to Howard Squadron, attorney for *The Star,*

> Some people in the entertainment world use publicity to build up a reputation and to make themselves a more valuable property. Then they want to protect their celebrity status, so they attempt to censor the press by getting it to publish only what they want. That's what Cher wanted to do. In her early days she'd sought publicity—and she didn't mind then if some of it was not always respectable, because at that stage she was hungry to build up her reputation as a celebrity. When she eventually became a celebrity, then she wanted to control the way she appeared in the press. In a sense she wanted to control the media (110).

The case *The Star* won was a victory for the press in general.

After a limited engagement in Central Park, during the summer of 1980, producer Joseph Papp opened his hit production of *The Pirates of Penzance* on Broadway. The show was a big hit, and it was especially notable because it starred popular singing star Linda Ronstadt as the heroine, Mabel. Linda's performance did not have a lot of depth and fire, but the role of Mabel is that of a demure little lass, and all of a sudden Linda Ronstadt was a bankable Broadway star. This was all the encouragement that Cher needed. If Linda could make the transition from pop and rock records to Broadway, why couldn't she?

For several years, Cher harbored ambitions of becoming an actress. However, no one could see beyond her TV series or her well-publicized role as a minimally talented but very famous celebrity. As she recalls,

Then the night before the show closed, I saw Linda Ronstadt do *The Pirates of Penzance*. She did it in Los Angeles for one night only. Watching her I thought, "If Linda can do this, what am I doing wasting my time? If the [movie] studio people won't take me seriously, then I'll go to New York and try my luck." I'd always wanted to be an actress. Not many people were encouraging, but some were. Francis [Ford Coppola], who used to play poker with Sonny, saw my show in Las Vegas once and asked, "Why aren't you doing movies?" But not many felt that way. Most took the view that if I hadn't begun acting when I was at the peak of my popularity, around 1975, why start now? Nobody understood that I'd got to the point where I had to find out if I had any talent. For years, I'd been popular in America, not because of my talent, but because I was famous. I kept on doing club work, and I built this house, but always in the back of my mind was the knowledge that soon I'd have to find out if I could really do anything. And when I saw Linda Ronstadt, I made up my mind. I'd go to New York, and even if I failed there I wouldn't care (52).

Cher decided to take the direct approach. If Joe Papp would take a gamble on Linda Ronstadt, why wouldn't he at least give her a chance? They met in New York City, and he said to her, "How do I know you're talented? There's no way I can tell from all that junk you've been doing over the years" (111). However, he decided to give her a chance. He presented her with a script of the play *I'm Getting My Act Together and Taking It on the Road* and told her to study and rehearse it, and to come back and audition for him.

I was terrified, so I spent a week rehearsing my audition with Lee Strasberg. When I finally did it, I think Joe Papp was impressed, but he had nothing for me. Then when we got back to his office, there was a message there that Robert Altman had called me. My mother knows Bob. She'd been trying to reach me in New York and called his number by mistake, and when Bob learned that I was planning to study acting, he got in touch (52).

"I needed a job in the worst way imaginable. I had been trying for eight years to get a job as an actress and received absolutely no encouragement," she proclaimed (112). And then, as though she willed it to happen, here was Robert Altman calling her to announce that he was casting a new

show, which was to be his Broadway directing debut. The play was called
Come Back to the Five and Dime, Jimmy Dean, Jimmy Dean, and there
was a part in it that would be perfect for Cher.

> Well, I read for him, and after a lot of discussion and a reading, he offered
> me a role in the play. But Ed Gracyzk [the playwright] wanted me thrown
> out right from the beginning, because I kept ad-libbing lines. He hated me
> at first. But I felt I had better things to say as my character. "You wrote this
> and took it as far as you could," I told him, "but I think I can take it fur-
> ther." Bob said, "Careful, you'll make him angry." Then, after the first run-
> through, Ed said, "Listen, you can say whatever you want to." He turned
> out to be a terrific guy (52).

Cher, Sandy Dennis, and Karen Black were cast in the principal roles
for *Come Back to the Five and Dime, Jimmy Dean, Jimmy Dean.* According to Robert Altman, he cast the three actresses with the reasoning, "Just
those names sound interesting together—it's an interesting combination.
I don't pick one actress for one part and another for another part. I chose
them all together. This is not 'The Cher Show' " (113). Even so, in the
October 22, 1981, issue of the *New York Times,* there was a story about
the upcoming play, and the headline read "Robert Altman to Direct Cher
in Broadway Debut" (114). It was the inclusion of Cher in the cast that
made this production so significant to the public. Regardless of what the
critics were to think, or whether or not audiences were going to respond,
Cher was in New York City working on her dramatic stage debut. She
was about to fulfill one of her dreams. Whatever the consequences were
going to be on opening night, Cher was about to become an actress now.

CHER: MOVIE STAR

In October 1981, Cher had just completed a six-month tour of the globe with her glitzy nightclub act when she packed her suitcases and moved to Manhattan. She came without Les Dudek, without her children—Chastity and Elijah Blue—and without her sequined Bob Mackie gowns. "I didn't come here to get parts," she explained in New York City.

> I came to learn how to act. I'd wanted to do it for years. No, I didn't have time—I was going to make time. Most people think I don't know how to act. People think I'm such a frivolous person. You know, after I got the part, I called my agency and asked if they could tell me about the play. They didn't know I already had the part; they said "Oh, you can't get in to read for that." That really pissed me off (113).

When Robert Altman first started to tell people that he was considering casting Cher, they thought he was nuts. "The producers said to me, 'Oh my God, she's too expensive for us, we'll have to give her a limousine!' I said, 'No. If she's going to be a New York actress, she has to learn how to ride a subway or take a taxi" (22). He was correct in following his instincts, and Cher threw herself right into the project.

By choosing this career path, Cher knew that she was turning her back on the huge salaries that headlining a Las Vegas act could bring her. While starring on Broadway in *Jimmy Dean,* she was paid $500 a week. However, she was living with her entire staff at the Mayflower Hotel on Central Park West, at a price tag of $8,000 a month. And, never once did she quit exercising her favorite lust: shopping. According to *Premiere* magazine, by the time the *Come Back to the Five and Dime, Jimmy Dean, Jimmy Dean* adventure was over, Cher was another $180,000 in debt.

Rehearsals for *Come Back to the Five and Dime, Jimmy Dean, Jimmy Dean* went into full swing right after Christmas. Cher was immediately impressed with director Robert Altman. He was already well known for such hit movies as *Nashville* and *M*A*S*H*, and for such non-hits as *Health, Popeye,* and *A Wedding.* Although his films weren't always sure-fire smashes, they are all consistently fascinating, for innovative casting and outlandish plot twists filmed with a wonderfully voyeuristic tone. Altman was the first director to cast Lily Tomlin in a movie—*Nashville,* garnering her an Academy Award nomination. He was also daring enough to cast Elliot Gould against type as Philip Marlowe in *The Long Goodbye.* Sandy Dennis had first worked with Altman in 1969 in *That Cold Day in the Park,* and Karen Black was one of the stars of his 1975 film *Nashville.* Now here were Dennis, Black, and Cher, preparing to face the Broadway critics with Altman at the helm.

"I can't say if I would've done this play if Bob weren't directing it," said Cher amid rehearsals. "All I can say is 'Thank God, it's Bob!' He accepts all of us—that's what's wonderful. 'We're O.K., he's O.K.' He'll stop and listen to anything we have to say. At rehearsals I'm fine, because I'm crazy about everyone I'm working with. But I'm exhausted every night. Yesterday I did my speech twice, and I was a mess afterward. A fucking mess" (113).

According to Robert Altman,

I never had any qualms about her. She had a natural ability, the guts and the confidence. It gets around to her desire to do things. If Cher says she's going to do something, she will do it. She had good instincts, and respect for her fellow actors. If I got her in a film tomorrow, I wouldn't expect her to be one iota different. The only thing that would surprise me would be if she did something badly (22).

On Saturday, January 9, 1982, Cher was still in rehearsals. She was working extra hard on her part as Sissy, and she decided to pop three huge multiple vitamins to make sure that she would keep her energy level and health in high gear. She chewed up two of the three vitamins she intended to take, but they tasted so awful that she swallowed the third one. However, it lodged in her windpipe, and she found herself choking to death. "I've never been so scared in my life!" she proclaimed. "I couldn't breathe. I tried eating a little piece of bread and taking a sip of water, but nothing happened. I started walking toward Bob. I remember getting dizzy and dropping the glass of water from one hand and the bread from the other." She mouthed the words "Help me," and Altman came to her rescue, applying the Heimlich maneuver. She coughed up the bread, and the pill moved in her throat, allowing her to breathe. "Alt saved my life, I could have died!" Cher later said (113). That night, however, she was definitely back among the living, boogying on the dance floor of Studio 54 with Liza Minnelli. That Cher, what a trooper!

Before the play opened, Robert Altman explained its extraordinary set. Like the unique casting of the play, the set was something that he had conceived. It was constructed so that two time zones existed. The past was happening upstage; the present was happening downstage. Said Altman, "We're going to have a lot of things going on simultaneously. We're going to really screw the audience up. It's split screen, double images. It allows you to show stream of consciousness and coincidence. It's fluid" (113).

Come Back to the Five and Dime, Jimmy Dean, Jimmy Dean opened at the Martin Beck Theater on February 18, 1982. Cher remembers that night quite distinctly as the only night during the play's run that she was frightened.

I felt I should be scared, but somehow I knew it would all be all right. People have said "If you fall on your face on Broadway everyone in the world will know it." I guess I was too dumb to know how terrible it would be if I were terrible. I was scared *only* on opening night, because everyone else was scared. But it went fine. But one night after we'd been doing the play for about six weeks, I looked across the stage and thought, "What am I doing here on stage with Sandy Dennis?" Then I thought, "Cher, if it's taken you this long to think that, then you'd better just keep going, because it's a bit late to be nervous" (52).

Cher knew full well that she could have announced to the world that she was all set to become a stage actress, and that no one may have ever given her the chance to prove herself. For that reason, she admitted that she was eternally grateful to the director who gambled on her ability. "So far as I'm concerned, Bob Altman was twenty-five feet high," she claimed. "He took a chance on me without knowing if I could do it or not. Even when I said afterward, "You took such a gamble on me,' his reply was, 'Don't be ridiculous. I knew as soon as you walked in that you could do it' " (52).

The cast not only featured the fun character actress Sudie Bond (*Swing Shift* 1984), but also costarred a then-unknown actress named Kathy Bates. Kathy would go on to become an Academy Award–winning actress for her portrayal of the villainess in Stephen King's *Misery* (1990), and she played unsinkable millionairess Molly Brown in *Titanic* (1998).

The play represented a huge cut in pay for Cher, but she was getting to do exactly what she wanted to do, starring on Broadway. "I got five hundred dollars a week," she recalled. "I was so dumb on the first preview night that while all the other actresses were having diarrhea and vomiting, I was only worrying about getting my make-up on too early, because I didn't want to be bored waiting around too long. Did I have a lot to learn" (115). For Cher, it was the best on-the-job training she could ever have received as an actress.

"I remember when she left Hollywood for New York," recalls Sally Kirkland. "Turning her back on her music career was another big move for Cher. The buzz around Hollywood was that she was selling all her property because she was going broke. She was working for Equity scale, and she gave up her glamorous life" (70).

Of this whole new experience of performing in a play, Cher claimed,

> I don't really know what I'm doing most of the time onstage, and if I stop to think about it, I won't know what I'm doing at all. When we started, everyone was talking about "preparation," and I didn't know what that was. What I do is sort of turn my mind to "pretend." I thought I'd hate having to be the same character every night, but then I found it was natural. There was a lot of freedom in it (116).

One of the things that thrilled her the most was how she was welcomed to town by several of the local Manhattan stars. In March of 1982 she reported, "I really enjoy not having to sing. I mean, I love to sing—I began as a background singer, you know—but having to sing for money takes the fun out of it. Carly Simon had a breakfast for me last Sunday— the sweetest thing anyone's done for me—and then for two hours we all sat around and sang. It was wonderful" (116).

Come Back to the Five and Dime, Jimmy Dean, Jimmy Dean was not an incredible smash hit during its run on Broadway, but it was one of the most intriguing and daringly different plays on Broadway that season. Not only did audiences flock to see it because Cher was in it, but the staging and the acting were riveting. Especially fascinating was the use of a split stage to denote the passage of time in two different time frames, September 20, 1955, and September 20, 1975. All the action took place at the luncheon counter of a tired-looking Woolworth's dime store, complete with one of those gurgling Orange Crush soda fountain machines. Behind it was an exact replica of the same set, with everything in reverse, as if the 1955 plot was taking place "through the looking glass" in an imaginary mirror behind the counter.

Cher was delicious as the counter girl of thirty-six who is unaware that life has been passing her by, all these twenty years she has held her job at Woolworth's in this dusty small town. When she announces that the *Ice Capades* is coming to town to hold auditions, her character, Sissy, jumps with joy at the prospect of a professional ice-skating career materializing to take her away from her tiny Texas hometown. Sandy Dennis was in her element as the neurotic who still carries the torch for actor James Dean twenty years after his death. And Karen Black, as the mysterious Joanne, dazzled with her bizarrely affected mannerisms. The play was thoroughly fascinating and entertaining to watch. It was especially impressive to see Cher totally focused, live and in person, bringing the bubbly laughing-in-the-face-of-depression Sissy to life.

While the critics almost unanimously didn't love the play, they all had favorable things to say about Cher. Frank Rich, drama critic for the *New York Times*, began his review with the statement, "Forget about whether or not Mayor Koch is going to run for governor. The *truly* momentous question of the month is 'Can Cher act?'" He then went on to call Cher's Broadway acting a "cheery, ingratiating, non-performance" (117). So much for the *Times*. Rex Reed, the acid-tongued critic for the *New York Daily News*, said in his inimitable fashion, "Cher finally made it to Broadway. What a pity that her first vehicle, *Come Back to the Five and Dime, Jimmy Dean, Jimmy Dean*, got totaled in a massive collision along the way." He did, however, go on to state, "Cher, on the other hand, gives the play the kind of naturalism it requires. If she learns to project with the same kind of ease and grace, she will have a first-rate characterization to her credit" (118).

Although the audiences were consistently good, the play was not sold out every night. According to Cher,

> Bob Altman put his own money into it to keep it open. I was the curiosity factor—they wanted to see if I could act. But I did bring people into the theater who'd never seen a play, people who didn't even know the proper

decorum for live theater. They'd yell out in the middle of a line—but I
could tell they really enjoyed it. God, that made me happy! This gay club
bought out the whole theater one night, and it was our *best* performance!
They cheered, they stood to applaud, but they listened (19).

She was thrilled with the whole process of being part of a Broadway
theatrical production. "I thought, 'People getting paid for this kind of
work, this is a cinch,'" said Cher. "I didn't like making the movie, but I
loved doing the play. That was the most fun I ever had in my life" (119).

Cher claimed that doing the play in Manhattan made her change her
mind about her famous wardrobe. "What I think affected my clothing is
moving to New York and meeting a lot of actresses and actors who don't
really care too much about clothing and don't make a big deal out of it—
a group of people you don't have to impress with your clothes." She
remembers one particular visit Geraldine Page paid her backstage when
she was doing *Jimmy Dean.*

She came running in looking like a rich bag lady with all these bags, an old
fur coat, her hair flying everywhere. She said, "Welcome to the street, kid!"
I like the fact that in New York you can go around any kind of way and people accept you. I really enjoy being able to walk around looking like a bum.
If I went into Beverly Hills looking anything but totally put together,
everyone would say, "Poor Cher, something must be tragic in her private
life. Did you see the way she looked?" (13).

The play only lasted for fifty-two performances, but it truly was the
vehicle that made Cher into an actress. Altman was so pleased with the
production that immediately following the closing of the show, the original cast reunited to capture the whole play on film. Although the movie
version is clearly a filmed stage play with an expanded set, it is truly entertaining. It made Cher a bona fide dramatic movie actress, and represented another huge step for her ever-growing career.

According to Cher, during the filming of *Come Back to the Five and
Dime, Jimmy Dean, Jimmy Dean,* she was uncertain of her vocal projection on camera. Stage acting is so much more broad and exaggerated, "I
cried a lot while we were making the movie," she later explained. "Bob
took so little notice of me. I really didn't know what I was doing, and I
was sure the camera would pick that up in my eyes. But apparently I was
all right. Afterward, Bob said, 'I didn't have to talk to you. You were doing
just fine'" (52).

While involved with the play and the movie version of *Jimmy Dean*, Cher began dating several different men. In rapid succession she was seen around town with hockey star Ron Duguay, actor John Heard, and singer John Loeffler.

> That was the first time I ever didn't feel like having a boyfriend. I was pretty wild. Then one day, I just sat down and thought, "God, this is just stupid and I really hate this, and I want a boyfriend right now." That was the morning of May twentieth [her birthday], because I'd just spent the night with this guy, and I was walking home from his apartment thinking, "This is ridiculous. This guy is crazy, and if I see him anymore, I'm crazy. The other two guys are O.K., but I don't really care. What I'd like is a boyfriend." That night I met Val Kilmer, and we were together for [one month]. My girlfriend fixed me up with him. We just met, and I said, "I don't date guys who are eleven years old!" and I walked out (4).

However, she was thirty-six, and Val was twenty-two, not eleven.

During this same period, Cher was still infatuated with being taken seriously as a rock star. That year she appeared on the album of an established rocker. It was a special guest performance on the Meatloaf album *Dead Ringer* (1981). Cher appears as a special guest soloist on the song "Dead Ringer for Love." In the raucous rock song, which was produced by Jim Steinman, Cher and Meatloaf trade fast-paced hard-rocking romantic come-ons to each other, and in the plot of this wild beer-hall brawl of a story/song, the two of them pick each other up at a bar amid several choruses glorifying "rock & roll and brew." There was also a raucous video produced of this cut, which really brought the story visually to life. Released in England as a single, the song "Dead Ringer for Love" hit Number 5 on the U.K. charts in February of 1982.

One night, during the Broadway run of *Come Back to the Five and Dime, Jimmy Dean, Jimmy Dean*, something miraculous happened. Even Cher was surprised. It had been eight years since Mike Nichols had flatly turned her down for the lead in his film *The Fortune*. Now, here he was, turning up backstage at the Martin Beck Theater after one of the performances, praising her acting ability and offering her a lead role in his upcoming film production, *Silkwood*.

Cher's lust for taking career risks was about to pay off in a big way. According to her mother, doing the play on Broadway was Cher's biggest gamble. "She was so scared she would fail that she got sick before performances," Georgia Holt remembers. "But she always sticks her neck

out. Whenever she's afraid, she goes ahead and does what's frightening
her" (21).

"Years ago, I went to see Mike about a movie," recalls Cher of her
encounter with director Mike Nichols. "He turned me down, and I told
him, 'You're wrong. Someday you're gonna be sorry, 'cause I'm really talented!' Then, when Mike saw *Jimmy Dean*, he walked into the dressing
room and said, 'You're right!' It was so funny because of all the time that
had passed" (13). Of their encounter in the Martin Beck Theater, she
continued, "That night Mike came backstage with big tears in his eyes,
and he said to me, 'I want you to be in my new movie with Meryl Streep.'
I think at that moment I lost my hearing first, then my vision" (120).

The way that Nichols offered the role to her came with one major stip-
ulation. She had to accept it on the spot without laying eyes on the script.
"Of course I say, 'Yes,' " she distinctly remembers.

> This was so cute—Mike Nichols called before he sent me the script and
> said, "It's a great part, but there's one thing about her—she's gay." I said,
> "Oh, O.K." It seems to me that an actress can play anything—a murderer,
> whatever—and what matters is doing a good job. The only time I worried
> was when I called my mother and said, "Mom, in this film I'm gay!" She
> said, "Oh, O.K." Then, when Mom saw the movie, she phoned immedi-
> ately. "Cher, you were wonderful, but I was so nervous, I was sweating! I
> thought you were going to be this dyke" (19).

> I've always thought people are people, whatever their sexual prefer-
> ence, and I knew I didn't want to play Dolly stomping around with a pack
> of Marlboros rolled up in my T-shirt sleeve, but I was all set to cut my hair
> short. Well, right away Mike said, "Let's not make a statement about Dolly
> with a butch cut. It'll be harder for you to bring her across, but let's don't
> help you with something obvious. Let's have you work to get everything
> out of her without externals." God, that was important! It let me say, "This
> is a *girl*, this is her way of life." And I don't think Dolly's gayness is the
> thing you remember the most about her (19).

Silkwood is the real-life story of Karen Silkwood and the events that led
up to her sudden and mysterious death in 1974. Karen worked at the Kerr-
McGee nuclear processing plant in Oklahoma. When she began organiz-
ing her fellow employees to demand union participation to question the
safety of their working conditions, the events in her life began to take a
tragic turn. It was clear in her mind that the "acceptable" levels of radia-

tion that the Kerr-McGee employees were being exposed to were in fact toxic, and she secretly traveled to Washington, D.C., to seek government intervention. It is generally suspected that the night her car was run off the road and she was killed, she was carrying documentation to prove her allegations of the safety cover-up to a reporter for the *New York Times.*

The role of Karen Silkwood was played by Meryl Streep, and her boyfriend Drew Stephens was portrayed by Kurt Russell. Cher played Dolly Pelliker, Karen and Drew's lesbian roommate. The character of Dolly is based on the real-life Sherri Ellis. According to Ellis, "I sold the producers of the film the character portrayal rights, and for $67,500 they can defame my character any way they want." When asked by reporters about her gay lifestyle, Ellis commented, "I don't feel my personal life is anyone's business" (121).

The real Drew Stephens served as an adviser on the film, and he met Cher on the set. Stephens reminded Cher that she had in fact met the real Karen Silkwood. Said Cher, "Drew told me he and Karen had come backstage after a Sonny & Cher concert. I didn't know that. I knew the vaguest nothing about her life and death. It really made me scared when I started reading about it" (121).

Also in the cast of *Silkwood* was Sudie Bond, who had been one of the actresses in both the play and the film *Come Back to the Five and Dime, Jimmy Dean, Jimmy Dean.* The supporting cast consisted of Diana Scarwid (*Mommy Dearest*), Fred Ward, and Ron Silver.

Of course, there were doubts about Cher's ability to portray the part of Dolly Pelliker. Could the sequined Las Vegas–TV performer really play such a low-keyed role with warmth, understatement, and credibility? Nora Ephron, who wrote the film's screenplay with Alice Arlen, admitted, "It was extremely high-risk casting. If it hadn't worked, it would have been devastating to the movie. Before shooting, people would ask, 'Who's in the movie besides Meryl?' We would say, 'Cher,' and they'd say, 'You're kidding?' We went through that for months. We just told people, 'Trust us' " (19).

Cher had her doubts as well. Poking fun at people's perceptions of her talents, Cher commented to Joan Rivers on *The Tonight Show* that it was a wonder she wasn't cast in a film opposite Pia Zadora instead of costarring with Meryl Streep.

> When I was packing my bags to go to Texas for filming, I said to my sister, "I cannot go and work with Meryl Streep! I cannot!" But she was so open

to me, and she had to be the one who was open, because I was so terrified. The first time I came on the set, she took me by the shoulders and gave me a kiss and said, "I'm so glad you're here." We got along so well, and it was strange for her because this is the first film she's working on with another woman (111).

From her first day on the set, one of Cher's biggest phobias came into play: her complexion and her use of makeup.

For a long time, I had *rotten* skin! [During] *The Sonny & Cher Comedy Hour* [I had] an allergic reaction to wearing heavy pancake crap all day under hot lights. My skin looked so bad, this doctor gave me X-ray treatments, which turned my skin different colors, so I had acid peeling to correct that. Nothing worked, and during *Jimmy Dean,* when I broke out again, I called Polly Mellen at *Vogue* [magazine] and asked who in this town was best for skin. She sent me to Mario [Badescu] for cleaning, then I used his products, and in a month my skin started to look great (19).

Now, here she was in Texas, and the decree came down from Mike Nichols, "*No* makeup" whatsoever for Cher. "Let me tell you, it wasn't my favorite look," she proclaimed.

I tried sneaking a little base on, but Mike'd always be watching. Finally I said, "Fuck it, he knows what's right." The first day of the shoot, Kurt asked me, "What are you supposed to be?" and I ran in the bathroom and cried. I'd waited my whole life to be in movies and, O.K., Meryl's no glamour queen either. This isn't *French Lieutenant's Woman,* but I looked like I worked in a stable. I am so convincingly ugly. It sure is easy to tear down an image (120).

According to Nora Ephron, Cher attempted to cheat and wear just a little makeup base, but everyone could see it, and Nichols put his foot down. "In one of the first shots in the movie, when she's going down the hall, I can see the makeup. It looks a little greenish," Ephron explains (121).

Cher finally relented and followed her enforced decree. "I'll tell you exactly what I did," she says.

I got up, showered, combed my hair straight down to let it dry that way so it was really nothing. Then I curled my eyelashes and put on a little base. I tried to get away with so many things and Mike always noticed it. There was nothing to hide behind in Dolly. There's no flash. That's exactly what was needed, so the public would see past "Cher" and accept me as an actress (121).

In the plot of the movie, Karen is in love with Drew, and Dolly is in love with Karen. When Drew walks out on Karen, Dolly tries halfheartedly to get Karen emotionally attached to her. There is one scene in which the two women sit on a porch swing and have a soul-searching talk about all of the things that are going wrong in their lives. The scene is one of the film's strongest segments, and we see the characters of Karen and Dolly stripped bare of any pretense. Cher's emotional acting in that particular scene is one of the reasons for the critical praise that was bestowed upon her after the film's release.

In another scene, Dolly accuses Karen of taking about as good care of her estranged children from a previous marriage as she did of Drew. Cher recalls of filming that sequence, "That was a rough day. There were long breaks, we wouldn't stay 'in character.' I'd do needlepoint, she'd do [knit] this green sweater and we'd listen to Michael McDonald records, or joke with Kurt. But that day we didn't talk to each other or anyone else. We just sat alone. Mike didn't talk to us either. At the end of the day I had a stomachache and Meryl had a headache" (121).

The filming of *Silkwood* took place between September and November of 1982. It had been quite a busy year for Cher. She had starred on Broadway, made two dramatic films, and stretched herself into a new realm of credibility. Would the public finally begin to think of her as something besides the other half of Sonny & Cher? This was certainly the start of Cher's coming into her own as an actress and an individual.

According to her, she felt like she was the production's cheerleader. "I was like the child, I was the darling girl. If any parts of it were funny, or could relieve tension, they were my parts, and so everyone was happy when I was around. And I didn't have to wear make-up or care if I looked great" (119).

Cher recounted in her book *The First Time* that a few weeks before *Silkwood* was due to open in theaters she received a phone call from Mike Nichols. He told her that the preview "trailer" for the film was running in a theater in Westwood, California, preceding a Tom Cruise film. He told her to go and see it, that it was very good. Cher went to the theater with her sister, and her manager. When the trailer came up on the screen, Meryl Streep's name flashed on the screen, and the crowd let out an "Ahhhh." Then Kurt Russell's name came up on the screen, and the audience said, "Ohhhh." Then Cher's name came up on the screen and the audience started laughing. Cher's sister Georganne started to cry. Her manager started to cry. And Cher was crushed.

According to her, when the film opened, she witnessed the same reaction. "When my name came on the screen everyone laughed. I was devastated, and yet I couldn't really get angry, because it was such an organic response. Everyone had that kind of reaction. It was painful beyond belief but it was interesting, because at the end when my name came up everyone clapped. This is an upward climb, this is an uphill battle" (119).

Sonny Bono, on the other hand, was having similar credibility problems. In the public's eyes, for the longest time, he would always be "Cher's ex-partner." On New Year's Eve, December 31, 1981, at a candlelight ceremony in Aspen, Colorado, after six and a half years of living together, Sonny married Susie Coelho. Embarrassingly enough, when Reverend Gregg Anderson performed the ceremony, he screwed up the couple's names by announcing, "Dearly beloved, we are gathered here to unite Sonny and Cher-ie!" Susie blurted out, "Who's Cherie?" but the damage was already done. Was she destined to always live in the shadow of Cher? Apparently so, and it was more than she could take. Her marriage to Sonny dissolved in less than three years.

On the subject of the public's opinion of her talents, Cher was quick to respond defiantly.

> People's perceptions of me are so limited. Do you think that when I was doing my Las Vegas act I was less or more a person than when I was doing *Silkwood?* I'm a worker. I work through the media available to me at the time. It was so painful to be constantly devaluated on the basis of external surroundings. You know what it is? I dress strangely. Many people don't understand about that, but it's something I like. I'm certainly not going to change (13).

In the middle of her stretching out as a film actress, Cher released her next album, *I Paralyze.* It was her hope that it would inject her right into the middle of the rock world, but it failed to make the charts. One of the best cuts on the album was the song "Walk with Me," which was very reminiscent of the songs that made Cher mentor Phil Spector famous. In the summer of 1981, Cher had stated,

> I've been spending quite a bit of time finding the right label, and the right producer for my next album. I believe I have found him, though. I needed to find a producer who was consistent, album after album. Then I thought, "I really love what John Farrar does with Livvy [Olivia Newton-John], and I adore all of Livvy's albums." So somebody said, "Yeah, but he doesn't record anybody but Olivia." So I got him to come over, we talked, and it's

set now. I'm looking forward to seeing what John wants to do. What John is going to write is going to be how he sees me; he's going to do his interpretation of "Cher," and that should be *very* interesting (20).

When the album was released in 1982, the only song that Farrar produced was the title cut, "I Paralyze," which failed to become the hit single that Cher had longed for. The rest of the album ended up being produced by David Wolfert. The album received almost no publicity and subsequently sold very few copies. *C'est la vie!* By the time *I Paralyze* was released, Cher was too busy with her new acting career to promote it, and the LP, which was her strongest and most consistent solo album in years, died on the vine.

When the film version of *Come Back to the Five and Dime, Jimmy Dean, Jimmy Dean* was released in late 1982, all of a sudden moviegoers were getting their first taste of Cher the movie star, and they were quite impressed. In fact, Cher was seriously mentioned as a contender for an Academy Award nomination for her portrayal of Sissy.

The studio that produced *Come Back to the Five and Dime, Jimmy Dean, Jimmy Dean* was actively campaigning to net her a nomination, along with Sandy Dennis. The major question was should she be considered for the "Best Actress" category, or for the "Best Supporting Actress" category?

"All of a sudden there seem to be dozens of contenders for the 'Supporting Actress' nomination," Cher commented in January of 1983. "I know a lot of worthy contenders are going to get cheated, and I don't want to be one of them. The studio has been campaigning to get Sandy Dennis a leading actress nomination for *Jimmy Dean,* but when you think about it, I did have more lines than she did in the movie" (122).

She was quick to give thanks to the whole *Jimmy Dean* project, both onstage and on film. "That gave me professional credibility for the first time in my life. For the first time, I didn't feel like an industry joke. You can be stupid about your life—and I have been many times—but not stupid enough not to know when you're considered nothing but a joke" (13). Well, finally in her career, Cher was having the last laugh.

When she was questioned by the press about her desire to win an Oscar for her work in *Come Back to the Five and Dime, Jimmy Dean, Jimmy Dean,* Cher commented, "Just a nomination would be enough. I want one so badly, I'd kill for it" (13). Well, she wouldn't have to go that far to obtain a nomination; she would simply have to wait for a year. For Cher, her greatest glories as an actress were just around the next bend.

REMOVING THE MASK

It had been more than twenty years since Cher first met Sonny Bono and became a bell-bottom-clad 1960s recording sensation. In the 1970s she was a glamorous television star. By the 1980s she became what she'd always claimed she wanted to be: a movie star. At the time it seemed like a long shot at best. Although other pop singers in the past had starred in movies—like Petula Clark, Diana Ross, and Olivia Newton-John—none of them made a successful long-term career of it. Yet for Cher, multi-media goddess, it somehow seemed like a logical progression—leaping from medium to medium.

Cher has never been one to take the conventional route to achieve any of her goals. The movie roles that have transformed her from a pop music princess into a bankable film commodity have been far from glamorous. The Cher of 1980s movie screens was drawn largely from the un-chic side of the tracks. Countergirl Sissy in *Come Back to the Five and Dime, Jimmy Dean, Jimmy Dean,* unadorned, gay plain-Jane Dolly Pelliker in *Silkwood,* biker mom Rusty Dennis in *Mask,* and pre-transformation Italian "old maid" Loretta in *Moonstruck,* all showed new shadings of Cher's personality. Where once she used costumes and makeup to become another character in front of TV cameras, now she was digging deep inside herself to bring these women to life on screen.

In the 1980s, she may have been seen in revealing Bob Mackie gowns, but they were worn for public appearances, not in front of movie cameras. Cher did her best to strip away the sequined surface of her former dazzling diva self and shed the designer skin that made her famous. Step by step, role by role, she was removing the mask she once hid behind.

I prefer not to play glamorous women in movies, because my heroes in film, for the most part, are usually people that you wouldn't know about unless someone like me brought them to the screen, like everyday kinds of people. If you're going to do this glamour stuff, which is totally make-believe, you don't have to be true to anything. That's what I like about both of the things that I do, because one of them is totally for fun, and it's superficial, and all about the excitement of the moment. The energy that you're giving off and the costumes are a great part of all that. The other part of the work that I do is about the reality of people's lives and getting inside them, and letting you see what's going on and how much the character is like the person that's watching. That part doesn't really leave too much room for costumes in my mind. I'd much rather be unglamorous when I'm making movies (39).

At the time Cher was able to make a fortune by performing for a couple of nights in a Las Vegas or Atlantic City casino showroom, but she temporarily chose to turn her back on glitzy singing gigs and a high income for her cinematic metamorphosis. When she was doing *Come Back to the Five and Dime, Jimmy Dean, Jimmy Dean,* Cher griped, "I have no money at all. Going to Broadway to do the play and film cost me a lot, because the pay was nothing, and I had to take my family with me. All in all, I must have spent around $84,000" (52). When she did *Silkwood,* she proclaimed, "They got me for a cottonball" (121). The "cottonball" was $150,000. When she did her third film, *Mask,* her fee was $500,000, plus a 5 percent take of the gross. For one week in Las Vegas, Cher was able to command up to $400,000, performing two shows a night. Las Vegas held no challenge for her. Starring in movies seemed like the ultimate gamble. Her films instantly began bringing her rewards that extended beyond the financial: a Golden Globe nomination for *Come Back to the Five and Dime, Jimmy Dean, Jimmy Dean,* a Golden Globe Award for *Silkwood,* a Best Supporting Actress Academy Award nomination for *Silkwood,* and a Cannes Film Festival "Best Actress" Award for *Mask.*

When *Silkwood* was released in 1983, Cher received a whole new crop of praise from amazed critics. The *New York Times,* which is quite conservative in its gushing accolades, heralded her portrayal of Dolly by announcing, "When you take away those wild wigs, there's an honest, complex screen presence underneath" (123).

The only anchor around her neck was that thirty-one-room Egyptian palace that she built in Benedict Canyon, and could not sell. By the time construction was finished, it ended up costing her more than $4 million, and no one seemed to be grabbing at the—then—$5-million asking price that she was trying to sell it for. "It took me four years to build, and in those four years I decided that I am not very much interested in what's going on in Los Angeles. I don't take advantage of whatever it has to offer. I don't hold parties and I'm kind of reclusive, no matter what you read," said Cher at the time. Although she found herself to be "cash poor" because of the house, she was quick to stress that she would not compromise her asking price. "I refuse to come down on the price. The price of things are the price of things. . . . my house is certainly worth it," she claimed (111).

However, her closest friends all realized that Cher had no money sense. She was also a self-admitted shopaholic. After the completion of *Silkwood*, Cher and Meryl Streep socialized together in New York City. Meryl recalls a short walk with Cher to pick up Meryl's son Henry at school one afternoon. "Not a long walk," said Streep. "Four blocks. And Cher spent two hundred dollars in four blocks, on a sweater, shoes, something else. I was horrified! I can't listen to her complain about money problems. She doesn't seem to realize that not having enough is the same problem as spending too much" (120).

Hollywood had been the home of much of Cher's outlandish behavior on and off camera. Her fights with the CBS censors about her exposed navel, her highly publicized attempts to wean Gregg Allman off drugs, and her flings with rock stars did not do much to endear her to the voting members of the Academy of Motion Picture Arts and Sciences. When it was announced in February 1984 that Cher was nominated for an Oscar for her work in the box-office hit *Silkwood*, it was not only a triumph for her as an actress, it was also a huge compliment from the conservative voting members of the Academy. Whether or not she won the award, just to be taken seriously by the old guard of Hollywood was a priceless honor for Cher, and she knew it.

It was in 1984 that Cher took her first acting prize, as Dolly Pelliker. The Foreign Press Association awarded her with a Golden Globe for her work in *Silkwood*—the first major award in her long career. At last she had validation that she had found her niche—as an actress.

Now that she was a film star, Cher began to attend all of the international cinema events. In the spring of 1984, she was one of celebrities present in London at the British Academy Awards. Grinning a wide smile for the cameras that night, Cher revealed that she had a mouth full of dental braces. She was on her way to a whole new look. Quoted in *People* magazine on her new "heavy metal" tooth look, Cher's only comment was "They won't be on for long" (124).

Straightening her teeth was just another step in Cher's on-going physical evolution. According to her in the early 1980s, "I believe in face lifts and nips and tucks and all that. If I need to have something done, I'll do it. I've had three breast lifts—one after each pregnancy, and one other" (125).

She was already plotting her next big comeback. According to her, "I've already been disposed of, so I want to bounce back. I'm like some of that trash that just won't go away" (126).

Cher's next film role represented another significant leap forward for her. It had originally been announced that she was to star in *Grandview U.S.A.*, the story of a girl who inherits an automobile demolition derby. One of the most alluring aspects of starring in *Grandview, U.S.A.* was that it would have paid her $650,000. With her extravagant lifestyle, she was in quite a financial mess. Accepting the role would have effectively erased her concurrent debt. However, when the shooting schedule was suddenly moved up—"before the cherry blossoms came off or something like that," recalls Cher, she backed out. According to her, if she went ahead and made the film, it would have broken one of her cardinal rules. "The one thing I said I could never do, which was to make movies just for the money" (22).

When Cher decided to pass on *Grandview, U.S.A.*, Jamie Lee Curtis ended up playing the part. The film went nowhere, so Cher didn't miss out on anything big. The film that she instead chose was *Mask*.

The plot of the film is bizarre, and just offbeat enough for Cher to really stretch out with her acting. *Mask* is about a strange real-life relationship between a mother and her teenage son. Neither character could be accused of being your average parent or child. Cher played Rusty Dennis, a motorcycle mama with a Hell's Angels–like troupe, who loves to get stoned out of her mind for recreation, or whenever the pressures in her life get to be too much for her to handle—which is quite often. Rusty's son, the real Rocky Dennis, died in 1978 of a rare congenital affliction known as craniodiaphysical dysplasia. The condition causes calcium deposits to form on the skull, resulting in an enlarged head and massive degrees of disfiguration. The victims usually succumb to the added pressure on the brain and spinal column.

Screenplay writer Anna Hamilton Phelan claims to have written *Mask* with an 8 × 10 photograph of Cher in front of her for inspiration. When director Peter Bogdanovich was signed for the project, he agreed with Phelan's idea of casting Cher. According to Bogdanovich, "I felt Cher's persona—or at least the persona people think is Cher—fit the character exactly. The woman had to be free, outspoken, tough . . . but also a lot more vulnerable than she lets on, which I think is also true of Cher" (67).

Cher received Phelan's completed version of *Mask* in December 1983.

> I got the script along with this really wonderful letter from [producer] Marty Starger saying that they [Starger and Bogdanovich] wanted me for the movie and they hoped I liked the script as much as they did. So I went upstairs and started to read it and when I got about halfway through I was so upset that I went right to the ending, and I was a mess. Then I went back to the middle, finished it, and I mean, I was hysterical. I cried and I cried and I cried. From the moment I read it, it just seemed very real (3).

Director Peter Bogdanovich was also very excited about the prospect of working with Cher. According to him, "What Cher has that immediately makes her a movie star are those extraordinarily soulful and penetrating eyes. When you move into a close-up with her, it doesn't matter if she's saying the line right. You think, 'With eyes like that, how could anyone not be saying the truth' " (22).

When the contracts were all signed, sealed, and delivered, one of the first things that Cher did to prepare for her challenging new role was to meet the real-life Rusty Dennis, the woman whom she was about to portray. According to Cher, "When I met Rusty, I really didn't ask her about who she was because I think that the best way to find out about someone is to ask them how they feel about everything else. She's just like one big dichotomy, and a real strange combination. She's taken a lot of drugs and she hangs out with bikers, but yet she's very metaphysical" (3). She adds, "She is tough but she has an edge of softness about her. She laughs a lot. She's soft-spoken and very warm, with a metaphysical side to her about finding her way through life. She is also quite a beautiful woman, even though, when she speaks, you hear those biker expressions" (127).

On the subject of meeting Cher, Rusty said, "My first impulse was to hug her, and I did. We rapped like two old friends—about the movie, the script, my life. We rapped about Cher's life, about mothers raising kids.

Personality-wise, Cher has an element of danger. You never know what she's going to say or do next. We share that element of danger" (128).

The film, which costarred Sam Elliott as one of Rusty's biker boyfriends and Eric Stoltz as Rocky Dennis, was shot around Los Angeles on a nine-week schedule. According to Cher, Rusty was often on the set as an unofficial creative consultant.

> She was never somber, absolutely never wistful about what we were doing. She feels Rocky is still around, and he had such a power and energy. She once told me she thought Rocky was in fact here on location with us, that he was cracking up at all the fuss over him. Everyone actually did have this feeling—and it really takes a lot for me to feel something strongly—that there was a higher presence around, an extra something that moved us (127).

The supporting cast for the film included screenplay writer Anna Hamilton Phelan as the "puppy lady," Estelle Getty of TV's *Golden Girls* as Rusty's mother, and Cher's ex-boyfriend Les Dudek as a biker named Bone.

In the past, Cher's costar Sam Elliott had mainly been known for his roles in several successful Old West TV movies and miniseries (*The Sacketts* 1979, *Shadow Riders* 1982), but was ready at this point to break into a high-profile legitimate film career. "I had never heard of him," said Cher, "but he was fabulous and I said to him, 'Sam, how come I haven't had the chance to see how fabulous you are?' And he said to me, 'How come it took you so long?' " (3).

According to Cher, her working relationship with director Peter Bogdanovich was quite easy, at least during the initial filming process.

> I don't really like being directed that much. I like having a certain amount of freedom with which to work. Peter tells you exactly what to do and you listen to it and then you do what you want to do. And I figured out how to work with him—he gives you line readings and then you go and do it the way you want to. And if it's as good as or better than what he expected, he'll let you do it your own way (3).

It wasn't long before her I'll-do-as-I-damned-well-please attitude got to Peter, and battle lines were drawn. Looking back on her experience of filming *Mask,* Cher was to state of her least favorite directors, "Peter Bogdanovich was my worst. At the time, I was so unsure of myself, and he wasn't very nice. One day he said, 'Just remember, this movie isn't about the woman, it's about a boy. I can cut you out [of the film].' I thought, 'I'm going to take that information and just stash it, and get real, real tough.' And I did" (61).

While she was filming *Mask*, Cher had an affair with actor Val Kilmer, for a mere matter of weeks. It was an unconventional affair, to say the least. "We went to a play, and then he never went home. We stayed together for a month, and we didn't even kiss. My daughter said, 'Mother, you're the weirdest woman in the world. I thought the first night you spent together you'd gone all the way" (22).

During their brief affair, Cher was able to take some of her real-life emotions and channel them into her screen portrayal of Rusty Dennis. At the time she had been living with Kilmer, and one day he walked out on her. "That was very painful, and it took me a long time to get over it, but it helped my acting a lot. I was also being beaten up [verbally] daily by Peter [Bogdanovich]. That helped too," Cher claimed (22).

However, it was during the postproduction phase of the film's creation that the real problems between Peter and Cher began to arise. First of all, real-life Rocky Dennis's favorite music was Bruce Springsteen's. Bogdanovich wanted to use Springsteen music in the film, but when a satisfactory financial agreement couldn't be reached between Universal Pictures and CBS Records, Universal opted to use the songs of Bob Seger instead. As it turned out, the music in the film was actually used as incidental music, and the replacement of Springsteen tunes with those of Seger was immaterial to the viewer—yet carried the same feeling. Second was the fact that Universal cut two scenes, totaling eight minutes of screen time. Bogdanovich threw a fit and waged a much-publicized war against his own film, and he urged Cher to do the same. Cher had worked very hard on the film, and she not only refused to put up with Peter's tantrum-like demands, she also came out and gave the film full press support by granting interviews in the film's favor.

"I'm not surprised Peter would serve his own interest before serving the picture's," proclaimed Cher, upon its release. "He's asked me not to do anything and to boycott everything. I said, 'You should get down on your knees and thank your lucky stars that I'm doing this, because one of us has to. This is a good movie' " (128).

Bogdanovich then dragged Rusty Dennis into the middle of it. She ended up speaking in favor of Peter, but she also underscored her comments by praising Cher. "They've cut two very important scenes—one's a song-and-dance scene that shows how me and Rocky used to clown around. Another scene, at a biker funeral, showed how he felt about death. To him, death was a form of freedom. The movie should be uplifting, but by taking those scenes out it's a little downbeat," said Rusty, who added, "The movie's good, no doubt about it. I think [Cher's] great in the movie, and deserves everything she can get out of it—an Oscar, whatever" (128).

Regarding Bogdanovich's complaints about Universal's editing, Cher explained,

> The one scene he keeps talking about is my scene; if I can live without, he should be able to live without it, but he was just amazed that studio people were screwing with his work. Basically, what I said was, "You know, you screwed with my work; now they're screwing with my work. . . . I don't really give a damn!" It's like being a slave and having someone sell you. When you're a slave, one master's as good as the next. He screwed up my work as far as I'm concerned, so for them to screw it up a little bit more . . . who cares? They really didn't hurt it as much as Peter hurt it in the beginning (130).

She further claimed at the time, "In the film, you hand in your work and then it becomes something totally different. You do the work on the thing and you have your scene, then they cut it, or change it, or take it out. OR they can redo the whole movie so it doesn't have anything to do with what you thought it was about" (130).

Cher admittedly put a lot of herself into her screen performance in *Mask*. In fact, one of her most memorable lines in the whole movie is "You must be confusing me with someone who gives a shit" (22). She said, "I was so close to Eric's Rocky character that on the last day of shooting, I was in tears, because I was never going to see Rocky again. Sometimes, just when I think I'm strong, I can get very emotional" (115).

When *Mask* was released in 1985, it became a big critical success. Jack Mathews of *USA Today* glowed, "Cher takes a career role and gives a career performance" (131). Rex Reed of the *New York Post* raved, "Cher doesn't call attention to her virtuosity, her no-fuss acting style matches Rusty's passionate lifestyle. The portrait she paints is of a woman who thinks of herself as one of the boys, but has a strong maternal instinct in spite of herself. . . . a Cher-delight" (132). And Kathleen Carroll of the *New York Daily News* exclaimed, "In Rusty, Cher has found a part that suits her as well as a black leather miniskirt. . . . Cher often stops to gaze at the camera with one of those mysteriously enticing Mona Lisa half-smiles, but she definitely puts her heart into this performance and the emotion shows through. And this is what makes *Mask* so appealing" (133).

In its first week of limited release in four theaters, *Mask* grossed $185,000. In May 1985, at the Cannes Film Festival, the film and Cher's performance continued to gain critical momentum. But also at the festival, the verbal mudslinging match between Bogdanovich and Cher continued. According to Cher, "When a director says his movie is not as good as it should have been, people may not be as interested in seeing it" (134). By that point, however, the film had already made over $37 million in ticket sales, so no one took any of Bogdanovich's gripes about the Springsteen songs or the missing eight minutes seriously.

"When I finally saw the film," Cher was to recall, "I cried all the way through it. By the very end I was sobbing and I knew no experience would ever be so special as that had been" (115).

On May 20, 1985, Cher won the "Best Actress" Award at Cannes for her portrayal as Rusty Dennis. She shared the honors with Argentine actress Norma Aleandro, who won for her role in *The Official Story*. Since May 20, 1985, was also Cher's thirty-ninth birthday, she thanked the assemblage for providing her "with the best birthday present of my life" (13).

"It is no secret that we didn't get on," Cher told the press of her relationship with her director. "Bogdanovich was so inconsistent. When he had his ideas and I had mine, I just went my own way. I won't work with him again" (13). Said Peter Bogdanovich in retaliation, "The main reason was that she didn't trust me; she doesn't trust men" (135).

Speaking of men, meanwhile there was a new man in Cher's personal life. He was Josh Donen, who is the son of director Stanley Donen (*Singin' in the Rain* 1952). She had been dating Val Kilmer up until 1984, and Josh was Val's agent. For a time, Cher and Eric Stoltz went out, and *People* magazine reported that the only reason Cher didn't film *Grandview, U.S.A.* was the fact that Stoltz wasn't cast opposite her. They instead made *Mask* together.

According to Cher, when she first met Donen, she found him to be "rude, but so funny that no one got his jokes. I couldn't understand why everyone liked him." She later changed her mind. "I won't mind having a child with Josh because he's young and he has never been married," said Cher of Donen at that time. "I've been married twice before and I if I never did it again it would be fine. The reason people get married is because the stigma is too much and they don't want their children to be bastards. Joshua wants to get married and I feel it's an awful lot of pressure" (127).

One of the reasons Cher arrived at this revolutionary way of thinking is that several Hollywood actresses, including Jessica Lange and Nastassia Kinski, recently had babies out of wedlock. Her opinion has obviously also been colored by the fact that her last marriage produced her son, whom she raised entirely on her own. In the mid-1980s, Cher said of Gregg Allman's role as father, "[Elijah] never sees his father. His father and I broke up when he was less than a year old. His father has never given him money for support. So it's like I had him, and that was it." She dismissed the whole institution of marriage by professing, "I haven't talked to Gregory in years. I couldn't care less if I never speak to him again in my life" (37).

After devoting the last couple of years to being taken seriously as a legitimate actress, in 1985 Cher began to pull out all the stops, dressing as bizarrely as possible. She began her foray into the world of unpredictable looks by cutting her black hair short and spiky and bleaching a skunk-like blonde streak across the top of it. Cher said, "I think my hair is fun and exciting and a little bit different. I know people who'd take to it immediately, because it's a bit foreign, but what people think about you isn't important. What's important is how you feel about yourself" (21).

Her daughter, who was sixteen at the time, couldn't believe what her mother had done. "Mom you can't!" was Chastity's immediate reaction. "You have to think about your career as an actress and what's best for your life. What will people think?" (21). This was the exact same situation that Rusty Dennis and her son Rocky found themselves in, in the film *Mask*. The mother seems to be the wild radical, and the child is the responsible, rational one. Amusing how art imitates life, and life imitates art.

On August 16, 1985, THE major event of the entire month seemed to be the wedding of Madonna and Sean Penn. Cher had gotten friendly with several of the young actors and actresses in Hollywood and, at the time, listed Sean as one of her closest friends. Cher was one of the select set of guests invited to witness the overpublicized event. Accompanied by her then "fiancé" Joshua Donen, Cher wore a tasteful black pantsuit, and a bright purple punk wig à la *Private Dancer* Tina Turner.

The non-royal wedding of the decade took place on the Pacific Ocean, at Point Dumme, and was marked by press helicopters buzzing the site for photographs. When it came time for Madonna to cut her five-tiered hazelnut wedding cake, she turned to Cher and asked, "Hey, you've done this before. Do you just cut one piece or do you have to slice up the whole thing?" Cher reportedly turned to Madonna and gave her a look that seemed to say, "As if I know?" (136).

Speaking later of abstaining from substance consumption, Cher was to say of the wedding, "I don't smoke, and while I can't say I don't drink, if someone said alcohol was gone from this earth, fine with me. I think the last time I had a drink was at Madonna and Sean's wedding. You needed it that day" (115).

While on the subject of weddings, it was clear that Josh Donen wanted to marry Cher, but Cher wasn't at all ready for the headaches. Her disastrous marriage to Allman really took the wind out of her sails on the topic of matrimony.

> I'm happy not being married. Marriage is more responsibility that I usually like to have. I'm really happy with him [Josh] not being married, and I don't want to ruin anything. I don't know if we'll get married. Maybe we will. We talk about it. Kind of like, "Do you want to go to the movies?" You talk about it until you either decide to or you breakup. I know I have a great time with Josh, and I enjoy being with him. He has more of all the things that I like so far, than anyone else I've gone with. So that makes me feel good about him (4).

In October 1985, Cher, along with Bruce Jenner and Tom Cruise, went to the White House to take part in First Lady Nancy Reagan's "Outstanding Disabled Achievers" press conference. The event was to focus on people who suffered from dyslexia. Cher professed, along with Jenner and Cruise, to having dyslexia, or an inability to read normally. She announced that she discovered she had dyslexia when she had Chastity tested and found that her daughter had similar problems. Said Cher of her own reading difficulties, "I see words and jumble them together. I see great billboards, billboards no one has ever invented. The brain has a way of compensating. I read my scripts very, very slowly, but I memorize them almost immediately. Now my problem is only annoying more than anything else" (137).

Aside from helping children who suffered from dyslexia, she also picked up a new boyfriend from the gig. In the spring of 1986, columnist Suzy reported that Cher was flying off to Chicago to accompany Tom Cruise on his latest film location. Possibly, Josh Donen's marriage proposals were getting to Cher, and she needed a break from their relationship.

In February 1986, when the Academy Award nominations were announced, there was great anticipation that Cher would be one of the five nominees included in the "Best Actress" category, for her work on *Mask*. This would have pitted her against her friend Meryl Streep, who was also favored for a nomination, for her portrayal of Karen Blixen (writer Isak Dinesen in *Out of Africa*). The "Best Actress" nominees were Streep, Geraldine Page (*The Trip to Bountiful*), Whoopi Goldberg (*The Color Purple*), Anne Bancroft (*Agnes of God*), and Jessica Lange (*Sweet Dreams*). It was Page who emerged the winner that year.

In the Academy Awards audience that night with Cher was her mother, Georgia Holt. Mom said, "When I was in the audience on Oscar night I was so proud I can't tell you. What's so great is she's living out her dreams" (138).

There was so much speculation about the reason why Cher and the film *Mask* were omitted from all the major award nominations. In fact the only nomination that the film received was for "Best Makeup." Several people have stated that the Academy snubbed *Mask*, boycotting any major nominations going to the film, because Peter Bogdanovich threw such a fuss over Universal's editing of the movie. Or was Cher omitted from the "Best Actress" category because of her "Las Vegas style" of dressing? Was she considered "inappropriate" for the honor just yet, in the eyes of the traditionally conservative older Academy voters?

Now that she was a former nominee—for *Silkwood*—Cher was invited on the show, to appear as the presenter of the "Best Supporting Actor" award that year. When she wasn't nominated for her acting in *Mask*, she thought for a moment about not going to the awards telecast at all. Then she came up with an even better plan. She was going to make certain that her appearance on the program would be one that no one was likely ever to forget. And she was right.

She phoned Bob Mackie, and told him of the idea she had for her Academy Awards outfit. She had a vision of paying homage to the American Indian. Her vision started with a feathered headdress, mimicking that of the Mohawk tribe warriors. It was to be accented with a cashmere blanket with black silk Indian symbols emblazoned on it.

At the time she was living with Josh Donen, and it was his father, director Stanley Donen, who was the producer of the Academy Awards telecast that year. She made Josh promise that he wouldn't be embarrassed by whatever it was that she was going to wear that evening. It wasn't until they were ready to leave the house that he finally got a glimpse of this creation.

It didn't matter to him that he was personally horrified, he feared that his father was going to have a fit when he caught a glimpse at Cher's getup. He was relieved when his father approached him at the venue and told him that he thought Cher's creation was hysterically funny.

Traditionally, the evening that the annual Academy Awards are presented is without a doubt the most glamorous night of the year for Hollywood. It was March 24, 1986, at the Dorothy Chandler Pavilion in Los Angeles, and—thanks to satellite technology—an audience of millions of people around the globe sat transfixed in front of their television screens, avidly watching the presentation of the Oscars.

As in previous years, the men were in sleek black tuxedos, and the women were trying to outdo one another with their expensive and elegant couturier-designed evening gowns. In the middle of the star-studded show came the time for the presentation of one of the major acting awards. The show's hostess, Jane Fonda, came out on stage, and announced, "To present the Oscar for Supporting Actor is one of the most glamorous people in this or any other business. And you'd better believe it. Wait till you see what's gonna come out here. Ladies and gentlemen, in a word—Cher" (139).

The TV cameras swept up a steep staircase located centerstage, and there she stood—the one and only Cher, dressed in an almost nonexistent black outfit that exposed more skin than it covered. Across her chest were five diamond-shaped pieces of studded cloth forming a bikini brassiere, the top of which was held in place by a spider web of thin, studded cloth strips. She was naked from her rib cage to her pelvis, exposing her beautifully trim stomach and sexy navel. The separate bottom of her outfit was formed of black diamonds of cloth, only inches in height, and worn over skin-tight black spandex pants. Draped across her left shoulder was a one-sleeved black cape, and on her feet were knee-high black satin high-heeled boots. Strapped around her neck was a black studded choker, and dangling from her earlobes were long black beaded earrings. Her lips were glossed a beige tone of red, and thanks to contrasting contact lenses, the pupil of her left eye was brown and the pupil of her right eye was green. Finally, to complete the unforgettable ensemble, piled high atop her head was a two-foot-tall Afro-like headdress of black bird feathers, harnessed into a Vampira-inspired widows-peaked, bugle-beaded black crown. She looked like a cross between Big Bird's evil twin sister and a Hell's Angels biker from Mars!

Every eye in the audience was glued to Cher as she self-confidently strode up to the podium and laughingly announced, "As you can see, I did receive my Academy booklet on 'How to Dress Like a Serious Actress'!" Her appearance on the almost three-hour telecast only lasted a handful of minutes, yet she had managed to steal the entire show. For weeks to come, the question "Did you see what Cher wore to the Academy Awards?" was asked more frequently than inquiries about the actual award winners.

Detroit gossip columnist Shirley Eder said of Cher's outfit, "I loved it, I loved it. It added the spice that it needed—that the show needed." On television, venomously amusing critic Rex Reed claimed, "I think she looked like Chief Sitting Bull in drag" (140). TV talk show host David Letterman made one of the funniest comments of all when he said on his program that Cher looked like she was dressed for Darth Vadar's funeral. Years later, people are still talking about that particular night. As recently as March 2000, *Entertainment Weekly* magazine called that very outfit, the all-time worst fashion statement in the entire history of the Academy Awards.

In an obvious spoof of herself, in the September 1986 issue of *Vanity Fair* magazine, and other publications, Cher was seen—with a straight look on her face—in one of the striking and now-famous Blackglama mink advertisements. Wrapped in a mink coat—and obviously naked underneath, Cher is wearing the outlandish Darth Vadar–inspired headpiece, through which runs the words "What Becomes a Legend Most?" In the past, since the late 1960s, the Blackglama mink advertisement had featured such other-era stars as Judy Garland, Gloria Swanson, Claudette Colbert, and all of the other grande dames of song and the cinema. Here was Cher, dressed in mink and a headdress worthy of a *Star Wars* appearance. The juxtapositioning of what she wore on her head and what she wrapped her body in makes this photo a classic in the series. If nothing else, Cher at least has a sense of humor about herself. The look of the ad is sheer class, yet the audacity of it is hysterically humorous.

The outlandish getup that Cher wore to the Academy Awards ceremony that year was obviously her way of stating, "If you think I don't dress like a 'serious actress,' I'm going to show you my interpretation of what one does look like!" It was really her own personal Declaration of Independence from any convention, past, present, or future. But then again, this is what makes her "Cher"—the talented star and indefatigable rebel. Thank God, some things never change!

10

WITCHES OF EASTWICK

There have been definite cyclical patterns in the career of Cher. There are spans of years where she is everywhere: new recordings, movies, television, magazine cover stories. And there are years at a time when she is nowhere in sight of the public eye.

After *Mask*, Cher seemed to go into one of her quiet periods. She was sent other scripts, but none of them seemed right for her. She was offered the starring role in the film *Baby Boom*. She passed on it, and the part went to Diane Keaton. "Diane was right for it. I wasn't," conceded Cher (22). Then she was offered the diabolical lead role in *Black Widow*, but again, it didn't feel right for her. Commented director Norman Jewison, whom Cher would later work with, "I'd never cast Cher as a femme fatale. She doesn't have the technique to play a character full of deception. She's just not devious" (22).

Throughout this post-*Mask* slow period, her public image was quite a dichotomy. On Valentine's Day 1985, she was in Boston accepting the Harvard University Hasty Pudding "Woman of the Year" award. As part of her fete, she was seen riding parade-style through the streets with two men in decidedly bad drag, as is the age-old custom. That same month she also led the list of Mr. Blackwell's annual "Worst Dressed Women." Another long-running tradition, Blackwell's list has usually featured Cher as one of its annual dishonorees.

Since her transition from television star/pop singer into a "serious" actress had represented a huge pay decrease for her, Cher began relying on different ways of augmenting her once-huge income. In late 1985, she teamed up with nutritionist Dr. Robert Haas, and together they sold the rights to a health-and-nutrition book. Dr. Haas is the author of the best-selling book *Eat to Win,* and Cher is Cher, so the publisher paid an advance of one million dollars. Hey, Jane Fonda was making money on her exercise books and tapes. Raquel Welch had an exercise tape too. So did Debbie Reynolds. Suddenly movie stars were all following Olivia Newton-John's 1981 song advice, let's get "Physical."

Speaking of their collaboration, Haas explained,

> She basically was burned out from doing *Mask.* . . . of course it's very demanding to do a movie, especially an emotionally charged movie like that . . . . but she also lost weight to play the part of a biker mom who was on drugs, and the way that she lost weight for the part was the wrong way, she simply starved herself, so by the time *Mask* was over, not only was she drained emotionally, but physically and mentally, and then she had gained weight back because usually when you starve yourself to lose weight, you generally put it back on plus some. So, Cher was now about eight to ten pounds overweight on that very small frame, which looks like a lot. So, we began working together and she saw results very quickly, lost the weight, and now has more energy than she ever had before (141).

Although she was now set to work on a health-and-fitness book, in actuality, what publishers really wanted was for Cher to write her own memoirs. She refused time and time again in the 1980s, stating, "People are asking me to do it. But everybody I'd be talking about is alive, and they'd be plenty pissed off. People don't like it so much if you tell every-thing about yourself when you're younger. I read a book about Bette Davis a long time ago—God, I didn't know she had such a rough life. It makes me feel not so all alone sometimes. Being a 'diva' is a very difficult job" (4). For the time being, her book in the works with Haas was as close as she was to come to writing her autobiography in the 1980s.

When she showed up at the Metropolitan Museum of Art in New York City for Diana Vreeland's costume exhibit gala in December 1985, Cher not only arrived in a Bob Mackie gown, she showed up with Bob Mackie on her arm. Cher has remained one of Mackie's most devoted clients, and she has always been one of his favorite mannequins.

In 1985 and 1986, television audiences witnessed the return of Cher. However, she was not hosting a new show or starring in a television spe-cial; she was plugging Jack La Lanne/European/Holiday Spas, in her new persona as a 1980s exercise guru. According to her at the time, she's always been into the health trip. "Exercising makes me feel good. I like to sweat, and I need to. I've got so much energy that it turns to negative if I don't do something physical. I get mean, and I can be a real cunt" (6). There were also full-page print ads of Cher in exercise togs, advertising the health spas in Andy Warhol's *Interview* magazine, with the diva looking fit and sassy.

After a year of no new movie releases, no albums, and no concert tours, suddenly Cher was back in the spotlight. During this era, Cher's most famous television appearance came in May 1986. It was her first guest spot on the television show *Late Night with David Letterman.* Up to this point, she had been invited onto the show dozens of times, but had declined every time. Finally, when she was again invited to appear on the program that spring, she agreed—but only if they met her financial requirement. It seemed that she had run up a hotel bill at posh Morgan's Hotel in New York City, which was—according to her—somewhere between $26,000 and $38,000. She told the show's producers that if they paid her hotel bill, she would agree to come on the show.

She was informed that they only paid "scale" to guests, which is in the vicinity of $700, so she declined. Finally, they agreed to pay off her extravagant hotel bill, and she agreed to the performance. When the show's producer, Robert Morton, asked her why she had never appeared on David Letterman's show before, she replied without hesitation, "Because I thought he was kind of an asshole" (25).

That night, when she came on the show, from the moment she appeared on camera, it was clear that David Letterman was not one of Cher's favorite people. He has always been known for his sarcastically antagonistic attitude toward guests. He likes to throw them off-guard and make them squirm. Obviously, Robert Morton had told Letterman what Cher had said about him. Not missing a beat, Letterman expressed amazement that finally, after several years of turning him down, she had consented to make an appearance. Cher pondered on camera, "I thought that I'd never want to do this show with you." An astonished Letterman asked, "Now why? Now, let's explore this a little. Why? Because you thought I was a, a. . . ."

"An asshole!" exclaimed Cher (142). Although they "bleeped" her comment, viewers could easily read her lips. She so befuddled Letterman with that reply, that he wasn't able to recover his composure for the rest of the program. Leave it to Cher to always say exactly what is on her mind.

Letterman was later to say of Cher's on-air comment, "It did hurt my feelings. Cher was one of the few people I really wanted to have on the show. . . . I felt like a total fool especially since I say all kinds of things to people. I was sitting there thinking, 'O.K. Mr. Bigshot, can you take it as well as you can dish it out' " (143). Thanks to Cher, he obviously developed a thicker skin, and learned painfully that "turnabout" is indeed "fair play."

May 20, 1986, was a very important date for Cher, as it was her fortieth birthday. Still in residence at Morgan's Hotel, she was awakened by the ringing of her telephone. It was director George Miller, who was in preproduction on his forthcoming film, *The Witches of Eastwick*. While she was still on the telephone with him, her best friend Paulette, Chastity, and Elijah came into her room with one of the hotel bellmen, carrying her birthday cake.

That night, Cher went out partying with her friends—including her assistant Debbie Paull—at the downtown Manhattan hangout Heartbreak. At the party, Cher sighted a handsome young man in his early twenties. Having broken up with Josh Donen at this point, she was currently single. The hot-looking young man's name was Robert Camilletti.

According to Cher, "I saw him in a restaurant on my fortieth birthday—actually it was a nightclub, Heartbreak. I said to a friend, 'Who is that boy? He's the most beautiful thing I've ever seen.' I didn't talk to him, but I knew I was thinking about doing this video, so I asked Debbie to get an eight-by-ten glossy of him" (115). Although Cher and Robert didn't have a conversation that night, she had it on her mind to look him up the next time she returned to Manhattan.

When she was asked at the time how she felt about turning forty, without batting an eyelash, she announced, "If I could be turning 25 instead of 40, I would certainly do that. . . . I'm not like Jane Fonda or any of these other women who say how fabulous they think it is to turn 40. I think it's a crock of shit. I'm not thrilled with it" (62).

Meanwhile, Cher was focusing on her upcoming role in the film *The Witches of Eastwick*, which was based on the book by John Updike. At the helm was Australian director George Miller, best known for his successful films—especially the Mel Gibson star-making projects, *Mad Max* (1979) and *The Road Warrior* (1981). "I didn't love the script," explained Cher, "but I wanted to work with Jack Nicholson" (144). Indeed, the all-star cast would put Cher in a production with three of the hottest names in 1980s cinema, Jack Nicholson, Susan Sarandon, and Michelle Pfeiffer.

Filming was to began in New England in July of 1986, with a 1987 release date.

Among the other alluring factors that made Cher want to work on *The Witches of Eastwick* was the fact that she was going to be paid a million dollars for being one of its stars. She may not have won an Oscar for her role in *Silkwood*, nor had she been nominated for an Academy Award for *Mask*, but through both of those films, she established herself as a huge box-office draw.

Her first obstacle was her instant clash with George Miller. According to Cher, "The director didn't want me—he only knew me as part of Sonny & Cher. But the movie company put pressure on him. I said to George, "I don't know where you've been; they didn't find me under a rock'" (115).

The plot of the story takes place in witchcraft lore–filled New England, where three single women are close friends. They are Alexandra the sculptress, Jane the cellist, and Sukie the local newspaper reporter. When the mysterious Daryl Van Horne arrives in town, and seduces all three of them, frightening consequences occur. Originally, it was Susan Sarandon who was to portray the character of Alexandra in the film.

Resigned to using Cher in the film, Miller's vision was to have Cher play the meek cellist, Jane. However, Cher had other ideas. "They always knew I wanted to play the role of Alex, and that I didn't even want to talk about the role of Jane," she claimed. When she threatened to pull out of the project altogether, she ended up getting her way. Cher was not happy with the movie, or the vibe on the set, but she was happy to be working with such a great cast. Although she never had fights with George Miller—once she was awarded the role she wanted—she was unhappy with several of the aspects of the film, and was less than thrilled with the studio she was working with. In typically Cher terms, she was to explain, "If I'd been fucked by my husband as much as I was fucked by Warner Brothers [Pictures], I'd still be married" (22).

In one of the first scenes in the movie, the three women get together amid a torrential rainstorm. When they start discussing it, they find that they were all wishing that a rainstorm would end the dreary outdoor event they had just come from. When they make this discovery of potential telepathy, Cher delivers the line, "It's not like it's gonna get us on *David Letterman*" (145). It is an especially amusing comment, since the real-life Cher had just gotten a ton of publicity from appearing on that very show.

Evil-spirited Van Horne turns out to be devil himself. When each of the seduced women begins to suspect his true identity, they all pull away from him. Frustrated by their rejection, Van Horne casts spells of his own on them as a threat to lure them back into his mansion and into his bed. The spell that Van Horne was to cast on the character of Jane called for her to awaken in her bed and discover that she was surrounded by over a thousand live snakes crawling on and around her. Susan Sarandon had no intention of getting anywhere near snakes, so the script was rewritten, and it was Cher who ended up with the snake scene. According to her, she had no problem with the 1,300 slithering nonpoisonous snakes—as long as she didn't have to do a scene with 1,300 insects.

During the filming, in the initial takes, the snakes kept getting up under the T-shirt that Cher was wearing. Fearless Cher even admitted that she was concerned for the snakes' safety, as she had to react violently as she threw back the covers of her bed when she awoke and found herself surrounded by the slithering creatures.

There were also several other special effects utilized in this black comedy of a film, including having the actresses floating through the air. According to Cher, "It was like filming a movie on Friday the 13th in the middle of a hurricane. But a movie doesn't have to run smoothly to be good" (119).

She was also to claim that director George Miller seemed to be more preoccupied with the way the special effects looked than what his actors were up to on camera. She was hoping to receive a stronger sense of direction from him regarding her acting. It was never to come, at least not to her satisfaction. "We all became friends on the film—Susan Sarandon, Jack Nicholson, Michelle Pfeiffer and the crew—but, I'm telling you, we didn't get a thing out of the director. It was a bitch," said Cher (115).

In addition to her on-the-set frustrations, while she was in the Boston area, working on *Witches of Eastwick*, Cher and Josh Donen were involved in an automobile wreck. According to the press reports, she and Donen were riding in a chauffeur-driven station wagon, when a car driven by Floyd Hardwick of Boston struck the car they were driving in, causing them to hit the car in front of them. Hardwick was arrested for drunk driving. They had just left the set, in nearby Cohasset. She was taken to South Shore Hospital in Weymouth, said a nursing supervisor. "Cher Escapes Accident with Minor Injuries," read the item in the *Tallahassee Democrat,* and several other major newspapers (146).

Cher was on a roll, and within one year she was to film three consecutive movies. Next on her plate was the sparkling romantic comedy, *Moonstruck*. Originally, Cher was reluctant to accept the part of Loretta, the slightly frumpy thirty-seven-year-old Italian widow who finds herself involved in the life of two feuding brothers. According to director Norman Jewison, he really wanted Cher for the part, but he had to trick her into taking it. He simply told her that if she didn't want the role, she shouldn't worry herself, as he had another actress in mind. But, he wouldn't tell Cher who the other actress was. Apparently, the mysterious identity of the other actress somehow forced her into making a decision and accepting the role. She reportedly nagged him throughout the shooting schedule to reveal the identity of the mystery actress. He repeatedly refused. After the filming was over, Jewison revealed that the part was originally meant for multiple Academy Award–winning actress Sally Field.

The original screenplay was entitled *The Bride and the Wolf*, but that bewitching "bella luna" that is so prominently featured in the film led to the film's name change. The film was sheer magic from the moment the cameras began to roll.

According to Cher, this was the most enjoyable film in which she had been involved. "*Moonstruck* was too silly, too much fun to be work," she claimed. "It was like getting paid lots of money to have a good time with a bunch of people you wouldn't have minded spending time with anyway" (119). And lots of money was exactly what she received for this role: a cool million dollars.

Another alluring point to working on *Moonstruck* was the fact that it was filmed in New York City. It gave Chastity and Elijah a sense of security to have their mother go to work every day, and come home every night. "I was lucky in New York when we did *Moonstruck*, because I was living in our apartment and both of them were there. Everyone was circulating in the house and the family was intact. I think children just want to know that you're at home so that they don't have to be there. As long as you're in the house, everything seems O.K.," Cher claimed (119).

Jewison had assembled the perfect cast for this bit of moonlit lunacy, including Olympia Dukakis as Cher's sage advice-sharing mother, Vincent Gardenia as her father, John Mahoney as Professor Perry, Danny Aiello as her inept fiancé, Anita Gillette as her father's girlfriend, and Nicolas Cage as Ronnie Cammareri—the passionate baker she falls in love with. However, Cage was not originally part of the cast; he only joined it at Cher's insistence.

Initially, the film studio had wanted to give the role her of her love interest, Ronnie Cammareri, to Peter Gallagher. Although she respected Gallagher, Ronnie had to come across as just a little bit "nuts" in the head. Cher felt that Gallagher was too cool and calm of a person to walk the fine line between sane and crazy. She felt so strongly about her casting choice that she told the studio she wouldn't do the film if Nicolas Cage didn't play Ronnie. Always one to stick to her guns in a battle, Cher naturally got her own way, again.

Norman Jewison was first enchanted by John Patrick Shanley's charming script. According to the director, "It read to me almost like a novel. He writes in long arias. Maybe Cher is the lyric soprano and Nicolas Cage is the tenor. Danny Aiello is the baritone and Vinnie Gardenia is the bass and Rose, the mother—Olympia Dukakis—can be the contralto and you bring them in with a triumphant fugue ensemble performance at the end" (147).

The chemistry between all of the actors in this film vividly, and comically, brought it to life. Throughout each of her 1980s films, Cher worked hard to become a brilliant ensemble player. *Moonstruck* showed off her acting skills to radiant perfection, and everything seemed to "click" with maximum comic effect. Cher also got along wonderfully with director Norman Jewison. He was later to claim, "Her comic timing is natural and almost infallible. I'll say so even though she nicknamed me 'the curmudgeon'" (22).

Moonstruck was filmed from November 24, 1986, to February 13, 1987. One of the most important things that Jewison did with the cast he had assembled, was to have them rehearse their lines together, like a big family. That way, when the cameras started rolling, there would be a camaraderie and a family feeling between them.

I took a studio on lower Broadway in New York and the whole cast worked together for about two weeks. If one of the actors in the film was also doing a play across town then someone else would read their lines while they were gone. At one point, Cher might be reading the dialogue of her mother in the film while someone else would be reading Cher's lines. In time, everyone knew not only their lines, but the lines of everyone else. This created a family-like atmosphere, which was very important to the film. I wanted to get to the point where all of the members of the cast *talked* alike, because that's the way families are in real life. . . . I wanted it to look on screen like these people *belonged* together. . . . As you watch the film, you can see the mother's character in Cher's character. I must say that it has been a long time since a family of mine really felt like a family (148).

When she first read the script, Cher was not certain if she could convincingly become the character of Loretta. "As much as I liked it, it wasn't like *Mask,* which I felt I just had to do. I was a little frightened because there seemed to be all kinds of possibilities and all kinds of risks here" (149).

In the film, Loretta goes through a metamorphosis, from ugly duckling to graceful swan. As with her own life, Cher was used to playing the swan. Instead of enjoying portraying the glamorized Loretta the most, she claimed, "But I much prefer playing her 'before' than 'after.' . . . The freedom is not interesting to me because that's something I know usually. Yet I don't think of her as being constrained, exactly. My idea was to play her more as bossy and controlled" (149).

Writer Shanley admitted that he was a bit startled when he first heard that Jewison wanted to cast Cher as Loretta. "Norman talked over his choices with me before any offers were made," he recalled. "Though I didn't have her in mind when I was writing the script, Cher couldn't be more perfect for the role of Loretta. . . . she's a very game actress and has allowed herself to look dowdy for some of this film." Before the film was released, he claimed, "The film will look great because the casting is right on the money" (150).

Originally, the character of Ronnie had the last name of Paolo in the script. However, when they were scouting locations in Brooklyn, for the bakery where several key scenes take place, they discovered the real-life Cammareri Bros. Bakery. It was one of the few in New York City that still used a coal-fueled basement oven. The site was too perfect, so rather than paint the bakery a new sign that read "Paolo," Jewison changed the characters' last name to Cammareri. While they were filming in the bakery, a real-life patron of the bakery barged in and demanded a loaf of bread. Recounted Jewison, "I said, 'Were trying to make a movie here,' and he says, 'I don't care what you're trying to make here! I came all the way from Wall Street and I want my bread!' I said, 'Allright, Cher, get the man his bread'" (151). By the time they were done shooting the scene, Cher and Jewison sold eight dollars' worth of fresh-baked bread for the bakery!

In the film, the characters seem to be believably Italian in their accents and their mannerisms. In several cases, this is a sign of good acting, because two of the principal players didn't have a drop of Italian blood in their veins. Cher, of course is Armenian/Native American, and Olympia Dukakis is Greek. According to Cher, having been married to Sonny Bono had given her a taste of what traditional Italian American families were like, not only the camaraderie but the conversational banter as well. "It kind of reminded me of Sonny's family. Everybody eating and talking and shouting, but you have such good times" (149).

One of the reasons that Cher and the other non-Italian actors were so adept and believable with their accents was the help of Julie Bovasso, who acted as dialogue coach on the film. Bovasso was also the actress who played the part of Cher's aunt, Rita Cappomaggi, in the film.

In the plot of the film, Cher's character Loretta is proposed to by Johnny Cammareri (Aiello), at the neighborhood Italian restaurant, The Grand Ticino (which is an actual restaurant in Greenwich Village—at 228 Thompson Street between Bleecker and Third Streets. If you go there, you will note that the movie's exterior shots of the restaurant were not filmed at the actual restaurant, as it does not occupy a corner location). Johnny promises to marry Loretta in exactly one month, as he is about to fly back to Italy to see his dying mother. His parting wish is that Loretta look up his estranged younger brother, Ronny (Cage), and invite him to the wedding. When she shows up at Cammareri's Bakery to meet him, she finds him impassioned with jealousy and grief.

Much to her surprise, there is instant chemistry between her and Ronny, and they make love in a fit of passion. The following morning the two of them wake up in Ronny's bed, shocked by what they have done. Ronny professes his love for her, and Cher's most memorable line comes when she slaps him across the face twice and commands, "Snap out of it!" Of this particular scene, director Jewison explains, "One of the best moments in the picture was 'Snap out of it!'—where she gives him two slaps. People were doing that [mimicking the film scene] in living rooms. It is the best kinetic moment in the picture, because of the way it's built" (152).

The next night, when the full moon comes up over Brooklyn, all sorts of lunacy occurs. Loretta's father takes his girlfriend to the opera, Loretta's mother flirts with Professor Perry at The Grand Ticino, Loretta's uncle and aunt rekindle the flame of their romance, and Ronny takes Loretta to the Metropolitan Opera to see *La Bohème*. Obviously smitten by Ronny's attention, Loretta precludes seeing the opera with a trip to the local beauty parlor for a complete makeover and the department store for a bewitching red dress.

One of the most moving scenes in the film is that in which tears well up in Loretta's eyes as she sits in the Metropolitan Opera House watching Puccini's touching *La Bohème*. The opera itself is so emotional that it is easy to imagine Cher watching the opera, reacting to the tragic plotline, and crying. However, in reality, the scene was shot with Cher, Cage, and a handful of "extras" staring at an empty stage, with director Norman Jewison telling Cher what was happening in the opera and her reacting to his words.

According to him, "The opera itself on stage we shot much later, and in another country [Toronto, Canada], in a different theater. So, I actually talked them [Cher and Cage] through the opera when they were reacting to it. In other words, I said, 'He's reaching out and he's going to take her hand,' and I played the opera in the background. . . . It was like shooting a silent movie" (152).

Said Cher of this most famous of Italian operas,

> And, of course, Nicky knew it really well, and Norman knew it really well, and me not knowing anything. Me being the cultural deficient that I am, I didn't know it. And we sit down, and the music starts playing and Norman starts explaining it, and he was doing such a great job of explaining it and the music was so fabulous that the scene really worked. I couldn't help from crying. I really like the way I cried in it, too. I think that it is my best work. And then, when we were finished, Norman was crying. So, I figured, "Well that must be pretty good." And that was a complete instance where if you look at Nicky, in that he is totally playing it close-to-the-vest. There's no overacting there (152).

Some of the other magical moments in the film are provided by the character players who surround the center action. Included on this list are the crazy old lady at Kennedy Airport who puts a curse on her sister's airplane and Loretta's grandfather (Feodor Chaliapin) and his dogs. Ironically, on screen Cher's character of Loretta was having an affair with Ronnie, the Italian baker. Amidst filming, every night she would go back to her apartment, to Robert, her Italian bagel baker. It was still another case of life imitating art, imitating life!

When *Moonstruck* was released, Cher volunteered to do anything she could to drum up publicity for the film. She was confident that this movie represented some of her finest work on camera, and she gave interview after interview to let people know about the film. "When we did *Moonstruck*," she was later to say, "MGM wasn't behind it 100 percent. And so I did everything I could put my hands on. I don't think I'll ever do as many interviews again. I don't feel like being violated. I just feel everyone knows enough about you" (119).

In between filming *Witches of Eastwick* and beginning work on *Moonstruck*, Cher had only one day off. Her third of three consecutive films in a row came with the courtroom drama *Suspect*. She had only one week off between filming *Moonstruck* and filming *Suspect*. This film had another well-known Australian director, Peter Yates, who is best known for his work with Steve McQueen in the detective action drama *Bullitt*. Her asking price for working on this film reportedly exceeded a million dollars.

Yates was well aware of Cher's dual personality: her need to be appreciated as a "serious actress" and her public persona as a human mannequin. According to him,

> Anyone who could be a personality and wear those clothes and who is also a serious actress has to be schizophrenic. I suppose [she has] a great need to be looked upon as a personality. But I just don't think she wants to take on the look of a serious actress in private life if she doesn't feel like it. It would be phony. And Cher has a strong detection against the phony (22).

Again Cher found herself in a film with an impressive cast, including Liam Neeson, Dennis Quaid, Joe Mantegna, and *Moonstruck* alumnus John Mahoney. Mahoney later found widespread fame in the 1990s as Kelsey Grammer's grumpy father in the TV series *Frasier*.

The role of Washington, D.C., defense attorney Kathleen Riley was a stretch for Cher. The film called for her to really rein in many of her natural instincts. Kathleen was neither bawdy, kooky, nor eccentric. She was a very straight and narrow, serious lawyer on a murder case. This was not the kind of role that one would naturally think of as a "Cher" role, which was obviously part of the appeal of accepting it.

Cher's character Riley is defending a mute homeless person (Neeson) who is suspected of murder. Against her own better judgment, she begins a personal relationship with one of the jurors, Eddie Sanger (Quaid). It seems that Sanger has evidence pertinent to the case, and Kathleen is torn between the likelihood of being disbarred for even associating with him, let alone sleeping with him. The plot thickens further when Kathleen discovers that the judge on the case has a strong personal motive for obstructing the truth about the case.

The director was thrilled with Cher's instincts for truly connecting with the character she was playing. According to Yates, "For instance, in the interrogation scene when she's facing Liam Neeson's character, the way that speech starts softly, builds, holds that long pause. A lot of people would have gone on without a pause. With Cher's 'Kathleen,' she is fighting an emotion, and it feels more honest. That is really what people do" (22).

He was also very impressed with her professionalism on the movie set. "She has a wonderful memory," Peter Yates claimed. "I'm dyslexic too, and I understand the enormous compensation that goes on with it. When you play in a courtroom drama, you have very long scenes. When other actors blow it, they typically blame the lighting, their costume, whatever. When she blew it, she'd just scream, 'Come on Cher! What the hell do you think you're doing' " (22).

When *Suspect* was released, it was the most un-Cher performance of her film career. It was a fascinating stretch for her to behave like a very focused defense attorney, on a case that could bring her triumph or ruin her entire legal career. She delivered a very believable and focused performance. However, she was the one who was the most disappointed with the results. She was later to complain, "It was disappointing. In my effort to be really real, I was really boring. I wasn't embarrassed but I wanted it to be more" (119).

Cher was later to state of this era, "You know I've covered the whole world in the last couple of years. I made three movies back to back" (115). Indeed, she had done exactly that—a trio of the best films in her career—in one year. Not since the 1930s and the old Hollywood star system had an actress made so many important career-making films in such a short period of time. As each of these three films was prepared for 1987 release, Cher's career was about to launch itself into the stratosphere.

11

MOONSTRUCK

In the time that Cher had been busy establishing herself as an actress, Sonny Bono had branched out a bit too. Since the end of their last television show together, *The Sonny & Cher Show* in 1977, he had taken several different acting roles on television and in movies. He sold a series idea to NBC-TV, called *Murder in Music City*. However, after the pilot was shot and run, the plug was pulled on the actual series. He acted in a miniseries called *Top of the Hill* and made appearances on shows like *The Love Boat* and *Fantasy Island*.

While taping a *Fantasy Island* episode Sonny started to reassess his career. When he was insulted on the set of the show by diminutive actor Herve Villechaize ("De plane, De plane"), he began to wonder whether or not he really wanted to remain in the television business. While the cameras rolled that particular day, Sonny's line, which he addressed to Villechaize, was supposed to be "It's a nice day, Tattoo." By mistake he said, "It's a nice day, Pontoon" (153). The next thing he knew he was being berated by Villechaize. "I have eight Gold records, and here I'm taking all this crap from a midget," he was later to complain (154).

However, roles he was interested in playing would surface from time to time. He went to Greece to film the 1979 movie *Escape to Athena*. It was a World War II film that costarred Roger Moore, David Niven, Claudia Cardinale, Stefanie Powers, Richard Roundtree, and Telly Savalas. It was about prisoners of war not only trying to escape their Nazi captors, but attempting to pull off an art heist as well.

In 1982 Sonny landed a small role in the satirical comedy film *Airplane II: The Sequel,* which was filmed on the Paramount Pictures lot on Melrose Avenue in Hollywood. Every day that he drove to the film studio, he passed the intersection of Melrose and La Cienega. Heading east from that intersection, Sonny passed an odd-shaped triangular block with a single-story restaurant on it. It had once been a hamburger joint, and most recently, it had been painted in pink and turquoise and called Chicken Olé. Now there was a very prominent sign on it that read "For Lease."

For some reason, Sonny was curious about the space, and on one of his trips past the block, he stopped to examine the building. He was later to confess that he had no idea what prompted him to stop in, but he felt compelled to do so. He tried the doors, looked in the windows, and did his own informal building inspection. He phoned the owner of the building, only to find that a woman was thinking about turning the place into a French restaurant. He told the owner that her plan would never work, because he envisioned the space as an Italian trattoria.

That night after his wife, Susie, went to bed, Sonny sat up sketching his idea of what the restaurant could look like, if he were to take it over. Whenever company came over to his house, it was Sonny who did the cooking, and garnered the compliments. He became obsessed with the idea of becoming a restaurateur. He signed the lease, repainted the place off-white, and accented it in Mediterranean colors of terra cotta and dark green. He changed the whole look of the place.

While he was busy making plans for his restaurant, in late 1982, Sonny decided that he really wanted to make amends with Cher. They had managed to divorce each other and still remain cordial. However, Sonny had this nagging feeling that they had not made amends for the breakup of their once-strong union. Cher was about to open her Las Vegas act at Caesar's Palace, and she agreed to meet with him. According to Sonny, she was still quite frosty toward him when they met in her suite. He sensed that she was very much on guard, even being in the same room with him. He told her that he wanted to put all of that behind them and move ahead. He also apologized for anything that he had done that had upset her or made her feel any animosity toward him. He anticipated that she would also tell him that she was sorry for anything that she had done or said that had upset or hurt him. She did not. However, he claimed that he felt better for having had that little meeting with her, and at least having extended the olive branch of peace.

In February of 1983, the doors to Sonny's new eatery opened, having been christened "Bono's." On the rainy opening night, several of his friends and supporters came to drink champagne and toast him on his latest venture. The guests that night included Donna Mills, Tony Curtis, Dick Van Patten, Valerie Perrine, Bert Convey, and Cher. There were also several press members and photographers. Cher reported to them, "When we were together, he made all the food" (35). Apparently, their meeting in Las Vegas had cleared the air between them enough to have her attend the opening of his restaurant, and wish him well.

For the first three months of operation the restaurant was a huge hit, booking reservations weeks in advance and turning down business. It appeared that again Sonny's instincts were absolutely correct, this time in getting into the food business. According to Sonny at the time, "It's like Rick's Cafe in [the film] *Casablanca* to me. Every night I drive to the restaurant, I visualize myself as Humphrey Bogart, and I see my friends" (155).

Not long afterward, a Houston businessman came into Bono's and convinced Sonny to open a Texas branch. The idea instantly appealed to him, and in 1984, the Houston version of Bono's opened its doors. Unfortunately, at almost exactly the same time the restaurant opened, the oil-based economy in Houston went belly-up, and Bono's/Houston went under.

Just as the second restaurant failed, Sonny's marriage to Susie Coelho also came to a crashing end. Susie had aspirations of becoming an actress and getting into show business, while all of Sonny's time was absorbed by the original Bono's and its short-lived Houston counterpart. In June of 1984, Sonny and Susie officially separated.

The following May, Sonny was in his restaurant, when he spotted a young woman sitting at one of the tables, having champagne with one of her friends. There was something about the woman that made him want to meet her. She turned out to be Mary Whitaker, and she had recently graduated from the University of Southern California with a degree in art history. Although Sonny was now fifty years old, and Mary was only twenty-two, within weeks of meeting, they were dating regularly, and seriously.

In September of 1985, while in Palm Springs, California, Sonny proposed marriage to Mary. He was getting his life in order, and onto a new path, at this point. However, there were several loose ends that needed attending to—notably his relationship with his two adult children,

Christy and Chastity. Since he had divorced his first wife, Donna, in the 1960s, he had very little contact with their daughter. One day, not long after he and Mary became engaged, out of the blue he telephoned Christy to tell her how sorry he was that he hadn't always been there for her, and to assure her that he loved her very much and hoped that he could make it up to her in some way.

While making plans to build a new house in Los Angeles on a lot they both loved, Sonny and Mary decided to stay at the house he owned in Palm Springs. However, it was a good two-hour drive from Bono's restaurant in Los Angeles. Finally, they decided to open a Palm Springs version of Bono's and simply take up residence there permanently. With that, Sonny found a perfect space on the north side of Palm Springs, where there was a tennis club. He leased the restaurant from the owners of the tennis club, and instantly plans were underway to open Bono's there. To fully make his break with Los Angeles, he closed the original Bono's on Melrose Avenue and invested a hundred thousand dollars in the Palm Springs site.

In February of 1986, Sonny and Mary were married in a family ceremony in Palm Springs. Later that year, Sonny was offered a role in a grade-B horror film called *Troll*. It was set to be filmed in Italy. He realized from the very start that this movie was not going to represent a career milestone for him, but it did come with an all-expense-paid trip to Italy. With that in mind, Sonny and Mary packed their bags and headed off to Europe.

Troll was about a cherubic child who is possessed by an evil troll. Under the demonic troll's spell, people turn into giant seed pods that sprout into new trolls. It was kind of a low-budget *Gremlins* meets *Invasion of the Body Snatchers*. The lively cast—which was obviously all game for an all-expense-paid holiday in Italy—included Michael Moriarty, Shelley Hack, June Lockhart, Anne Lockhart, and Julia Louis-Dreyfus. In other words, at the same time that Cher was filming the brilliant *Moonstruck*, Sonny was filming the completely forgettable *Troll*. What different paths their acting careers had taken.

When Sonny and Mary returned to Palm Springs from Italy, they were disappointed to find that the tennis club they were leasing the restaurant from had gone bankrupt, and they either had to purchase the entire property or lose all of the money they had invested. As the saying goes, "in for a penny, in for a pound," so Sonny purchased the entire property, tennis courts and all.

Meanwhile, Sonny and Mary also wanted to make improvements in their living accommodations, and they purchased an older home in a once-grand neighborhood. Between construction improvements on the house and work on the new restaurant, Sonny was given a negative taste of what the local government was like in Palm Springs. The city forced work on the house to come to a halt because Sonny didn't have the right permit. Then he couldn't add a second floor to the house because of some other ordinance, even though other homes in the neighborhood had second floors. Then he wanted to put up a new sign by the front entrance of the restaurant. Again, he was denied permission, due to another ordinance.

Finally, tired of fighting city hall, Sonny decided that the only way he could make positive changes in the city ordinances was to run for mayor. While he made plans to begin his political career, another movie offer came in out of the blue. It was from avant-garde filmmaker John Waters, who at this point was famous for his series of cult classics starring rotund drag queen Divine. Among the most famous Waters/Divine collaborations are *Pink Flamingos* and *Polyester*. *Pink Flamingos* is most famous for one of the closing scenes, in which Divine is seen eating fresh dog excrement.

Sonny was to confess that when he first received the script for the film entitled *Hairspray*, he had no idea whom John Waters was, and he had to ask the young man who was managing Bono's restaurant whom he was. Sonny loved the script for *Hairspray* and thought it would be fun to appear in it, as the husband of Debbie Harry. However, when he was told about Divine's final meal on camera in *Pink Flamingos*, he became concerned that being in *Hairspray* might hurt his bid at becoming the mayor of Palm Springs.

Before Sonny gave John Waters an answer about *Hairspray*, he decided to phone up the director to make certain that there weren't any hidden elements of the script that might prove embarrassing to his upcoming campaign. Waters assured him that not only would no one be consuming poodle droppings in the film, but there would be no dogs allowed on the set. With that, Sonny agreed to accept the role. *Hairspray* was a significant film for several reasons. First of all it marked the professional debut of a talented new actress, Ricki Lake. Unbeknownst to everyone at the time, it was also to be the final screen appearance by Divine. And, most importantly, it was to be the first time Sonny Bono was the star of a hit film.

Hairspray—like all of John Waters's films—takes place in the director's hometown of Baltimore, Maryland. It centers around a 1960s TV dance party program—à la *American Bandstand*—and two teenagers vying for attention on it. The protagonist was played by teenage Ricki Lake, and her mother was none other than the over-the-top Divine. Sonny played the role of Ricki's rival's father. One of his most amusing scenes in the movie comes when he attempts to conceal a bomb in the gigantic beehive hairdo of his wife (Debbie Harry).

John Waters is known for the bizarrely creative casting of his films, and *Hairspray* was no different. Sonny's costars in this hysterical movie included Pia Zadora, Ric Ocasek of the group the Cars, Jerry Stiller, and soul legend Ruth Brown. According to Waters, he wrote the role with Sonny in mind and was ecstatic that Bono accepted that part.

Although Sonny may have made peace with Cher, their divorce, their legal battles, and everything else in their lives as a couple, Cher obviously still had not. Like a spoiled girl complaining about her parents, during this era she was still taking potshots at him in public, and in the press. In 1986 she stated her opinion of Sonny by exclaiming, "I don't like him. I don't like what he became and I don't really like who he is. Maybe it's not who he is, but who he is with me. It's hard for me to say it, too. I don't hate him. I went through that for a while. But I don't really want to be around him now" (62).

Sonny, on the other hand, proclaimed,

> What upsets me even more is that I've always been unaware of the awkward way she felt about me. When I did the [*Sonny & Cher Comedy Hour*], I put the whole focus on Cher in order for her to attain the career she's desired. She has wanted a lot of things. She's wanted to be a rock & roll star, a TV star, a movie star. She's gotten all of them. It's so painful when she gets on national TV and says things like, "I always wanted to become a movie star, but I was too controlled by Sonny." I hocked all of our furniture and the valuables to write and finance a movie for Cher to star in [*Chastity*]. I practically went broke trying to prove she had the talent that everyone now knows she has. She's an incredible actress. I always knew that. I think it's because she has that tremendous drive. She keeps seeking and attaining. She has a kind of power. She has a source all her own and she knows it. I wish her well, but I just wish she would enjoy it and leave me alone (156).

According to Cher at the time, "I'm a woman who's found herself, and who's a better person because of it. I've made some awful mistakes, but I think I've profited from them" (13). It was the most creatively fertile period of her cinematic career—three films in one year, two of them breaking the million-dollar asking price for her services. She was at the top of her game, and she was doing everything that she could to maximize it.

Throughout all of this increased activity, her strongest relationships in the mid-1980s were with her children, Chastity and Elijah. Teenage Chastity, for a time, lived in New York city with Lee Strasberg's widow, Anna, and attended the High School of Performing Arts, of *Fame* notoriety. On the subject of motherhood, circa the mid-1980s, Cher claimed,

> Maybe I could have done a better job. I get frightened, then I'm around them and I see they're really good kids. I see edges in their personalities I hope will round off, aspects they'll grow through. I'm not so bowled over by my love for them that I don't see their strong and weak points. But I feel they both have an innate strength that will pull them through—I see Chastity's toughness coming from me, and Elijah's vulnerable, poetic spirit from Gregory. He was the gentler, nicer parent than me—when he was straight (127).

Elijah, at the time, had only seen his father on three occasions. One day he argued to Cher, "Mother, he's not too busy to pick up the telephone!" when she tried to make excuses for Gregg Allman. "That really blew me away that he could say that!" she replied in awe (120).

Cher simply shrugged her shoulders over the question of what kind of mother she has been. "I'm convinced they're going to write *Mommie Dearest* books one day," she says. "But it's like this: I did the best I could" (36). Sometimes Cher was clearly the mother, and Chastity was clearly the daughter. However, there were also times that that the roles reversed, and Cher at the age of forty seemed more like the child, and Chastity at fifteen acted more like the parent.

"Sometimes Chas drives me crazy too," Cher said at the time.

> She wanted combat boots last year! But people have to have their own expression. I'm living proof. Actually, my daughter is so traditional, it's frightening that she can be my daughter. I think it's a backlash. I told her one day, as I was looking in the mirror—"Chas, I'd like to get a Mohawk. I'd really like to get a Mohawk. I'm going to get a Mohawk. I've made my decision." She threw herself against the bathroom door and hollered, "You've got to think of your work. It would be limiting—you're an actress now." Then she stared at me and said, "Wait a minute, you should be

throwing yourself at the bathroom door, and I should be wanting a Mohawk" (115).

With regard to her relationships with the men in her life, Cher was to claim, "Men are luxuries, not necessities. I'm happier with a man, but I don't fold up and die if I don't have one around." Of her many publicized affairs, she quickly retorts, "People thought I was sleeping with the entire Mormon Tabernacle Choir" (67).

In addition to being linked with all of the men she had dated, there were also persistent rumors that Cher was gay. In the mid-1980s she flatly denied the inference. "I have my share of problems, but lesbianism isn't one," she explained.

> Sometimes I read stories about me and they make me upset. One really upset me. It said that I was having an affair with some chick. . . . I find women attractive, but I haven't seen any women I'd really like to make it with. I have a real strong thing toward men. My best friends are women, but I can have a good relationship with a woman without going to bed with them (18).

The rumors most likely stemmed from the "masculine" way she carried herself. Although she wore very glamorous clothes, she was not very "girlie" in her mannerisms or her speech. She said at the time, "I can be very independent if it's necessary and most of the time I am. But I would much rather be taken care of . . . . it's weird. My behavior is very 'masculine,' because I do exactly what I want. I don't give a shit who knows it or who cares. As long as I'm happy doing it, everybody can kiss my ass, you know. . . . I don't answer to anyone but myself" (6).

While she didn't feel that she had to explain herself, Cher was highly displeased with the person that the press perceived her to be in the mid-1980s. According to her, "God, I am so sick of 'finding a new life.' It seems like every time someone writes about me, it's me with a NEW life. Every time I get a new boyfriend, I get a 'new' life" (130).

Whenever the subject of her fascination with younger men came up, she became very defensive. "Listen, the fact is that older men never asked me out," she said. "Also, I'm happier with younger men; they are definitely more fun. On my birthday, every man I've ever been with—except for my two husbands—calls me or sends me presents or flowers. I've had good relationships with all of them" (115).

Meanwhile, by the end of August 1986, while Cher was still working on *The Witches of Eastwick,* Sean Penn and Madonna were working on a workshop production of a play called *Goose and Tom Tom,* by David Rabe, at Lincoln Center. Cher was invited to the Labor Day weekend closing night performance. She didn't have anyone to go with, and that young man she had seen at Heartbreak on her birthday in May came to mind. According to Cher, "I just thought, 'I'm going to ask that guy to go with me.' I told Debbie [Paull] to call him up and tell him that it's not a date, that I just wanted him to go with me to see a play" (115).

After inviting Robert to go with her, Cher had run into Melanie Griffith, who was also in town. The two of them ended up attending the play with Camilletti. After the play was over, the three of them went to the closing night party, and then Cher and Robert went back to her suite at Morgan's Hotel, where she was still staying at the time.

Since he was only twenty-two when they met, Cher kept telling herself that he was just a nice guy she could hang out with whenever she was in Manhattan. That night at Morgan's, the two of them ended up talking until 3:30 in the morning. At that point, he leapt up and suddenly announced, "I gotta catch a train to Queens" (115). The reason he had to make his hasty exit was that he had to leave Manhattan to open the bagel shop.

The following day, Cher was due to leave for California, but by the time she got up, she decided to postpone her trip one more day. That evening she and Melanie Griffith had dinner and then met Robert and a friend of his, named Steve, at Heartbreak. From there, the foursome moved on to the China Club. While at the China Club, Cher suddenly felt awkward, and thought to herself that she really shouldn't get involved with someone who was so much younger than she was.

When she suddenly announced to him that she had to go back to her hotel to pack for the next day's flight, he asked if he could come with her. She had offered to let him read the script to *Moonstruck,* which she was going to come back to New York to begin filming, right after she was finished with *The Witches of Eastwick.* So, she agreed. Back at the hotel, they went up to her room, and she gave him the script she had promised him. However, when she went to shake his hand "goodbye," he informed her that this was not the way he wanted the evening to end. Well, one thing led to another, and he ended up spending the night with her.

She indeed left the next day for California as planned. After five days of thinking about Robert, she telephoned him from the West Coast. What developed was a long-distance telephone relationship. At the time, she was filming interiors for *The Witches of Eastwick* in California. Then she flew back to New York City, and purchased the apartment in Greenwich Village.

With work on *Witches* wrapped, Cher moved back to New York City and took possession of the loft space she had purchased, and the relationship with Robert escalated from there. When she was shooting *Moonstruck,* she would film all day, come home, shower, get in bed, sleep for a while, and wait for Robert to come home. At this point he had quit the bagel shop and was now working as a doorman. Later, he was employed as a bartender. However, the die had been cast, and he was forever to be known in the press as Cher's "bagel boy."

As usual, Cher could care less what the media thought of her latest *amour.* "We struck up a phone relationship, I guess," Cher was to explain amid her relationship with Robert.

> You know, he was making bagels at the time. And I thought, "What will my friends say if I go out with him?" But the more I got to know Robert, the less I cared what anybody thought. He may have talked like one of the *Lords of Flatbush,* but he had so many great qualities, I couldn't believe it. Then I met his parents and I understood what a good family he came from. His father, Frank, is really funny; I mean, he doesn't want his wife to play the lottery, because she might win and ruin everything, when they're so happy with their lives already. It's one great Italian family, and that's why Robert is so good, so moral. I met him in May [1986], and I didn't fall in love until, well, sometime between Thanksgiving and Christmas (115).

Although he was nearly half her age, Cher had an instant bond with Robert.

> I feel safe with him, real comfortable. He's really protective of me. He tells the truth, his morals are impeccable, and he has a great heart. I think I trust him more than anyone I've ever known. I don't know if we'll stay together—it's not a goal. Robert's not the best relationship I've ever had, but this one is the biggest Band-Aid. It's liniment, lotion, incredibly healing. I love his simplicity—he makes me feel peaceful (22).

Robert once told Cher that he was "just a mook from Queens" (25). After that, her pet name for him was always "Mookie." They didn't read the same books, and he hadn't been to the kind of places she had been to, or experienced the kind of life she had led. She was a hugely successful media star in a publicly quiet phase of her career, and he was just a nice young man starting his adult life. Yet, somehow they found enough common ground between them to truly enjoy each other's company. They would walk around the Village together, go out to triple-feature movie marathons, or go out to eat at funky little restaurants. In New York City, it is easy to have total anonymity, and the two of them enjoyed each other's company.

At the end of 1986, as Cher's relationship with Robert was just getting underway, she was looking forward to a calendar year in which she was going to have three major motion pictures released, and she was already making plans for her return to the recording studio. Cher had been in the business long enough to know what happens when you are riding the wave of a huge success—you have no privacy, and the press hounds you every step you make.

Cher told Robert that he should enjoy their time together, because, if any of her forthcoming 1987 projects suddenly took off in a big way, they were going to have absolutely no solitude whatsoever. She had an idea that these three films were going to have a profound effect on her career, but she had no idea just how successful she was about to become. Yet she sensed that she was standing on the threshold of one of the most rewarding periods of her life, and what a wild ride it was going to be.

12

I FOUND SOMEONE

From 1987 to 1988, Cher found herself in exactly the position she had for so long desired. She had become acknowledged as one of the most "bankable" actresses in films, alongside such contemporaries as Jessica Lange, Goldie Hawn, Meryl Streep, Susan Sarandon, Jane Fonda, Michelle Pfeiffer, Kathleen Turner, Sissy Spacek, Barbra Streisand, and Sally Field.

Yet to the public it seemed that she had disappeared altogether. She hadn't been seen very much in the public eye since the 1985 release of *Mask*, with the exception of occasional TV appearances. She had spent the past year filming almost nonstop, preparing her unprecedented cinematic triple whammy of *The Witches of Eastwick, Suspect,* and *Moonstruck*. This trio of films presented three distinctively different screen roles for Cher: the vengeful sculptress in *Witches,* the determined but torn lawyer in *Suspect,* and the pragmatic spinster in *Moonstruck.* Not only were movie audiences treated to Cher's acting versatility, but they also got a glimpse of her new nose.

"I had made it smaller after *Mask*," she was to reveal. "It's basically my same nose, just a little smaller version." According to her, she didn't mind her nose when she was a television star on the small screen in the 1970s. However, seeing herself blown up on the movie screen was another story. "I kind of liked it," she said of her own nose. "I thought it was interesting. But you blow it up to be three feet [tall], and it started to be a little bit of a problem" (157). It didn't seem to be a problem for anyone else, but Cher was amid her lifelong quest for perfection, and her forays in plastic surgery and other appearance-altering procedures were just part of it.

On April 3, 1987, Cher was one of the stars of an hour-long television special called *Superstars and Their Moms*. Not only did Cher appear on camera with her mother, but Georgia Holt was the co-executive producer of the show. Among the other stars who appeared with their mothers were Bill Cosby, Cybill Shepherd, Whitney Houston, Tom Selleck, and sisters Phylicia Rashad and Debbie Allen. The show was hosted by Carol Burnett and her daughter, Carrie Hamilton.

Said proud mom Georgia Holt of her own daughter, "The positive is watching your kid get started, like watching them learn to walk. . . . For eight years in Hollywood, no one would let Cher read for a film. Now, she's done three back-to-back" (138).

Finally in June of 1987 the fruits of Cher's labors began to blossom forth, with the theatrical release of *The Witches of Eastwick*. This odd mixture of black comedy, supernatural doings, and sexy dialogue proved a delightful summer hit with audiences, and with critics as well. Giving the film three and a half stars (out of four), Roger Ebert in the *Chicago Sun Times* claimed,

> This movie plays like a plausible story about implausible people. The performances sell it. . . . It's [Jack] Nicholson's show. . . . he plays the devil: a role he was born to fill. . . . The women are played in the movie by Cher, Michelle Pfeiffer and Susan Sarandon, and they have a delicious good time with their roles. These women need to be good at double takes, because they're always getting into situations that require them. When they're together, talking up a storm, they have the kind of unconscious verbal timing that makes comedy out of ordinary speech (158).

"Nicholson's back. And that old Jack magic has us in his spell," wrote Rita Kempley in the *Washington Post*. "He is undisputedly the star of *The Witches of Eastwick*, despite formidable competition from his coven played by Cher, Michelle Pfeiffer and Susan Sarandon" (159). And in that same paper, Desson Howe wrote "Jack is crackerjack. . . . Sarandon (as music teacher Jane Spofford), Cher (earthy sculptress Alexandra Medford) and Pfeiffer (fertile town reporter Sukie Ridgemont) turn in excellent performances" (160).

Eager to promote *Witches of Eastwick*, Cher enthusiastically granted several press interviews to kick off her three-film streak. The day before she began promoting *Witches,* Cher was busy on the other side of the camera, making her debut as a video director. As she had been considering on her fortieth birthday, she directed her new boyfriend, Robert, and herself, in the video for her upcoming single, "I Found Someone." Becoming a director was another goal that Cher also longed to attain, and this was to be her professional entry into directorship.

Although *The Witches of Eastwick* was well received when it was released, Cher's expectations for it were higher. "It didn't come out quite the way I expected," she claimed, "very few of them do" (144).

In October of 1987, *Suspect* hit the theaters. It did well at the box office, but was not a big hit. While Cher drew generally good reviews, the film was criticized for its plotting. Roger Ebert's review in the *Chicago Sun Times* reflected this exact stance, when he wrote, "*Suspect* is a well-made thriller, but it was spoiled for me by an extraordinary closing scene where Cher, as the defense attorney, solves the case with all of the logic of a magician pulling a rabbit out of a hat. . . . *Suspect* is fun when Cher and [Dennis Quaid] interact, she does a convincing job of playing a lonely career woman" (161).

Film critics in the city where *Suspect* was filmed were far less forgiving. Two separate reviewers for the *Washington Post* had problems with the film's plot, and with Cher's portrayal. Hal Hinson wrote,

> In taking the part of Kathleen Riley, the beleaguered public defender in *Suspect,* Cher must have thought she would turn people's heads around with a potent range and diversity of her talent. . . . There's a sort of reverse vanity that draws performers to parts like this, and in Cher's case, the sheer plainness of the woman is what must have first attracted her. . . . As Kathleen, Cher is trapped trying to play the one thing she's not—dull. . . . On occasion, she gives Kathleen a chance to sass and talk back. But she can't find anything of herself in this woman, and the performance is dogged, joyless (162).

Taking the same stance in the same newspaper, writer Desson Howe claimed,

> Peter Yates's *Suspect,* a Washington courtroom drama, breaks down under cross examination like those cornered witnesses at the end of *Perry Mason.* . . . Cher's advances toward Serious Actresshood, via *Come Back to the Five and Dime Jimmy Dean, Jimmy Dean* and *Mask,* are slowed by her paper-thin role as a liberal beauty who must represent the beast. . . . But for the most part, this case, which includes a convenient last-minute taped

confession and a lifeless Cher–Quaid romance, should have been thrown out of court (163).

While *Suspect* was doing respectable business in the movie theaters, Cher was busy launching a totally different kind of project—a new album. Concentrating on her movie career for the past couple of years, she was amid one of the longest albumless periods of her entire career. She hadn't recorded any new songs since 1982's *I Paralyze*. Having released thirty-six albums (twenty-two solo, eleven with Sonny, one with Gregg, one with Black Rose), Cher had announced in 1985 that she had signed a new recording deal with her ex-beau David Geffen's record label. She already racked up eleven Gold and three Platinum records in her past, and she was ready for a couple more.

Interestingly enough, as nasty as Cher's mid-1970s affair with David Geffen had ended, in the ensuing years, they had patched up their friendship. Since that time, David had long ago left Asylum/Elektra Records, and had started his own label, Geffen Records. He managed to lure several of his favorite performers into signing with his new label, including Neil Young, Joni Mitchell, and Elton John.

Speaking of their affair, and the evolution of their mid-1980s friendship, Cher explained,

> I know everybody thinks it's bizarre. But it was great. David was one of the best relationships I've ever had. He was different than he is now, because he was only thirty when I met him. He wasn't very sure of himself, and he certainly wasn't very sure of having a relationship with me. Neither of us intended it to happen. We just fell in love. We've said the meanest things to each other, and we always come back to being really close friends (8).

Geffen was also glowingly kind when speaking about her. "Cher is an incredibly loving person, and incredibly willful" (8).

Not only was she willful, she also had a clear idea of what she wanted to do musically. She had no intention of repeating her past successes, or her past failures. She hadn't had a major hit on the charts since 1979, when "Take Me Home" became a huge smash. Her two subsequent album forays into harder rock, *Black Rose* and *I Paralyze*, were more in the direction that she wanted to move into. Listening to both of those albums back to back, and then listening to her debut album on Geffen Records, one notices a musical progression. She now longed to be less like the musical persona of Bette Midler and more like that of Joan Jett.

Although she had sold millions and millions of records in the past, she remained her own harshest critic. "I'm a really good performer if you watch me work, but I'm not nearly as good if you listen to me," she claimed.

All of my past hits were really embarrassing to me. I don't think I would even listen to "Dark Lady" or "Half Breed"—it's just not my kind of music. I'd rather listen to Bob Seger. I've always been ragged on in this business. The critics have always hated my albums—except for the fans who are turning out to be the most important anyway. I always wanted to be a better singer and I never was. That always drove me crazy. For me, going into the recording studio is a terrible experience (164).

The music scene had changed from the early to the late 1980s. The stripped-down, back-to-basics punk rock sound that Cher had emulated with the group Black Rose had become slicker, more synthesizer-based rock and roll. Simple and subtle ballads had been replaced in the Top 10 by power ballads in the style of Anita Baker and Whitney Houston. In-your-face women rockers like Madonna ("Like a Virgin") and Joan Jett ("I Love Rock & Roll") were concurrently confronting their listeners with frankness and a powerful vocal delivery. Now, more than ever before, pop songs like "Half Breed" and "Dark Lady" sounded like the products of a bygone decade.

There hadn't been a new Cher album in the stores in over five years when 1987's *Cher* was released. Having shifted her focus from music to movies, Cher appeared to have ended her recording career. How ironic that it was actually her old boyfriend, David Geffen, who was responsible for her huge 1987 musical comeback. In 1975, with the *Stars* album on Warner Brothers Records, Geffen had made a valiant attempt to make Cher a respected rock and roll entity. It had taken twelve years, and now with the brilliant *Cher* album, he not only made good his promise, he exceeded it—giving her the first million-selling Platinum album of her career. He brought back Cher in a big way, on both sides of the Atlantic Ocean.

The album hit Number 32 in America and Number 26 in the United Kingdom. It proved to be a consistent best seller in her career, with three consecutive hit singles "I Found Someone" (Number 10/U.S.), "We All Sleep Alone" (Number 14/U.S., Number 47/UK), and "Skin Deep" (Number 79/U.S.).

A brilliant ten-cut disk, *Cher* not only reestablished her as a rocking diva of the first degree, the project teamed her with some of the hottest

songwriters, producers, musicians, and singers in the business. Five separate producers worked with Cher on this album, producing separately
or in collaboration with each other. They included newcomer Michael
Bolton, Desmond Child (who was the lead singer of Desmond Child &
Rouge in the 1970s and was to help make Ricky Martin a huge star in the
late 1990s), Peter Asher (who was one-half of the 1960s duo Peter &
Gordon and is responsible for producing all of Linda Ronstadt's biggest
hits), and Jon Bon Jovi and Richie Sambora (of the group Bon Jovi).

Cher had chosen five out of ten songs either written or cowritten by
Desmond Child. She had first recorded two of his songs on her *I Paralyze* album ("When the Love Is Gone" and "The Book of Love"). This
album also marked the first time that Cher recorded the songs of Diane
Warren. On her four albums for Geffen Records, Cher was to record
twelve songs by Warren. The only songwriters she has recorded as many
songs by are Sonny Bono and Bob Dylan. And, speaking of Sonny Bono,
on this album, she recorded a new interpretation of her first million-selling hit with him, "Bang Bang (My Baby Shot Me Down)." This new version of her classic 1960s hit was essentially Cher with the whole group
Bon Jovi backing her. She gave the song a gutsy new attitude, making it
one of the high points of the album. Additionally, she dedicated this
album to her much-maligned ex-husband, writing in the liner notes,
"This Album Is Dedicated With Love To Sonny Bono for the first time,
and John (His High Kaladness) Kalodner for making me do it again."
John Kalodner, who is credited on all three of her original Geffen
albums, had worked for years at Atlantic Records and in the 1980s moved
to Geffen Records as an A&R person. Signing Cher to a recording contract on Geffen was largely his doing.

This album also found Cher supported vocally by several exciting
guest stars, including Maurice White of the group Earth, Wind & Fire,
who provided the "vamp" vocals on "Skin Deep." By far, the most stir-
ring song on this album is the all-girls song "Perfection," which finds
Cher leading her own vocal trio, where she is joined by Bonnie Tyler
("Total Eclipse of the Heart") and her old pal from the Phil Spector
days—Darlene Love ("Today I Met the Boy I'm Gonna Marry").

Since the 1960s, Darlene's once-fabulous singing career had hit rock
bottom, and she had worked as a cleaning woman in the 1970s to support
herself. In the 1980s her luck had changed, and she experienced a comeback as a regular star singer in New York City at the Bottom Line, and as
an actress. Like Cher, she too was amid a career rebirth. That same year,

1987, Darlene was one of the stars of the film *Lethal Weapon,* playing Danny Glover's wife. She has appeared in the subsequent *Lethal Weapon* films, and has since revived her singing career. In the 1990s she penned her own autobiography. "Perfection" was a wonderful reunion song for Cher and Darlene, and their voices blended well with Bonnie Tyler's raspy growl.

Cher's 1987 Geffen comeback album was also the third time she had released an album simply entitled *Cher.* The distinctive Matthew Rolston portrait of the diva on the cover, in a black leather jacket, perfectly personified her new rock image for the late 1980s and early 1990s. Released amid her successful run of three back-to-back hit movies, the 1987 *Cher* album only further heralded the return of one of the music world's most enduring stars.

When it was released in New York City on Christmas Day 1987, *Moonstruck* was an instant hit, both critically and at the box office. The press on it, when it went into general distribution on January 15, 1988, was overwhelmingly glowing from the very start. On the television show *Siskel & Ebert at the Movies* the pair of critics called *Moonstruck* "a treasure," ecstatically proclaiming, "Cher is absolutely brilliant. It is the best work she's ever done" (165). Roger Ebert, in his own printed column in the *Chicago Sun Times,* called it a "magical" film, noting,

> The most enchanting quality about *Moonstruck* is the hardest to describe, and that is the movie's tone. . . . at the heart of the story, there is Cher's astonishing discovery that she is still capable of love. . . . The movie is filled with fine performances—by Cher, never funnier or more assured. . . . In its warmth and in its enchantment, as well as in its laughs, this is the best comedy in a long time (166).

Rita Kempley, reviewing the film for the *Washington Post* claimed, "*Moonstruck* is a great big beautiful valentine of a movie, an intoxicating romantic comedy set beneath the biggest, brightest Christmas moon you ever saw. . . . Norman Jewison, whose last movie was *Agnes of God,* creates his comic masterpiece with this infectious ethnic romance . . . Cher creating a fairy-tale realist, captivating yet cautious" (167).

When the nominations for the 1987 Academy Awards were announced, Cher's portrayal of Loretta in *Moonstruck* was at the top of the Best Actress list. Also nominated in the Best Actress category were Glenn Close for *Fatal Attraction,* Holly Hunter for *Broadcast News,* Sally Kirkland for *Anna,* and Meryl Streep for *Ironweed.* Meryl Streep was so instrumental in helping Cher become a serious actress in *Silk-wood*, and now she and Cher were competing for the same award.

Meanwhile, by tossing his hat into the Palm Springs mayoral race, Sonny Bono had opened himself up for all sorts of ridicule in the press. But, by now he had developed a very thick skin against negative criticism. Like Clint Eastwood and Ronald Reagan before him, he was trading the task of actor for that of politician. During his campaign in the lush desert resort town, he inevitably ran into comments about Cher, his most famous show business identity being that of being Cher's ex-husband. He dealt with these comments with a great sense of humor.

At this point in time, Sonny and Cher had very little contact with each other. If it were not for their daughter, Chastity, keeping each of them informed of the other's activities, each wouldn't have known what the other was up to—save newspaper coverage of their latest endeavors. Sonny was genuinely startled in early 1988 when he received a phone call from one of the producers of the TV show *Late Night with David Letterman*. Usually it was Cher who appeared on such shows. After chatting Sonny up on the phone for a few minutes, the producer asked Sonny if he would consider appearing on the program, with Cher. The producer then told him, if he had any reservations about appearing on the program with his ex-wife, would he please consider what such an appearance could mean for his political campaign. He considered it for a moment, and then agreed.

A week after saying "yes" to the *Letterman* appearance, Sonny received another call from out of the blue, and this time around, it was the diva herself—Cher. She immediately cut to the chase and announced to him that she was very concerned about the upcoming appearance, confessing that she was slightly freaked out with anxiety about reuniting with Sonny, live on-camera, with half of the world tuning in to watch this uncomfortable moment.

She told Sonny that she knew his sense of humor, and she knew David's, and it left her slightly worried, especially since the last time she was on the program, she called Letterman "an asshole" on national television. He did his best to calm her down, and between the two of them, they decided on a game plan that Cher could live with: he would go out and test the waters of the interview and talk about his bid for mayor, and then she would come on the program after Sonny had broken the ice.

A few days later, Sonny received still another surprising phone call, again from the producer of *Letterman*. This time around the conversation was another out-of-the-blue request. This time she asked Sonny if he would consider singing with Cher on the program. He was a bit dumbfounded, and even tried to put off the question. He suggested that perhaps Cher would be happier doing a cut from her latest album instead of a duet with him. The producer then rephrased the question "If Cher will sing with you, will you sing with her?" (35). Again, he agreed.

Sonny's wife, Mary, was seven months pregnant at that point, but gladly accompanied him on the first "Sonny & Cher" event she was to witness in person. With that, together they flew from Palm Springs to Los Angeles, and then on to JFK Airport, where they were chauffeured into Manhattan. All along the way, Sonny thought about this odd reunion with Cher, which was to be televised before millions of onlookers.

The following morning, Chastity came to visit her father at his hotel room, very excited about seeing him and that afternoon's TV taping. Like all dutiful daughters, her big concern involved what Sonny was going to wear for the appearance. With that, Sonny and Chastity spent hours shopping for the right outfit for him, finally deciding on a pair of black baggy pants, and a hot-looking patterned silk shirt.

When Chastity, Sonny, and Mary got off the elevator at NBC Studios in Rockefeller Plaza and were immediately mobbed by a wall of press photographers, it started to sink into Sonny's consciousness just how big an event this was going to turn out to be. It turned out to be an emotional event for everyone involved, the brief but touching reunion of Sonny & Cher.

Cher hadn't sung in front of a live audience in six years, and hadn't been seen on camera with Sonny Bono in nine years. Her backstage entourage that night included her boyfriend Robert, her girlfriends Paulette and Deborah Paull, eleven-year-old Elijah Blue Allman, and her long-time hairstylist, Renate Leuschner-Pless.

Cher greeted Sonny backstage, and after a few seconds of awkwardness, they picked up where they had left off, like old friends who were reunited after an altercation. Sonny said hello to Robert, whom he had met once before, and Cher acknowledged the upcoming birth of the newest Bono baby. Cher was also enthused to have Sonny hear a tape of her latest single, and had someone in the sound booth program it for her. Cher then rehearsed with bandleader Paul Shaffer, and it was time for the show to start.

As planned, Sonny was the first one on the program. David Letterman introduced him as the writer of ten Gold records, and a candidate for mayor of Palm Springs. Amid thunderous applause, Sonny came out onto the set and began chatting with the ever-unpredictable Letterman. After a brief bit of bantering about politics, Letterman got down to the subject on everyone's mind: Sonny & Cher.

"What happened?" Letterman asked Sonny, "Where did it all go wrong? You were responsible. You molded her. You had the look, the sound. You wrote the songs. You had the idea for the television show. . . . And then, one day—Bingo—it all goes south on you" (168).

Sonny thought for a few seconds and replied, "I ask myself that every day. No, no really. It's just too hard for two people to have a marriage and to be in show business. Comes a time when you lose the relationship and discover you're a business. I look at Sonny & Cher almost as two other people. I love them, like any other fan" (168).

When David Letterman introduced Cher, she came out and performed one of the songs from her 1987 *Cher* album, "I Found Someone," and then joined him and Sonny at the interview desk. Cher was wearing a micro-mini dress, black fishnet stockings, pointed black high heels, and a white jacket festooned with chains and metals. Around her waist she wore a metal belt that clung to her shapely hips.

When she sat down to be interviewed, seated between Sonny and Letterman, David started right in, poking fun at her costume and making jokes about her tattoos. Irreverent Letterman immediately began sparring with Cher regarding her life and her career. When he asked her how she felt being back together with Sonny—on this show—professionally for the first time in ten years, she snapped back at him that she felt "nothing" (168).

In his 1991 autobiography, *And the Beat Goes On*, Sonny claimed that he froze when she flippantly said that. "She quickly recanted and said she was joking. But I didn't know. Cher had an icy, unemotional, calculating side to her. I hoped she felt something, but then experience had taught me better" (35).

Then Cher replied, "We have a very strange relationship that no one will understand. I don't understand it. Sonny says that he doesn't understand it either."

"Do you ever think of getting back together again?" Letterman asked.
"In what capacity?"
"Married."
"I don't think Mary would like that, she's pregnant," Cher replied.
After zinging comments back and forth to each other like two tennis

players in a dead heat, volleying one-liners, finally Letterman asked the question that everyone was anticipating would be asked. "Is there any chance that you two would sing for us?" (168).

Cher tried to get out of it, by claiming that she had a sore throat, but Letterman still pushed. "None of this has been discussed," David claimed.

Although her comment was "bleeped" by the censors, Cher zinged back at him, "You're full of shit."

"I can't believe the way she speaks," Letterman said to Sonny.

Bono laughed and replied, "This is a dirty show, I'm leaving" (168).

Sonny got up from his seat to move over to where the band was cued and waiting, and as a wave of deafening applause, whistles, and shouts from the audience cheered them on, Cher—almost reluctantly—agreed.

As a duo, since the 1960s, Sonny & Cher had sung the song "I Got You Babe" to each other hundreds of times. Yet this night, for the first time in ten years, and for what was to be the last time ever, they sang the song that made them both household names. Cher, in her own autobiography *The First Time*, recalled looking out at the audience, and she noticed that half of the crowd had tears in their eyes. Then she looked at Sonny midsong, and he too was misty-eyed. According to her, she thought to herself, "I've got to hold myself together—I don't want to do this publicly" (25).

The brief minutes that Sonny and Cher spent together singing "I Got You Babe" provided millions of viewers that night with one of the most touching experiences on television in whole decade of the 1980s. For the time that it took them to warble their way through this—their signature song—they touched the hearts of their fans. They were once again the act the world over knew as "Sonny & Cher," and standing next to each other singing that one song, they made time stand still. After the applause swelled, and the television show cut to a commercial break, it was over. Once again Sonny Bono, and the singularly named Cher, had made TV history.

Right after the taping of the *David Letterman* show, it was an oddly askew group who was gathered backstage, for the first and only time. "Well, that was kinda exciting," Sonny was overheard saying to a passerby in the green room backstage (22). It was a truly awkward moment. There stood Sonny Bono, age fifty-two, with his new bride, Mary, who was twenty-five. And with them was Cher, forty-one, with her new boyfriend, Robert, age twenty-three. The two men shook hands, and—oddly enough—the four of them had almost nothing to say to each other. Afterward they all went their separate ways. What the television audience saw that night was almost the entire extent of Sonny and Cher's relationship with each other at the NBC Studios. Like two comets in the night, they passed for a few moments in the stratosphere, and then went off in different directions.

Cher and Robert left the studio and were whisked away in their waiting limousine. Chastity said goodbye and left to meet some of her friends. And Sonny and Mary grabbed a cab and went out for a steak dinner at Smith and Wollensky. As quickly as it had happened, the historic reunion of Sonny & Cher was over. That night, when the program was broadcast, ratings went through the roof, and once again the duo was big news.

It was shaping up to be a big year for Sonny and Cher, together and separately. The same week that the Academy Awards were announced, the Palm Springs mayoral election was held. The day of the Academy Awards, Sonny telephoned Cher to predict that she was going to take the trophy that evening for her work on *Moonstruck*. When she arrived at the Shrine Auditorium for the awards presentation that evening, there was a huge traffic jam, so Cher and Robert had to jump out of their car and walk from the street in a hurry so they didn't miss the beginning of the show. The first award to be given out that evening was that of Best Supporting Actress, and Cher didn't want to miss the opportunity to see if her on-screen mother, Olympia Dukakis, was going to win in that category. Cher was thrilled to witness Dukakis take her trophy for portraying the role of Rose Castorini in *Moonstruck*. That evening, *Moonstruck*'s screenplay writer, John Patrick Shanley, also took an Academy Award for his work on the film in the category of Best Original Screenplay.

This particular year, the producers of the Academy Awards moved the category of Best Actress to the very end of the show. Cher spent much of the evening squirming uncomfortably with anticipation. On the telecast, she and Nicolas Cage gave out the Oscar for the Best Supporting Actor, to Sean Connery. When it finally came time for Cher's category, it was Paul Newman who was awarding that particular trophy that year. He read the nominees—Cher, Glenn Close, Holly Hunter, Sally Kirkland, Meryl Streep—and Cher recalls that at that point, she had lost all of her sense of reality, the sounds she heard and the sights she saw were suddenly surreal.

Paul Newman ripped open the envelope containing the name of the winner of the award, and he took a deep breath. In those few seconds, Cher was later to explain that by taking that breath, she was convinced that she had lost, because it doesn't take very much breath at all to say her one-syllable name. Time seemed to be moving in slow motion in her head, as Newman announced, "Cher for *Moonstruck.*"

Robert, her date for that evening, leapt up out of his seat, and with him, the entire audience rose from their seats, applauding and cheering with delight. Cher immediately stood up, kissed Robert, hugged her children, turned to walk up to the stage, and promptly tripped on the shawl of her elaborate outfit, stumbled, and lost one of her earrings.

When she reached the podium and held her Oscar for the first time, all thoughts of her much-practiced acceptance speech went right out of her head. She forgot to thank the Academy, or director Norman Jewison, but managed to thank—by name—her makeup man and her hairdresser, and Meryl Streep for all that she had taught her.

When she was done giggling and stumbling through her thank you's, Cher went backstage to be greeted and interviewed by the press. Arriving backstage she ran into Audrey Hepburn, who had been her idol ever since she first saw *Breakfast at Tiffany's.* Hepburn smiled and said to Cher, "I'm so glad you won—I wanted you to win." According to Cher, that encounter with Hepburn was worth just as much to her as the trophy itself!

As officials from the Academy attempted to take Cher's trophy from her, in order to add the engraved plaque with her name on it, she refused to give it up for one minute. This night was a dream come true for Cher, and she was bound and determined to enjoy every minute of it.

True to Cher form, the outfit that she wore that night was eye-popping to say the least. The amount of skin on her body that was covered by anything opaque was about the size of a tiny bikini. In another Bob Mackie creation of lace and gauze, as she posed with her trophy that night, she was about as close to being stark naked as you could get and still be considered dressed. The black "shawl" she had wrapped around her wrists and looped behind her, covered more of her forearms than any of her shapely body parts. With a few sewn-on sequins, and some dangling bugle beads, curly-haired Cher was beaming a genuine smile the whole evening in her bare-as-you-dare creation.

With regard to Cher taking the Oscar that night, Sally Kirkland says jokingly, "If it had been anyone else who won, I might have been upset!" She then explained,

Actually I am friendly with all of the women I was nominated with that night. Cher I knew before the Oscars. Holly Hunter and I know each other. I met

Meryl Streep at Raul Julia's memorial, and I have met Glenn Close. To be nominated in the same category as all these great women, was an honor. I will never forget that outrageous outfit Cher wore that night. She has to be years and years ahead of her time. And, she always makes certain that she is going to remain youthful and accessible to the rock & roll world. On one level I was devastated, and on another level I was not. How could I not remain friends with Cher? She went from Broadway to *Silkwood* to *Mask*—and everything she had done was such a 180 degree turn from where she had been, and what people expected from her. *Moonstruck* was such a perfect film for Cher, and I was happy for her victory (70).

Several days later, the horrific gaffe of having not thanked either Norman Jewison or the man who wrote the words that she spoke—John Patrick Shanley—sank in finally. To make amends for her glaring omission, Cher took out a full page ad in the legendary show business newspaper *Variety*, to properly thank them for helping her obtain her ultimate dream of winning an Academy Award for her acting.

It was an incredible month for Sonny & Cher fans. Not only was it a magical time for Cher, but—to the amazement of many—Sonny Bono was elected mayor of the city of Palm Springs, California. While Cher was reveling in her Oscar glory, Sonny and his fourth wife, Mary, were celebrating his electoral victory. The truly ironic thing about Sonny winning his mayoral race is the fact that prior to this time, he had never before registered to vote!

After winning the Oscar, Cher seemed to be taking inventory of her life from the vantage point of this new personal and professional plateau she found herself upon. She was in one of those rarefied places in life where she seemed to hold all of the cards, and control all of the variables. The role she claimed in the mid-1980s to want to portray next on the screen was that of famed American painter Georgia O'Keeffe. On the other hand there was also talk about a musical with David Bowie. She had yet to launch production on her own version of *The Enchanted Cottage*, but whenever she was asked what her dream projects were, she always mentioned it with fondness.

In the movie realm, Cher was far from finished stretching out into new horizons. Even at this point she was telling everyone who would listen that she wanted to produce and direct films. According to her, "I know it sounds incredibly pompous, but I'd like to direct a film. I don't know that I have any talent in that area, but I have a hunch that I might because I have ideas about film that I don't see other people exploring" (169).

At the time she was very secure in her relationship with Robert. She said at the time, "You know it never mattered that he was making bagels or bartending. Everybody asked me how we deal with our relationship, so I asked him, and he said, 'Tell them we deal with it fine. You're 41, and I'm 23, and I'm madly in love with you and you love me, and we have a great life. If other people have a problem with us, then they have to work it out alone'" (115). When she was asked by *New Woman* magazine if their relationship was serious or not, in her own inimitable fashion, no-bullshit Cher replied, "Oh, hey, we're just fucking around, that's all, sixteen months of fucking around" (115).

In fulfilling her burning desire to establish herself as an actress who was respected in Hollywood, she had more than proven her talent and her worth. She was at an age where she was truly comfortable in her own skin, perhaps for the first time ever. "I thought 40 was a bitch and I wasn't too thrilled with that, but here I am, 41, and I'm pretty happy. I can say I am an actress now. I'm doing all the things I want to do," she claimed (115). Finally, after over twenty years in show business, Cher was finally admitting to herself that she had "arrived."

LOVE HURTS

Having won the Academy Award for *Moonstruck* and scored a huge comeback album, in 1988 Cher was on top of the world. She was happily experiencing the highest point in a long and enduring career that consists of huge peaks and valleys. She had worked long and hard to be taken seriously as an actress of style and substance. She had also struggled in the music business to be seen as a full-fledged rock and roll star. With 1987's *Cher* album she had done just that. From this vantage point, it seemed that there was no stopping her career momentum, or her appeal.

Fueled by her movie and TV fame, during the year 1988, Cher continued to keep a strong public presence through her hit records. In June of that year, her latest single, "We All Sleep Alone" made it to the Top 20. On September 7, 1988, Cher performed at the fifth annual MTV Awards, which was staged at Universal Amphitheater in Universal City, California.

During 1988 Cher seemed to be interviewed by every magazine under the sun. The only two she seemed to have missed were *Popular Mechanics* and *National Geographic*. She continued to spout her views about everything from drugs to motherhood. This was truly her year, and she wasn't about to miss out on a minute of it—every headline-grabbing moment of it.

"I don't believe in drugs," she proclaimed in *New Woman* magazine that year, "They're a big waste of time. I've seen lots of people do drugs and I've never seen one person benefit from it, not one iota. It didn't make them happier, more creative, it didn't make them anything. Life is all your have, and if you ruin it in the beginning, how tragic" (115).

With regard to her role as the mother of two teenagers, Cher explained, "Let's face it, I'm not around constantly. But I try, really try, to make up the time whenever I can. And I've never abused my children. I think I spanked Chastity once, and though I could kill Elijah sometimes, the one time I slapped him I rushed to my room afterward, sat there, and thought, 'This is impossible.' I've never lost control again" (115).

Cher continued to speak her mind, right off of the cuff. Concerning her own honesty, she told *Premiere* magazine in 1988, "If I don't want to tell you something, I'll tell you why, but I won't lie. Even though I have lied in my life. I don't remember when. But I try not to do it, because it doesn't make a lot of sense. It's kind of hard to tell a reporter, 'This is none of your business.' I mean, I do. Actually, I do a lot" (22).

The middle 1980s were chic and glitzy years. Top-rated TV shows like the opulent prime-time soap operas *Dynasty* and *Dallas* flooded the airwaves with women in huge, puffy-shouldered designer gowns. After years and years of Hollywood stars slumming it in blue jeans, glamour was back in a big way. Even men were wearing rhinestone lapel pins and more ostentatious jewelry. In cities like Manhattan and Hollywood, women were dressing more chicly and elegantly than they had in decades. It was also the era of celebrity-endorsed perfumes. Elizabeth Taylor reportedly made more money in the 1980s from her line of Passion perfume, eau de toilette, lotion, and perfumed dusting powder than she had from her movie career. Every fashion diva—from Paloma Picasso to Cher—quickly got into the act. Cher's line of perfume was aptly called Uninhibited. The elaborate bottle featured Cher's name written in script on a metallic front plate. The screw top to the bottle was a jewel-encrusted crescent moon pointing upward and holding a metallic disk in its points. Cher looked great on the cosmetic pages of Sunday newspaper supplements, and suddenly everything seem to be blossoming with the scent of the ever-uninhibited Cher.

To assure the proper launch of her perfume line, Cher held a New York City press conference, which Bob Mackie created a special costume for. When Cher arrived at her Trump Tower press event, she was dressed as Egyptian queen Cleopatra, with a jewel-encrusted ancient Egyptian wig and see-through harem pants. Although it was already autumn in New York, Cher was again captured by photographers wearing a costume that cost thousands, yet presented her as nearly nude.

In the *New York Times,* Cher's perfume was presented for sale, with the sales pitch, "Discover Uninhibited at Macy's: Only Cher could inspire a fragrance this provocative, this prophetic. A futuristic flagon, filled with the very essence of adventure. Of risk-taking. Everything that Cher is about. And, just maybe everything your special lady's about too. There's only one way to find out" (170). However, finding out what "Uninhibited by Cher" smelled like was not for the budget-conscious. One-half a fluid ounce of the perfume sold for $65, an ounce for $175, and 1.7 ounces. for $300! The eau de toilette spray went for $30 and $45. The eau de toilette pour presented three ounces for $42.50.

It was also an era with more celebrities than ever before hawking goods and services in television commercials and print ads. Cher enthusiastically got on the bandwagon in 1988 when she was the star of TV and print ads advertising Jack La Lanne/Holiday Spas. In the TV commercial, Cher was seen extolling, "If it came in a bottle, everyone would have a good body" (115).

Since she was on an exhibitionist bent, it would seem that this would be a perfect time for Cher to up her price for performing, and book herself for either a concert tour or a Las Vegas engagement. However, in 1988 she announced to the press that booking herself at a casino was the furthest thing from her mind. "I didn't want to play Vegas for another twenty years," she claimed, "even though I was making fabulous money. I didn't want people to tell me I wasn't capable of more. Nothing in life is easy, O.K., but I had people, even people who supposedly loved me, come out with, 'Cher, can't you be satisfied with being rich and famous' " (115). Obviously not.

After the incredibly successful year she had lived through in 1988, Cher had big plans to begin a new album and a new movie. However, she found that she was so wiped out that she could barely get up every morning. "I was so sick I thought I was going to die. I went to doctor after doctor," Cher claimed (8).

Finally she did have her ailment defined as being the Epstein-Barr virus, which mysteriously saps your energy. Cher was later to report,

The [next] record took much longer because I got really, really sick for the first two months of 1989. I was really sick and couldn't even get out of bed. So they had to postpone the movie I was doing, we had to put off the record. Finally, everything started coming together. About a year and a half ago, when I did a record, three movies, everything worked well. This year, it was a little more difficult. Now, I'm putting together the live show and I'm starting to have meetings with movie people. But I can't find a moment to have those meetings. Everyone's kinda angry with me because everyone thinks I'm fucking off. The truth is I don't have a moment to "take a shower." . . . if we were friends I would have said, "take a shit" (164).

According to Cher, she was startled to have suddenly lost her vitality. "I was constantly sick and had no energy. I was someone who went full-tilt boogie when others were dropping like flies. But I should have figured out another way" (171).

After two months of rest, Cher directed her recharged energy into her next movie role, and her next record album, *Heart of Stone,* which was released in June of 1989. "Once I actually started the album, I stayed with it," Cher explained at the time.

We started this record in such a weird way, because the first thing I recorded was "After All," and that was such a long time ago. They needed the song for the movie soundtrack. [Album coordinator] John Kalodner listens to the songs first and gives them to me and I choose the ones I like. In this case, the producers came with their own songs. Desmond [Child] came with his material and Michael Bolton came in with his songs. And you know that if you pick a Michael Bolton song, he's gonna produce it. I had as much artistic control as I wanted, but I didn't take enough. I love the songs, and I think my performance isn't bad, but the music isn't exactly what I wanted it to be. I tend to like music that's a little harder. . . . The only change I would make on this album would be to make the music a little harder. I'd make it more guitar-oriented. My first love in life is rock & roll. I can do that style of music easily, but I'm having to work my way there (164).

In rock and roll terms, Cher's *Heart of Stone* album was a perfect one. Assembled using nearly all of the same producers as she had on the *Cher* album, it contained six different cuts from Diane Warren's songbook, either written solo or with cowriters Michael Bolton, Desmond Child, Jon Bon Jovi, and Richie Sambora. The songs were nearly all recorded with the same "power ballad" approach that had made Cher's previous album such a self-assured hit. The one main exception to this formula was the song "After All," which was the theme song to the movie *Chances Are.* A duet with Peter Cetera of the group Chicago, it is more of a delicate ballad and was produced by Peter Asher.

Aside from the hit singles, *Heart of Stone* also featured several exquisite cuts that made this one of her strongest albums ever. Among these songs is "Love on a Rooftop," written by Desmond Child and Diane War-ren. Directly mimicking Phil Spector's famed "Wall of Sound" recording formula, this electrifying cut echoes the pounding beat and forceful vocal delivery that once made the Ronettes so exciting in the 1960s. In fact, the song was originally introduced by Ronnie Spector on her little-known 1987 album, *Unfinished Business*. However, Cher's dynamite version of this song takes the lamenting tune of days gone by and turns it into an anthem of hope.

Propelled by the amazing number of five separate hit singles, *Heart of Stone* ultimately sold over two million copies in the United States alone, hitting Number 10 in America and Number 7 in the United Kingdom. At the time, in America, this was her highest-charting solo album ever and the biggest-selling one of her whole career, as either a solo artist or as one-half of Sonny & Cher.

This relentless string of hits showed her off as a strong and confident belter of rock songs with crackle and excitement. "After All" (Number 6/U.S.), "If I Could Turn Back Time" (Number 3/U.S., Number 6/UK), "Just Like Jesse James" (Number 8/U.S., Number 7/UK), "Heart of Stone" (Number 20/U.S., Number 43/UK), and "You Wouldn't Know Love" (Number 55/UK). Furthermore, both "After All" and "If I Could Turn Back Time" were certified Gold million-sellers by the RIAA in the United States.

One of the reasons for the huge success of the song "If I Could Turn Back Time" was the totally outrageous video that was filmed to promote it. Cher still had a sexy body, and she chose to show it off in a way that topped even her four most famous flesh-revealing outfits—the "Half Breed" loincloth, the "Take Me Home" Viking drag, the "Prisoner" slave-in-chains, and her see-through *Moonstruck* Oscar-accepting costume.

Said her designer, Bob Mackie, "When we design the costumes for her, it has nothing to do with fashion. It has nothing to do with anything but the fact that we are attempting to present to the world this . . . crea-ture in her own right" (8). If that wasn't the truth. This outfit alone restated the fact that there is truly no one in show business even remotely like Cher!

Shot aboard a U.S. Navy ship, this video gave the sailors a show quite unlike any they would have expected from a forty-two-year-old Academy Award–winning movie star. While dancing and prancing aboard the ship's deck, and straddling cannon barrels, from below the waist, Cher appeared to be wearing two pieces of ribbon about an inch in width, joined at the crotch and leaving little to the imagination. To say that she had "bikini waxed" was a sheer understatement. The "If I Could Turn Back Time" video was in fact so risqué that it was banned by MTV and was allowed to be shown only after midnight. Always one who loved to shock her fans, this time around, Cher had truly outdone herself.

When her video was banned, Cher remained uncharacteristically blasé about it. "When they pulled my video from MTV, I understood it," she claimed. "I didn't care that they banned it. I really didn't. It might not be suitable for very small children" (8). However, she claimed that she simply had a side of her personality that somehow needed to shock her audience.

> Sometimes I get really tired and don't have the energy to play Cher. Some-
> one once asked me how I was able to wear that revealing outfit on the new
> video. But it's weird because that's not really me. In my private life, I'm
> really shy and introverted as a person. I can do things in my public life that
> I could never do in private. Cher could play to a hundred thousand peo-
> ple, but I would have trouble talking to one person. They're both me, but
> "Cher" is just such a different part of my personality. One's private and
> one's something else that I don't understand at all (164).

In true Cher form, that year the pop diva had the distinction of being named 1989's "Worst Dressed Female Rock Artist" by *Rolling Stone* magazine. The same publication, in its 1989 annual Critic's Awards, declared "If I Could Turn Back Time" the year's "Worst Video." Criticisms like this seemed to just roll off her back like water on a duck's feathers.

> What I do, I do for myself and my fans—the new ones and the die-hard
> ones. The other people, the critics, what they say is like the poison of the
> business. But you have to take that along with the good. Sometimes the
> critics just try to be cute or try to make a name for themselves. There are
> so many silly things that go into it that you don't know what the fuck they're
> trying to do. I think my fans have been unbelievable, because they just
> stuck by me when it looked like I was dead to the world and never com-
> ing back (164).

In the album liner notes of *Heart of Stone*, Cher doubly credits John Kalodner. According to her,

> John Kalodner's name is on the album twice. And, can I tell you some-
> thing? If his name was all over, it was stamped on every part of the album,

it wouldn't be too much as far as I'm concerned. The only reason I'm on Geffen Records is because of John Kalodner. I'd be on Desert Island Records if not for him. I didn't want to make the first album. I didn't want to get back into the record business. I'm not nearly as good a singer as I am an actress. As a singer, I could never do what I really wanted to, because I wasn't good enough. But I was smart enough to hear that I wasn't cutting it vocally (164).

One of the most bizarre aspects of the *Heart of Stone* album packaging was the artwork on the original version of it—which is now something of a collector's item. The cover was an artist's drawing of Cher seated on the ground next to a rounded, heart-shaped stone. However, if you look at the illustration from afar, you can see Cher's body positioning connects the silhouette of a dead man's skull. The way the waistband of her dress wrinkles, teeth are formed, and the white-faced sketch of her face forms the skull's eye socket. There is a famous Victorian illustration of a woman at a vanity table, but if you look at it from afar, it too forms the silhouette of a human skull. This illustration was very similar, but starred a forlorn-looking Cher. It was fascinating, yet hideous at the same time. Commenting on artist Octavio Occampo's grim front and back cover designs, Cher claimed, "I think the album cover is a fiasco, but I'm crazy about it. It's like one of those gigantic mistakes that got totally fucked, but when I look at it, it's so me. I think it's ugly, but I like it a lot" (164).

When Geffen Records went back to press the next run of *Heart of Stone* albums, the artwork had been completely changed. The ugly illustration was gone, replaced by a new portrait of Cher, by Herb Ritts. The album had already been certified Platinum in America when the artwork switch was done.

While Cher was in the recording studio working on her second album for Geffen Records, her relationship with her Bagel Boy, Robert Camilletti, was heading toward a crashing finale. While her fame was in the less-than-meteoric phase, they had found it easy to live together and go out in public together without any major incidents. Robert had not only costarred in Cher's "I Found Someone" video, he had also landed a couple of featured roles in movies. He had also worked as a disc jockey at dance clubs. However, ever since Cher had won her Oscar in 1988, she was pursued by the press, stalkers, and the paparazzi even more relentlessly than ever before. When a rumor circulated that Cher and Robert were about to get married in a top-secret ceremony, the intrusive press encroached even further.

In order to approach or leave Cher's Benedict Canyon home, which she lived in at the time, one would have to come down a long driveway. It was becoming increasingly more and more difficult for Cher and Robert to come and go out of the place without some kind of confrontation. Even the contents of their garbage cans were scrutinized by the press. Living in Cher's universe was beginning to become a suffocating experience.

On one particular occasion, a press photographer in a car nearly ran Cher and Robert off the road and into a ditch, just trying to get a photograph. The following day, Cher had a doctor's appointment, so they devised a plan to have Robert drive Cher's car out first and divert the photographers at the gate. Their plan worked well on the exit phase. However, when Robert returned to the house to meet Cher, a pair of photographers jumped out at him and caused him to crash the car. He wasn't hurt by the crash, but was angered intensely and took off on foot to pursue the photographers. After they fled, Camilletti sabotaged their car by yanking the phone out of it.

When the police arrived to investigate, the photographers claimed that Robert had threatened to kill them, so they had no choice but to take him down to the police station in handcuffs. Cher followed the police car down to the station, while Robert was booked, and she was going to post bail. However, as Cher sat in the police station, she found herself surrounded by a sea of press photographers flashing cameras at her. Meanwhile, in his cell, Camilletti was taking his own dose of verbal abuse from a cop who came up to him and commented, "Oh yeah, you're the Wop that's fucking Cher" (25).

Cher bailed Robert out, and they went home. However, he announced to her that he was done living in a fishbowl with her and that he was going home to Brooklyn. She was later to philosophically say of her affairs with younger men, "Val [Kilmer] left me. Robert [Camilletti] left me. The two of them were really young, and they were both looking for their own identity, and I'm a big shadow. The men I pick aren't very impressed with my lifestyle. I always pick men who are more work-ethic sorts. I like straight men" (8).

On March 18, 1989, Cher was one of the stars of the HBO-TV special *Comic Relief III*, a benefit for the homeless. The show was hosted by Billy Crystal, Whoopi Goldberg, and Robin Williams. The other stars to perform live at Universal Amphitheater included Arsenio Hall, Shelley Long, Gary Shandling, and Martin Short.

When *Heart of Stone* was released in the stores, Cher began a 1989 concert tour to promote it. The first of her appearances on this tour was in front of a crowd of 16,000 people at an outdoor amphitheater in Mansfield, Massachusetts. It was also her first concert appearance in eight years. That night, the concert was held to celebrate the tenth anniversary of a Boston radio station, WXKS-FM. When Cher reached the part of the show in which she was going to perform the song "We All Sleep Alone," she announced from the stage, "This next song has particular meaning for me, because I just broke up with my boyfriend" (172). Backstage that night, a resolute Cher was quoted as saying of her breakup with Robert, "It's okay. That's life" (144). *People* magazine snidely swiped, "As for Camilletti, he's still spinning discs, perhaps dreaming of someday running for Mayor of Palm Springs" (173).

Up to this point, Cher had always prided herself on being a dynamo of boundless energy. The idea of launching a concert tour, promoting her new album, promoting her perfume, promoting health spas, and beginning work on a new movie just seemed like business as usual for her. She was only forty-three years old, and in tip-top shape—why not go for it? With that, she plunged herself into that 1989 concert tour.

One of the most exciting aspects of the tour was that Cher's son, thirteen-year-old Elijah Blue Allman was featured as a background guitar player. If your mother and your father are both rock stars, why not get into the family business? Also, Cher delightfully included fellow Phil Spector–days alumna Darlene Love as one of her background singers on this particular tour.

With her boundless enthusiasm, Cher worked with director/choreographer Kenny Ortega to create a spectacle of a rock show. Said Ortega at the time,

> [It's] a tense gig, put together in a relatively short period. Everybody was handpicked by Cher. I set up dancer auditions for her, and with the musicians, she saw maybe 70 guitar players, and sat through every one of them. And, she didn't want a heavy metal show, but she liked the idea of a "heavy" set, something monstrous she could play with and we could climb in. Then two days before we left L.A., she said, "Kenny, let's get props, let's get crazy" (174).

The concert tour was a huge success. The top ticket prices for her shows were $200, and scalpers were asking—and getting—up to $600 a ticket. In August of 1989 Cher headlined at the Sands Casino Hotel in

Atlantic City, New Jersey. She may not have wanted to become a "Vegas" act again, but by playing Atlantic City, wasn't she actually contradicting herself? Oh well, that's so Cher.

While she sold out shows across the country, she seemed to consistently be dogged by critics from coast to coast during her 1989–90 tour dates. One of the problems seemed to be the fact that there were now so many different versions of "Cher" that it was becoming increasingly more and more difficult to work them all into the same show. There was the teenage pop singer Cher, the glamorous TV star Cher, the singer of trashy story-songs Cher, the unglamorous roles Cher had played on the silver screen, and the scantly clad leather-and-studs Cher she had been promoting via her concurrent pair of Geffen Records albums. To roll all of these different personas into one multimedia extravaganza, the diva and her troupe relied on extensive video footage projected onto the huge projection screens like the Jacksons had made famous during their 1984 Victory Tour.

In these concerts, Cher turned her back on her biggest pre-1980s hits—like "Half Breed," "Dark Lady," "Gypsys, Tramps and Thieves," and "Take Me Home." Instead she presented her own interpretation of hard-rocking songs like Bob Seger's "Fire Down Below," Bruce Springsteen's "Tougher Than the Rest," the Eagles' "Take it to the Limit," and a clever cover of Gregg Allman's "I'm No Angel." If there was anything to be viewed of herself from before the 1980s, it was covered on the video clips. Cher used the extra minutes while they ran to make another dramatic costume change.

Reviewing her show at New Jersey's Garden State Arts Center in August of 1989, David Hinckley of the *New York Daily News* found her entertaining, but uninspiring.

> They cheered the Lady Godiva Cher and the Bon Jovi Cher. They cheered the video clips of the 1965 Cher singing "I Got You Babe," with Sonny. They cheered excerpts from *The Witches of Eastwick*. With no incentive to pick just one, then, Cher has thrown them all into this show. . . . The result is a production so lavishly Cher-centric it makes Madonna look modest. . . . by inviting all these Chers along, she's ended up with a celebration of her name—and a rather bloodless show (175).

Months later, on the other coast, Mike Boehm of the *Los Angeles Times* came away with a similar impression, reviewing her show in June of 1990 at the San Diego Sports Arena. Boehm claimed it was one big ego-fest.

> In a lazy hour on stage, some of which she spent singing, Cher was interested only in spotlighting what's least substantial about herself. . . . Cher's concert was so much like a testimonial that rubber chicken should have been served. . . . Instead of trying to delve into a song, changing the dynamics, shading tones—doing the things that good singers do to communicate feeling—Cher just kept belting (176).

One can almost imagine Cher herself reading these reviews and saying out loud, "Fuck the critics, my shows are for my fans, and not the critics." You know what? She was right. Fuck 'em if they can't take a joke. Cher might be a legitimate twentieth-century diva, but let's not confuse her with Maria Callas.

On September 6, 1989, Cher appeared in one of her trademark risqué outfits at the sixth annual MTV Awards. That month the RIAA certified her song "If I Could Turn Back Time" Gold for selling over a million copies, as it reached Number 3 on the American record charts. It was her biggest American hit in years.

By late 1989, Cher had a new man in her life. He was someone she had worked with, and became friends with first. All of a sudden she found herself dating Richie Sambora of the rock group Bon Jovi. He had been a producer and a performer on her last two albums for Geffen Records, and he seemed to be in her life at a time when she needed someone. They had attended the MTV Awards together, and, according to an article in the *Star* newspaper, the very next day he went out and bought Cher a diamond ring.

The article, entitled "Cher Says 'I Will' After Rocker Richie Dazzles Her with $10G Ring," shocked Cher's publicist with the notion that her star client was engaged. Said Lois Smith, "I don't know anything about this. He's on tour and Cher's in Boston, getting ready to work on her new movie, *Mermaids*. Both their schedules leave them little time to see one another. They were together at the MTV Awards, but I don't know if they can say more than 'hello' on the telephone right now until Christmas because of the way their schedules are" (177).

Although Cher and Sambora continued to date on and off, their romance didn't end up lasting very long. Ironically, after over fifteen years of Cher always having a boyfriend by her side, she was about to enter a long phase of being a single career woman.

In October of 1989, while "If I Could Turn Back Time" hit Number 6 in England, Cher was busy filming her latest movie, *Mermaids*. She was very anxious to get in front of the cameras.

I couldn't find anything that I wanted to do. I was desperately looking. There are not a lot of great scripts and there are so many women in my area. There was two years between *Mask* and *Witches*. I don't want that to happen again. But I care a lot about this phase in my life. I've done things just for money and I'm not ashamed of it, because your work is what you do to put clothes on your back and feed your kids, but, like, I don't ever want to do TV again. Cable [TV] I don't think of as television, I'm talking about network TV. TV for me—I say it and it will probably be the next thing I do, because I always make these great pronouncements and then I'm totally full of shit—it's stifling to do TV for as long as I did, and I ended up hating it. I don't ever want to do that with movies, and therefore, because of my age and because I'm a woman, I'm not going to get the best script out of 30 scripts. I'm going to hope that I get the best script out of two or four scripts and I'm going to wait a long time for them (119).

With regard to the forthcoming *Mermaids*, she explained,

It's very reminiscent of *Moonstruck*. It's a sweet look at people who are totally out of their minds and doing the best job that they can, but they're just cracked. The story's not even mostly about me. It's about Emily Lloyd, and I play her mother. It's a little bit bigger than Jack Nicholson's part in *Terms of Endearment,* but then you can't imagine *Terms of Endearment* without Jack Nicholson (119).

The filming of *Mermaids* was fraught with problems and delays. Originally, the director slated for *Mermaids* was Lasse Hallström (*My Life as a Dog*), but he was replaced with Frank Oz (*Little Shop of Horrors*). Almost instantly, Cher and he did not get along. Finally Richard Benjamin (*My Favorite Year*) was brought in to helm the project. According to Cher, "Look, I'm only difficult if you're an idiot. If you don't know more than I know, then I'll probably be difficult. I know you're not supposed to say it, but nobody ever says anything if an actor gets fired, but a director gets fired and everybody has a heart attack" (8).

Winona Ryder's character narrates *Mermaids,* and much of the action is presented from her perspective. Although the family is Jewish, Ryder longs to become a nun. Throughout the film, Ryder never refers to Cher's character as "Mom" or "Mother"; she is addressed and discussed as "Mrs. Flax."

As Mrs. Flax, Cher, wore a Marlo Thomas–styled *That Girl* dark flip wig, and inappropriately too-tight and too-low-cut clothes. Instead of cooking dinner for her two young daughters, she cuts up bagels and other food—like Maraschino cherries and marshmallows—and skewers them with American flag toothpicks or colorful *hors d'oeuvres* toothpicks. Describing one of her dishes of toothpick-assembled finger foods, she explains the menu as including "cheese ball pick-me-ups and marshmallow kabobs."

According to Cher, she didn't have to look very far to find an inspiration for her characterization—Georgia Holt. "My mother *was* Mrs. Flax," she proclaimed. "She dressed really provocatively. We lived with all women in our house, too. She had three best friends, and they were beautiful women. My God, these women were knockouts! It was sort of like me and my girlfriends, I guess" (8).

Holt was later to comment,

When I saw *Mermaids*, I went, "Jesus Christ, is that the way I did with my children?" And Cher says, "Mother, do you know how many times you made us move?" But I was always trying to move us to a better place. And I also don't remember, you know, being a sex machine. Maybe I was. When I went in to get a part, my agent always told me to wet my lips and pad my bra, do that number, and that's what I did (8).

Once *Mermaids* was filmed, Cher was back on the road in 1990, resuming her North American "Heart of Stone" concert tour. On March 31, 1990, the tour opened at the Starplex Amphitheater in Dallas, Texas. The tour ran until August 29, 1990, closing in front of a sold-out audience of 14,966 at Toronto, Canada's Exhibition Stadium. Ultimately, Cher performed in front of sold-out crowds in thirty-five North American cities.

The week of July 5, 1990, Cher's *Heart of Stone* album was certified Double Platinum for over two million copies sold in the United States alone. In October of 1990, Cher was in the British Isles for a short concert tour, and on the nineteenth of that month, she performed at Wembly Arena. She also packed in standing-room-only crowds for her appearances in Birmingham, England and Dublin, Ireland.

After Cher's short-lived affair with Richie Sambora fizzled, she moved her best girlfriends, and her sister, into her huge house. There was certainly more than enough room for them all. In 1990 Cher explained of her everyday all-girls slumber party, "Paulette [Betts] and I 'live together' live together," she said. "And [workout partner] Ange Best is almost always there. My sister was there for a long time, but now she's getting married. We're like *The Golden Girls*. Paulette is Rose, Angela is Blanche. I'm Dorothy. And Georganne is Sophia. We've even got robes monogrammed with our *Golden Girls* names" (8). Both of her children, Chastity and Elijah, were of the age when they were off living their own lives, and having her best girlfriends around her made her feel better, especially in light of her recurring health problems.

The only other woman in show business at that time who commanded as much media coverage was Madonna. In many ways, Madonna had become adept at adopting Cher-like career moves. With as much as they had in common, it was rather surprising that they didn't become closer friends. Madonna was not one of Cher's favorite people. "I must say, I understand Madonna," Cher explained in 1990. "But, I can't say that I like her. I understand wanting to make something out of yourself and working really hard and having people make it really difficult for you. But she's too rude. For me to like Madonna, she'd have to be nicer" (8).

In 1990, Cher continued to make uncomplimentary statements about her ex-husband Sonny Bono. Only two years before, on the *Letterman* show, it appeared that they had buried the hatchet. Yet, in the November 1990 issue of *Vanity Fair* magazine, Cher blasted Sonny by saying, "I don't talk to Sonny anymore unless I have to. Sonny didn't even love me, I don't think. He just didn't want me to get away from him. I certainly don't miss him. It just seems like another person was with him, when I look back on it. It's amazing when you get old—you do have all these lives. If I met that person now, I'd tolerate her" (8). Is it any wonder that Cher's fans are often left confused by her pronouncements?

That same year, Cher publicly admitted that she had been undergoing therapy to try and help her deal with her hectic life. She said at the time,

> I'm in therapy and I think that's good for me. It's been about two years. A couple of years ago I had three surgeries in a row, which made me feel unbelievably bad. It was supposed to be two surgeries, but it turned into three. There was a process between the last two that I had to go through, and it was the worst experience of my life. I was reading [the book] *The Road Less Traveled,* and out of the blue I called the doctor who wrote it, Scott Peck. I said, "Hi I'm Cher. I'm having a really rough time. I need some help" (8).

By the end of 1990, Cher was ready for some major changes in her real estate holdings. She sold the spacious New York City loft that was located above Tower Records, off of Broadway in Greenwich Village. Rap record producer Russell Simmons purchased the apartment from her for $1.6 million. She had also finally sold her Mulholland Drive mansion—the Egyptian-influenced house that nearly bankrupted her—to Eddie Murphy for $6.5 million. With her capital gains, she purchased a nice little pad in Aspen, Colorado, for $2.5 million and a Malibu manse, which cost her only $3 million. While she lived there, she began construction of a new dwelling on a two-acre cliff looking out on the ocean. According to her, "I cut the plans down to 12,000 square feet from 16,000" (8). That Cher, so practical.

She said at the time, "I call what I want from my new house 'prehistoric futuristic.' I like things made of stone and I like everything one color—very beige. I'm using the house that I'm living in now as a prototype for the next one. I just do it as I do it. It's like designing my beads" (8).

Cher was relieved to unload the Egyptian palace of a house. According to her, "I don't like being in situations that I cannot get out of. As much as I loved it, there were times when I was almost bankrupt in that house. When I was desperately trying to sell it, I couldn't. I'm going to build the house again, just in a different reincarnation" (119). With regard to selling it to comedian Eddie Murphy, she explained, "It's weird. One day he was in the house and said, 'This house is so peaceful and beautiful.' I expected him to be this really punky guy and he was so ethereal, and so it seems to me that if he could see the beauty of the house, he should have it" (119).

When *Mermaids* was released in December of 1990, it received decidedly mixed reviews from the critics. Roger Ebert in the *Chicago Sun Times* found it to be quirky but enjoyable.

It's a story told by a teenage girl whose mother avoids becoming known as the town tramp only because she changes towns so often. . . . The mom in *Mermaids* goes by the name of Mrs. Flax, and is played by Cher, but in an eerie sense played as Cher, with perfect make-up and a flawless body that seems a bit much to hope for, given the character's lifestyle and diet. . . . And yet, perversely perhaps, I found this an interesting movie. I didn't give a bean how it turned out, and I found a lot of it preposterous, but I enjoyed that quality (178).

Desson Howe of the *Washington Post* hated it—a lot. "This movie," he wrote, "doesn't come of age so much as die of it. It's awash in mediocrity, waterlogged with innocuousness. . . . Cher seems to have her mind on other things. She phones in her performance. . . . Last and definitely least is the inspiration-free direction of hack-helmsman Richard Benjamin" (179).

However, in that very same paper, writer Hal Hinson loved it.

The strength of June Roberts's sprightly, inventive script—which came by way of Patty Dann's novel, with some custom modifications based on Cher's relationship with her own mother—may have been the project's salvation. . . . All of the women characters here are seen as exotics . . . for some this notion might be hard to swallow. But Cher, who's the most otherworldly of modern actresses, makes the suggestion seem altogether reasonable. Her Mrs. Flax is deliciously trashy—kitsch in high heels (180).

A decade later, viewing the film *Mermaids* reveals it to be a fascinating bit of cinema fluff, a highly entertaining comedy film that is short on depth, but full of tears and laughs. It is especially fun to see Cher working with Winona Ryder and Christina Ricci, as her daughters. Both Ryder and Ricci blossomed into two of 1990s' cinema's brightest stars, and to watch them on screen with Cher—at her most Auntie Mame–like—is a delight. However, at the time, *Mermaids* was not a huge box-office hit.

The one aspect of it that was a major hit, however, was the song "The Shoop Shoop Song (It's in His Kiss)," which Cher recorded for the movie's soundtrack album. She had gone into the recording studio with producer Peter Asher and sung her own versions of a couple of 1960s hits. When it was released as a single in the United States, "The Shoop Shoop Song (It's in His Kiss)" only made it to Number 33 on the charts. However, when it was released in England, it zoomed up to the top of the record charts, and became the biggest-selling single of her British recording career. It was also the first time she had ever hit Number 1 on the British charts.

On January 26, 1991, Cher was seen on tape at military bases in the Middle East in a specially produced two-hour armed forces video program. Taped in the living room of her Malibu house, she was the star of *Cher's Video Canteen,* on which she hosted twenty-two video clips by such artists as Bonnie Raitt, Janet Jackson, John Fogerty, Paul Simon, and Van Halen.

On February 4, 1991, Cher was the star of her first network television special in twelve years, as CBS-TV broadcast *Cher at the Mirage,* a concert TV special. Among the songs that she sang during the special was her version of the song "Many Rivers to Cross." She had finally broken her promise to stay away from Las Vegas for several years. She ended up with a great concert video from the deal, which she released as a video cassette. Throughout the beginning of 1991, Cher continued to tour North America.

In March of 1991, she was in an operating room at the Medical City Dallas Hospital in Dallas, Texas. No, this wasn't one of her plastic surgeries, it was to be there for a young girl she had befriended, Marie Jatejic, and it was a delicate operation on the girl's face. Ever since she had filmed *Mask* in the 1980s, Cher had made the Children's Craniofacial Association (CCA) one of her pet charities. According to her, "There are all kinds of worthwhile charities. But I can't spread myself too thin. I have to feel committed. If you look at one of these children, knowing that the only thing that keeps them from living a normal, happy, productive life in society, is money, it seems a shame" (181). On February 10, 1992, Cher appeared on the American syndicated television program *The Maury Povich Show* and pledged an astonishing $450,000 toward the Children's Craniofacial Association.

Once Cher became the honorary chairwoman for the CCA, in several of the cities she performed at in concert, local organizations would bring children afflicted with the physical ravages of this disorder and allow them to hang out with Cher. Along the way, there were several children, and adults, who genuinely touched her heart. She met Marie Jatejic when she was on tour in Australia. There was something about Marie that kept the child in Cher's thoughts. With Cher's personal intercession, Marie was able to have an expensive operation to try to give her a more normal life, and to feel better about herself. Usually squeamish about watching a medical operation, Cher put her fear of hospitals aside, and was there for Marie. "It's hard to see them trapped in these little faces. You can really see the change in Marie's life. Her operation was one of the highlights of my life" (182).

In June of 1991, Cher released her third LP for Geffen Records. Her twenty-sixth solo album, *Love Hurts,* took a similar approach to her previous Platinum-selling albums on Geffen Records, the hard-rocking "power ballad" styling of the songs and a team of different producers working toward a cohesive collection of dynamic cuts. Highlights on this

album include Diane Warren's brilliant composition "Love and Understanding," and "A World without Heroes," which was written by Gene
Simmons and Paul Stanley of KISS with Lou Reed, and Alice Cooper's
producer, Bob Ezrin.

When the album was released in June of 1991, it instantly hit Number
1 in England, becoming her first LP to debut at the top of the charts in
that country. And it stayed at Number 1 for five weeks. Although it only
peaked at Number 48 on the American album chart in *Billboard,* it was
certified Gold. In America in 1991, Cher's popularity on the music charts
was starting to cool down. While she was to continue to be bigger than
ever before in England, and in Europe, her recordings seemed to fall on
deaf ears in the United States.

As a special marketing ploy, the *Love Hurts* album was not only
released with regular CD packaging, it was also available in a special limited edition package. This special collector's version was housed in a
hinged wooden box with thirteen special Cher Tarot cards, bearing additional Gothic artwork and the album liner notes. The Cher Tarot cards
were bound together with a rice paper ring, on which was printed the
quote "I hate and I love. Why I do so, perhaps you ask. I know not, but I
feel it and I am in torment," by Gaius Valerius Catullus, 84–54 B.C. It was
the complete Cher experience: listen to the music, play with the Tarot
cards, learn the philosophy.

Love Hurts had the distinction of yielding four separate hit singles,
with varying results on the music charts on each side of the Atlantic. They
were "Love and Understanding" (Number 10/UK, Number 17/U.S.),
"Save Up All Your Tears" (Number 37/UK, Number 37/U.S.), "Love
Hurts" (Number 43/UK), and "Could've Been You" (Number 43/UK).

Cher was aggressive in her attempts to promote the album. On
June 14, 1991, she was interviewed on the television program *CBS This
Morning.* At this point in time, probably the only other woman in show
business who had the impact and staying power of Cher was Madonna.
When she was asked her opinion of Madonna, part of her frank answer
had to be "bleeped," but for anyone who could read lips, Cher's complete
reply was,

> There's something about her that I don't like. She's mean, I don't like that.
> I remember having her over to my house a couple of times, because Sean
> [Penn] and I were friends, and she was just so rude to everybody. It seems
> to me that she's got so much, that she doesn't have to act the way she acts,

like a spoiled brat all the time. It seems to me when you reach the kind of acclaim that she's reached and can do whatever you want to do, you should be a little more magnanimous and a little bit less of a cunt (182).

On June 16, Cher debuted the first single off her new album on the Fox-TV program *Backstage Pass to Summer.* On June 17, she was seen in Britain on the BBC1-TV program *Wogan.* On July 27, 1991, Cher was a guest on the NBC-TV program *The Tonight Show.* By August of that year, *Love Hurts* had been certified Gold in America. In November of 1991 alone, she was also seen on the TV programs *Sally Jesse Raphael, Late Night with David Letterman, The Tonight Show,* and *Dame Edna's Hollywood.* Alas, the *Love Hurts* album was the least successful of her trio of Geffen Records studio albums in America.

In October, high-fashion critic Mr. Blackwell assessed fashions since the 1960s and awarded Cher the honor of being named the "Worst Dressed Woman of the Last Three Decades." According to Blackwell, "From toes to nose, she's the tacky tattooed terror of the 20th Century. A Bono-fide fashion fiasco of the legendary kind" (183). In the December 15, 1991 issue of *People* magazine, Cher graced the pages of the publication's "Best and Worst Dressed of 1991" spread. Showing her tattooed behind through fishnet stockings and a thin thong, wearing knee-height high-heeled boots, a long black wig, and little else, Cher's photo appeared on a page headlined "The Stars, The Moon." It was thumbs down for Cher's "mooning" fashion statement, taken from the promotional video for her song "Save Up All Your Tears." Talk about cheeky!

That same year, Cher also released her first book, *Forever Fit.* In it she revealed her exercise tips, low-calorie recipes, and all of her secrets for maintaining a remarkable figure. Conspicuously missing from her health and fitness tips was her biggest body-maintaining regime, countless thousands of dollars in plastic surgery, body-part lifts, and very expensive dental work. However, as Cher was to point out at the time, "If you never take care of your car, someday it's going to break down. You can buy a new car, but you can't buy a new body" (184).

In time for Christmas 1991, Cher released her fitness video cassette *Cherfitness—A New Attitude.* According to her at the time, "I made this video for myself. I put together the best trainers that I could. I believe in being driven by the best." With regard to her training perspective, Cher explained, "I based this program on my own cross training technique. It's in modular increments, so if you don't have a great deal of time, or you just need to concentrate on one area of the body, no sweat" (184).

In March of 1992, superstar manager Frank DiLeo was interviewed by *USA Today* about his featured role in the forthcoming film *Wayne's World*. DiLeo had become quite the cigar-chomping legend in the 1980s when he signed the then-hot Michael Jackson for exclusive representation. Since parting ways with Jackson, DiLeo had gone on to appear in a series of films as an Italian mobster, including a role in 1990's *Goodfellas* as gangster Tuddy Cicero. He bragged to *USA Today*'s Karen Thomas about his then-current roster of stars, including Laura Branigan, Al B. Sure!, and Richie Sambora. He also talked about the client he had just signed, Cher. "She was looking for somebody to get more involved in her music career. She wants to do better. She likes doing albums, maybe even better than movies" (185). Reportedly, their first work together was to be the promotion of her next single, "Could've Been You."

In April and May of that year, Cher was busy promoting herself in Europe via an eight-week-long concert and public appearance tour. She played in twelve countries and to sold-out audiences in each of them. That year, the British recording industry declared *Love Hurts* to be Triple Platinum. On April 11, Cher was one of the international celebrities to attend the grand opening of Euro Disney in France. On the twenty-fifth of April her latest British single, "Could've Been You," hit Number 31, just prior to her May 6 and 7 dates at Wembly Arena.

Cher was due to headline at the Paramount in New York City on May 27, 1992, but following the exhausting European tour, she was suffering from bronchitis and sinusitis. With all of the tabloid coverage about her mysterious illness, her fans were beginning to worry about her health. To make up her canceled dates at the Paramount Theater, Cher returned to New York City to perform in Madison Square Garden on October 27, 28, 30, and November 1, 1992. She reportedly grossed $1,068,078 for her performances.

On July 2, the RIAA in the United States certified her first Geffen Records album, *Cher*, Platinum for over a million copies sold in her native country. On October 26, Cher made a surprise phone-in appearance on CNN's *Larry King Show*. The show's guest that particular day was presidential hopeful and third party candidate Ross Perot. She dialed up the call-in show to let Perot know that he had her vote in November when it came time elect the next president of the United States.

"Hi Ross, it's Cher," said the diva to the politician on King's chat show.

I would be willing to give up everything I'm doing and come and be one of the volunteers as long as I know that if I got into it, you wouldn't quit. If something doesn't happen, then I can't imagine what's going to happen to the rest of my children's future. . . . Whether you like it or not, you are the focus. It's like you are the father of this patriot movement. Whether you like it or not, you have to be there (186).

When King asked her, "You'd give up part of your career for this?" Perot replied, "Now don't do that Cher. But I would love to have your help" (186).

In 1992 Cher was again up on the silver screen, in a major hit motion picture, Robert Altman's wildly successful *The Player*. Starring Tim Robbins, *The Player* is a refreshingly delightful murder mystery set in Hollywood. While actors like Whoopi Goldberg and Lyle Lovett play detectives trying to solve this intentional death of a screenplay writer, a virtual "who's who" of real Hollywood celebrities appear as themselves. It became *THE* film to be seen in that year, and Altman's scene-stealing cameo stars included Burt Reynolds, Steve Allen, Jayne Meadows, Harry Belafonte, Shari Belafonte, Anjelica Huston, Marlee Matlin, Rod Steiger, Jeff Goldblum, Lily Tomlin, Andie MacDowell, David Carradine, Jack Lemmon, Susan Sarandon, Julia Roberts, Bruce Willis, Sally Kirkland, and Cher.

In *The Player*, all of Hollywood has turned out for a gala event calling for everyone to dress in "Black & White Only, Please." Naturally, it is Cher who, in *Jezebel*-like fashion, is the one star who shows up in flame red. In a low-cut, tattoo revealing, fire-engine-colored, beaded designer gown, she comes sweeping up to the event. Cher is seen three times amid the plotted action at this black & white only event. Cher's one audible line is uttered to her date that evening, actor Peter Gallagher. She turns to him and says, "Well, are we having fun yet?" In a later scene shot at the same event, Academy Award–nominated actress Sally Kirkland is viewed chatting with Cher.

According to Kirkland,

In that scene from *The Player*, we are seen on camera together, talking at a Hollywood event. During that scene, I took that as an opportunity to congratulate her about the Oscar. That was the first time I had seen her since that big night at the Academy Awards, and it was my moment to congratulate her. While the camera was on us in *The Player*, we were probably talking about holistic or spiritual things, because we both share that in common (70).

In spite of all of her high-profile activity in the United States, at this point Cher had completely cooled off on the record charts. Between the stripped-down "grunge rock" sound coming out of Seattle and the 1990s resurgence of back-to-basics country music, the kind of hard-rocking power ballads that Cher had recorded on her three Geffen Records albums was suddenly passé. However, she was still huge news in Great Britain and Europe. In December of 1992, Geffen Records released her first hits compilation, *Cher's Greatest Hits 1965–1992.*

The British-only sixteen-song album was such an extraordinary look at Cher's career that it became one of the most sought-after import albums in the United States. The album featured eight of her biggest hits from her three Geffen Records; her rocking duet with Meatloaf, "Dead Ringer for Love"; two of her biggest hits on MCA, "Dark Lady" and "Gypsys, Tramps and Thieves"; and her trademark Sonny & Cher anthem, "I Got You Babe." In addition, it contained the biggest European hit of her long career, "The Shoop Shoop Song," and three previously unreleased songs—each of which went on to become British hit singles during this same period of time. When *Cher's Greatest Hits 1965–1992* was released in Britain, it debuted at Number 1, echoing the Number 1 chart entry of her 1991 *Love Hurts* album. It seemed that in England, Cher could do no wrong.

Not long after "Could've Been You" had failed to become a major hit on either side of the Atlantic, Cher and her new manager Frank DiLeo parted company. Unfortunately, he was unable to point her career in an upward direction on the music charts. By the time that *Cher's Greatest Hits 1965–1992* was released, her long-time business partner Bill Sammeth was credited in the liner notes as being her manager.

The three new songs were "Oh No Not My Baby," "Whenever You're Near," and "Many Rivers to Cross." "Oh No Not My Baby" had originally been a 1964 hit for Maxine Brown and was written by Carole King during her initial 1960s streak of songwriting magic at the Brill Building in New York City. Cher's version of the song is the perfect follow-up to "The Shoop Shoop Song." Cher has always done very well when she is reinterpreting classic songs from the 1960s, particularly those songs that were written and arranged with girl singers or girl groups in mind. Cher has in the past interpreted "Rescue Me," "It's a Cryin' Shame," "Will You Love Me Tomorrow," and "Baby I'm Yours." Her single version of "Oh No Not My Baby" went to Number 33 on the British charts. "Many Rivers to Cross," which was originally written and sung by Jimmy Cliff, was recorded live at the Mirage during her TV special in Las Vegas, and went to Number 37 on the British charts in January of 1993. *Cher's Greatest Hits 1965–1992* became the biggest-selling European album of her entire career. According to her, "It came out in Europe. It went, I don't know, gazillion Platinum. But it also had the biggest song I've ever had, 'The Shoop Shoop Song' " (61).

On February 16, 1993, Cher was in London, where she accepted an award for the Artist Formerly Known as Prince, who was named Best International Solo Artist at the twelfth annual BRITS Awards. The event was held at Alexandria Palace. On March 6, her single "Whenever You're Near" made it to Number 72 on the British pop charts.

With all of her radio and record sales success in England, Cher's career had drastically shifted. Instead of being looked at as a classy Academy Award–winning actress, she was seen as more of a living tabloid soap opera star. Stories like "Cher Stricken by Terrifying Mysterious Illness" (*National Enquirer*, July 4, 1989), "Cher Finally Finds Lover Her Own Age—Rock Star Eric Clapton" (*Star*, August 13, 1991), and "Cher Bounces Back from Devastating Disease" (*National Enquirer*, August 13, 1991) seemed to define her public career more than her music or her acting. This is all without even mentioning the headlines that her daughter, Chastity, was creating during this era. Headlines like "Cher's Lesbian Daughter Chastity in Late-Night Catfights with Gal-Pal Roommate" (*Star*, December 11, 1990) presented a whole new angle for keeping Cher's name on tabloid covers.

It was also impossible not to notice the excessive plastic surgery and appearance-altering work she consistently had done to herself during this era, including an increasing number of tattoos. One couldn't help but notice that the face and the image of Cher began to evolve in the early 1990s. Thankfully, she didn't become a grotesque-looking clown, like Michael Jackson, but her work on her body seemed to be veering out of control. In 1989 she had admitted, "I had my nose done. I had my tits done. I wore braces. I'm not embarrassed to say stuff that I've had done, because I don't care what people think about it" (119). However, it didn't take Sherlock Holmes to discover that she didn't just stop there.

Whenever she was questioned about her plastic surgery, however, Cher tended to become very defensive—as though, like the tale of "The Emperor's New Clothes," no one was supposed to notice that she had spent the last ten years acquiring a brand new face. "I don't know why people are preoccupied with my cosmetic surgery," she said in amazement in 1990.

I really don't. It mystifies me that people would care what I do to my body. I remember when I was young, all the people that were popular—Sandra Dee and Doris Day—were people I really couldn't identify with. So then you feel inhibited and you feel ashamed, or you feel less good because you don't look in style, so I think what you have to do is create your own style (8).

In the early 1990s Cher had her teeth capped, which drastically changed the shape of her mouth. Then, to top it off, she began to have her lips puffed up via the current new fad with Hollywood actresses, collagen injections. An entire generation of her fans, who had grown up loving her unique jagged-tooth smile, were suddenly seeing Cher as someone entirely different than the woman American television audiences had once fallen in love with.

And then there were her tattoos, which everyone had ample opportunities to see through the skin-revealing fashions she wore. Most prominent on Cher's body was a large tattoo on her left upper arm. It was an artist's drawing of a necklace with a heart-shaped pendant, which was tattooed on to look like it was draped on her arm in a nonconcentric fashion.

According to Cher, her favorite tattoo parlor at the time was one called Red Devil. It is an all-female "inking" salon, located on La Brea, in Los Angeles. "I don't know why I like tattoos so much," she said at the time. "I know it's crazy. I can't defend them. I've had some of my tattoos for 20 years. I love getting them. The women at Red Devil do piercing too. Now, I'm really frightened of piercing. That seems so extreme—like noses and lips and belly buttons and nipples and tongues" (8).

In 1992 and 1993, the physically revised Cher embarked on one of her most ill-timed and ill-chosen career moves, that of TV product spokeswoman. First of all, there was her print and television advertising campaign. Sunday newspaper coupon supplements were full of photos of the puffy-lipped new-nosed Cher selling a sugar substitute. "There's Sugar, the Pink Stuff and Equal. I Choose Equal" said the headline of the coupon-bearing advertisements. ("The Pink Stuff" refers to Equal's sugar-substitute competitor and manufacturer, Sweet & Low.)

According to Russ Klettke of NutraSweet, the company approached Cher about doing the ads. Cher had used Equal in one of the recipes in her 1991 book with Robert Haas, *Forever Fit.* "We read about it in a review in *People* magazine," he revealed. "She's known to speak her mind. What she says, people basically believe it. And when you're working with a celebrity, you want people to believe it" (187).

Bill Reishtein of the advertising agency Oglivy & Mather explained that the agency had passed on the idea of having Cher sing in the ad. Instead they took the plain-talk approach. What television audiences didn't see on camera was professional reporter Jeanne Wolf of TV's *Current Affair* interviewing Cher and prompting her straight talk. Of not getting to see Cher sing or act in the ad, Reishtein said at the time, "People see that all the time. They know she does those things. What they don't get to see is her being a real person talking. That's the most interesting part of the commercial" (187).

Time and time again, in the beginning of 1990s, Cher's energy was zapped by the effects of the Epstein-Barr virus. She found that her glands were swollen and that her immune system was shot. She was on a regimen of antibiotics, and for a two-year period, she was up and down with exhaustion. Still, she kept dragging herself out of bed and launched herself into project after project. When offers, like the Equal non-sugar sweetener campaign came around, Cher viewed them as easy, quick, and painless ways to make large chunks of money.

In the fall of 1992, while all sorts of celebrities were seen selling cosmetics and other items on stations like QVC and the Home Shopping Network, Cher too tossed her hat into that ring. She was seen over and over again on television selling her own line of Lonely Hearts jewelry, based on her new necklace tattoo.

With the spread of cable and satellite television feeds in the 1990s, there were more TV stations than ever before. Television programming known as "infomercials" started gaining popularity, and programming frequency. In the early 1990s American television audiences were suddenly bombarded by several celebrity-driven half-hour- or hour-long television commercials made to look like informational variety shows. Dionne Warwick reportedly made a huge amount of money on her phone-in fortune-tellers hotline *The Psychic Friends Network*. Victoria Principal of TV's *Dallas* made a huge income selling her Principal Secret cosmetics. Ali MacGraw, Meredith Baxter, and Lisa Hartman sold Victoria Jackson cosmetics. Mary Wilson of the Supremes and Davy Jones of the Monkees teamed up to sell CDs of 1960s pop music. It was only a matter of time before Cher became involved.

Cher has a friend in Los Angeles who is a hairdresser, Lori Davis. Davis was getting ready to launch her own line of shampoos, hair conditioners, and hairsprays, and she had the money to film an infomercial. With several celebrity clients in Los Angeles, Davis asked Cher if she would be the celebrity hostess on an infomercial produced to sell her hair-care products.

Cher's agent, Ronnie Meyer, tried to talk Cher out of doing the commercial, as it might hurt her career to suddenly be selling shampoo on late-night TV. Cher rationalized that it was a quick, easy way to collect a paycheck, and so she agreed to do it. On the infomercial, in a living room setting, Cher conducted a "girls talk" session with Lori Davis and two of her best friends. In the context of the infomercial, Cher would ask Lori about different hair-care problems, and—naturally—Lori had some expensive product in her hair-care line to address just that problem.

In Cher's mind, it seemed quite simple. After all, she had done TV commercials for health spas, what difference could this make? Unfortunately, she didn't realize that these infomercials were going to be run on several television stations, over and over and over. One minute Cher was a hard-rocking, Oscar-winning superstar. The next minute she was hawking shampoo on late-night TV.

David Letterman razzed her mercilessly on his TV program. *Saturday Night Live* especially skewered her in a comedy skit parodying the Lori Davis Hair Products infomercial. Their version featured late comedian Chris Farley, in full drag and a wig, as the rotund Davis. In an instant of poor judgment, Cher had suddenly turned her career into a joke. Her credibility was suddenly shot. The movie offers came to a screeching halt.

Cher was later to look back on this period of her life as though she'd broken a mirror for bad luck. She was officially amid seven years of career bad luck. She made jokes about how she should have tried selling something more "meaningful" than shampoo on TV, something substantial like the Planet Hollywood theme restaurants. "Well there wouldn't have been a problem had I not done the infomercial," she said.

> I mean, the infomercial was possibly the stupidest thing I ever did. But, O.K., so I did a stupid thing, so kill me! Let's negate my entire career and let's look back on all my work and say it was a fluke or I'm just tacky. I paid a really stiff penalty for the crime. I could have killed somebody and gotten away with less. But the truth is, it's all about how things appear. The reason I said Planet Hollywood is because the press that's done for Planet Hollywood makes it look like these celebrities are not just selling a product. The fact is they are out there selling a product, it just looks cool. But, in our society, it's much more important how things look instead of how they really are. I was stupid; I chose the wrong thing (23).

In the United States, the laughably dreadful Lori Davis hair-care infomercial ads proved to be the straw that broke the camel's back in the public's eye. The nonstop TV deluge of these continually broadcast ads wrote the book on overexposure. "I became a joke on *Letterman* and *Saturday Night Live*. My career took a huge nosedive, went right in the toilet. I couldn't have been dumber. It was a huge, devastating misjudgment of what people would accept from me" (171). Even the *New York Times* referred to her Lori Davis debacle as "an embarrassing interlude as an infomercial queen" (24).

It had been a long, wild ride for Cher the last couple of years, starting with her phenomenal 1987–88 streak of success on film, on record, and in her personal life. It had taken her five high-activity years for her coast downward from the top. *Moonstruck* had made her into a movie star, but between the Equal ads, the Lonely Hearts jewelry, and the Lori Davis hair products, it was as though Cher had transformed herself into something akin to a fashionably dressed used-car salesman. After a downward spiral that began in 1991, for the next seven years things would continue to be decidedly hit and miss for Cher.

14

CHASTITY'S SONG

While a flurry of activity was going on in Cher's life, the two people she is still most closely associated with—Sonny and Chastity Bono—were living their own soap opera lives. In addition to all of the tabloid coverage that Cher was receiving, regarding her health, her boyfriends, her plastic surgery, and her new career as a merchandise spokeswoman, she was also linked to her ex-husband's blossoming political career and to revelations about her daughter's awakening sexuality.

As a high-profile politician, amid his four-year elected term as the mayor of Palm Springs, Sonny not only made friends and allies, he also found himself to be the political enemy of many others. But, such was the thankless lot of a career in politics.

Among the things he was able to accomplish while in office was establishing the Palm Springs International Film Festival as an annual event. He is also responsible for outlawing thong bikinis in public places. In the middle of his term as mayor, in 1989, he successfully fended off a political recall vote whose organizers hoped to have him deposed from office. According to *Time* magazine, the point of contention was that Sonny had failed to significantly bolster the languishing downtown area of his sleepy little desert town. One conflict arose when he deposed three of the members of the Palm Springs Visitors & Promotion Board, all of whom were amongst his detractors. *Time* also referred to him as "Mayor Bonehead" (181). This threat to his budding political career blew over, and Sonny emerged successful and proved himself a worthy leader who was concerned about his community.

In July of 1991, when a horrible bus crash occurred in his town, Mayor Bono was at the scene of the accident, tending to the victims. The accident involved a busload of Girl Scouts and ended up claiming the lives of six people. On November 4th of that year, Bono was honored by the National Disaster Conference for personally heading to the scene of the crash and assisting in rescuing several of the victims. In addition, Sonny reportedly donated a full year's worth of his $15,000 mayoral salary to the Palm Springs Police Department's antidrug program.

In August of 1991, Sonny published his autobiography, *And the Beat Goes On*. The memoir gave him the chance to tell his side of the story with regard to his musical career, his marriage to Cher, his divorce from Cher, and the accusations and rude comments that his ex-wife—Cher—was still hurling in his direction. Sonny painted Cher as someone who was so ego-driven that she was often cold, calculating, and ungrateful. Of their initial breakup, Sonny was to state, "She resented me. She hated sharing the spotlight. She really wanted to be bigger than Dylan and Jagger. Only she wanted that fame and attention and adulation all for herself" (35).

In 1992, Sonny unsuccessfully ran for a seat in the U.S. Senate. Bob Dole was quoted as saying at the time, "When I first heard he was running, I thought, 'Gee, they must be kidding' " (188). He may have lost that particular political bid, but Sonny Bono's political career was far from over.

Nearly thirty years since it was originally recorded, in 1993, the Sonny & Cher recording of "I Got You Babe" was prominently featured in the Bill Murray and Andie MacDowell comedy film *Groundhog Day*. Based on the success of the film, the song was once again released as a single in England and made it to Number 66 on the UK music charts.

In 1994, Sonny again found himself in a political race, for the post of congressman in California's forty-fourth district. Republican candidate Bono defeated Democrat Steve Clute, 56 percent to 38 percent, to win the congressional seat in the United States House of Representatives. It was time for the next chapter of his life: Mr. Bono goes to Washington.

That was the end of him putting his attention toward the Palm Springs edition of Bono's restaurant; he had bigger things to do. Cher wasn't the only half of Sonny & Cher with a knack for reinventing herself. In his own more low-keyed way, Sonny too was a brilliant survivor. His 1990s tenure in Congress was another high point in a career that had many successful phases.

Cher used this as an opportunity to further zap her ex-husband. She was quoted in the *Washington Post* as stating, "Politicians don't work for the people; the system works for the politicians. It's a huge crime to be so greedy and to let the people down and the country fall apart. Politicians are one step below used car salesmen" (189). This comment was coming from a woman who was concurrently using her vast talents, fame, beauty, and creative energy to sell overpriced designer shampoo on television.

While all of this high-profile drama was going on in her parents' lives, Chastity was having her own personal struggle—with her sexual identity. "I was conscious as a very young child that I was different from other girls, different from the person my Mom expected me to be," recalls Chastity (16).

When Chastity was a little girl, Cher loved to dress her up in frilly, girly outfits. When she was old enough to voice her own opinion, she preferred more tomboy-like outfits. Sonny didn't care if she felt more comfortable in more boyish clothes. Cher however, protested. "She criticized my baggy pants, T-shirts and boy's sneakers. I was hurt and angry that she didn't accept me for who I was," claimed Chastity. "I first realized I was gay around my 13th birthday, when I saw a lesbian love scene in the [1982] movie *Personal Best*. But I was still hesitant to explore my sexuality and terrified of sharing my discovery with my mother" (16).

Then there was Cher's role as Meryl Streep's gay roommate in the film, *Silkwood*. According to Chastity, "My mother was playing a lesbian in *Silkwood* at the time, and I remember reading over and over the scene where they're out on the swing talking together. I had a big crush on Meryl. It's hard not to" (64).

According to Chastity, she felt pressured into her first attempts at having sex with men. "The only time I ever slept with a man, I was 16," she reveals.

> I did it because I was sick of everybody saying, "How do you know you're gay if you've never slept with a man" so I could say, "Well, I did it, so now I know." He was a marine, which is the most hysterical thing. I get shit from every woman I've ever been with: "The one guy you fucked was a *marine*?" I went on one other date with a guy after that, in Palm Springs. I was totally in love with this girl at school, but she was not comfortable

with the whole lesbian thing. I met this guy who was the son of one of the people who worked in my Dad's restaurant. He was an arts student, good-looking, bohemian, long hair, gentle. I thought, "Well, if I could be attracted to a guy, this would probably be the kind of guy—he's not rough and rugged." We went to see some movie, and I thought about this girl from high school the whole time. It put me in a really bad mood, and I just wanted to go home. I thought, "You know what? I gave it another shot, and it's just not happening" (64).

By the time she was sixteen years old, she began to act on her gay sexual urges. "Mom and I were staying at Tom Cruise's house, and he had two lofts," Chastity recalls.

Mom slept in the one, and I slept in the one with the kitchen. Mom came in to get something to drink, and this girl and I were on the pull-out sofa bed making out. Instead of rolling away from each other and pretending that we were just sitting there talking, we both jumped up like dorks. Mom walked in, saw us jump up, and went right back out. She never confronted me about it, but the girl with me told her, "Oh, we fell asleep, and you scared us.' My Mom's always hated her, because she knew something was up (64).

"Two weeks later, on my 17th birthday, she picked a fight with me, prob-ably about my clothes, and then told me she wasn't going to my party. It wasn't until years later that she finally admitted that the real reason was that she was devastated after walking in on me" (16).

This episode was to drive a wedge between Cher and her daughter. Sonny was the first of Chastity's parents to know that she was gay. "He was the first one in my family to know," she was to reveal. "I was reading this lesbian book, and he saw it in my room. He picked it up and said to me, 'Is there something that you want to talk to me about?' So I told him, and he was like, 'Oh, I knew.' He was really great about it" (64).

Still, Chastity couldn't seem to confront her mother on the issue. "She didn't understand it," Chastity explains. "Actually, Mom took me to a shrink at one point because she was worried about my being gay. I was spending all of this time with [lesbian family friends] Joan and Scotty. Of course I knew I was gay at that point, but I didn't tell her, and I didn't tell the shrink because I knew that would be a bad idea" (64).

Much to everyone's surprise, when Cher did find out, she completely freaked out. Chastity was in New York City at the time, and Cher was in

California. In a heated telephone conversation, Cher screamed at her daughter, "How could you do this to me? Why didn't you tell me what was going on? I had to find out from your father!" Finally she commanded, "I want you to leave the apartment right now" (16). Chastity packed a suitcase and moved in with a group of her friends.

It took Cher about a week to cool down and get things in perspective. What seemed to hurt her the most is that everyone else around her knew before she herself did. Part of the problem was Cher's own self-absorbed denial. She realized that her daughter was a bit of a tomboy, but she was not anywhere near being emotionally ready for this revelation.

While Chastity was off on her own in the late 1980s, she put together a band, which evolved into the short-lived rock group known as Ceremony. They were eventually signed to Geffen Records, Cher's label, and released one unsuccessful album.

While she was in New York City pursuing her own recording career, and attending New York University, Chastity would hang out at several Greenwich Village gay and lesbian bars. Although her mother and father were world-famous, she didn't think that anyone was paying attention to her whereabouts. Before long, Chastity dropped out of school to devote her full attention to her rock group, and her affair with her first girl-friend.

According to Chastity, both of her parents strongly disliked her first girlfriend, Heidi.

> Mom hated my girlfriend before Joan. At one point she wouldn't let her in the house. Later Mom told me, "I couldn't understand why she treated you the way she did, and your taking it was just too difficult for me to watch." My Dad felt the same about her. He never forbade her to come in his house—that's not his style—but he didn't like her. Nobody liked her. She treated me like shit. I was basically her glorified slave (64).

Said Cher of Heidi "I didn't think she was very nice to Chastity. She didn't show her any respect" (61).

Unfortunately for twenty-year-old Chastity, this exact era was one in which several self-appointed media representatives began "outing" celebrities for being gay or lesbian. This forced several singers and actors to declare their sexuality. Among them were Elton John, Melissa Etheridge, the Indigo Girls, and Janis Ian.

It was also an era where the editor of *OutWeek* magazine began regularly "outing" celebrities on the cover of its magazine. His name is Michelangelo Signorelli, and he made Chastity Bono one of his targets. "Michelangelo—whatever the fuck his name is—Signorile . . . so he wrote this article in *OutWeek* [magazine]. It's a great article, actually, and he was right on the money, but it really pissed me off at the time," she was later to admit. By presenting the facts, Chastity's secret was open for further scrutiny.

"I got a call from my mom's publicist," recalls Chastity.

> She'd gotten an advance copy of the *Star* and read it to me. My first reaction was, "Can't we stop it? Isn't there something we can do?" She said, "No, it's done, they're running with it." My Mom was completely freaked out. She had warned me, "This could happen, be careful." And here it happened. Before that I used to go out to the bars, and I would go out to gay pride events and stuff like that. . . . She always told me, "Be careful. If this ever got out, I don't know if you could handle it." But I didn't think it would happen, because it had really never happened before. You didn't have that shit before me (64).

Her first instinct was to deny the rumors. "Then the publicist had me do an article with the [*National*] *Enquirer* that said I wasn't gay. So that was totally embarrassing, stooping to the level of giving an interview to the *Enquirer*" (64).

The February 13, 1990, issue of the *National Enquirer* featured the headline-grabbing cover story "Branded a Gay, Cher's Daughter Chastity Fights Back—THE TRUTH ABOUT CHER, MEN & ME—Exclusive Interview." In the article, Chastity is quoted as claiming,

> I live in an apartment in Greenwich Village with two other women—but they've been my friends since I was a student at NYU and it's a typical economical arrangement. I like to pay my own way and you show me a 20-year-old who can afford to live alone in New York. I date men. I don't have a steady boyfriend—I go out with guys I find appealing, and I go out with them for however long we like each other (190).

"I lied," Chastity recalls.

> But at that point I didn't feel bad about lying because I was just so pissed off that it even happened, that they were invading my privacy that badly.

I lived in total fear with my shades drawn. I was being followed and hounded. No, I really didn't have any guilt about lying. I was pissed. I hated the gay community. I was beyond angry because I found out that it was a gay man who leaked the original story. They were getting quotes from people in the gay community saying, "Oh, I saw her at this club." This gay bar called the Cubbyhole had its bathroom wallpapered with my tabloids. They were selling T-shirts of me at Gay Pride [events] (64).

Chastity admits that she was horrified to learn what the press could legally do when it was printing stories about the private lives of public figures. Although she had been a public figure all of her life, this was all coming at her during a time in which she was struggling to find her identity.

Most people who are stars wanted first to be artists, and in our society we raise famous artists to the level of stars. Because you have a particular talent at something and are making a living at it, why does that give the media unfair advantages over you that they wouldn't have over an ordinary person? I learned a lot about what the press could legally do when I was outed, because they couldn't say the name of the girl I was with. They blacked out her face because she was not public domain. I was. I was the daughter of Sonny & Cher (64).

Throughout the early 1990s, Chastity became one of the tabloids' most regularly covered celebrities. Among the headlines from this era are "Sonny Blames Cher for Daughter's Gay Nightmare" (Globe), "Cher Told Daughter Chastity Filmed Lesbian Movie" (Star), "Cher Defends Lesbian Daughter" (Star), and "Cher's Lesbian Daughter Chastity in Late-Night Catfights with Gal-Pal Roommate" (Star).

While she was busy denying all of the rumors, Chastity's love life went down a tragic path. After she broke up with her first girlfriend, Heidi Shink, Chastity began an affair with family friend Joan, who was her mother's age. No one was more surprised at the affair than Chastity herself. "Here was this woman that I had loved for years who had loved me," she was to recall. "Our relationship turned romantic and sexual" (64).

Unfortunately, while she and Chastity were lovers, Joan became fatally ill. "Looking back on it now," says Chastity, "I think that's why it happened because she was going to get sick and she needed somebody who had the time and the love and the patience to take care of her and help her through and to get on to the next place" (64). Joan became very sick in July of 1993. She had already been diagnosed with Non-Hodgkins lymphoma once before, in 1989. Surprisingly, Cher was fine with Chastity's relationship with Joan. She had gotten over her initial fears about her daughter's sexuality. Recalls Chastity, "She was really cool. I told her, 'I'm seeing Joan,' and she started laughing. She said, 'Well, I think this is going to be a very good life experience for you" (64).

While Joan was still ill, Chastity met her next girlfriend, Laura. "The first time I ever met Laura was at a Hollywood party. One of my dearest friends works with her at E! Entertainment. I was still with Joan, and Joan was healthy." After Joan died, Chastity put her focus on her rock band. At one of the band's performances, Laura reentered her life. "She was at a gig I played, and we talked a little," Chastity recalls. "I was kind of ready to have something for myself again. She was able to talk to me in ways that my friends couldn't—about what had gone on with Joan. She was so compassionate and open. At the time I thought she was an angel sent to me to get me through my grieving. It was an instant connection" (64).

Finally, by 1995, Chastity was tired of being hounded by the tabloid newspapers about her sexuality. On the cover of the April 18, 1995, issue of *Advocate* magazine, Chastity publicly admitted she was gay. With a relieved smile on her face, Chastity looked radiant on the cover of the magazine, which heralded its exclusive interview with the headline "Chastity Bono Out At Last."

She said at the time,

> I definitely feel that if k. d. lang, Melissa Etheridge, the Indigo Girls, and Janis Ian hadn't come out, I wouldn't be coming out now. I'm certainly too wimpy to be the first person on the block to do something. However, maybe my being one more person doing it is going to make another person do it. It's like that silly hair commercial "Tell two friends, and they'll tell two friends, and so on, and so on" (64).

After Chastity had made her public announcement, she felt relieved of the burden of hiding her personal life. She became a contributing writer for the gay and lesbian newsmagazine the *Advocate* and later worked for organizations including the Human Rights Campaign and GLAAD (Gay and Lesbian Alliance Against Defamation). As much publicity and media coverage as Chastity received for her courageous pronouncements about her personal life, even more publicity was generated by her famous parents' reactions. Ironically, it was conservative Sonny who was able to handle it in stride, and it was Cher was felt upset and hurt by her daughter's actions.

Cher even surprised herself with her strong reaction.

> I think one would expect—I would even expect—for it not to make any difference to me, and for me to handle it easily. If you had asked, "Who will handle it better, my father or my mother?" no one would have said, "Oh, Sonny Bono is probably going to be the one who comes through it like a champ, and Cher is probably going to fail on all scores." But, I freaked, and he was cool. I was also really upset that I was the last person to know. I felt stupid in that way, and I felt really fucked. I hated that everybody in the family knew but me (26).

After all of the nonconformist activities of her very public life, what was it that upset Cher the most, the fact that Chastity was a lesbian, or that Sonny knew about it first?

> I don't know that it was more than anything else, it was just that for so long I was hoping it wasn't true, and then when it was true, I just felt I had done something wrong. *If I had been a better mother.* . . . —all of the stupid things that people from Ohio are supposed to feel, not mothers who are Cher, who have lots of gay friends and all that shit. As far as I was concerned, I really wasn't supposed to feel that way, because it wasn't liberal of me at all. It wasn't really who I thought I was, but it didn't make any difference. Those were my feelings and even though I am not very proud of them, that is what it was for me; that was my experience, and I cannot try to lessen it by pretending that it wasn't. Nor am I ashamed of it. I was surprised by it. The reason I am not ashamed by it is that I was in so much pain about it, and I don't really know why. But it was genuine, unbelievable pain (26).

When Cher was finally able to reconcile her feelings, Chastity interviewed her for a cover story in *Advocate* magazine. "Emotionally, I just didn't want it to be the truth," said Cher in the 1996 article.

> I was talking to my friend the other night about this. I was telling him my reaction, and I was saying that I thought I would have had a much different reaction based on my so-called philosophy. But when it comes to your own children. . . . I think that whatever my reaction was, it was a disappointment to me. But that's what it was. No, your being gay was not something I was hoping was a fact of life (26).

With all of the gay friends she had in her life, what were Cher's fears based upon? "I don't think gay life in the olden days was able to be nearly as healthy as it is becoming. I didn't want you to have a deviant lifestyle; I didn't want you to be breaking new ground. I think maybe some part of me that was real Americana was hoping you were going to get married and have kids—or not get married and have kids" (26).

Cher also voiced her concern that Chastity had opened herself to further prejudice. According to her, "Unfortunately, for a lot of people in America, when they think of gay, they think of drag queens going down Christopher Street [in New York City], stuff that is so over-the-top that they can't relate to it on any level. If people have a hard time with the way I dress and look, it is very difficult for them to see grown men dressed like that" (26). Most of all, Cher felt that she had done something wrong in her children's upbringing. "I felt guilty," she claimed, admitting, "Both their childhoods were not exactly Betty Crocker" (24).

Chastity was also able to see the irony in much of what her mother's life had been about, and had represented to millions of people around the world, both gay and straight. "My Mom got pregnant with me during a movie she made called *Chastity*," she pointed out. "I've never seen it, but I hear that it has some type of lesbian overtones. Nothing overt, but it's about a young girl discovering herself" (64). Cher had been surrounded by gay men and women all her life. She had even portrayed a lesbian on the screen in *Silkwood*. It was as though she could handle it in other people's lives, but not her own daughter's life.

Cher had been less upset when Chastity quit school after only a handful of classes at New York University. Said Chastity,

> It's weird because she's an extremely educated person for having no formal education. Education, unfortunately, wasn't stressed very much in my family. I think because they were so successful at not needing it, they didn't see the point in it for me. Not having it worked great for them. Look where they are now. My Dad's a congressman, and he doesn't even have a high school diploma (64).

What infuriated Cher even more was the fact that the tabloids had forced her into a corner, and made both she and Chastity confront the subject in front of the countless millions of readers of the *Star*, the *National Enquirer*, and the *Globe*. "I've also had a problem with those newspapers," admitted Cher.

The couple of weeks that that stuff came out, there were also some things that weren't of as much interest to people—about Elijah being a Satanist, and a guy who cut off his ear and sent it to me. Fuck it. I'm tired of dealing with those people. It's just so difficult to prove that they are doing it with complete malice. I'll tell you something if Chastity joined the Ku Klux Klan, then I would be out of my mind. There are certain things that I think are bad and certain things that I don't really care about. It would be a lot more important to me that Chastity be a good person than what her sexuality is. She is everything I would want her to be—sensitive, smart, talented. But it made a lot better story to say that I was out of my mind about it (8).

Chastity says of her own experiences of being a target of paparazzi photographers, "The first time my girlfriend and I were followed by street photographers, she wanted to bash them. But I said, 'No. Then you would be the lesbian Sean Penn. Just grin and bear it' " (191).

Finally, Cher was able to get over her hurt and anger, and to accept Chastity as her own person and not as an extension of herself. Today, Cher and Chastity are closer than ever. Says Cher of her daughter, "[She is] one of the coolest people I've ever known" (24).

Looking back on her mother's negative reaction, in 1997 Chastity was to state,

> Now, I'm glad she reacted badly. People can more easily relate to it. They can say, "Well, even Cher had a hard time." But she was able to get past it. I really believe a lot of responsibility in coming out is on the gay person's shoulders. Often we come out and that's it. We're still not sharing our lives. Our parents have an "I know it, why talk about it?" attitude, so we exclude parts of our lives from them. To help the parents' process, we have to share our lives on a regular basis. It's amazing how it changes the relationship. When I was 18, my Mom wasn't like a friend. She was a parent. As I became confident with myself, I started showing what I was doing, and our relationship became completely different. We're friends now. We talk a lot. I had always thought we were just kind of different and didn't understand each other. I didn't realize how much of the responsibility was mine. I didn't let her get to know me (191).

In 1998 Chastity published a book called *Family Outing*, in which she spoke very frankly about her sexuality and her famous parents' very separate reactions to her revelations. With regard to Cher's having "freaked out" at the news that her only daughter was gay, Chastity claimed, "But it actually strengthened her support in the gay community, because her response was so primal and almost textbook for the parent of a gay child—and she got past it" (192).

Although Sonny Bono openly embraced his daughter's controversial lifestyle choice, it was to cause political problems between father and daughter. In 1996, Chastity made this statement about Sonny: "He was talking to me at one point about gays having a minority status. I was very antigay then, because this was right around the tabloid time, and I was feeling, 'Fuck anything gay.' But now, of course, my view is different. I think we do need to be protected. We are a minority. But I haven't really talked about that since with him" (64). Politically, now that Sonny was a conservative Republican on Capitol Hill, he was against giving gay people special rights in America. Although he loved his daughter, this left them at odds politically.

According to Chastity,

As far as my Mom, it was the opposite. We did not have a great relationship growing up. I knew that she loved me, but it was strained. We were very different, and I didn't have very high hopes for ever having a close relationship with her. But when I finally came out, I stopped censoring what I talked about with her. I let her get to know me for the first time as a whole person. In doing that, I got to know her, and all of a sudden our differences didn't seem like such a big deal. It turned everything around, and now I'm just super close to her (193).

When Chastity confronted Cher about making a statement to her gay and lesbian fans, Cher replied,

The most important and hardest thing in the world to keep remembering is to be honest about who you are—but that is the most rewarding thing. For some of us it is harder than for others. Being gay and being proud of it might take more energy, but it is so much more rewarding than trying to deny who you are. . . . Being who you are is not always popular. I know too. I have been on the popular side of being me and on the unpopular side of being me (26).

Due to a very public "coming out," the relationships between Sonny and Cher and Chastity shifted a bit. Some of it was favorable, and some of it was unfavorable. Regardless of what the outcome was to be between all three of them, Chastity's actions, and her levelheadedness toward doing the right thing, caused each of them to grow emotionally.

15

IT'S CHER'S WORLD

Concurrent with all of the drama that was going on in Chastity's life, Cher's own very hectic life and career were continuing right along at full velocity. From 1993 to 1998, she continued to be involved in one project after another. Although her popularity was waning a bit, and at times it seemed that she had withdrawn from the public eye, her activities and her creative output continued to move forward.

Through an organization called the United Armenian Fund Relief Organization, on April 28, 1993, Cher flew to Armenia. She had grown up knowing that she was of Armenian descent; however, she never knew firsthand what the country was like. She did know that Armenia was a grim and desolate place; a 1988 earthquake rocked the country and left its residents broke and hungry. At this point, the Soviet Union, which once ruled over it, had fallen apart, and so had the economy there. To top it all off, they were now at war with their enemies, the Azerbaijanis.

Cher was first of all curious to see where her ancestors had come from. And she wanted to see what she could do to shine some light of hope and charity upon the Armenian citizens. Cher and her party left from London's Heathrow Airport and flew in an ancient 707 cargo plane that had seats bolted in the back of the cabin. With them they took dried food, medicine, clothes, and toys for the children. Mattel Toys had donated Barbie dolls and Hot Wheels toys toward the cause. In addition, the plane also had to be filled with enough food for Cher and her party, as the resources of the country were so depleted that there was little or no food there to buy. On the way, Cher recalls that the plane ride was so turbulent that all of the passengers had to carry their own oxygen canisters just in case of mishap.

It was a harrowing landing in Yerevan, Armenia, and all along the way, Cher stopped to wonder to herself how on earth she had gotten talked into this goodwill project. However, when she arrived there, she saw that although the people had little, they were all humble and polite. Cher was deeply touched by this experience, and it certainly served as a reality check for her as an American, and as a wealthy international star.

Everywhere she went people asked her all kinds of questions about America, and what it was like to live there. Were there really cowboys there? What was Jack Nicholson like? What did teenagers wear there? Everything about life in America fascinated them. Cher walked around in wonderment, seeing an entire country filled with people with coloring and facial structure identical to hers.

She also went to several orphanages and was deeply touched by the sad eyes of the children she found there. All of the orphanages were full of children who had lost their parents in the recent war, and there was never any hope of anyone adopting them. Cher found her trip a hauntingly bittersweet one. She had finally seen the land of her ancestors' roots, but what she found there was a country in shambles.

For the rest of 1993, Cher kept a pretty low profile. In January of 1994 she found herself back in the Top 40 on the American record charts. It was her latest teaming, with not one, but two male media stars, Beavis and Butt-head. As the obnoxious cartoon stars of the animated series on MTV bearing their name, the characters of Beavis and Butt-head, like *The Simpsons* and *Ren & Stimpy* before them, recorded their own album, *The Beavis and Butt-head Experience.* Well, at least Cher has a sense of humor about herself, or how else could we hear her singing the immortal lyrics "I got you Butt-head" on the airwaves?

With the exception of the fictional, precociously obnoxious cartoon characters grunting and snorting throughout, this particular hard-rocking cut is actually a fun new version of "I Got You Babe." Rather tastelessly, Cher and Beavis and Butt-head use the song to roundly put down Sonny Bono. While the ending music to the song plays, the following dialogue unravels.

Butt-head: So, like Cher. . . .

Cher: So, like Butt. . . .

Butt-head: Is it true you like used to be married to that Bono dude [pronouncing it "Bon-O" like the member of U-2]?

Cher: It's Bono. Sonny Bono.

Butt-head: Is that like that dude that's like a cop in San Diego?

Cher: No, he was the mayor of Palm Springs.

Butt-head: He's a wuss.

Cher: Yeah, well yeah.

Beavis: He sucks.

Cher: Yeah, well, kinda, yeah.

Cher wasn't about to allow an opportunity to zap Sonny to slip through her fingertips, even it if meant facilitating two cartoon dorks in insulting her ex-husband. And, to top it off, the album was on Geffen Records, headed by Sonny's old nemesis, David Geffen. Ever since their reunion on the *Letterman* show in 1988, Cher seemed to be on a relentless quest to put down Bono whenever she could.

In 1994 Cher was one of the "guest stars" in Robert Altman's next all-star cinema extravaganza, the satirical film about the world of high fashion *Ready to Wear (Prêt-à-Porter)*. The film starred Julia Roberts, Tim Robbins, Sophia Loren, Marcello Mastroianni, Kim Basinger, Anouk Aimée, Stephen Rea, Forest Whittaker, Lauren Bacall, Linda Hunt, Sally Kellerman, Tracey Ullman, Rossy De Palma, Lyle Lovett, Lili Taylor, Rupert Everett, Teri Garr, Harry Belafonte, Danny Aiello, and an international host of stars. Naturally a who's who of the fashion and modeling world was also featured: designers like Christian LeCroix and Jean Paul Gaultier, and models like Naomi Campbell and Jerry Hall. Fashion mavens from all over the world converge in Paris for a week's worth of *haute couture* events in the fabled City of Light. Cher was seen in another cameo appearance, arriving at one of the fashion events.

Three fashion editors (Hunt, Kellerman, and Ullman) vie for the attentions of a famous fashion photographer (Rea), the head of the Fashion Counsel is murdered, someone is being blackmailed, designers are having nervous breakdowns, and it seems that the entire cast is caught hopping in and out of bed with one another. Altman is a genius at assembling large casts of notable celebrities and weaving several stories together in an entertaining mix. He has a lot of fun with this high-profile melange of a cast in *Ready to Wear*. One of his famed devices is to have certain themes or recurring events running throughout his pictures. In this film he pokes fun at modern Paris's most notable flaw: the lack of clean-up-after-your-dog laws. Every few minutes someone else in this film laughably steps right into canine excrement on the sidewalk. Here is an assemblage of the world's most chic and cultured elite, and still they are walking through dog shit.

Cher is first seen on a television monitor, arriving at one of the Bulgari fashion events, looking smashing in black leather pants. Next, we see her being interviewed by Kim Basinger, who portrays perky but stressed television personality, Kitty Potter. "I'm as much of a fashion follower as I am a perpetrator," says Cher, appearing on camera as herself. She then tells Kitty, "I'm a victim as well as a perpetrator of all of this. And I think it's not about what you put on you body. I think it's more about what you are on the inside" (194). It's ironic but amusing to hear this humble statement coming from the collagen-enhanced lips of a woman who—in her lifetime—has worn countless millions of dollars worth of clothes. At this point in history, Cher's career-long wardrobe budget has already far exceeded that of even Marie Antoinette!

On October 8, 1994, Cher was one of the stars to perform in Memphis, Tennessee, at a mega-star-studded concert event called *Elvis Aaron Presley The Tribute*. The show, which was staged at the Pyramid Arena, was broadcast live as a pay-per-view event. Other than seeing "the king" perform when she was eleven years old, this was to be the closest she was to come to being a part of his legend. The evening was to make a lasting impression on her, and it was to give her the inspiration to record an Elvis-oriented song on her next solo album.

Also that year, Cher was heard on the album *The Glory of Gershwin*. Produced by Beatles producer George Martin, the concept was to team famed jazz harmonica player Larry Adler with some of the hottest stars of contemporary music and to record the classic songs of George and Ira Gershwin. *The Glory of Gershwin* was also an eightieth-birthday celebration in song for Adler. On the album, Sting can be heard singing a jaunty 1920s Charleston-style "Nice Work if You Can Get It," Kate Bush can be heard warbling "The Man I Love," Elton John sings of "Somebody to Watch over Me," and Cher proclaims "It Ain't Necessarily So."

The liner notes state, "Each artist chose the song they wanted to sing. They then negotiated a musical arrangement with Martin and turned up at the studio, where recordings were conducted live, in the presence of a full orchestra. None of them had ever worked this way before. Cher was not the only one to ask, 'What am I going to be singing while *they're* there?' In any event, she loved it" (195).

In an album filled with fun highlights, probably the most lusciously surprising cut is Cher's. The exquisite strings and full orchestra backing her, and a completely flattering arrangement, shows her off to delicious advantage. Cher starts the song soft and understated and warms it up to a vampy finale. "It Ain't Necessarily So" makes one realize how much better her ill-fated 1970s standards album *Bittersweet White Light* might have been if George Martin had been at the helm.

To top it all off, in the fall of 1994, Cher launched her own short-lived mail-order company, entitled Sanctuary. It was a marketing idea to sell various "Gothic"-themed products. The cover and the artwork of her 1991 album *Love Hurts* had been designed with very Gothic touches— Gothic patterns, hearts, flaming torches, Tarot cards, all of that dark era of knights and mysticism, with a slight witchcraft bent. It was Cher's way of leaping onto the Gothic bandwagon, and selling some candles and gargoyles along the way. Sanctuary didn't end up to be a huge success for Cher, but it was certainly another creative notch in her multimedia belt.

Only Cher could spend a calendar year in the company of such diverse compatriots as she did in 1994. From Beavis and Butt-head, to the height of the Paris fashion world, to Elvis Presley, to George Gershwin. It was just a typical year in the life of the world's most flexible pop diva.

The week of March 25, 1995, Cher was back in the Number 1 spot on the British record charts. This time around she was singing with Chrissie Hynde and Neneh Cherry, with Eric Clapton on guitar. The song they recorded together was a touching all-star version of the Judds' inspirational country hit, "Love Can Build a Bridge." Between Cher's vibrato, Chrissie's gravelly growl, and Cherry's snappy delivery, this trio of rock divas sounds great together. "Love Can Build a Bridge" was originally recorded as a benefit for the homelessness charity Comic Relief, and became one of the three biggest British hits of her entire career. Yet the single wasn't even released in America—and at present is only available in the United States as an import.

Having recorded three excellent Gold and Platinum rock and roll albums on Geffen Records (and her recent Number 1 British *Greatest Hits* album), and producing over a dozen hit singles on the charts from them, Cher left Geffen Records.

In 1995 she released her thirty-first album, *It's a Man's World*—in

Europe only. It was her first album for Reprise Records. Her last four singles never even made the charts in America, but she was currently bigger than ever in England. The *Love Hurts* and *Cher's Greatest Hits 1965–1992* albums and the singles "The Shoop Shoop Song (It's in His Kiss)" and "Love Can Build a Bridge" were all huge Number 1 records in the United Kingdom in the early 1990s. Yet she had never had a Number 1 album in America and hadn't scored a Number 1 U.S. hit single since "Dark Lady" laughed and danced its way up the charts in 1975.

Instead of even courting the American musical market, Cher blew off the notoriously fickle and jaded United States and aimed all of her attention at the British marketplace, where she was still considered a musical trendsetter and hit maker. Her decision proved right on target. In America, one lousy review in *Rolling Stone* magazine might sink an album before it was even given a listen.

Cher cultivated the British media by making television appearances aplenty to make sure that everyone in England knew that she had a new album. On December 24, 1995, she was the star of her own UK-only holiday television special, *Christmas with Cher* on the ITV network. On January 9, 1996, she was seen performing the song "One by One" on *National Lottery Live* on BBC1-TV.

The fourteen-cut *It's a Man's World* album was released in Europe in time for Christmas 1995, and reached Number 10 in England in February of 1996. It produced four hit singles on the British singles charts: "Walking in Memphis" (Number 11), "One by One" (Number 7), "Not Enough Love in the World," (Number 31), and "The Sun Ain't Gonna Shine Anymore" (Number 26).

When the American version of *It's a Man's World* was released in June of 1996, so many alterations had been made to it that it is not the same album at all. First of all, it was resequenced, some of songs were drastically remixed, dramatic introductions were sheered off, and three of the songs—"I Wouldn't Treat a Dog (The Way You Treated Me)," "Shape of Things to Come," and "Don't Come Around Here Tonight"—were dropped altogether.

For anyone who has only heard the American version of *It's a Man's World*, listening to the European one is a real revelation. It is more multi-textured, and has a lot more music on its tracks. "Not Enough Love in the World" has an entirely different feeling to it, featuring Cher singing to sparse and stripped-down tracks with an organ, which is reminiscent of Procol Harum's "A Whiter Shade of Pale," one of her favorite songs.

The original version of "One by One" has very dominant background chorus vocals repeating, among other things, "dear daddy, dear daddy." There is also a saxophone solo in the middle of the British version that is entirely missing in the American version of the track. "Angels Running" starts off slower with Cher's voice, and percussion embellishments. It also features stripped-down instrumentation in the beginning, and two musical bridges that are absent from the U.S. release. "What About the Moonlight" likewise has a completely different intro and new musical tracks throughout. The American version has heavier chorus vocals, and the European version has only Cher on the intro with very basic tracks. And the song "Gunman" has Cher reading several verses at the top of the song and at the ending, both of which were removed from its U.S. counterpart. To top it all off, those who purchased the American version of this album missed La Cher on the song "Shape of Things to Come" delivering the sage advice, "Come on baby, get your ass in gear."

The European version is also very different physically from the subsequent American release entitled *It's a Man's World*. When the album was released in the States, Reprise Records bought a full-page full-color advertisement to announce the new Cher LP, presenting a blowup of the Cher-dressed-as-Eve photo. The headline read "It's a man's world. Yeah, right" and the name "Cher" spelled out in sleek, hot-pink letters.

According to Cher, *It's a Man's World* was a complete departure for her. "[It] was me experimenting with me. I didn't want to sound like I've always sounded on records, because I'm kind of bored with it. Some songs like 'If I Could Turn Back Time,' I like, but on a lot of albums, I think I'm kind of pukey! The problem with having a really distinctive voice is that if you like it, great, but if not, people can't stand [your album,] and you're blown out of the water the first three songs" (196).

She explained to *Billboard* magazine's Jim Bessman how she tried to sound like something different than the highly identifiable power-ballad vibrato voice she had promoted on her Geffen Records recordings. "I worked really hard to have more control and not use my vibrato and other things. I didn't like my voice. It's still me—you know it's me, and there's no getting around it. But on some songs, like 'One by One' and 'The Gunman,' you don't know it's me right away" (196).

It's a Man's World featured songs in an exotic, but generally somber vein. "It's kind of a sad record," she admitted. "I have two speeds—really sad and kick ass—but this is a bittersweet kind of album" (196). One of the most effective songs on the album is Cher's new version of the

Walker Brothers' 1966 hit, "The Sun Ain't Gonna Shine (Anymore)." She was the first to admit that she was around for the first version of this song. "I've been doing this for 32 years now," she said. "I was there when it hit the first time Sonny and I played with them on TV" (196). Her interpretation of the song had that old Phil Spector feeling to it, creating a distinctive beat and a very "Wall of Sound"–sounding backing track.

To come up with the kind of album that she wanted to record, Cher worked with some of London's hottest contemporary record producers, including Christopher Neil, Greg Penny, Stephen Lipson, and Trevor Horn. With regard to using four different producers, Cher explained, "I don't like working with one producer. I like the idea of producers picking songs they like, because that way they do their best job in the songs they pick, whereas if they do the whole album, it seems that they only love their songs, and the rest they just do" (196).

Even in its altered state, it was a shame that this album never caught on in the States since it is undeniably one of the best albums of her career. Unlike her trio of hard-rocking studio albums for Geffen Records, *It's a Man's World* is pure pop music, 1990s style. Her singing on it is more controlled and more effectively moody than she had sounded since her *Foxy Lady* album in 1972.

When it was initially released in America, the first pressing of the *It's a Man's World* CD was engraved with a "limited edition" hologram of the cover image of Cher as Eve in the Garden of Eden with a ripe red apple and huge live snake draped across her chest and wrapped around her arm. The week of July 13, 1996, the album made its debut on the *Billboard* charts at a promising Number 64, but never made it any higher. That same week, the single "One by One" made it up to its peak, Number 52. The one bright aspect of the release was that the disco remix single version of "One by One" became a Top 10 dance hit for Cher.

It's a Man's World was a hit with Cher's critics. Stephen Holden wrote in the *New York Times*,

> From an artistic standpoint, this soulful collection of grown-up pop songs, a version of which was released in England last November, is the high point of her recording career. Capped by an iconoclastic rendition of " 'It's a Man's, Man's, World," James Brown's ode to male supremacy, the album evokes the hard emotional lessons learned by a woman who has loved too well, but not wisely. . . . the album suggests that Cher, who has been saddled with the tabloid image of a boy crazy perpetual adolescent, has achieved a kind of emotional maturity (24).

Even fickle *Rolling Stone* magazine described it as *"It's a Man's World,* her first in five years, on which her voice sounds better than ever" (61). To promote the album, Cher starred in a stylish video for the song "Walking in Memphis." However, it went unnoticed in the United States. In Britain, she scored four Top 40 hits; in America she couldn't even muster one. Not even her crackerjack hot video—of Cher dressed like Elvis Presley himself and singing the song "Walking in Memphis"—sparked any interest in America.

Only her five-cut CD single of "One by One" gave her any visibility in America. In one of the "Americanized" remixes of the song, the American branch of her new record company felt compelled to add a guest solo by rapper Melle Mel in the middle of the song to try to appeal to the stateside audiences. It did little or nothing to help her American record sales on the pop charts.

One of the songs that she was the proudest of was her touching interpretation of the 1991 hit "Walking in Memphis." In 1999, amid her victorious "Believe" concert tour, Cher was to intro it by saying,

> This next song that I'm gonna do has a very sad beginning, but a really cool ending. So, there's a man—a singer, a really good singer named Marc Cohn, and he did this song called "Walking in Memphis," and he had a huge hit. And then later—years later, I thought, "I'll do it.'" And I had a huge "bomb." It was like a major "bomb." Not exactly like in the infomercial category, but very close to it. I just want to get the reference straight, so everyone knows what I'm talking about (197).

Cher had her own lifelong Elvis Presley fixation, and performing in Memphis at the 1994 Presley tribute made her recording of this song all the more important to her. It was a personal tribute to her initial rock idol. Cher recalled seeing him in concert when she was eleven years old and explained,

> Elvis is the definitive rock & roll attitude. He was the real deal, and people have expanded on it, but the baseline was a rebellious guy who looked different. There's been the Sonny & Cher version of Elvis, the David Bowie version of Elvis, the Marilyn Manson version of Elvis, but basically you're getting back to a guy who didn't look the same and had an attitude, and everyone's just copped on that and done their own version (23).

To complete her Elvis homage, Cher starred in her own video of "Walking in Memphis." She is seen in the video singing the song as though she is narrating it. Dressed as a girl singer in fishnets, Cher was filmed sitting on the first step of a Greyhound bus in high heels, looking like a brunette Marilyn Monroe in the publicity stills for the 1956 movie *Bus Stop*. In the rest of the action, Cher is seen as an Elvis impersonator. As a "drag king," Cher makes a striking man in two-toned shoes, and ultimately in blue suede shoes.

When Chastity Bono interviewed her mother in 1996 for *Advocate* magazine, she asked Cher to describe her *It's a Man's World* album. "Oh, I don't know—who knows what it's like?" said the modest pop diva. "It's music. I sing it, you know. It's too hard for me to say, 'Oh, it's a fabulous album!' Who knows? It's kind of good though. It doesn't suck" (26).

Although Cher had asked to be released from Geffen Records, her long-time ally, David Geffen, was quoted in the *New York Times* as having said, "Cher is the proverbial cat with nine lives. She's really a very delicate piece of machinery. People think she's tough, but the truth is she's a pussycat who has had to feign toughness in order to keep from being killed" (24).

Speaking of her recording career up until that point, she was to explain, "As a wife, mother and recording artist who was gigging constantly, I had to juggle so many balls at once that I didn't have time to think. It's not been a deep musical career, and I've always dressed kind of bizarre. But I think my voice has gotten better, and so has my choice of music" (24).

In between the fall 1995 release of the European version of *It's a Man's World* and the June 1996 release of its shorter American version, two very important things happened in Cher's life: her return to the movies and her fiftieth birthday. First up on her agenda was the film *Faithful*, which opened in New York City on April 3, 1996.

While battling the Epstein-Barr virus, launching an infomercial career, and watching Chastity be bedeviled by the tabloid newspapers, Cher had reportedly turned down two very important films in the late 1980s and early 1990s: *War of the Roses* and *Thelma & Louise*. It is interesting to imagine Cher in both of these films. It was ultimately Kathleen Turner who played the lead in 1989's *War of the Roses*, a movie about a bitter divorce. And what would have been more interesting than to see Cher play the role played by Susan Sarandon in 1991's *Thelma & Louise*, or the role played by Geena Davis?

After two cameo roles as herself in *The Player* and *Ready to Wear*, Cher chose as her return to cinema 1996's *Faithful*. Six years had passed between *Mermaids* and *Faithful*. What was the big creative gap about? "Well, first of all," she explained, "I was sick [with Epstein-Barr virus]. Also, it is so hard sometimes having no private life and being in the public eye so much. Being under scrutiny and having every move you make not only talked about but lied about. When you get too hot sometimes, it's not comfortable" (26). She also felt that she had been juggling too many activities at once. "It seems like I should have enough time for both music and films," she surmised, "but one usually ends up taking the back seat" (196).

Faithful is a highly entertaining little film, but it is clearly adopted from a four-character play, and 99 percent of the action is in dialogue. It is all too often entertaining for the wrong reasons. Since Cher is in almost every frame of this film, there is ample screen time to examine the contours of her face. Although she and Chazz Palminteri talk nonstop for the first hour of the film, one cannot keep one's eyes off of Cher's face. First of all, her lips are so oddly puffed up from collagen injections. Then there was her mouth, which had morphed—in the last decade and a half—from the jagged-toothed smile of her youth into a Chiclets-like row of perfectly spaced piano keys. It also appeared in this film that her face was so taut from plastic surgery that it didn't move—or couldn't move—when she speaks.

Faithful was written as a play by Chazz Palminteri, and this film was co-executive produced by scandal-ridden New York City nightclub owner Peter Gatien (The Limelight) and coproduced by Robert De Niro. It was directed by Paul Mazursky, and costarred Cher with Palminteri, Mazursky, and Ryan O'Neal, the latter as the husband who wants her dead. Cher plays red-haired Maggie, who is confronted with an intruder to her house (Palminteri) who informs her that her husband wants her murdered and that he is the hired killer. In the ensuing dialogue, Palminteri confesses his self-doubts and talks to his therapist (Mazursky) about his many conflicts. Cher subsequently attempts to seduce him into letting her free. At several points, one is not certain who is setting up whom in the plot of the film. Was it really Ryan who hired the killer? Did Cher hire the killer to look like her husband was plotting to kill her? Was Cher going to commit suicide, but wanted to hire a killer and subsequently implicate her husband? Together they hatch a plan to get rid of Cher's conniving husband (O'Neal) in this talkative black comedy of errors.

The advertisement in the Arts & Leisure section of the *New York Times* for *Faithful* depicted Cher as bound and gagged, outlined with four red concentric circles forming a bullseye. The headline read "After 20 years of marriage, she thought she was the target of her husband's affection. She was only part right." Her husband wasn't the only one who was gunning for Cher in this movie; there were the film critics to consider.

"Even loyal fans of Cher may be tested by [this] new film," wrote Barbara Shulgasser in the *San Francisco Examiner*.

> "I love Cher. What can I do? I am powerless to do anything but give her a lot of leeway. But leeway is insufficient in the case of *Faithful*. *Faithful* requires a governor's pardon. . . . Cher is looking a little too collagened to seem real, but given the many convolutions of her career, she probably sees herself as way beyond real anymore. She still has that dry, deadpan and jaded affect that plays well on screen (198).

Mike Clark in *USA Today* claimed, "This is Cher's first movie since *Mermaids*, and something beyond normal aging seems to have taken hold. Since our visual choices in the first hour are all but restricted to Cher, pro killer Palminteri and a very handsome house, facial immobility takes on added significance. . . . If I had *Diabolique* and *Faithful* in theaters simultaneously, I'd hire a hit man to take myself out" (199).

In the *San Francisco Chronicle* Peter Stack said, "Even Cher's good looks can't save *Faithful*. . . . *Faithful* seems as if it ought to be more fun than it really is" (200). And, Stacey Richter reported in the *Tucson Weekly*, "Palminteri and Cher have a nice chemistry between them and the movie has a decent number of satisfying moments. I just wish the actors didn't keep saying the word 'faithful' over and over, with unsettling emphasis" (201).

Weeks later, Stephen Holden of the *New York Times* wrote, "This dark marital comedy, in which she stars with Ryan O'Neal and Chazz Palminteri, died at the box-office two weeks after it opened last April" (24). Indeed, that is exactly what happened. Even Cher knew that it was not a great piece of filmmaking. "It was no loss," she said. "At least the reviews said it was nice to see me acting again" (24).

Not long after the brief run of *Faithful* came May 20, 1996, Cher's fiftieth birthday. As it approached, did she dread it? "I guess so," she admitted. "And then I thought, 'Well, this isn't so bad.' I was really nervous about turning 40, but that was the best year of my life. I did three movies, an album, I met Robert, my kids were still at home, and it was just a blast" (61). After it was over, she had to admit, "I thought it was going to be awful. But it was a day just like any other day, and I was having a really good time" (24). However, when *Rolling Stone* magazine asked her to name something good about becoming fifty, Cher flatly replied, "I can't think of anything good about being 50" (61).

One of the aspects of this milestone birthday that annoyed her the most was that she wasn't in a relationship when it took place. According to her that year, "Rob [Camilletti] was my best relationship ever, and when we broke up I was devastated. But we're still best friends. Since Rob, I have had one relationship [Richie Sambora], and it was great, but it lasted for about a minute and a half" (24).

In September of 1996, Cher was one of the celebrities who was heard on the Kid Rhino record album *For Our Children Too*. This all-star children's album of nursery rhymes and story songs also featured Celine Dion, Elton John, Faith Hill, Natalie Cole, Seal, and Carly Simon and James Taylor. Cher's contribution to this album was the song, "A Dream Is a Wish Your Heart Makes," from the 1950 Disney animated film *Cinderella*. The profits from the album went to the Pediatric AIDS Foundation.

Regardless of the lukewarm reception of her latest album, the crash of her latest film, and the sting of turning fifty, what Cher was most excited about was her film directing debut. *If These Walls Could Talk* was an all-star film for, by, and about women, and one of the most important moral issues of the twentieth century, abortion—and more specifically a woman's right to make decisions about her own body.

When Demi Moore's production company contacted Cher originally, it was to offer her an acting role. She told them she would only accept it if she could direct as well—and they agreed.

A trilogy film, *If These Walls Could Talk* centered around three different abortion issues in three different decades. Explained Cher,

> It's about this house in the period of the '50s, the '70s, and '96. The women in it find themselves with unwanted pregnancies. It is Demi Moore's project, and Demi plays the woman in the '50s, and Sissy Spacek plays the woman in the '70s, and Anne Heche plays the young girl in the '90s. I play the doctor. I loved doing it. I love the subject matter, and I love directing, and I really love working on something that is meaningful (26).

Although she can be conservative with some of her politics, and liberal with others, it wasn't a stretch to guess what side of the fence her sympathies were on when it came to abortion rights.

> If you saw my film, you know how I feel. It's nobody's business what happens to any woman's body but hers. It's her responsibility—not that she's

going to be happy with whatever choice she makes—but she has to be the person to make it. That you could legislate someone's body is almost an impossibility for me to comprehend. I guarantee if men could have babies, we wouldn't have to worry about these laws (23).

During the elder George Bush years, specifically in 1989, Cher had already gone on record with regard to defending women's rights and being militantly pro-choice. "This is my country, right or wrong this is not my government, right or wrong. I was thinking, 'If they ever overturn Roe vs. Wade, am I going to become a militant? Am I going to be out there marching and going to jail? Absolutely, I'm not going to stand for that for a second!" she claimed (119).

According to Cher, one of the reasons that this film project was so important to her was the fact that she herself had an abortion in the 1970s before she had become pregnant with Elijah. She wanted to tell this story with honesty and realism. According to her

I made fifty decisions a day when we were doing *If These Walls Could Talk*. It was fun keeping all those plates in the air, but it was also relentless. . . . When we were done shooting for the day, I had to watch the dailies, to make sure I had everything I needed. Then I went home dead and exhausted (25).

The film's cast included some of the biggest women's names in 1990s Hollywood, including Sissy Spacek, Demi Moore, Anne Heche, C. C. H. Pounder, Shirley Knight, Jada Pinkett, Lindsay Crouse, Diana Scarwid, and Cher. Even the directors were women. While Nancy Savoca directed the first two segments of this film, the third segment was directed by Cher.

In the "1996" episode of *If These Walls Could Talk*, Cher, in her role as an abortion clinic doctor, gets to deliver the line, "I remember what it was like when it was illegal for women to make this decision. I don't want to see those days come again" (202). It was a line Cher could have scripted herself. Amid the plot of the Cher-directed segment, there is an abortion clinic protest, and a large, angry crowd is gathered. In this particular segment, there is a photographer at the forefront of the crowd, clicking pictures. The photographer is played by none other than Cher's ex-boyfriend Robert Camilletti.

Two other familiar faces from Cher's film career are also seen in her section of *If These Walls Could Talk*. They are Craig T. Nelson and Diana Scarwid—both of whom appeared with Cher in *Silkwood*.

Directing this film segment was an important step that Cher had always wanted to take, ever since she first started working on major movies in the 1980s. How did she like being on the other side of the camera for a change? "Oh, I loved it!" she proclaimed.

> And, I'd love to do it again at any time. I want to work on meaningful projects. It's great to do things that are fun and entertaining, but it really also has to have an equal part of something that will make people feel something important and meaningful. Film is such a great way to sneak up on people and show them how other people feel, people that they might not even have the chance to meet or associate with or think they could be friends with. It's a great way to change opinions (23).

As a director, Cher came through with flying colors, and *If These Walls Could Talk* became the most-watched original movie in HBO cable-TV history. The movie has a surprise ending, when a gunman comes into the clinic for vengeance. As the credits of this fascinating and somewhat disturbing film are rolling, Cher's song "One by One" plays.

With regard to Cher's entry into the world of directing, Chazz Palminteri claimed,

> When you become a star, and you're not hungry anymore, one of the things that keeps you a star is your work ethic. Cher's very regimented. She gets up at a certain time, works out, has a chef that cooks certain things for her to stay in great shape, has a voice teacher come every few days for a singing lesson and a chiropractor who gives her adjustments. She's also one of the smartest people I've ever met. Mark my words, she will become an A-list director one day, guaranteed (24).

When Cher had been asked in 1989 what kind of movie roles she longed to play, she confessed that she only wanted to find important leading roles. She pondered, "I would like to have played [General George] Patton in *Patton,* Rocky in *Rocky* and Vivian Leigh's part in *Gone with the Wind"* (119). However, the ten years that followed *Moonstruck* had been frustrating ones for fans of Cher's films. She had appeared in five films, and only two of them, *Mermaids* and *If These Walls Could Talk,* provided her with enough material to really work with on screen. She reported in 1996, "I'm getting scripts and stuff like that, but I don't want to make the same mistake like when I did *Faithful,* and wasn't sure that I should be doing it" (26).

In one of her strangest career moves, in 1996 Cher was one of the celebrities to lend her voice to a computer game called "9." A product of Tribeca Interactive, this particular computer game follows several fictional characters through a disaster-filled resort house. Among the other celebrities heard on this interactive screen game are Christopher Reeve, James Belushi, and Steve Tyler and Joe Perry of Aerosmith. Cher's a rock star! She's a movie star! She's a computer game! Who else but Cher could make so many multimedia moves, and still keep it somehow cohesive?

There were lots of projects that she was involved in during the first seven years of the 1990s, but it hadn't been her most creative era. So, trapped in the public's perception of her, and the weight of her own fame, did Cher ever get tired of being "Cher" the star? According to her, "Yeah, I did that for four, five years. How long have I been gone. . . . I just puttered around. I don't know. I was kinda happy not to be 'Cher' for a while" (61).

Assessing the decade of the 1990s from a 1996 standpoint, Cher admitted at the age of fifty, "I've had huge ups and downs in my life, and I've made some stupid, stupid mistakes and bad choices. But no matter what I'm going through at the moment, somehow I always think the future is going to be better, and somehow it always is" (24).

The year 1997 was one of those years in which Cher seemed to disappear from the public eye again. After a movie that the critics savaged, and an album that was a smash in Britain yet only moderately successful in America, and her cinematic directing debut, it was a year without high-profile Cher. However, amid the silence, there was talk about an important new movie role, and discussion about some new directions for her next album.

On January 6, 1998, Cher flew to London, where she was recording her next album. She was scheduled to make a public appearance at the department store Harrod's. For its annual storewide January sale, the store had a tradition of featuring a huge star to kick off the event. The big star that year was someone who was a pro when it came to the sport of shopping—Cher. Little did she know at the time, but following a relatively low-keyed twelve months, she was about to become one of the most seen and most talked about stars of 1998 and 1999. Her life was about to leap back in the fast lane and take several unexpected turns, one after another.

16

FAREWELL TO SONNY

Ever since Sonny Bono had been elected to Congress in 1994, he was a welcomed addition to the Washington, D.C., scene, not only as a legislator, but as the brunt of an endless barrage of jokes and jibes in the press. If anyone had the image of this half of the 1960s duo of Sonny & Cher as a dyed-in-the-wool radically liberal post-hippie singer/songwriter, their preconceptions were quickly dispelled.

Always a conservative thinker when it came to laws and government, he was still against drugs and generally too far along the right-wing path on any issue. He was also very vocal with regard to upholding laws that prevented gay couples from marrying. This was to drive a wedge between him and his daughter Chastity. It also gave his ex-wife Cher more ammunition when she wanted to publicly put him down for his politics.

Known for his sense of humor by television audiences who had grown up with his image on the screen, Sonny the politician had it all in perspective. Commenting on his latest career path, Bono laughed, "The last thing I thought I would be is a congressman, given all the bobcat vests I used to wear" (154).

Among the things that drew voters to him was this sense of humor, and his ability to see politics for what they were. When he was making his unsuccessful 1992 attempt at running for a seat in the U.S. Senate, he was asked of his qualifications. In the April 22, 1992, issue of the *Los Angeles Times,* Sonny stated, "What is qualified? What have I been qualified for in my life? I haven't been qualified to be a mayor. I'm not qualified to be a songwriter. I'm not qualified to be a TV producer. I'm not qualified to be a successful businessman. And so, I don't know what 'qualified' means. And I think people get too hung up on that in a way you know" (203).

What he was qualified for was getting people's attention and speaking his mind in a way that made sense. When Sonny won the election in 1994, he headed off to Washington, D.C., to make his voice and opinions heard. According to the December 12, 1994, issue of *U.S. News & World Report*, when he was presented his congressional ID badge, he was quoted as saying, "That's cool" (203).

As he became more and more interested in politics, he and his wife, Mary, attended a function where Senator Phil Gramm, Republican from Texas, spoke. Recalled Sonny, "I wanted to be a Senator and went to one of his affairs and he said something like, 'You can't eat corn if you ain't a pig.' I said to my wife, 'What the hell does that mean' " (203).

One of the first things he wanted to do in Congress was to attempt to cut through a lot of the legal jargon and "mumbo jumbo" that lawyers-turned-congressmen loved to hurl about, simply to make it sound like they knew what they were talking about. Sonny had the distinction of being one of two non-lawyers on the House Judiciary Committee. In the middle of the Judiciary Committee's debate about a crime bill, Bono interrupted the proceedings to announce that he had enough of the "legalese" he had heard that day. "Boy, it's flying in this room like I can't believe today. Now certainly everyone has demonstrated their ability in legal knowledge, so wouldn't it be nice if we vote on this thing and just pass this thing" (204).

He said, from his perspective on both politics and show business, "I don't know if politicians have the grip on reality that entertainers do. [Entertainers] know if they disregard a message from the people they could lose their careers" (204). According to him at the time, he was familiar with life on both sides of the streets. "I was with Sam Cooke the night he was killed. That's the streets. You get a strong perception of the dues that have been paid" (204).

From the time he arrived in Washington, everyone seemed to know who he was, and they were all curious to see him in action. Obviously, this wasn't the first time that a Hollywood actor changed jobs and went into politics. But this was certainly the first time a rock and roll star from the 1960s had been elected to Congress. Whether his fellow congress-men and congresswomen agreed with his politics or not, he soon found himself beloved by everyone for his warmth and honesty. One of his first really high-profile functions was a Press Club Foundation dinner, held in January of 1995.

According to several sources, his address at this particular dinner was key in winning a favorable reputation in the Capitol city. One of his main issues in Washington was his dislike of bureaucracy and red tape. Explaining the evolution of how he got into politics in the first place, in his address, Bono said,

> I wanted to get a license to put a sign on my restaurant. I couldn't get back in show business, so I thought I would cook pasta for the rest of my life. I was fortunate enough to get married again and marry a beautiful woman, so I didn't care. I've got a great-looking wife, way better looking than Cher. She's taller, and she's 33. Anyway, we bought a restaurant, moved down to Palm Springs, and I was going to retire and kick back. And I wanted to get a sign, and I went to the city and said I would like to get a sign. They said, "You would?" I said, "Yeah." "You would?" I said, "Yeah." "What do you want exactly?" I said, "I want to get a sign." "Do you realize what you're asking for?" I said, "I think so. I would like to get a sign that says 'Bono Restaurant.' " And he said, "You don't just get a sign. This is city government." I said, "I'm sorry." He said, "Fill this out and bring it back tomorrow." So I brought it back tomorrow. And he said, "Come back in three more weeks." Then he said, "Don't come back for a while." So, I started not to like this guy. We bought the restaurant, so I was making payments now, but I couldn't open it because I couldn't get a sign. So that's when I became fascinated with politics. . . . I never saw anything so confusing in my life, and illogical. So finally I went there and said, "Listen, I worked out our problem." And he said, "You can't have worked out our problem." I said, "I have," and he said, "You can't." I said, "I have." He said, "We have to work out your problem." I said "No, I worked it out. I'm going to run for mayor and fire you." I ran for mayor and I fired him. But, I'm not totally heartless. He's my gardener now (203).

Regarding that particular speech, Representative Joe Scarborough, Republican from Florida, stated, "Sonny had a sort of reputation as somebody that wasn't exceptionally bright. Then the guy turned around and delivered what I thought was 30 minutes of just brilliant humor. And my opinion of him changed in a second" (205).

Sonny was so popular in his own California district, and in Washington, that in 1996, he ran again to stay in his congressional post, and again won. Since he had claimed credit for eliminating a reported $2.5-million deficit in Palm Springs while he was the mayor, his voting base was very impressed with the job that he was doing.

However, not everyone who loved him agreed with his political stance. One of the most defining issues that he addressed in Congress was the introduction of what was called the Defense of Marriage Act, in 1996. It gives the individual fifty states the right to deny same-sex marriages, regardless of what other states subsequently vote to recognize.

In the *New York Times* (July 9, 1997), his daughter Chastity aired her own views on this subject.

I would have a lot more respect for him if he really was anti-gay and voted this way, as opposed to being so great about it, which he was when I came out. He said stuff to me like, "Sometimes you have to go according to the people who got you there," the constituent thing, that old excuse. And when I told him that job discrimination against gays is legal in 41 states, he actually said to me that that was unconstitutional—while he was a Congressman. Frightening (191).

"The problem with my father is that he is hypocritical," Chastity said to the British publication *OK!* (206). As 1997 came to a close, Chastity and her father were at odds with each other.

Cher was also very critical of her ex-husband's politics. She stated publicly that she couldn't believe that Sonny had actually become a Republican, let alone a congressman. Although she disliked his politics, she had to admit that there would always be a lifelong bond. Cher said on CNN in 1997, "No one is ever going to understand our relationship but Sonny and Cher. I have a bond that's close to Sonny, nothing will ever break it. Sonny and I could sit down in a room and in two seconds be making jokes. It was a bond before we knew each other, and it's going to be a bond when we're both dead" (207).

As December of 1997 rolled around, everyone's attention was taken by the Christmas and New Year's season. Cher was planning her next album. Chastity was working as a consultant on the controversial ABC-TV sitcom *Ellen*, whose star, Ellen DeGeneres, had just recently announced that she—and her fictional TV character—was a lesbian. And Sonny Bono, Mary, and their two young children were looking forward to a post-Christmas ski holiday.

Sonny had been skiing in the Lake Tahoe area for over two decades, and he loved the peace and relaxation that came from sailing down the beautiful tree-lined snow-covered mountains of California and Nevada.

In addition to the great skiing, there is also a breathtaking view of the huge freshwater lake from the top.

According to Anne Bego, who was skiing at Heavenly resort the first week in January of 1998,

> I was standing in line to get on the chair, and I heard a familiar voice from behind me. It sounded just like Sonny Bono. I turned around, and there he was, talking to someone. There were no bodyguards, no fans, nothing that would draw anyone's attention to him other than the sound of his voice. He appeared to be there just to ski and have a great time, like the rest of us. He was obviously enjoying the skiing and the serenity of the mountains, and no one seemed to be bothering him or trying to get his attention (208).

On Monday, January 5, 1998, Sonny, Mary, and their two children got up, put on their ski gear, and headed for Heavenly Ski Resort. As was often their pattern, Sonny would ski off onto more difficult turf at the top of the mountain, and Mary and their two children would take their time on more child-friendly slopes. This was the case on that particular day. Sonny was last seen alive by his family at 1:30 p.m. (Pacific Standard Time), taking the ski lift ahead of his wife, nine-year-old son Chesare, and six-year-old daughter Chianna. As was their habit, if they got separated, they would all meet at the bottom of the hill later in the afternoon.

Experienced skiers have a habit of going off the packed-down snow of the official trails. Lured by fresh snow, they will ski off past the warning signs and into the danger of the trees. Only minutes after getting off the chair lift at the top of Upper Orion slope, Sonny took such a turn off of the beaten track, where other skiers stayed. That particular turn was to end in tragedy.

According to Mary Bono, they all got to the top of Upper Orion, and got separated. "Sonny took off," she explained, "and he skied so beautifully. He hadn't fallen all week, and his form was unreal. Chesy took off after him and then, the strangest thing—Chesare caught an edge and started to fall" (209). Her attention was diverted by her son losing his balance. And then Sonny was gone from sight.

When she didn't see Sonny, Mary just figured that he had skied ahead of them. Sonny turned off into the trees near the top of the slope, apparently lost control, and struck a tree with such downhill velocity that the force of his head against the tree stripped bark from it. Unbeknownst to his wife and children, they had skied right past him and were unaware there was a problem. At first, Mary was concerned, but not worried.

In spite of all of the outrageous outfits that had come before, Cher sported her wildest one yet on the cover of 1979's *Take Me Home* album. (*Casablanca Records/MJB Photo Archives*)

Cher enraged feminist groups when she released her 1979 *Prisoner* album with this naked sex slave photo on the cover. (*Casablanca Records/MJB Photo Archives*)

Cher in 1980, walking down Fifth Avenue in New York City with famed guitar player Les Dudek. Together they formed a short-lived rock band, Black Rose. (*AP/Wide World Photos*)

By 1980 Cher already had her sights set on becoming a film star. She had secured the rights to the 1940s film *The Enchanted Cottage* in hopes of starring in it. (*Harry Langdon/Casablanca Records/MJB Photo Archives*)

Cher's road to becoming a serious actress began with the Broadway play *Come Back to the Five and Dime, Jimmy Dean, Jimmy Dean.* Cher on December 29, 1980, during rehearsals, with her costars Karen Black and Sandy Dennis (left) and their director, Robert Altman (right). (*AP/Wide World Photos*)

After the Broadway run of *Jimmy Dean,* Altman captured Cher and her costars on film. (*Playbill*)

A trio of legendary ladies: film stars Lillian Gish and Lena Horne at the 1982 Tony Awards with Broadway star Cher. (*AP/Wide World Photos*)

After seeing Cher in *Come Back to the Five and Dime, Jimmy Dean, Jimmy Dean,* film director Mike Nichols offered her a lead role in *Silkwood.* Portraying the role of lesbian factory worker Dolly, Cher was forbidden to wear makeup, which horrified her. (*Anchor Bay Entertainment/MJB Photo Archives*)

Meryl Streep as Karen Silkwood, Kurt Russell as her boyfriend, and Cher as her roommate. Together, the three portrayed real-life workers in a Texas nuclear plant. (*Anchor Bay Entertainment/MJB Photo Archives*)

In *Silkwood*, movie audiences were able to see Cher in a whole new light as an actress. She was also nominated for a "Best Supporting Actress" Academy Award for her performance. (*Anchor Bay Entertainment/MJB Photo Archives*)

Cher accepting the Golden Globe Award for her performance in *Silkwood*, January 29, 1984. (*AP/Wide World Photos*)

Cher and Sam Elliott in *Mask*. As the mother of a seriously deformed but magical child named Rocky, Cher's performance touched movie fans deeply. (*Universal Pictures/MJB Photo Archives*)

Real-life biker-chick-mom Rusty Dennis gave Cher a role she could really sink her teeth into in 1984's *Mask*. (*Universal Pictures/MJB Photo Archives*)

Kind of a drag: Cher at Harvard picking up the annual Hasty Pudding Award, February 13, 1985. (*AP/Wide World Photos*)

In the 1980s Cher changed boyfriends almost as quickly as she changed hairstyles. With TV executive Josh Donen at a party at Manhattan's Palladium following the MTV Awards, September 14, 1985. (*AP/Wide World Photos*)

After *Silkwood* and *Mask,* Cher went back to her fashion chameleon ways. For a short time in the 1980s she even went blonde. (*Steve Granitz/Celebrity Photos*)

With her favorite designer Bob Mackie on her arm, Cher sweeps into New York City's Metropolitan Museum to attend the opening of "The Costumes of Royal India" exhibit in 1985. (*AP/Wide World Photos*)

Sporting one of the most bizarre outfits of her entire career, Cher was a
presenter at the 1986 Academy Awards when Don Ameche (left) won his
Oscar. (*AP/Wide World Photos*)

Susan Sarandon, Michelle Pfeiffer, and Cher in the 1987 hit film *The Witches of Eastwick*. (*Warner Brothers Pictures/MJB Photo Archives*)

Cher as public defender Kathleen Riley in 1987's *Suspect*. Portraying a lawyer, Joe Mantegna is seated on the right. (*TriStar Pictures/MJB Photo Archives*)

In *Suspect,* Cher's character becomes illegally involved with one of her jurors, played by Dennis Quaid (right). (*TriStar Pictures/MJB Photo Archives*)

Both Olympia Dukakis (left) and Cher won Academy Awards for their work in the 1987 film *Moonstruck.* (*MGM Pictures/MJB Photo Archives*)

If she could turn back time! Throughout her career Cher has sported "cheeky" outfits like this one, which showed off all of her attributes, and several of her tattoos. (*Nancy Barr/Retna Photos*)

With Winona Ryder (left) in the 1990 film *Mermaids*, Cher portrayed a kooky early 1960s mom. The soundtrack album provided her with her biggest-selling single up until that point, "The Shoop Shoop Song (It's in His Kiss)." (*Orion Pictures/MJB Photo Archives*)

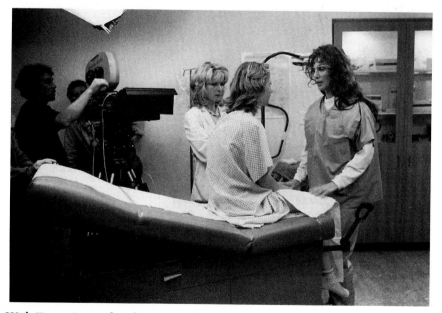

With Diana Scarwid and Anne Heche, Cher starred in her fourteenth film, the highly acclaimed *If These Walls Could Talk*. Cher made her directorial debut in this three-segment film, and also portrayed an abortion clinic doctor. (*HBO Pictures/MJB Photo Archives*)

(Harry Langdon/Casablanca
Records/MJB Photo Archives)

(AP/Wide World Photos)

(AP/Wide World Photos)

(AP/Wide World Photos)

(AP/Wide World Photos)

The many faces of Cher. Her fans have stuck with her through plastic surgery, divorces, and even tragedy. Although they had feuded for years, when Sonny Bono suddenly died in a tragic skiing accident in 1998, his passing touched Cher in a way that was startling even to her.

Cher was as effervescent as the bubbles in a glass of champagne in the 1999 film *Tea with Mussolini*. (*Philippe Antonello/G2-MGM Pictures/MJB Photo Archives*)

With costar Lily Tomlin in *Tea with Mussolini*. (*Philippe Antonello/G2-MGM Pictures/MJB Photo Archives*)

Cher as Elsa Morgenthal, an affluent art collector, in *Tea with Mussolini*. (*Philippe Antonello/G2-MGM Pictures/MJB Photo Archives*)

"The kids were so cold they were crying," recalled Mary at the bottom of the hill. "I said, 'O.K., he had to have skied to the bottom. He'll be there waiting for us' " (209). However, three hours later, as the sun was setting and the ski resort was getting ready to close the slopes for the day, Mary became worried and reported her husband's disappearance to the Ski Patrol. She figured at this point that the worst thing that could have happened would be that he had a broken leg.

At approximately 6:45 p.m., Sonny Bono's body was found in a wooded area between two trails. He was in a foot of snow and had been dead more than five hours. Sgt. Lance Modispacher, of the Douglas County Sheriff's Department, said of Bono's family, "[They] skied past him and didn't notice. He was in such an area of trees that you wouldn't see him" (210).

According to Douglas County, Nevada, sheriff, Ron Pierini, "death was immediate" and "there is no indication of any substances or alcohol." Describing the circumstances of the accident, and the length of time before medical professionals were on the site of the accident, Pierini reported, "There are trees all over the place. Even if paramedics were on the scene, it would not have done any good" (211).

Finally, members of the Ski Patrol reported back to Mary, who was still at the bottom of the mountain. "They told me they found a body in the mountain, and I said, 'Please let me go up.' Then, the minute I got there, I saw his feet and his legs and I knew it was him. I got to see him, be with him on the mountain. They let me be with him for an hour and a half" (209).

While all of this was happening, Cher was on her way to London, for her scheduled Harrod's department store appearance. She was in her hotel suite when the phone started ringing. It was Chastity on the line from America. Cher recalled her daughter's somber words to her " 'Mom, Dad's dead.' I got completely hysterical. I just started sobbing and collapsed to my knees" (171).

She had her representatives phone the owner of Harrod's, Mohamed Al Fayed, to inform him that she was too distraught to make her scheduled appearance. Al Fayed was more than sympathetic, having just lost his son Dodi in the car crash that also killed Diana, Princess of Wales, only months before. Wearing dark glasses, and clutching a tissue for her tears, Cher headed back to London's Heathrow Airport and flew to Los Angeles. She was met there by a limousine and was driven to Palm Springs.

Sonny's third wife, Susie Coehlo, was on her way to Palm Springs as well. When Cher arrived at the house Mary and Sonny shared, she was still unsuccessfully fighting the tears of sorrow. According to family friend and former Sonny & Cher record producer, Denis Pregnolato, "Cher walked in and went straight to Mary and Chastity and the family. Everybody hugged and cried" (188).

Although they had been divorced for twenty years, indeed Cher and Sonny still had a bond that no one, not even their families, could quite understand. In spite of all of the critical things that Cher had said about Sonny, she still loved him very deeply. According to Chastity, she was startled by her mother's emotional state. "I'd never seen my mother in that shape. She's not a big crier" (171).

Public statements of sadness and mourning flooded in from across America. Sonny was first remembered for his contributions to rock and roll music. Ronnie Spector was to recall, "He didn't give up. Sonny & Cher became huge and when that went away, he went into politics. He just kept plugging on." La La Brooks of the group the Crystals remembered, "Whatever he had to do to please Phil [Spector], he did. And, it paid off" (36). Of his business sense, Darlene Love eulogized, "He was a smart, funny man who didn't take himself too seriously. He's the reason there's a Cher" (205).

Ronnie Spector recalled in late 1989 how Sonny came to New York City to appear in concert with herself and Darlene Love at the Bottom Line. It was a special Christmas concert to celebrate the twenty-fifth anniversary of the release of the Phil Spector album *A Christmas Gift for You*. "I said, 'Sonny, you're the Mayor [of Palm Springs] now. I can't believe you came to the show.' He said, 'I could not *not* do this. I had to be a part of the music" (205). Sonny Bono will always be remembered as someone who never forgot whom his true friends were.

California Democrat Rep. Jane Harman said upon hearing of his death, "We won't forget his freshness, his humor, his ability to not take himself too seriously, but to take issues very seriously. I think he was an excellent member of Congress, one of the nicest guys. And Sonny, we'll miss you, Babe" (188).

According to politician Bob Dole, "If you're going to sum it up, he was the life of our party. He loved people, liked politics. He felt he had accomplished a great deal in just getting here—and he had" (188). Controversial Speaker of the House Newt Gingrich said, "We all feel that we lost a very good friend. He was building a real fan club in Washington" (211). Even President Clinton eulogized Bono the politician by stating, "He made us laugh even as he brought his own astute perspective to the work of Congress" (210).

In her own statement to the press, Chastity Bono claimed, "Although my father and I differed on some issues, he was very supportive of my personal life and career and was a loving father. I will miss him greatly" (206).

Being at Sonny's house in Palm Springs was a haunting, surreal event for Cher. She found so much memorabilia that threw her back to a long-forgotten time in her life. "Son saved everything," she said. "I saw his old bobcat vest. I remember the day we found it, what car we were in, how the breeze was blowing. It's so long ago it's like another solar system," she claimed. "Look, I never thought it would be like this. As long as he was here I could bitch at him, be angry. That was in this compartment, this was in that compartment, everything's tidy. But if people believe things are tidy, they're insane" (171).

During her time in Palm Springs that week for the funeral, Cher stayed in a bungalow at Sonny and Mary's house. In between her own bouts of crying, Cher was there to comfort both her own daughter, Chastity, and Sonny's widow, Mary. Reportedly, Cher and Mary, who had only briefly known each other up to that point, bonded as friends in mourning.

In the local newspaper, *The Desert Sun,* Mary was quoted as saying,

> It's more a sisterly thing than a rivalry. Cher has been a constant source of comfort for me. It was funny. We spent a couple of hours together, talking, and she asked me what I was going to wear. I said, "I'm going to wear a conservative dark suit. What are you going to wear?" She says, "I'm going to go like 'Cher.'" I said, " 'That's great. The two of us will personify his life with our wardrobes" (212).

The press coverage on the death of Sonny Bono was massive. As a stunned public returned to work after the New Year's weekend, it was the biggest story of the first half of January 1998. It was teamed that week with the tragedy of a member of the Kennedy family, Michael Kennedy, who was also killed in a freak skiing mishap.

In a town that celebrates celebrity, New York City featured Sonny and Cher cover stories the entire week: "I MISS YOU BABE! Cher Distraught after Sonny Bono Dies in Ski Accident" (*New York Post,* January 7, 1998), "IT'S TWO STRANGE—Sonny Bono Dies in Eerie Repeat of Tragic Ski Accident That Killed Michael Kennedy" (*New York Daily News,* January 7, 1998), "CHER'S TENDER TRIBUTE—Through Tears and Smiles She Remembers Her Best Friend Sonny" (*New York Daily News,* January 10, 1998), and "Cher's Moving Eulogy to Sonny 'He Was the Greatest' " (*New York Post,* January 10, 1998).

276   CHER: IF YOU BELIEVE

According to Cher, she was especially leery about seeing Sonny in his casket. She knew that it was going to a painful moment. "He had these really cool hands, and I looked away and went, 'Oh fuck it. I'll just look at him.' So I thought, 'I don't want this to be the last thing I see.' He looks like such a Republican, and I'm going to really hate that" (171).

What the public seemed to be anticipating all week was whether or not Cher would be speaking at her ex-husband's funeral. She had said such harsh things about him in the last ten years, yet obviously was grief-stricken about his sudden death. Finally, it was announced that she was definitely going to deliver the eulogy at the funeral, which was to be held on Friday, January 9, 1998.

When saddened, red-eyed Cher went up to the pulpit, it was an emotional moment indeed. She carried with her several handwritten yellow legal pad pages. Of her written statement, she was later to claim, "I didn't want to blow it. I felt I had to repair all the damage and misconceptions about Sonny" (171). America watched the touching and emotional eulogy on television, as Cher gave the most important performance of her life. She was incredibly nervous, and afterward reported, "I had no control. My face was making all kinds of movements, I had to lock my legs and grit my teeth. I was terrified" (171).

In front of her family and friends, Cher began her eulogy by stating, "Please excuse my papers, but I've been writing this stupid eulogy for the last 48 hours, and of course I know this would make Sonny really happy." Speaking about their first meeting she said, "He walked into this room. I swear to God, everyone else just washed away in this soft-focus filter. Like Maria saw Tony at the dance [referring to the characters in *West Side Story*]. . . . Of course at this time he was talking to a girl who thought that Mount Rushmore was a natural phenomenon, so we were definitely a marriage made in heaven" (213). She spoke of her love for him, their marriage, and their differences.

With tears in her eyes, and intermittently sobbing, Cher, who spoke for several minutes, said,

I wanted to tell Mary and Chesare and Chianna how proud I am of them, and of what he made of himself after we were separated and his accomplishments. I know that a person just doesn't decide to become a Congressman in the middle of his life and then be one. But it was just like Sonny to do something crazy like that. He was the greatest friend. When I was young, there was this section in *Reader's Digest* called "Most Unforgettable Character I Ever Met." For me, that person is Sonny Bono, no matter how long I live or who I meet. That person will always be Sonny for me (213).

Chastity Bono was especially upset over the fact that at the time her father died they were divided about their differences in opinion.

I felt sad about a lot of things that my Dad did. I never really talked to him about gay issues until I did my *Advocate* [magazine] interview with him, and I felt badly about that interview. I thought it made him look bad, and as his child, I didn't want to do that. I also felt badly that he was so clueless on our issues. When he cosponsored DOMA [Defense of Marriage Act, the anti-gay marriage bill], I took it very personally. I put a tremendous amount of distance between us and then he died before we were able to resolve it. Growing up, we were so close. I thought he was the greatest thing in the world. When you have such high expectations of somebody and they let you down, it hits you that much harder (193).

My older sister, Christy, who's always trying to keep the family together, talked to him right before he died, and she said, "You really should call Chas." And he said, "Yeah, I'm gonna do that." What's really interesting from a spiritual side is that the famous medium James Van Praagh did a reading with my mother recently [1998], and one of the things he said to her was that my Dad said, "I wish I listened to Christy. I should have called Chas." This was something that my Mom didn't know about. The only people that knew about that conversation were the three of us. . . . When he first died it was much harder, and I had to make my own peace with it. At first it was devastating. I felt terrible and guilty because I felt that I didn't do everything that I could to work on the relationship, although he was equally to blame. At his funeral service I was having this dialogue with my Dad in my head, and I just kept saying, "My God, we fucked up. We were so stupid. Why did we let this happen?" It was hard. There was an open casket, and I'm not a big crier at all, but I broke down. One of the things my Mom used to say was that my Dad and I had the same hands, and I held his hand, and it was so cold. That made me feel terrible. At this point I feel that I've worked through it, and I feel more peace about it, but I still wish that it had gone a different way (193).

According to Cher, she had no idea that the CNN television news network was going to have cameras rolling at Sonny's funeral until right before she arrived there. Viewing a teary-eyed Cher delivering such a moving testimony after years of berating Sonny publicly made several people question her sincerity and her motives. Several months later, she claimed that the public and the press think that they know her, but they really don't know the person within. "I think it hit home for me the most when people thought I was acting at Sonny's funeral. That's the definitive experience of people getting it so wrong that you just don't know where anybody's coming from. I was so blindsided by that. And that day, I actually did give a thought to packing it in and saying, 'You know what? Fuck all you guys, you don't get it anyway. I'm out of here' " (214).

Sonny's death had been one of the most emotional experiences in her entire event-filled life. "[I] almost moved out of the country and gave up show business when the reports started coming in that I was acting at Sonny's eulogy," she was later to angrily state (144).

For a woman who had lived the majority of her life in front of TV cameras, movie cameras, and microphones, Cher was startled by the outpouring of media attention Sonny's death brought to her, both sympathetic and then critical of her. Would this leave her too devastated to continue her career? Would she pour herself into her work with feverish determination? How would Cher emerge from this tragic event that would obviously force her to take a long, hard look at her life?

Sonny Bono had died at the top of his game. He was amid his fourth successful career when he died instantly. This fact hit Cher very hard. Was this going to force her into her shell, or would it force her onward to even greater achievements? Inquiring minds wanted to know.

17

BELIEVE

After Sonny's death in January 1998, the spotlight was back on Cher, after over a year of relative silence. The past year had been a relatively quiet one by "Cher" terms. Following the funeral, everyone in the universe seemed to be asking, "What has Cher been doing lately?" She was about to deliver her answer in a big way.

Following the funeral, she seemed to have a whole new vantage point on her former husband and singing partner. Before she moved on with her career, she obviously wanted to put some of the negative things she had said about Sonny well in her past. In the spring of 1998 she reported to *People* magazine, "We both said some nasty things. We were flippant, full of ourselves, wanting to come off smart. I was pissed off and didn't pull punches. We made great copy" (171).

Sonny's widow Mary Bono also found herself in the spotlight right after his death. While Cher was still in Palm Springs for the funeral, after it was all over, the two women reportedly reminisced about Sonny for an hour and a half. According to Mary, "We talked about how we both realized Sonny's strength." When she asked Cher what she thought about her running for Sonny's vacated congressional seat, Cher replied, "If this is something you need to do, you do it" (215). The *National Enquirer* quoted Mary as stating, "Cher has been unbelievable. She has given me the strength to go on. I look at her as more of a sister than my husband's ex-wife. I couldn't have gotten through this without her" (216).

In mid-January, Mary and their two children appeared on *The Larry*

King Show, where she announced that she would indeed be running for her late husband's congressional seat. She also told King that she was planning on taking her young children skiing again very soon. "It's sort of like getting back in an airplane after a crash," she explained. "But, I think it's important. I also think it's very important to talk with the children about everything. There is no question my children can ask that I would not answer" (217).

On Tuesday, January 27, 1998, President Bill Clinton, in his annual State of the Union address, eulogized Sonny Bono at the top of his speech. While Cher had spoken of the singer and songwriter she had married and loved, Clinton spoke glowingly of the congressman whom Washington had grown attached to over the past couple of years. Mary Bono was in the audience during the speech, and was shown on camera during the network telecast of the event.

With her hat in the ring, Mary Bono became the Republican candidate running to fill her husband's vacated seat in Congress. Oddly enough, her Democratic competitor was also a show business veteran, Ralph Waite, who was best known to TV fans as "Pa" on *The Waltons*. Mary shared many of the same political views as her late husband Sonny. She believed that the government was wastefully bloated, and spent too much money on itself, and she was dead set against the so-called "free trade" agreements with Mexico, as it took jobs away from the farm workers in her own home district.

Speaking of her campaign tactics, the *New York Times* found that, like Cher, Mary had her own sense of style. According to that newspaper, "On the campaign trail, Bono wears stylish Norma Kamali suits and matching Ferragamo pumps" (218).

Although Cher may have given a thumbs-up to her fashion sense, Mary claimed to be opposed to government funding for legal abortions. This was only the beginning of their differences in opinion. On April 7, 1998, when the special election was held to fill Sonny's vacated congressional seat, Mary Bono successfully won.

Within Mary Bono's first year in office, she made several well-meaning statements about Sonny, which totally pissed Cher off. The most notable allegation was the fact that she claimed Sonny was in the habit of abusing prescription drugs, particularly painkillers. She went so far as to imply that if Sonny hadn't been under the influence of such drugs, he may never have slammed into a tree that fateful day in January.

The feud got started when Mary Bono gave a press interview regarding the pain pills, claiming that occasionally Sonny had taken up to twenty a day. It became a big issue when her comments were published in *TV Guide*. In that publication, Mary claimed she was "100 percent convinced" that the pills contributed to his collision with the tree. She went on to say, "What he did showed absolute lack of judgment . . . that's what these pills do" (219).

That was all it took for Sonny's mother, Jean Bono, to get into the fray. In a *Star* newspaper article entitled, "Mystery of Autopsy Report Who Killed Sonny Bono" (December 8, 1998), Jean was quoted as saying, "What Mary has done is despicable. She has blackened my son's name in front of his children, his family and his friends when he's not around to defend himself. She says my son abused all these prescription drugs and that his behavior was erratic. But the autopsy report plainly states there were only minute traces of drugs" (219). Mama Bono wasn't the only one upset.

Cher was not only mad at the press for thinking that she was using Sonny's funeral for her own self-promotion, she was especially mad at Mary Bono for opening her mouth about this issue, whether it was true and accurate or not. Said a bristlingly frosty Cher, "You know what? Fuck everybody! I don't care what anyone thought about my motives at the eulogy. I don't really care what anybody says about me. But there's a rule. I'm not Sicilian, but I lived with Sonny long enough to know that some things belong in the family. Some things stay in the family. And she broke that rule" (144).

Mary had her own say on the topic as well. She was especially frosty regarding the fact that Cher had made peace with Sonny via famed psychic James Van Praagh and then announced the fact in a cover story in *People* magazine. Being a no-nonsense kind of gal, Mary thought that the whole notion of using a medium was absurd. "Why couldn't she say he was a good man before he died?" Mary proclaimed. "To say that Sonny has forgiven her is just ridiculous! She's just promoting herself. Cher's always been the best at self-promotion. She's the ultimate spinmeister" (220).

To put a public sense of closure to her grieving for Sonny Bono, on May 20, 1998, CBS-TV broadcast the hour-long special, *Sonny & Me . . . Cher Remembers*. According to her at the time, she willingly went down memory lane to put her life back into perspective. "I couldn't wait not to be Sonny & Cher," she said about the special, "But I don't mind going back. It's my choice now" (171).

For her, it was the greatest loss of her adult life. She felt like she lost "my father, my husband, my brother, the father of my child, my partner, and my best friend" (16). Although they had rarely seen each other since the 1970s, she had always felt some sort of strange connection with Sonny. "Most of the time, I just don't think of him as dead," she claimed.

I don't remember to talk about him in the past tense. Even though I know he's dead, I feel somehow closer to him now than I've felt in a long time. He somehow has more relevance to me now. It took a long time to get over my anger. But we had the strangest relationship. I mean, [when we divorced] he had me in court trying to prove I was an unfit mother. And on the day he lost the case he walked out and grabbed me and kissed me on the lips. Kissed me hard. I was really angry, but we were like kids. We just let things go. We ended up laughing hysterically. We had just spent hundreds of thousands of dollars in court, but it was like a joke. It was always a game with us (144).

In 1998, Cher finally released what was supposed to be her own in-depth autobiography. However, when *The First Time* hit bookstores, fans and critics were disappointed to find that it wasn't the full story they were anticipating, but a compilation of short vignettes including "My First Solo Recording" and "My First Shopping Spree." Unfortunately, the book left huge gaps in time completely unexplained. Cher also left out anything she didn't care to discuss, from boyfriends to plastic surgery.

Cher's 1998 to 2000 comeback was nothing short of miraculous. In true Cher form, it was a complete multimedia sweep: the biggest album of her career, the biggest single of her career, a critically acclaimed movie, a starring role in the VH1 *Divas '99* television special, a sold-out international tour, and—finally—her first Grammy Award.

The key to the whole tidal wave of success that struck for Cher was her *Believe* album. It was the LP's executive producer, Rob Dickens, who talked her into turning her back on arty rock and roll this time around and devoting an entire album to dance music. Not since the golden days of 1970s "disco" had this been done by a major artist of the stature of Cher.

According to Dickens, "I thought, every gay guy I know is a huge Cher fan. They just love her as an icon. She has this huge gay following and they love High-NRG dance records. So the idea was to repay their faith and loyalty to her over the years, to make a record for them" (144). This was not exactly what Cher had in mind. She was reluctant to agree at first, but he finally talked her into it. What the hell, what did she have to lose?

Regarding her relationship with Dickens during the recording of the ten cuts contained on *Believe,* the diva herself confirms, "We argued the whole way through" (144).

It was the title cut that was to become the cornerstone of her new wave of success. There were already six writers credited with having written the song "Believe," so why not add her own pen to the task? Explained Cher, "I was singing in the bathtub, and it seemed to me the second verse was too whiny. It kind of pissed me off, so I changed it. I toughened it up a bit. I wrote the lyrics, 'It takes time to move on, it takes love to be strong/I've had time to think it through and maybe I'm too good for you.'" (144). It was also Cher's idea to take the chorus and put her own voice through a synthesizer to come up with the audio effects that make this cut so memorable.

Only three of the songs were written by people she had worked with before, including Diane Warren and Desmond Child. Cher chose Warren's composition "Takin' Back My Heart," which was cut as an up-tempo ballad. And producer Todd Terry had her rerecord one of her trademark songs, Warren and Child's "We All Sleep Alone," redone as a High-NRG dance number. Mark Jordan, who had written the song "The Same Mistake" on her *It's a Man's World* album, contributed the catchy and pulsating "Taxi, Taxi" to the *Believe* disk.

Judging by the results of *Believe,* the three sets of producers had a blast making this, the ultimate Cher dance album. Junior Vasquez produced "The Power," and Todd Terry was responsible for the songs "Taxi, Taxi," "Love Is the Groove," and "We All Sleep Alone." The rest of this brilliantly executed album was produced by Mark Taylor and Brian Rawling. In addition to the infectiously catchy title cut, the Spanish guitar-driven "Dov'è L'Amore," the defiantly bold "Strong Enough," and the techno blast of "Runway" made this a true 1990s classic.

As they did for her album *It's a Man's World,* Warner Brothers/Reprise Records chose to release *Believe* globally before bringing it out in America. It proved to be a stroke of marketing genius. Rather than even give *Believe* a chance to fail in America and ruin everything, it came to the United States last, and arrived as a bona fide worldwide smash.

Released in autumn of 1998, both the album and single versions of *Believe* instantly hit Number 1 in England. But that was only the beginning. The song was to hit Number 1 in twenty-three countries around the globe. And the album was to be certified a Gold or Platinum smash in thirty-nine separate countries. The list is nothing short of astonishing: Argentina—

Platinum, Australia—Double Platinum, Austria—Double Platinum, Belgium—Platinum, Brazil—Gold, Canada—Septuple Platinum, Chile—Gold, Colombia—Gold, Czech Republic—Gold, Denmark—Quintuple Platinum, Finland—Gold, France—Platinum, Germany—Double Platinum, Greece—Gold, Hong Kong—Gold, Hungary—Platinum, Indonesia—Platinum, Ireland—Triple Platinum, Israel—Gold, Italy—Triple Platinum, Japan—Gold, Korea—Platinum, Malaysia—Gold, Mexico—Double Gold, Netherlands—Gold, New Zealand—Double Platinum, Norway—Platinum, Poland—Platinum, Portugal—Double Platinum, Singapore—Gold, South Africa—Double Platinum, Spain—Quadruple Platinum, Sweden—Double Platinum, Switzerland—Double Platinum, Taiwan—Gold, Thailand—Gold, Turkey—Triple Platinum, United Kingdom—Double Platinum. Cher was back—in a big way!

It was already an around-the-world hit by October of 1998. When it was released in America the following month, no one was quite certain what would happen. Well, Cher hit the jackpot again, when in the beginning of 1999 "Believe" became the Number 1 song in the United States, and in fact, *Billboard* magazine was later to tally it as the Number 1 song of the entire year! To top it all off, the single "Believe" was Number 1 for twenty-one weeks on the Hot Dance Music/Maxi-Single list. In America alone, the *Believe* album peaked at Number 4, sold over four million copies, and remained on the charts for a year and a half.

Was Cher excited and surprised by this feat? You had better *believe* she was! "Well, yeah!" she proclaimed.

> When the song came out in Europe, it went to Number One immediately, and I wouldn't have expected that either. But when we came to the U.S., and stations didn't even want to play it, that made it really hard. And also the song was released in November [1998], which is a really awful and competitive time to come out, so we knew that it was either going to be a miracle or we were totally screwed. And I would say it's kind of on the miracle side (23).

Not since 1984, when Tina Turner went from "nowhere" to "everywhere" with her triumphant *Private Dancer* album, had there been such a massive worldwide comeback. According to Cher, "I remember when Tina did the same thing, around 12 years ago. Every once in a while it happens. I think it happens more for the Rolling Stones and Aerosmith. I'm sure it happens a lot more with male artists" (23).

Well it was certainly her turn now. The Cher global assault of the senses continued throughout the year 1999. In January she gave American television audiences a delicious dose of the song "Believe" when she performed it on the American Music Awards telecast. That same month, Cher was seen on America's traditionally top-rated broadcast event of the year, football's Super Bowl game. In 1999 it was Cher who sang the national anthem; millions and millions of football fans (and die-hard Cher fans) watched and listened to her sing "Oh say can you see. . . ." at the kick-off of the game. Although it appears that the music and singing at the Super Bowl is being performed "live," it never is, as it is always pre-recorded. Fearing mechanical glitches, on a program where every second costs a fortune, Cher's vocal tracks—like everyone else's before her—were lip-synched to tape. Any singer will tell you that "The Star-Spangled Banner" is notoriously one of the most difficult songs to sing—in any key. Well, she sure sounded and looked great on the football field that day!

In February, Mary Bono got to deliver Sonny's spin on the Sonny & Cher saga when the television biographical made-for-TV movie *And the Beat Goes On* was telecast. Since Mary was credited as the "co-executive producer" of the film, this certainly did nothing to endear it to Cher. An interesting take on their union, based on Sonny's book of the same name, it didn't do anything to hurt her career, but it certainly painted her as being ambitious and self-centered. Reviewing the movie in *Entertainment Weekly* magazine, Ken Tucker claimed "*And the Beat Goes On* is designed less to make Sonny look like a saint than to make Cher look like a cruel ingrate" (221).

And, what did Cher think of all of this? According to her, she refused to watch it. "I swear to God I wasn't interested," she proclaimed. "I enjoy the great drag queens who do me. I think that's sweet. I feel a connection with them. I had no connection with that movie. Besides, I lived it. I don't have to see somebody's idea of what it was. I know what it was" (192).

In March of 1999, Cher's follow-up single to "Believe," the anthem to self-assurance, "Strong Enough," entered the British charts at Number 5. As for "Believe" before it, Cher released a clever and glitzy video version of the song, which received heavy rotation on video programs around the world.

On April 13, 1999, VH1 broadcast its television extravaganza, *Divas Live '99*, starring Tina Turner, Cher, Elton John, LeAnn Rimes, Faith Hill, Brandy, and Whitney Houston, along with guests Chaka Kahn and

Mary J. Blige. The special, which also yielded an album, video, and DVD, helped to herald Cher's brilliant return to the top.

Tina opened the show, strutting into the Beacon Theater in New York City singing her hit "The Best." Accompanied by Elton on piano, she then launched into her signature song, "Proud Mary," only to be joined onstage by none other than Cher. To see that trio of superstars on one stage together was truly the highlight of the whole show. Cher's only other performance on the special was her dramatic rendition of the fiery "If I Could Turn Back Time." Interestingly, neither Tina, nor Elton, nor Cher were part of the big ensemble number, "I'm Every Woman," which was lead by Whitney.

Backstage at the telecast, Cher used her media time wisely, announcing her first big concert tour in years, to commence that June in Phoenix, Arizona. When she was interviewed backstage, it was remarked how she was in fashion again. Asked how to define the cycle of her career being hot, Cher laughed, "When the moon is full, and my ass is in Jupiter—I don't know." With regard to what her fans could expect from her concert tour, she replied, "It won't be plain or sedate, or tasteful" (222). According to VH1, *Divas Live '99* was the most popular, and most watched, program in the television network's history, and Cher's presence was a huge part of making it exactly that.

One of the most dramatic career decisions that Cher made during this period of time was a sudden change in management. Although her longtime manager, Bill Sammeth, was credited on her *Believe* album as being her personal manager, by the time the *Divas Live '99* special aired, she had signed with Roger Davies. It was Davies who had masterminded Tina Turner's career up to and throughout her huge comeback of 1984. Reportedly, Sammeth was stunned by the news that he would be losing his star client suddenly, at the very peak of her success. According to *Entertainment Weekly* magazine, Cher terminated his services just prior to her appearance on the Super Bowl telecast in January.

"Take Me Home" producer Bob Esty, who has remained close friends with Billy Sammeth, explained of Sammeth's sudden firing,

> He was with her, literally holding her hand for twenty years. He was involved in the *Believe* album, setting up the whole thing, even talking her into doing it. And, she was getting ready to do this tour, and I think what happened was Roger Davies came on the scene, of course, smelling an opportunity, and sweet-talked her by telling her what she wanted to hear about how much she could make. Maybe she was thinking that Billy wasn't

in that league as far as big rock style concerts, even though Billy handled all the Cher shows over the years. But this was arenas—this was another whole thing. So, she unceremoniously fired him—completely out of the blue as far as Billy was concerned. He went up there to her house and Cher said, "You're through." So, he was hurt. She'd done it before, and then a week would go by, and it's "Billy I didn't mean it." But this time she meant it, and went with Roger Davies. Coincidentally, I saw Billy in Key West, when I was doing a musical there, and he was so devastated and unhappy, and just couldn't understand why she did this. Now, I got this story from Billy, so I am sure there is another side to the story (101).

He sued her, she countersued him, and now her relationship with Bill Sammeth is over.

At long last, on May 14, 1999, Cher was back in movie theaters with a hit film, and a classy one at that, *Tea with Mussolini,* directed by Franco Zeffirelli. Costarring a glittering cast of Oscar winners and nominees, this film was an effervescent treat to watch. And, for anyone who blinked in 1996 and missed *Faithful,* it seemed as though Cher had been missing from the big screen the entire decade—since 1990's *Mermaids.*

Every one of the five principal women in this bittersweet remembrance of a film had previously danced with Oscar for one film or another. Cher (Best Actress winner) found herself starring on screen alongside Judi Dench (Best Supporting Actress winner), Maggie Smith (Best Actress and Best Supporting Actress winner), and Best Supporting Actress nominees Joan Plowright and Lily Tomlin.

The plot and script of the film were drawn from the personal diary of Zeffirelli, and the action begins in prewar Italy, 1935. The central character, Luka, a little boy who is the illegitimate son of a local businessman, finds himself without a mother when his own dies. His father, who is married to another woman, does not recognize him as his son due to the social stigma of fathering a child out of wedlock. Luka is also tormented by his father's vulture-like wife. Cher, Dench, Smith, Plowright, and Tomlin all come to the rescue, taking turns doubling as his surrogate mother. In the middle of all of the action, World War II breaks out, and everyone finds themselves scrambling for their own safety and dignity.

Portraying the role of a wealthy American in Florence, Cher is a dazzling delight to watch on screen. She is sumptuously costumed in 1930s hats and flowing gowns, and she even gets to sing the song "Smoke Gets in Your Eyes" amid the action. Cher's character of Elsa stupidly signs away all of her belongings to an Italian gigolo, and when the United

States declares war on Mussolini's Italy, she is incarcerated along with the British women. To make matters worse, it turns out that Elsa is Jewish as well, and is sought by the Nazis. It is right after Cher sings "Smoke Gets in Your Eyes" that she gets to deliver her most memorable line. When one of her suitors asks her, "Are all American women as alluring as you?" she answers wryly, "Alas, no."

In *Tea with Mussolini,* Cher gets to make one stunning entrance after another in glamorous outfits. Since three of her costars are charming but dowdy-looking older British women, and the other a drably mannish American lesbian archeologist (Tomlin), she is set off with gem-like sparkle scene after scene. "Yeah, I am very unforgettable," Cher says on camera at one point. And, yes, in this film, she certainly is just that. Even her final exit scene is a dramatic one, escaping to Switzerland in a rowboat in the middle of the night.

The reviews for this film were also consistently good. Although not every critic loved the structure of the film, they were generally entranced by Cher. Mick LaSalle of the *San Francisco Chronicle* found it

> Warm, spontaneous and heartfelt . . . the second thing to mention is Cher, who is wonderful in the film. Cher hasn't had an important role in years, but *Tea with Mussolini* should turn things around for her. I've never been a fan. But with this movie I finally "got" Cher. It's a role that allows her to be seen, that lets her create a vivid character while showing off what is best about her as a screen personality. . . . Plowright is lovely, but somehow it's Cher who lingers in the mind when the film is over. She suggests an intelligence behind the free-spirited Elsa, a wisdom partly innate but earned, too. No one can be that generous without having gone through rough times, but she's too classy to show it. Playing the essence of good times, lewdness and open-hearted enthusiasm, Cher manages to embody all those frivolous virtues that Mussolini's fascists were intent on destroying (223).

Roger Ebert of the *Chicago Sun Times* didn't love the movie, but he enjoyed the performances. He thought that "the movie is heavier with events than with plot," yet found "the ladies supply quite enough entertainment all on their own. . . . I liked the performances of the women (including Cher, people keep forgetting what a good actress she can be)" (224).

James DiGiovanna, in the *Tucson Weekly,* snidely observed, "Played by Maggie Smith in her usual stiffly regal style, Lady Hester is fond of fascism and afternoon tea, and despises Americans, Jews and crassness.

Thus, she is triply irked by the arrival of crass, Jewish-American singer Elsa, played by crass, Native American singer Cher." He also points out, with regard to the Jewish vs. Nazi angle in the film, that "it seems odd that only the wealthy and beautiful Elsa (well she's supposed to be beautiful, though Cher's post-modern approach to plastic surgery strikes me more as 'scary' and 'weird') is affected by this situation" (225). Oh well, you can't please everyone.

Speaking about *Tea with Mussolini,* prior to its opening in March in London and in May in America, Cher was in the dark as to how it would fare. According to her at that time,

> I just put one foot in front of the other and do my work. You never know. When I was making this album [*Believe*], there was nothing that would lead anyone to suspect it was going to be big. I made it in this funky little studio in England, about as big as my bedroom. It was really low-key. And the movie in Italy was a really quiet production. You know, it's just work until it comes out, and then it's either a hit album or a bomb. You just don't know. Or you could be in a huge movie, with a $100 million budget and it could be nothing. You just don't know with art. Art's a strange thing (23).

Discussing his casting choices for this film, director Franco Zeffirelli said of Cher, "She was heaven-sent. We had already cast the three English ladies, but we were still fighting to find the right American lady. There was the usual list—Glenn Close, Diane Keaton, Susan Sarandon. But then I wondered, 'What happened to Cher?' You know, her career goes up and down like the waves of the ocean. I didn't know if she was available" (144).

When Cher did finally see the edited film, her first reaction was to be—as she would put it—pissed off. She felt that much of her best work on camera ended up on the cutting-room floor. "My scenes were cut to ribbons," she proclaimed. "They were much longer when we filmed them. They made more sense. Now they seem disjointed. But maybe I'm looking at my performance and judging the film by it. I don't know. I shouldn't knock it. A lot of people really like the movie (144).

According to *TV Guide* magazine, Cher's final scene in the film, in the rowboat, was "soooo Garbo." She also received glowing congratulations from several of her acting compatriots. Said Cher, specifically about the rowboat scene, "I got the coolest message from Ben Kingsley, who was going on and on and on about that and I thought, 'What movie did he see'" (192).

Cher's 1999 month-by-month global domination of every media out-
let on planet Earth reached an all-time frenzy. She seemed to appear on
every magazine cover and every television show within reach, from
VH1's *Behind the Music* to *Rosie O'Donnell*. In May 1999 she was in
Monte Carlo for the World Music Awards, wearing silver pants, silver-
and-white jogging shoes, and a black cherry–colored red wig. On June
16, 1999, Cher kicked off her *Believe* concert tour. Sold out in every
American city it was booked in, it was a massive success with her fans.

It was an elaborate and exhausting show for Cher to mount and perform week after week. Toward the end of July, she was so exhausted that
she was forced to postpone several of her scheduled dates in certain
cities, including Detroit (July 23); Moline, Illinois (July 24); Indianapolis (July 27); Cincinnati (July 29); Tinley Park in the Chicago area (July
30); and St. Louis (July 31). According to her record company, Warner
Brothers, she was "under the weather, hit by an undisclosed illness"
(226). But, by the beginning of August, she was back on her feet again,
making her fans "believe" in her—show after show.

The American leg of the tour ended up in Las Vegas, at the MGM
Grand, where the last concert was broadcast "live" over HBO, on August
29, 1999. Before the year was over, Cher's Vegas concert had become an
elaborate video cassette and a DVD package. Both the video and DVD
packages included a 3-D cover illustration of the diva.

Cher's *Believe* tour stageshow delivered all of the aspects of her life
and her career, from music, to fashion, to television, to film. Instead of
discussing her career as a part of Sonny & Cher, she let a presentation of
clips from *The Sonny & Cher Comedy Hour* present that aspect of her
life for her, while she was busily changing into a new outfit and a new wig.
The same was true of her many movie roles. Another taped segment,
which was shown on several huge projection screens around the venue,
displaying her varied cinematic personas. Paul Mercovich, who was one
of the keyboard players in her touring band, sang the duet "After All"
with Cher in concert.

What most people didn't realize, however, was that Cher's "live" special wasn't really broadcast "live" at all. It had been in fact taped the night
before, and then broadcast. Yeah, like anyone cared. However, critic Ken
Tucker in *Entertainment Weekly* had fun griping,

> Why complain that a "live" concert isn't "live" when you're dealing with a
> star who rarely wears her own hair and scored her first hit song in more

than a decade by mechanically distorting her voice. . . . For this tour, Cher has surrounded herself with a batch of distractingly cornball dancers who must cavort for minutes on end while Cher is backstage getting new hair and duds. . . . Cher in *Tea with Mussolini* had more spontaneity than Cher in Las Vegas (227).

To express her feelings in "Cher" terms, she really didn't *give a shit* about what the critics thought about her concert; it was a huge hit with her fans, and the numbers brilliantly attested to that. Probably the best reviews she could get came from her own children, Elijah and Chastity.

I think I'm cool, but I am sooo uncool to my children. I'm like, so corny. I embarrass them to no end. Everything I do embarrasses Elijah. But you know what he said about the concert? "My friends and I actually thought your show was good, Mom. It was good." That's better than a rave review in the *New York Times*, because he never has anything good to say (192).

Chastity likewise agreed. "[I'm] not generally astonished by what my Mom does," she said, "but seeing the *Believe* concert gave me one of those rare opportunities to disconnect, to forget who I am, and be totally blown away by her. I had a ball watching the crowd—kids, old people, straights, gays—everybody loved her" (193).

After HBO's hugely successful *Cher in Concert* special proved a hit in "the colonies," Cher headed across "the pond" to Europe, where she "wowed" her fans in Europe. By the time the year 1999 came to an end it was tallied that over 1.5 million fans bought tickets to see Cher live in concert, in a seven-month period. In addition, HBO claimed that the *Cher in Concert* telecast was the highest-rated original program in the past two years.

Since 1999 was the "Year of Cher," every record label under the sun was scrambling to get in on the bonanza while she was hot. Because Cher had recorded for many different labels over the years, just about every record company had something to offer. Even *I Paralyze*, which had been long forgotten, found its way back onto a CD. MCA repackaged her 1973 *Bittersweet White Light* album and turned it into a seventeen-song all-ballads retrospective called *Bittersweet—The Love Songs Collection*. It took the nine cuts from the original album, added Irving Berlin's "What'll I Do," "The Way of Love," and six other cuts, and gave it a new cover, liner notes, and a classy package.

Geffen Records in America compiled its own *If I Could Turn Back Time/Cher's Greatest Hits* disc, which included all of her biggest hits from her three solo albums on that label, plus "The Shoop Shoop Song (It's in His Kiss)" and several of her 1970s hits like "Dark Lady," "Take Me Home," and "Half Breed," as well as Sonny & Cher's "I Got You Babe." As an added treat, this album also included a never-before-released song written by Diane Warren, entitled "Don't Come Crying to Me."

Imperial Records jumped on the Cher bandwagon with its own *Bang, Bang—The Early Years*, which took eighteen cuts from her original Sonny Bono–produced solo albums, featuring the biggest hits from this era and including "Dream Baby," "Elusive Butterfly," "Alfie," "Hey Joe," "Needles and Pins," and "It's Not Unusual." Universal Music Records took eight cuts from her pair of Casablanca solo albums, plus "Bang Bang" and "You Better Sit Down Kids," and released an album called *Take Me Home* (not to be confused with her hit 1979 album). This brief "hits" disc was packaged using the original *Take Me Home* golden Viking warrior cover of the original album of the same name.

In Europe, record labels were likewise getting into the act. Magic Records in France released a pair of Cher solo albums, 1998's *Sunny*, and 1999's *With Love, Cher*. The first one featured twenty cuts from the 1960s, and the second one followed the next year with fourteen cuts. These two disks are especially fun because they brought several of her non-hit album cuts to compact disc for the first time, anywhere in the world. Among the time-capsule-like cuts that fell in this category were "Pied Piper," "Homeward Bound," "I Want You," "Milord," "Girl Don't Come," "Sing for Your Supper," "I Will Wait for You (Love Theme from *The Umbrellas of Cherbourg*)" and "There but for Love." In Germany, Spectrum Records re-released the *Black Rose* album, completely intact, for the first time on compact disc. However, instead of the black-and-white-and-purple artwork on the cover, depicting Cher's stiletto high heel and tattooed ankle, it was packaged with a photo of Cher in concert and marketed as a "Cher" album, instead of as a Black Rose group album.

However, the best full-circle Cher retrospective album of the 1990s came from WEA/Universal Records in Germany. It was simply titled *Cher/The Greatest Hits*, and it was distributed throughout Europe. Released in 1999, it opens with "Believe" and ends with a hot remix of "Dov'è L'Amore." This one traces her entire Geffen Records career, plus the European version of "One by One" and the beautiful trio of Cher, Chrissie Hynde, and Neneh Cherry singing "Love Can Build a Bridge." It also highlights the 1960s ("All I Really Want to Do," "The Beat Goes On," and "I Got You Babe") and the 1970s ("Gypsys, Tramps and

Thieves"). According to *Billboard* magazine in January 2000, following the 1999 Christmas season, *Cher/The Greatest Hits* had already sold over three million copies in Europe since its November release date.

While all of this was going on, Cher was featured on three other high-profile albums in 1999. The patriotic album *Sing America* included her rendition of the "Star Spangled Banner," which she had recorded for that year's Super Bowl kick-off. The album *VH1 Divas Live '99* contained her singing "Proud Mary" with Tina Turner and Elton John and her solo performance of "If I Could Turn Back Time." And during the holiday season, Cher was heard singing Phil Spector's "Christmas (Baby Please Come Home)" while Rosie O'Donnell sang the chorus on the hit Yule season disk, *A Rosie Christmas.* It was great to hear Cher interpreting yet another Spector classic. Not only was the arrangement very "Wall of Sound"–sounding, but the same vocal distortion that was used on the song "Believe" was used here as well. It was Cher saluting her past by choosing a Phil Spector tune to record, while tipping her hat to the sound of her own 1999 hit.

In addition, *Cher in Concert* was released as a video cassette and as a DVD package, just in time for the Christmas season as well. Both formats featured a 3-D reflective cover, which featured the diva in a brightly colored red wig with a strange little unsymmetrical widow's peak protruding from the bangs.

Cher was one of six celebrities who appeared on the cover of the September 20, 1999, issue of *People* magazine, with a headline heralding the "Best & Worst Dressed '99." The magazine's appointed fashion critics found Cher to be dressing "not age-appropriate," "tacky," and "not occasion appropriate." Seeming to have traded gowns, Bob Mackie spangles, and stilettos for pantsuits and low-heeled shoes, her fashion statements put her in the Top 10 of the year's "Worst Dressed" celebrities—along with Madonna, Mariah Carey, Val Kilmer, and Shania Twain. Hey, it ain't easy being Cher—or dressing like her.

Although Cher was amid one of the high points of her entire life during 1999, Sonny's sudden and unexpected death made her think about her own mortality. The *Star* newspaper, in its December 7, 1999, issue, reported that Cher had selected and placed a down payment on a funeral plot, which she intends on making her own final resting place. Naturally, for Cher, being Cher, even this was nothing out of the ordinary. She has reportedly chosen the most famous cemetery in Paris, France, Pere Lachaise. Known as the eternal address of such celebrities as songbird

CHER: IF YOU BELIEVE

Edith Piaf, controversial British writer Oscar Wilde, and Doors rocker Jim Morrison, Pere Lachaise is a historical site in "the city of light." According to the article, she put down a $4,300 down payment on the plot she personally chose. There is, however, one small detail that Cher needs to deal with; if she intends to be entombed at Pere Lachaise she has to either live, or die, in Paris to be buried there. Cher is of course a woman who is used to getting her way, so she is certain to think of some way of getting around this prerequisite. Obviously, she has several years to work on getting around this particular obstacle.

It was Cher, Cher, Cher, Cher, Cher, everywhere you looked in 1999. In addition, when all of the end of the decade, end of the century, and beginning of the new millennium tallies were published, Cher was heavily featured in all of the coverage. In England, Cher was acknowledged as the biggest-selling female recording artist—ever. Not only was "Believe" the biggest global hit of the year, but Cher was crowned the only woman in history to have a Top 10 single in the 1960s, 1970s, 1980s, and 1990s. When *Pollstar* magazine, a concert industry publication, reported who were the hottest acts in America in 1999, they ranked her in the Top 10 of the year's biggest concert attractions. They claimed that she earned $37.7 million from concert ticket sales alone. Now, that is pretty damned impressive, to say the least.

It had been an incredible tour for her, performing fifty-five shows across North America alone. During the subsequent European leg of the tour, she performed thirty-five shows in thirteen different countries.

After the astonishing year that she logged in 1999, what was it that made her hot some years, and not so other years? Even she couldn't answer that question completely. "It depends on the year, basically," she said in an attempt to explain. "It would be a good study, because it's been weirdly extreme. Some years I'm the coolest thing that ever happened and then the next year everyone's so over me, and I'm just so past my 'sell by' date" (214). Cher had waited a long time to be back on top, and in 1999, she completely "worked it" to the max!

IF I COULD TURN BACK TIME

Cher started out the year 2000 in an equally active fashion. The first week in January, when the 1999 Grammy Award nominations were announced, she was right there on the list. She was nominated in four different categories, including Record of the Year, Best Pop Album, Best Dance Recording, and Best Remixer of the Year for the "Club 69 Future Anthem Mix" of "Believe."

That same month, she announced that she was returning to the concert halls for another round of her triumphant *Believe* tour. The twenty-one additional concerts would occur across the United States and Canada. She began January 28 in Salt Lake City, Utah, and ended up on March 4 in Philadelphia, Pennsylvania. Reviewing her show at the massive new Staples Center in Los Angeles, Tony Gieske in the *Hollywood Reporter* called the show "a night of trailer park surrealism and mellow bellows" and proclaimed, "she has never looked sexier or more svelte. . . . Glad we got you, babe" (228). Indeed, judging from the thunderous round of applause and the full standing ovation she received that evening, she was a huge hit in her hometown.

In the first months of the new century, the avalanche of repackaged Cher albums continued to appear in music shops. In America, MCA Records released *The Best of Cher/The Millennium Collection*, which featured her biggest solo MCA hits, as well as the full-length (6 minutes, 46 seconds) "Take Me Home" and "All I Ever Need Is You" with Sonny. In Germany, Geffen/Universal Records released *Cher/Millennium Edition*, which teamed a baker's dozen of her 1970s MCA cuts with four of her 1980s Geffen Records cuts, including "Love on a Rooftop."

On February 23, 2000, the Grammy Awards were handed out, also at the Staples Center. Cher was conspicuously missing from the telecast. Although she was not there in person, her song "Believe" took the trophy as the Best Dance Recording of the year. This was—astonishingly—the first Grammy Award of her career.

On March 26, 2000, Cher was one of the presenters at the first Academy Awards of the twenty-first century. Wearing a beautiful and full-length black velvet gown, Cher looked radiant. The long-sleeved, off-the-shoulder gown was worn with a necklace-like chain belt, with a large stone-encrusted crucifix that dangled in her lap. For Cher, this was quite a change of pace. When she got up to the podium to present an award, she commented on how adult and grown-up she was dressing this year, and then assured the crowd that she would never let it happen again. For Cher, wearing something tasteful and sedate was perhaps the most surprising move that she could possibly make.

By far the most surprising thing about Cher's personal life—as the old century ended and the new one began—was the revelation that she had been without a boyfriend for over six years. Several magazines went so far as to proclaim that the once wild Cher was—unbelievably—"celibate." "Well, it's not true," she explained of that rumor. "I don't even know how that celibacy thing got started. I think I told the writer I hadn't had a boyfriend in, oh, I don't know, how many years. But I wouldn't even think of being celibate. I would just think of it as not having a boyfriend. 'Celibate' sounds like you're a nun" (191).

However, she was the first to admit of love,

> [It's] harder to find when you're older. I live in Los Angeles, where newer is better and older is useless. But I guess if grass can grow through cement, love can find you at every time in your life. . . . I'm not the love-the-one-you're-with type. [Being alone] is definitely a deficit, but I certainly don't have the time or energy to share my privacy with some asshole I'm not crazy about. I'm just looking for someone with a great sense of humor who's really creative, fun, sensitive and sweet (171).

Cher was quick to explain that there were certain advantages to being single for a change.

Well, the pros are, you don't have to brush your teeth before you go to bed, and you don't have to shave your legs for weeks at a time, and you can go home and veg out and have control of the clicker [television remote control]. And the cons are, there's not someone who tells you how adorable you are and rubs your head and goes into a crowded press conference and stands at the back and winks at you so that you think, "I can get through this" (214).

Still, those around her were starting to get a little bit concerned. Her own sister, Georganne, claimed, "Cher hasn't been out enough in recent years. You don't meet people in your living room. You have to go out, and she's been a bit reclusive" (171).

One of the dichotomies that exist with Cher is the perception of wild flamboyant Cher, which is her public image, and of the behind-closed-doors Cher, the laid-back private person. The "public" Cher seems like a difficult character for any man to just ask out on a casual date.

According to Bob Esty,

Cher's not at all wild. Although she dresses wildly, she's very conservative in how she lives her life. She loves to dress up and go out. And I'm sure she has a great sex life when she wants to. I got to know her mother a little bit, she's fabulous. And Georganne, her sister, is beautiful and wonderful. And I think Cher always felt like the odd one, and separated from everyone else in the world. She's a loner woman. And when you're a huge celebrity and that, I'm sure it can get very lonely. She's basically shy, and thinking all of the time (101).

Says Esty of Cher's solo status, "I just wish Cher, one day would meet someone, like a Sonny, but who would give her the other side too, the security and the love. Kind of a 'Mr. Right.' Because—as we all know—it's lonely at the top" (101).

In the late 1990s, Cher had begun constructing a massive new house in Malibu, set on a cliff that overlooked the Pacific Ocean. She began making plans to move in, with ample space for friends to stay as well. Although it was nearly completed by the year 2000, she continued to make modifications to it and to the grounds well into 2001. The house itself is a brown structure, and everything in it is either painted, carpeted, or upholstered in shades of brown and beige. For a woman who is so colorful and flamboyant in her lifestyle and dress, one would expect flame red or brilliant orange—but brown? According to her it was a warm and calming color to live amidst.

In November of 2000, gossip columnists were reporting that Cher's bouts of loneliness were being combated by her moving a new roommate into her massive Malibu manse: Rob Camilletti. *Star* magazine, and other publications, were claiming that Rob's acting career never became what he had hoped, and that he was working as a bartender at a Los Angeles bar called the Sunset Room. It was also reported that in 1999, "when Rob wanted a hair transplant, generous Cher picked up the $20,000 tab" (229).

In an article in the *Star,* entitled "Lonely Cher Butters Up Bagel Boy" (November 28, 2000), one unidentified source was quoted as saying, "She's been waiting for Rob to grow up a little before starting over with him" (229). Whether or not Rob's taking up residence in Cher's huge brown and beige *casa* was a platonic, or a romantic, arrangement wasn't explained by Cher at the time. Obviously, the Cher and Rob saga is far from finished.

Among her closest relationships now are those she shares with her children. Chastity has moved up to San Francisco, with her current girl-friend, Laura Lamastro. She is, however, a frequent visitor at her mother's Malibu home. Her son, Elijah, moved out for a while, seeking his own independence. But, as Cher explains, "He did leave for, like six months but then he came back and now everyone says, 'He's never mov-ing out.' I wouldn't mind if he got married and brought his wife home to live" (192).

Like Chastity before him, Elijah has his own rock band. The band is called Deadsy. According to him, he isn't seeking the kind of widespread and massive success that his mother has. "I used to get swarmed at the airport, and it was annoying," he claims. "I'm not into my Mom's whole fame thing. I don't ever want to be, like, crazy famous. I want my band to be ridiculously big, but I don't want to be an icon" (192).

Cher says of her son, "He's a really smart, really talented, really strange person. He marches to his own drummer more than any person I've ever met—except maybe Sonny" (144). According to Chastity, "She's had to be a lot stricter with him" (171).

Not long after Sonny Bono's death in 1998, Chastity became embroiled in the whole controversy regarding the very controversial *Ellen* TV show. As a consultant on the show, she found herself in a posi-tion to deliver her opinions to the press, as she saw fit. When the once light and amusing television series took a different path in its 1997–98 broadcast season, Chastity found it to be a bit too militantly gay, and a lot less entertaining.

Ultimately, she ended up aggravating the show's star, Ellen DeGeneres. Explaining her stance at the time, Chastity said, "Well, I don't want to say 'less gay.' I want to say, 'Just go a little slower.' I don't think her character should have been not gay. She came out as a gay woman, and she should have absolutely been gay. But there are ways to have deferent subplots, ways to do it" (193).

Instead of finding support for her opinions, she ended up being misinterpreted. Although she was astonished by the criticism that she personally took, she was able to see the whole issue in perspective. "Look at my Mom's career," Chastity explained.

> She made the decision to do *Moonstruck,* and she won the Academy Award. Then she made the decision to sell hair care products because it was really good money, and it turned out to be a really bad decision. But she's still the same person who won the Academy Award for *Moonstruck.* People can just turn on you so quickly. . . . It hurt my feelings that people were so quick to judge. [Openly gay comedian] Lea DeLaria really went after me. [She said], that I had the I.Q. of a sea sponge, and "Chastity Bono can bite my ass," which is probably the most repulsive thought I can think of. There's no danger of that happening. And then, of course, there was Ellen. I called her and explained what happened, and I tried to reassure her how much loyalty I had to her show. She listened, but as soon as she starting doing press [interviews], I was the enemy. That was really hard, because I still have so much admiration for what she did. It's hard to have one of your heroes turn on you in such a harsh way. In June [1998] I saw the documentary, *The Real Ellen Story,* and once again she was talking in a negative manner about me. I put a call in to her and talked to her assistant and said, "Let's just sit down and talk about this. I'll buy you a beer, and let's sit down and get past this." I wasn't her enemy; I was an ally of the show. She just couldn't see that. She's not at that point. I don't know if she will ever be (193).

However, growing up as Cher's daughter, she was used to living in a show business fish bowl. She had been doing it for her entire life, so this was hardly something new. "People assume it must be difficult," Chastity claimed, "but I don't have anything to contrast it to, it's all I know. To me, it's complete normalcy. Would it have been nice to have her around more when I was growing up? Absolutely. But she had a lot of responsibility and was supporting many, many people. She did the best she could" (191).

Although it doesn't look like it is going to happen anytime soon, Chastity claims of Cher, "She'd love to be a grandmother. She loves playing with her assistant's nephew and going off to the toy store for friends' kids. But she's never pressured me, and I don't feel ready to make that kind of commitment" (171).

Cher mania continued throughout the year 2000, with a highly publicized television appearance on *Will & Grace,* the announcement of a new twenty-first-century Cher doll, Cher's very personal new album which was made available only on the Internet, two significant new compilation albums in the stores, and talk of a new movie role for television.

In August 2000 the show business trade papers, *Variety* and the *Hollywood Reporter,* announced that talks were underway for Cher's next screen role. This time around it was to be a glitzy, big-budget, made-for-TV production of the Tony award–winning Broadway musical *Mame.* It would feature Cher as the titled star of the production: the outlandish "Auntie" Mame Dennis. Goodness knows that she has behaved like Auntie Mame all of her life. This seemed like a perfect role for her. If the project unfolds as originally discussed, Barbra Streisand would produce the film for ABC-TV. According to *Daily Variety* at that time, "Streisand has officially advised the network she'll only be involved in the project as producer. Hopes were high for Streisand's involvement, but she has decided it was not to be. . . . They'll move to casting a big star for the musical—Cher is on the short list" (230).

In November of 2000, Cher chose to make her follow-up album to the hugely successful *Believe,* a deeply personal one. It was an album that she had originally recorded in the early 1990s, but it was rejected for release by her current label, Warner Brothers Records. She decided to entitle it *Not.Com.mercial,* because that was exactly what it was—out of tune with what was currently going on the music scene. However, she was very "cutting edge" in the fact that she chose to sell to her fans exclusively via her own website: www.cher.com.

The most ironic aspect of the *Not.Com.mercial* album's Internet-only sales method is the fact that Cher herself claims that she is beyond "computer illiterate." According to her, she has no clue what to do with a computer after switching on the power button! "I'm not very Web savvy because I'm dyslexic, so I can't make heads or tails of it," she explains. "I can't type. I have a hard time seeing letters. If they make the software where you can talk into it, I would love that" (231).

Cher herself wrote eight of the *Not.Com.mercial* album's ten songs. In the spring of 1994, she was invited by Miles Copeland to participate in a "writer's retreat" near Bordeaux, France. Recalls Cher, "Even before I left my house [for France], there was magic. The week before my trip I would wake up in the middle of the night and write, and write, and write" (232). She flew to Paris, rented a car, drove down through the French countryside for two hours, and arrived at the castle where this creative retreat was to take place. There she joined several other singer/songwriters including Brenda Russell, Patty Smyth, country star Ty Herndon, and Pat McDonald.

When she came back to the United States, Cher was so excited about the new material she had written that she teamed up with Bruce Roberts to produce the tracks for what she intended to be her next album release. When Warner Brothers Records passed on releasing it, Cher simply put it on the shelf for six years, until she was in a position to release the album herself. She explained. "It's totally uncommercial. It's a part of my personality that never really gets exercised. I just wrote everything the way I felt it. Like my song about Kurt Cobain. One morning I woke up and heard Courtney Love reading his [suicide] letter on the radio. And so the next morning, at 5:00 a.m., I just wrote this song all in one sitting. Then I put it to music" (144).

Although some Cher followers might be surprised to find that she could write songs, many of her fans will recall that she penned the tune "My Song (Too Far Gone)" from her *Take Me Home* album in the 1970s. "I write all the time," Cher explains. "I wrote one of the verses in 'Believe,' I rewrite things in my movies all the time because I have a pattern of speaking that people don't get exactly." Why has it taken so long for her to do some concentrated writing? According to her, "Because I'm a little flighty" (231).

Since Cher had just released *Believe*, the most successful album of her entire four-decade career and a completely in-character Cher-goes-disco release, one would think that she might want to stay in the dance music genre for her follow-up project. Never one to follow the obvious path, Cher preferred to simply release *Not.Com.mercial* on her own, and let the chips fall where they might.

With regard to not wanting to be pigeonholed into one particular genre of music, she explained, "Artists have more than one side, and sometimes people get locked into one thing, and there's no place for anything else, because [radio stations and MTV] are so regulated. . . . That's a brilliant thing that the Web can do: It's a place for things that have no place" (231).

For anyone who has not heard any of the cuts from the *Not.Com.mercial* album, the logical question to ask might be: "Are the songs so awful that they couldn't be released conventionally?" The answer is "no." The music is well-recorded, the lyrics are straightforward and very heartfelt. However, the songs on this album are totally different in style from the entertaining pop hits that have made Cher a star. Also, knowing that this album was not going to be offered in department stores or played on radio stations, Cher was able to pepper the songs with as many four-letter words and expletives as she pleased. And she did exactly that.

The album opens up with the song "Still," which is a great mid-tempo rock ballad of lost love. It is directly followed by the CD's most controversial song, "Sisters of Mercy," on which Cher spends five minutes blasting the nuns at the Catholic orphanage her mother placed her in as a baby. Explains Cher,

> I wrote this song for my mother. After she had me, she got pregnant again. My father took her to Scranton, Pennsylvania, and he left her. I was six or eight months old. So she took me to this Catholic orphanage. She was completely on her own and went to work in this all-night diner for a dollar a night plus tips. She made this arrangement for the nuns to take care of me. Then, my father didn't come back, so she got an abortion. And, she almost died, so for three weeks she couldn't get out of bed. When she came back to see me, the mother superior wouldn't let her. She said, "You are not a fit mother, and you have to put her up for adoption." My mother said the [nuns] were so cruel to her. She was so without any resources, and she felt the weight of this huge establishment against her. That's why I wrote the song (233).

Cher's song lyrics so upset some devout Catholics that a number of church members managed to publicly jump into the fray. Sister Camille D'Arienzo, who is the president of the Brooklyn New York chapter of the real life Sisters of Mercy organization, went on record in the *New York Post* to make a statement. According to her, "If her charges [of cruelty by the nuns] are true, then there is no one of us who would not express sorrow. If they are not true, such harsh criticism, while being unfair, also carries a warning to all . . . who are responsible for the care of all people young or elderly. She's an artist, too, so there also lingers the question of how much imagination preys into an artist's memory" (234).

The song "The Fall (Kurt's Blues)" was written about the suicide of Kurt Cobain. "Fear to Fly" was about the World War II veterans who defended the free world in the 1940s and were often shunned by society when they returned home once the battle was won. Similarly, the song "Our Lady of San Francisco" is about a homeless woman she once encountered in the City by the Bay. One of the best cuts on the album is "Disaster Cake," which Cher penned about one of Chastity's lovers. Explains Cher, "I wrote the song about Chastity's ex-girlfriend, Heidi. She was staying at my home trying to get her life together. I tried to talk to her, but people have always got to learn for themselves! Around my house we call it 'learning the hard way' " (232).

The *Not.Com.mercial* album rounded out its eight Cher-penned songs with two from friends. One of them was "Born with the Hunger," which was given to her by Shirley Eikhard. The other was her 1970 recording of the Sonny Bono composition "Classified 1A," which was the disastrous single that was released just prior to "Gypsys, Tramps, and Thieves."

During the time period in which Cher released *Not.Com.mercial* on the Internet, two new Cher compilations of note were released. In the United States, MCA Records rolled out a two-disc collection called *The Way of Love*. Among the forty songs on this "best of" collection were all of her MCA-released hits from the early 1970s, four Sonny & Cher cuts from the era, and the three biggest hits from her Imperial Records days in the 1960s—including "Bang Bang (My Baby Shot Me Down)." *The Way of Love* also marks the third album appearance of "Classified 1A." The one song on this two-disc compilation that makes its album debut here is the long-forgotten "B" side of the "Classified 1A" single, the Sonny Bono–written and –produced song "Don't Put It on Me." The conga-driven ballad is one of the album's highlights. It is obviously the product of their middle-of-the-road lounge act days.

Also in stores in time for Christmas 2000 was the non-hits Cher compilation called *Behind the Door 1964–1974*, from Australian-based Raven Records. Included on this twenty-five-cut album are sixteen songs from the 1960s and nine from the 1970s. The producers who assembled this album intentionally wanted to release a Cher album that didn't include any of the singer's hit singles so that it could be played next to a Cher hit album without overlapping tracks.

Before the controversy from Cher's song "Sisters of Mercy" had a chance to cool off, the "Dark Lady" diva made one of her most high-profile cross-marketing appearances, on the top-rated American television show *Will & Grace*. Not only did she make a brief appearance on the program itself, but the TV show was also used to market the latest Cher collectable item: the forthcoming Barbie doll series Cher doll. Although the doll was not going to be available to the public until the spring of 2001, it made a notable debut on national television.

The special Cher episode of *Will & Grace* was broadcast on November 16, 2000. The character of Jack gives his friend Will a new Cher doll for his birthday, knowing that Will wouldn't want it—allowing Jack to keep it for himself. In several of the successive scenes, Jack is seen playing with the doll, and doing very affected Cher impersonations. Finally, it leads up to a scene at a coffee shop, where Jack has provided his Cher doll with a seat at the table all her own, complete with a children's "booster" chair.

The real-life Cher shows up, looking very classic "Cher," complete with bell-bottom jeans and a fall of waist-length straight hair. She tells Jack that even she thinks it's a little bizarre that he is talking to her doll as if it were a real person. However, supposed Cher expert Jack doesn't realize that he is actually talking to the real Cher. He then accuses her of being a drag queen. This comment leads to a comical competition between Jack, imitating Cher, and Cher, just being herself.

Finally, in disbelief, the real diva tells Jack to "get a life" and then turns to leave. However, unable to let the job go unfinished, Cher turns back to Jack and sings a chorus line of her signature song "If I Can Turn Back Time." When Jack still doesn't "get" it, he in turn does an over-the-top impersonation of Cher singing the same lyrics. Unable to resist driving her point home, Cher is compelled to slap Jack on the face, reciting her famed *Moonstruck* line: "Snap out of it!"

Although she's on camera less than two minutes she manages to steal the whole show, while effectively plugging the new Cher doll. The Cher doll instantly became the most highly anticipated collectable doll of the new century! According to the *New York Times*, "[It was] a decision by Cher to donate her fees from the sales of the [Cher doll]. Mattel said the organizations receiving those donations would include a foundation that fights facial and cranial disorders among children and a foundation raising money for the National World War II Memorial in Washington [D.C.]" (235).

When the year 2001 debuted, *America Online* ran the New Year's resolutions of several media stars. Cher expounded upon several new album projects she hoped to record and release by the end of the year. "I want to do a live album at Carnegie Hall of old standards, like the ones I used to do on *The Sonny & Cher Show*. And I want to do a country album with all the really great country artists. A Christmas album too. That's what I always say, 'Ok, this is the year I'm going to do those three albums' " (236).

In May of 2001, when the new collectable Cher doll hit toy outlets, it turned out to be quite a work of finely crafted art. According to the Mattel Toys website, the doll is dressed

> in a daring lavender gown designed by Bob Mackie. The Cher doll achieves incredible likeness to her namesake. True to life details including authentic face sculpting, dramatic face paint, and a gorgeous mane of black hair. And the dress—a stunning lavender ensemble fit for this legendary entertainer. Crisscross halter, floor-length skirt and a fabulous feather boa make a bold statement. Silvery swirled detailing accents the gown, adding just the right amount of sparkle to this already breathtaking doll (237).

To say the least, Cher's huge late 1990s comeback was an inspiration to many of her hit-making contemporaries. Says former LaBelle singer Sarah Dash, "I still enjoy her talent today. She has really given me the incentive, because, of our peers, for her to come back in such a big way, was truly fantastic. Santana *and* Cher. I mean don't rest on your laurels! I am anxiously awaiting to see her again, and find out what she does next" (84). Supremes star Mary Wilson is among Cher's biggest supporters. "I don't know how she did it, but I'm just glad that she did, because she's just one of those people, that you don't expect that from—and she came through with it," says Wilson of Cher's return to the top (238).

According to actress Sally Kirkland,

> Cher has been through a lot of ups and downs. It is hard for me to identify with someone who has had it too easy, and hard for me to identify with someone who doesn't get back up and fight for what she believes in. She is definitely the type of person who has a lot of tenacity. Cher just keeps reinventing herself, and she has been amazingly feisty about keeping in the limelight and remaining true to herself. Role models like her come few and far between. I identify with her for standing up for women, and consistently aligning herself with good causes (70).

Now that Cher is at an all-time high in her career, will she be content to rest on her laurels for a while? According to her,

> I keep hoping I'm going to catch that Frank Sinatra wave and never have to prove myself again. You know, that one big wave Sinatra hit, and then

he was "Sinatra" forever and ever? But I'm really fine with the peaks and valleys. It's the valleys that make me—force me—to reach further. I live an artist's life. It's not supposed to be smooth and nice and tidy and neat. I don't like the valleys very much when they're happening and I'm always surprised when I peak again, but I just keep doing it (192).

Yet, isn't her life much more interesting as a roller coaster, than if it suddenly all became smooth sailing? "Oh, it's a lot better to read about than it is to live," she insists.

Yeah, it makes good drama, but it's really difficult, especially when everybody's saying, "There is no way Cher is gonna pull it out this time," and I also find myself thinking, "Shit! There is no way I'm gonna pull it out this time!" But I'm responsible for my own downfalls, because I am a very strange combination of stability and instability. Emotionally, half of me is solid and down-to-earth, the other half is Judy Garland. But I'm fine with it. I'm good with it, actually. I have lemons, and I make lemonade (192).

Although she is at the peak of her career, she still feels hemmed in by people's preconceptions of her. She is also frustrated being the age she is currently. "I hate my fifties," she claims.

They suck. I never felt older until I hit 50. And the way I first noticed was through my work. When I was 40 I was playing opposite somebody who was 21, and nobody noticed. But at 45, as you start to look older, all you can do is look good for your age. There's a certain span of time—and I'm very much there—when you have to wait till you can play the Shirley MacLaine/Anne Bancroft roles. So what am I supposed to do? Like, go camping for 10 years. . . . When you turn this age, you've been there, done that, bought the T-shirt, got the poster, been the poster. You have to figure out new, creative ways to stay vital, interested, have new dreams. Maybe I'll come back as a cowboy. Maybe next time I'll do better (171).

More film directing seems to be an obvious option for Cher. "There's a place for me to make my talent visible. I don't know if it's in front or behind the camera, but I know I can contribute," she claims (171).

It is interesting to note that many of Cher's biggest-selling songs, like "Take Me Home" and "Believe," resulted from her literally being talked into recording them. It is as though the kind of music Cher thinks she ought to sing isn't always what people want to hear her singing. With regard to her complaints while recording the *Believe* album, Bob Esty explains,

> I heard she hated the experience, like the *Take Me Home* experience, again. But at least this time, I hope, that she's come to realize that when you are good at something, and people like you doing it, you've got to accept it. Maybe it's not your favorite music. And maybe you don't understand why people like it, but they love it and love her. I was thrilled to find out that she was going to perform "Take Me Home" in her act. She is bigger than any of the rock acts she is emulating, and they all want to be her! I hope she is having a good time with the music she is doing now, because everyone else is sure enjoying listening to her do it (101).

As of late, Cher has also become weary of her tattoos. She has also publicly stated that she is considering getting them removed. "When I got them, no one else had them. Now everyone has them. They're not so fabulous anymore" (171).

While Cher has worn wigs ever since her days on *The Sonny & Cher Comedy Hour,* in the mid-1990s, she began wearing them exclusively for all of her public appearances. Since that time she has been experimenting with blonde wigs, red wigs, black wigs, and white wigs. "You know, I've worn wigs my whole life when I work, so they don't ruin my hair," she explains.

> And that's how I keep my hair really nice. I don't spray it, I don't tease it, I don't put lots of crap in it. I just wear it straight and long. I buzzed it and dyed it white once a long time ago, but mostly, it's long now. But I have really cool wigs, colored striped wigs and everything, because it's fun to be able to be more current. But I don't want to be bothered with that kind of shit when I'm alone. I just want my hair. It happens that this year [1999], my hair is pretty "in." "Cher hair" is coming back in a big way and I just happen to still have it (23).

Since she seems to perpetually be on the all of the "worst-dressed" celebrity lists, does she have any style regrets? She claims, "I don't, because style's not big enough to have regrets about. You go, 'Oh, that was a stupid dress,' and you move on. Or you say, 'Oh, that was great,' and you move on. Style is what you've got on the outside and it's just for fun or to make some sort of a statement; but it hasn't got very much to do with who you are on the inside" (23).

Cher claims that it isn't easy being Cher—especially when she dresses to be noticed, which she generally does. Her every public appearance seems to be prefaced with the anticipation of, "What will Cher wear?" As she explains, "It's just one of those things where you don't know what you're letting yourself in for. You try to make an impact on people, and then you do make an impact, and then you're screwed" (212). Now that she's been a fashion mannequin for the entirety of her public career, in 1998 she announced, "[I'm] not as into fashion, the quantity of it, as I used to be. I don't have to be" (171). Yeah, right, like anybody is gonna believe that.

In fact she claims that she has no regrets whatsoever. "Too few to mention. No, I've had lots of them, but it's the old, 'You can't cry over spilled milk,' because you can become your own regret archivist, and who's got time for that? Try to just log it somewhere and not repeat the mistake too many times" (214).

Has she ever longed for anonymity?

Sometimes I hate not having any privacy. But I don't know that I hate being Cher because that's who I am. I do wish I'd created myself smaller. Some people have great private lives, too. I didn't create that somehow. I didn't know the penalty for being too large. I wish I'd created [a public/private persona like] Michelle Pfeiffer or Mel Gibson—people who when they're off screen, they're off screen. I've created something that was too flamboyant (23).

There are also times in which she longs to be in a different line of creativity. "If I could be anything," she says, "I'd be a painter, because then I could just do my work and not need anybody to do it and not have to be judged at the moment of doing it" (119).

If Cher would pick her favorite song that she has recorded, what would it be? Hard-pressed to pick just one, she replies, "There are two, and neither one of them was a hit. One was 'I Paralyze,' and the other was 'Save Up All Your Tears'" (214).

When I listen to music, it's mostly the sound that gets me first, and if the lyrics are fabulous, well then, that's a bonus. But my favorite song is "A Whiter Shade of Pale" by Procol Harum, and I still have no idea what the fuck they're talking about. . . . The moment the organ comes in, I'm just toast. . . . I'm pretty eclectic. I like Marilyn Manson, too. I look at Marilyn Manson like a mother would, like I'm sure his mother looks at him. I don't make a moral judgment; I just like the images. You know, I don't like the content very much, but I think it's a phase he's going through (214).

Since that song "Believe" has become her new anthem, does Cher herself believe in life after love? According to her, "Definitely. I've experienced it. It's been a long time; I've never been alone this long" (214).

Now that she is in her mid-fifties, can we look forward to her continuing to tour when she is sixty or seventy? "Oh, I can't envision that," she says.

This is just such a hard job. How Tina Turner can still do it blows my mind. Every night, for a nonstop hour and a half, I'm singing, dancing, running around backstage, ripping off my clothes and changing costumes nine times. I'm constantly moving. But, I'd rather take a gun and shoot the roof of my mouth off than just come out on-stage, stand there in one outfit and sing. That is sooo not me. I'm not a singer—I'm an entertainer. I'm there to make it sparkly. Maybe when I get really old, I'll teach. Maybe I'll teach acting to kids. The arts can keep kids from making terrible mistakes in their lives (191).

As much as she loves acting in movies, she also admits that she can be difficult if things don't go her way.

If you're a man and you're a strong negotiator in a group of men, they respect you for that and even admire you. If you're a woman, they just think you're a bitch. And, also, men wouldn't try to pull some crap with other guys that they normally try to get way with when they deal with women. It's hard, because I don't think it's really a woman's way for the most part. You have to pretend to be tougher than you are. I do a lot of acting. The truth is, I'm usually the easiest person in the world to get along with on the set or wherever I'm working. I'm not a prima donna. But I don't like having my eagerness or my gentleness being mistaken for weakness and then having someone try to mess with me. It really makes me cranky (23).

Ever since Sonny Bono's untimely death in 1998, Cher has been singing a different tune when she thinks of him. Where once she would do her best to be snide about him, she now sees their relationship with different eyes. She now admits, "Oh, God, I wouldn't be here if I hadn't met Sonny. I definitely wouldn't be here. It's weird. If something happened to your mother and then I asked you what your relationship meant to you, it's just part of you that's hard to explain. It is what it is, but it's inside me" (23).

If we are to believe that Cher is now self-confident and happy with herself, then what's up with all of the plastic surgery? Is she finally done with it? Hopefully she is happy with the work that she has had done, and she will leave well enough alone. Although she downplays the work that she has had done on herself, the photos of her show undeniably dramatic changes over the years.

Ponders social critic and author Camille Paglia, "Because of her working-class background, a mass audience of women have a deep empathy with her emotional life. If Cher's a joke, she made herself so by having too much surgery. Until she altered her nose she looked like an Indian princess. Then she started looking less and less like herself and started to drift, like Michael Jackson, into a solipsistic fantasy" (24).

And then there are times when she is incredibly frank. According to Lily Tomlin, "It's a really interesting dichotomy. I remember after she divorced Gregg, she did this performance in an amphitheater. She had blow-ups of all her tabloid covers and she went through them all and told the audience what really happened. Even when you go out to dinner with her, she tells you so much personal stuff so flat out you're amazed" (144).

Several years ago, Cher read a critical article about herself that claimed that after the nuclear holocaust, the only living creatures on the planet will be "cockroaches and Cher" (24). After getting over the shock of seeing such a statement in print, she was able to see the humor in such a prediction. Given the indestructibility of Cher's career, it is a bizarrely complimentary conclusion to draw.

What is it that makes Cher a star? Is it her singing? In musical terms, she doesn't have the technically best voice in the world, but the voice she does have is distinctively expressive, filled with emotion, and undeniably unique. "Gypsys, Tramps and Thieves," "Dark Lady," "The Way of Love," "Half Breed," "Take Me Home," "I Found Someone," and "Believe" aren't so much songs as they are dramatic performances set to music.

Is it her body? One has to admit—she has never lost her figure. She still looks great, and always has. We have never seen a fat version of Cher, or one who is disheveled or unkempt. She is rather the opposite. Sometimes she is glamorous, and sometimes she dresses like she thinks everyday is Halloween, but she always dresses and behaves like a star.

Is it her acting? She has delivered several great performances in her film career, with her strongest work appearing in *Mask, Silkwood, Moon-*

struck, Mermaids, and *Tea with Mussolini.* As a stage star, she was a delight to watch in *Come Back to the Five and Dime, Jimmy Dean, Jimmy Dean.* Although some might argue that she isn't the most flexible actress on the screen, whenever she appears in front of a movie camera, she is undeniably mesmerizing to watch.

Is it her living soap opera life, which has decorated the headlines since the 1970s? What would the legend of Cher be without the headline-grabbing twists and turns in her personal life? What would her life story be like without her affair with Sonny Bono, her disastrous marriage to drugged-out Gregg Allman, or her love affair with the infamous "Bagel Boy"? Then there are her mysterious illnesses, her controversial plastic surgery, Chastity's sex life, her dreadful infomercials, and her dramatically candid statements about whatever she chooses to expound upon.

The key to Cher's success isn't any one of these, as much as it is a by-product of all of these things. For an entire generation who grew up watching Sonny & Cher on television in their unique and strange outfits, Cher will always be that lanky thin girl with long brown hair and bell-bottom pants. For those who grew up in the 1970s, she is perpetually the wise-cracking wife of Sonny. For those who fancy the movies, it is Cher as Loretta in *Moonstruck* who immediately comes to mind. For 1980s rock fans, the thought of Cher in that barely-there "If I Could Turn Back Time" thong certainly leaves an indelible impression. And, now we all have the millennium-era Cher to ponder. She's that bewitching temptress of many haircolors, and many fashionable personas, all set to an effervescently pulsating beat.

She is an Academy Award–winning actress. She is now a Grammy Award–winning recording star. She is truly one of the most colorful characters of the twentieth century. You never know what she is going to wear, or what kind of frank pronouncements are going to spring from her mouth. She is a fashion chameleon, a completely unique song stylist, and she lives the glamorous life of a classic Hollywood star. There has never been anyone quite like her. She is the diva for all seasons. She is Cher.

SOURCES OF
QUOTED MATERIAL

(1) Mark Bego's interview with Cher, March 1, 1979, the Pierre Hotel, New York City.

(2) *Soho Weekly News*, March 8, 1979, "Bob Weiner," gossip column item.

(3) *The Movie Magazine*, Spring 1983, "Cher: Tender Moments with a Motorcycle Mama."

(4) *Us*, July 1, 1988, "This Is My Life and I Get to Do Everything I Want," Mark Morrison.

(5) *People*, April 10, 1978, "Cher, at 31, Faces Up to Feminism and New Hope That There's Light at the End of the Tunnel of Love," Lois Armstrong.

(6) *After Dark*, February 1979, "Conversations with an All-American Vamp," Brant Mewborn.

(7) *Chicago Tribune*, February 15, 1976, "Mother Wants Life to Be Better for Cher," Elaine Markoutsas.

(8) *Vanity Fair*, "Cher: Starred and Feathered," Kevin Sessums, November 1990.

(9) *National Enquirer*, 1980, "Cher's Father Admits I Was Hooked on Heroin for Years," Bob Temmey.

(10) *People*, February 10, 1975, "Uncaged at Last, Cher Wings a TV Solo Where Sonny Crashed," Barbara Wilkins.

(11) *Ladies' Home Journal*, 1975, "Cher—Georgia Holt Has Been a Maid, a Waitress, a Six-time Loser at Marriage. Still, She Raised Her Daughter Cher 'To Be Somebody,'" Ron Horner.

(12) *New York Post*, May 28, 1985, "The 9 Faces of Cher," Stephen M. Silverman.

(13) *Cher!*, by Mark Bego, Pocket Books, New York, New York, 1986, © 1986 Mark Bego.

(14) *TV Guide*, December 25, 1976.

(15) *USA Today*, May 1, 1985, "Cher Owes It All to Dumbo."

(16) *Cher Exposed: Her Life in Pictures*, American Media Inc., Tarrytown, New York, 2000.

(17) *Time*, March 17, 1975, "Cher."

(18) *Playboy*, 1975, "Playboy Interview: Cher."

(19) *Cosmopolitan*, January 1984, "Cheers for Cher," Tom Burke.

(20) *Los Angeles Herald Examiner,* June 5, 1981, "Cher's Dream: To Be the Ethel Merman of the '80s," Darcy Diamond.

(21) *McCall's,* July 1985, "Cher Takes Off Her Mask," Barbara Lovenheim.

(22) *Premiere,* February 1988, "Why You Can't Laugh at Cher Anymore," Jan Hoffman.

(23) *Celebrity Style,* May 1999,"Cher," Michael Slezak.

(24) *New York Times,* June 30, 1996, "Queen of the Comeback, Cher Tries Yet Again," Stephen Holden.

(25) *The First Time,* Cher as told to Jeff Coplon, Simon & Schuster Publishers, New York, New York, 1998.

(26) *Advocate,* August 20, 1996, "Cher: The *Advocate* Interview," Chastity Bono.

(27) *Sunday Tempo,* January 15, 1984, "Cher Taking Off the Make-Up to Apply Her Acting," Candice Russell.

(28) *Behind the Music,* TV series, "Cher," first broadcast April 11, 1999.

(29) *New York Post,* May 31, 1985, "Pimply Cher Shared Sonny's Toothbrush and Undies," Stephen M. Silverman.

(30) *Ladies' Home Journal,* 1974, "Cher's Own Story," Lyn Tornabene.

(31) *TV Guide,* April 12, 1975, "Cher . . . without Sonny," Rowland Barber.

(32) *Look at Us,* by Sonny & Cher, compact disc liner notes, Sundazed Records, 1998. Sonny Bono interview with Ken Sharp, July 12, 1991.

(33) *Rolling Stone,* May 24, 1973, "As Bare as You Dare with Sonny & Cher," Chris Hodenfield.

(34) *McCall's,* June 1974, "What Really Happened to Sonny & Cher," Nellie Blagden.

(35) *And the Beat Goes On,* Sonny Bono, Pocket Books, New York, 1991.

(36) *USA Today,* January 7, 1998, "Tradition Shaped Bono's Career," Andy Seiler, Arlene Vigoda, and Ed Martin.

(37) *Rolling Stone,* March 29, 1984, "Cher Wants to Be Taken Seriously," Lynn Hirschberg.

(38) *The Wondrous World of Sonny & Cher,* Sonny and Cher, compact disc liner notes, Sundazed Records, 1998. Sonny Bono interview with Ken Sharp, July 12, 1991.

(39) *Details,* August 1989, "I Got Clothes, Babe," Michael Schmidt.

(40) Imperial Records, press biography, 1965, "Cher."

(41) *Star,* August 20, 1985, "Cher's Secret Past," Brian Haugh.

(42) *KRLA Beat,* July 7, 1965, "Cher vs. the Byrds," Derek Taylor.

(43) *Star,* August 27, 1985, "Cher's Ex-Con Father Was Blackmailing Her for $500 a Week," Brian Haugh.

(44) *The Wondrous World of Sonny & Cher,* Sonny and Cher, original liner notes by Sonny & Cher, ATCO Records, 1966.

(45) *In Case You're in Love,* Sonny and Cher, compact disc liner notes, Sundazed Records, 1998. Sonny Bono interview with Ken Sharp, July 12, 1991.

(46) *Star,* newspaper, September 3, 1985, "Sonny's Ego Trips over First Movie with Cher Start Bitter Bust-Up," Brian Haugh.

(47) *TV Guide,* magazine, quoting a Sonny & Cher cover story originally dated March 18, 1972, in the magazine's January 24–30, 1998, Sonny Bono cover story, "Sonny Remembered," Fred DeCaro.

(48) *New York Times,* 1967, reviewing the movie *Good Times.*

(49) *Leonard Maltin's 1998 Movie & Video Guide,* Signet Books, New York, New York, 1997.

(50) *New York Post,* August 9, 1969, *Chastity,* review of the film by Archer Winsten.

(51) *Cue,* August 16, 1969, *Chastity,* review of the film by William Wolf.

(52) *Los Angeles Times,* December 5, 1982, "Cher Discovers Acting—and Critics Discover Cher," Roderk Mann.

(53) *Cher: 3614 Jackson Highway,* album liner notes by Cher, Atlantic Records, 1969.

(54) *Sonny & Cher Live,* record album, Kapp Records, 1971.

(55) *All I Ever Need: The Kapp/MCA Anthology* by Cher & Sonny and Cher, compact disc liner notes, MCA Records 1995.

(56) Mark Bego's interview with Daniel Eastman, 1985.

(57) Mark Bego's interview with Bart Andrews, 1985.

(58) *New York Post,* 1971, review of *The Sonny & Cher Comedy Hour.*

(59) *Daily Variety,* 1972, "Hollywood Style," by Army Acherd.

(60) *People,* 1994, "Cher without Sonny: Can the Show Go On?" Nellie Blagden.

(61) *Rolling Stone,* September 19, 1986, "Cher Q&A," Jancee Dunn.

(62) *Vanity Fair,* May 1986, "Très Cher," Arthur Lubow.

(63) *The Operator: David Geffen Builds, Buys and Sells the New Hollywood,* Tom King, Random House, 2000; as excerpted in *People* magazine, March 6, 2000.

(64) *Advocate,* "Chastity Bono: Out at Last/Virtuous Reality," Judy Wieder, April 18, 1995.

(65) *TV Guide,* June 1, 1974, "The Party's Over," Rowland Barber.

(66) *New York Post,* May 30, 1985, "Team Splits Up—But Show Still Goes On," Stephen M. Silverman.

(67) *Us,* April 8, 1985, "Cher Unmasked," Nina Leeds.

(68) *TV Guide,* quoting a Sonny & Cher cover story originally dated June 1, 1974, in the magazine's January 24–30, 1998, Sonny Bono cover story, "Sonny Remembered," Fred DeCaro.

(69) *Newsweek,* June 10, 1974, "Newsmakers" item.

(70) Mark Bego's interview with Sally Kirkland, May 2, 2000, Hollywood, California.

(71) *Esquire,* February 1976, "The Winning of Cher," Julie Baumgold.

(72) *National Enquirer,* June 24, 1975, "Cher's TV Clothes Cost Up to $30,000 a Week," Robert G. Smith.

(73) *New York Daily News,* February 9, 1975, "Will Cher Be a Long-Playing Single?" Kay Gardella.

(74) *Variety,* 1975, review of *The Cher Show,* "Cher Is Back—& a Winner," Bob Knight.

(75) *Los Angeles Times,* February 16, 1975, "Three Cheers for Cher and Her New CBS Variety Show," Cecil Smith.

(76) *Newsweek,* 1975, review of *The Cher Show,* "Cher and Cher Alone," Harry F. Waters.

(77) *Good Housekeeping,* 1975, "Cher: Super Star! Super Mom?" Joseph N. Bell.

(78) *New York Sunday News,* January 25, 1976, "Only on Sunday," Bob Lardine.

(79) *TV Guide,* June 5, 1976, "The Lives and Loves of Salvatore and Cherilyn, Part IV," Rowland Barbar.

(80) *Good Housekeeping,* 1976, "Cher Talks about Cher," Mary Fiore.

(81) *Viva,* 1978, "Gregg Allman: Cher's Sometimes Ex Sings the Blues," Elliot Mintz.

(82) *Chicago Tribune,* April 16, 1975, "Dad Sues Cher."

(83) *Long Island,* February 20, 1977, "Cher: Women Should Feel Some Kind of Worth," Larry Grobel.

(84) *TV Guide,* quoting a Sonny & Cher cover story originally dated June 5, 1976, in the magazine's January 24–30, 1998, Sonny Bono cover story, "Sonny Remembered," Fred DeCaro.

(85) Mark Bego's telephone interview with Sarah Dash, April 28, 2000.

(86) *People,* September 8, 1975, "Now That Cher Has Helped Show Him the Way, Gregg Allman Takes to the Road Again," Jim Jerome.

(87) *People,* December 5, 1977, "Chatter" gossip item, "Paternity Toot."

(88) *Rolling Stone,* November 4, 1976, "The Sorrowful Confessions of Gregg Allman," Patrick Snyder.

(89) *New York Post,* September 16, 1977, "First Look at the New Cher."

(90) *People,* September 9, 1977, "Hey, Who Is That Lady with Howard Himmelstein? She Came Dressed Not to Kill but to Boogie."

(91) *Us,* January 10, 1978, "Cher & Gregg: The Losing Fight to Save Their Marriage," Elliot Mintz.

(92) *People,* 1977, "Chatter" item.

(93) *Celebrity,* July 1977, "Cher & Other Dolls," Rick Mitz.

(94) *New York Daily News,* March 22, 1978, "Cher Plays It Single and Special," Kay Gardella.

(95) *Star,* April 11, 1979, "Cher: My New Life," Robin Leach.

(96) *Star,* December 5, 1978, "Superstar Cher Splits $4 with Sonny and Plans for a Golden New Year," Robin Leach.

(97) *People,* 1979, "Chatter" item.

(98) *People,* October 22, 1977, "She Still Shakes—Not Knits—Booties, but Cher's Approaching Domesticity with Gene Simmons," Lois Armstrong.

(99) *Ladies' Home Journal*, April 1979, "Cher," Varina M. Druce.

(100) *Rolling Stone*, October 16, 1980, "Cher Plays It Low-Key with Black Rose," Jim Farber.

(101) Mark Bego's interview with Bob Esty, Los Angeles, California, April 25, 2000.

(102) Mark Bego's interview with Barbara Shelley, 1985.

(103) *New York Times*, March 7, 1979, "TV: Cher and Fantasies," Tom Buckley.

(104) *Los Angeles Times*, June 24, 1979, "Selective, Striking, Shy—All Très Cher," Roderick Mann.

(105) *Los Angeles Times*, June 8, 1981, "Cher: Lots of Flash, No Heart at the Greek," Paul Grein.

(106) Mark Bego's telephone interview with Randy Jones, May 1, 2000.

(107) *People*, 1980, gossip item.

(108) *New York Daily News*, October 7, 1980, "Cher: Rockin' and Rollin' to a New Life," Andy Secher.

(109) *Us*, November 11, 1980, "She's Got Herself a New Guy and a Whole New Shtick as a No-Name Rock Singer. But Cher is Cher. . . . " Michael Musto.

(110) Press statement of Howard Squadron of the *Star* newspaper, 1980.

(111) *Los Angeles Herald Examiner*, January 11, 1983, "Cher Looks Ahead to a Whole New Career."

(112) *Los Angeles Herald Examiner*, December 18, 1983, "Cher Finally Gets Some Respect," Hal Hinson.

(113) *New York*, February 1, 1982, "Cher and Altman on Broadway," Jennifer Allen.

(114) *New York Times*, October 22, 1981, "Robert Altman to Direct Cher in Broadway Debut."

(115) *New Woman*, February 1988, "Cher Delight," Jim Watters.

(116) *New York Times*, March 12, 1982, item in the "Arts & Leisure" section of the paper.

(117) *New York Times*, February 19, 1982, review of *Come Back to the Five and Dime, Jimmy Dean, Jimmy Dean*, Frank Rich.

(118) *New York Daily News*, February 19, 1982, review of *Come Back to the Five and Dime, Jimmy Dean, Jimmy Dean*, Rex Reed.

(119) *The Cable Guide*, "Cher Struck," Jay Gissen, March 1989.

(120) *People*, 1985, "Cher Finds a New Life," Jim Jerome.

(121) *On Cable*, December 1984, "Do You Know Me?" Michael Reeves.

(122) *New York Daily News*, January 20, 1983, "Cher's Not Selling Self Short in '5 and Dime,' " Marilyn Beck.

(123) *New York Times*, 1983, reviewing the film *Silkwood*.

(124) *People*, April 16, 1984, "Star Tracks" gossip item.

(125) *Star*, March 24, 1981, "Why I'll Stop at Nothing to Keep My Body Looking Young and Sexy."

(126) *Star*, April 9, 1985, "Cher Rockets Back to the Top with a New Man & Plans for Another Baby," Brian Haugh.

(127) *People,* 1985, "Cher's Got Critics Raving over Her Risky Role—And Off-screen She's Got a Loving New Man," Jim Jerome.

(128) *USA Today,* March 14, 1985, "Cher's Role Thrills the Real Life Rusty."

(129) *USA Today,* March 21, 1985, "Cher's Seriousness Is No Act," Tom Green.

(130) *Los Angeles Times,* April 8, 1985, "Cher Earns Share of Spotlight," Deborah Caulfield.

(131) *USA Today,* March 8, 1985, "The Profound Truth Lies Behind *Mask,*" Jack Mathews.

(132) *New York Post,* March 8, 1985, "*Mask:* A Cher-Delight," Rex Reed.

(133) *New York Daily News,* March 8, 1975, "The 'Elephant Boy's' Story," Kathleen Carroll.

(134) *USA Today,* Mary 15, 1985, "Festival Face-Off over Mask," Jack Mathews.

(135) *People,* June 3, 1985, "Fair Cher?" Fred Bernstein.

(136) *Madonna: Blonde Ambition,* Mark Bego, Cooper Square Press, 2000.

(137) *USA Today,* October 31, 1985, "Cher's Battle with Dyslexia."

(138) *USA Today,* April 30, 1987, "Turning the Spotlight on Stars' Moms," Matt Roush.

(139) *The Academy Awards* presentation, Los Angeles, California, March 24, 1986.

(140) *Kelly & Company,* TV show, WXYZ-TV, Detroit, Michigan, March 28, 1986, Shirley Eder and Rex Reed as guests discussing the Academy Awards.

(141) *Kelly & Company,* TV show, WXYZ-TV Detroit, Michigan, February 24, 1986, Marilyn Turner interviewing nutritionist Robert Haas.

(142) *Late Night with David Letterman,* television show, May 1986, CBS-TV.

(143) *Indianapolis Star,* Indianapolis, Indiana, July 7, 1986, [quoting *People* magazine item], "Letterman Recalls His Loss of Poise at Cher's Hands."

(144) *Entertainment Weekly,* April 23, 1999, "Hip to Be Cher," Benjamin Svetkey.

(145) *Witches of Eastwick,* film, directed by George Miller, 1987.

(146) *Tallahassee Democrat,* Tallahassee, Florida, August 4, 1986, "Names and Faces" column item "Cher Escapes Accident with Minor Injuries."

(147) *New York Times,* December 11, 1987, as reproduced in the production notes included in the DVD copy of *Moonstruck.*

(148) *Box Office,* January 1988, as reproduced in the production notes included in the DVD copy of *Moonstruck.*

(149) *Los Angeles Times,* March 1, 1987, as reproduced in the production notes included in the DVD copy of *Moonstruck.*

(150) *Backstage,* January 13, 1987, as reproduced in the production notes included in the DVD copy of *Moonstruck.*

(151) *Moonstruck, Original Press Kit,* 1987, as reproduced in the production notes included in the DVD copy of *Moonstruck.*

(152) *Moonstruck,* audio commentary included as a bonus track on the DVD copy of the film, MGM Pictures, 1998.

(153) *New York Post,* January 7, 1998, "Death on the Slopes II—He Made the Most of What He Had," David Hinckley and Thomas Galvin.

(154) *TV Guide,* January 24–30, 1998, "Sonny Remembered," Fred DeCaro.

(155) *People,* May 16, 1985, "Loving Linguine as Time Goes By."

(156) *Star,* June 18, 1985, "Sonny Blasts Back 'I Nearly Went Broke to Make Her the Star She Is Today'," Audrey Lavin.

(157) *USA Today,* October 22, 1987, "Cher Rocks, Rolls and Directs," Jeannie Williams.

(158) *Chicago Sun Times,* June 12, 1987, *The Witches of Eastwick,* review by Roger Ebert.

(159) *Washington Post,* June 12, 1987, *The Witches of Eastwick,* review by Rita Kempley.

(160) *Washington Post,* June 12, 1987, *The Witches of Eastwick,* review by Desson Howe.

(161) *Chicago Sun Times,* October 23, 1987, *Suspect,* review by Roger Ebert.

(162) *Washington Post,* October 23, 1987, *Suspect,* review by Hal Hinson.

(163) *Washington Post,* October 23, 1987, *Suspect,* review by Desson Howe.

(164) *Music Connection,* September 18, October 1, 1989, "Cher," Kenny Kerner.

(165) *Siskel & Ebert at the Movies,* TV show, as quoted in the *New York Times,* December 25, 1987, reviewing *Moonstruck.*

(166) *Chicago Sun Times,* January 15, 1988, *Moonstruck,* review by Roger Ebert.

(167) *Washington Post,* January 15, 1988, *Moonstruck,* review by Rita Kempley.

(168) *Late Night with David Letterman,* television show, February 28, 1988.

(169) *Los Angeles Times,* January 19, 1984, "It All Finally Falls into Place For Cher," Kristine McKenna.

(170) *New York Times,* Macy's department store catalog, copy advertising the perfume "Uninhibited—by Cher," February 1989.

(171) *People,* May 29, 1998, "Being Cher," Jim Jerome.

(172) *Time,* June 19, 1989, "Solo, For Now," an item on the "People" page, Emily Mitchell.

(173) *People,* June 19, 1989, "Solo Again, Cher No Longer Acts in Concert with Rob Camilletti."

(174) *USA Today,* August 18, 1989, "Cher's Sizzling Tour/Pouring Her Heart into Her Show," Jeannie Williams.

(175) *New York Daily News,* August 25, 1989, "Memo to Cher: Let Loose," David Hinckley.

(176) *Los Angeles Times,* June 23, 1990, "Cher: Glitz Not Gold," Mike Boehm.

(177) *Star,* October 3, 1989, "Cher Says 'I Will' after Rocker Richie Dazzles Her with $10G Ring."

(178) *Chicago Sun Times,* December 14, 1990, *Mermaids,* review by Roger Ebert.

(**179**) *Washington Post,* December 14, 1990, *Mermaids,* review by Desson Howe.

(**180**) *Washington Post,* December 14, 1990, *Mermaids,* review by Hal Hinson.

(**181**) *People,* December 23, 1991, "From Cher, with Love," Jim Jerome.

(**182**) *CBS This Morning,* television show, June 14, 1991, interview with Cher.

(**183**) *Encyclopedia of Rock Stars,* Dafydd Rees & Luke Crampton, 1996, DK Publishing, New York.

(**184**) *People,* December 23, 1991, advertisement for the video cassette *Cherfitness—A New Attitude.*

(**185**) *USA Today,* March 2, 1992, " 'World' is DiLeo's Oyster," Karen Thomas.

(**186**) *USA Today,* July 20, 1990, "Cher, A Perot Booster."

(**187**) *USA Today,* February 11, 1992, "Cher Sweet on Equal in NutraSweet Ad."

(**188**) *People,* January 19, 1998, "Sonny Bono: His Improbable Life and Sudden Death/Last Run," by Karen S. Schneider, Todd Gold, Jeanne Gordon, Lyndon Stambler, Elizabeth Leonard, and Margery Sellinger.

(**189**) *Washington Post,* circa 1990, exact date unknown.

(**190**) *National Enquirer,* February 13, 1990, "Branded a Gay, Cher's Daughter Chastity Fights Back—THE TRUTH ABOUT CHER, MEN & ME—Exclusive Interview," Steve Herz and Patricia Towle.

(**191**) *New York Times,* July 9, 1997, "Growing Up in Public: From Babe in Arms to Gay Advocate," Alex Witchel.

(**192**) *TV Guide,* "Cher the Experience," Michael Logan, August 21–27, 1999.

(**193**) *Advocate,* "Chastity Lets Loose/The Sudden Adulthood of Chastity Bono," Gabriel Rotello.

(**194**) *Ready to Wear,* film, directed by Robert Altman, 1994.

(**195**) *The Glory of Gershwin,* album liner notes, Mercury Records, 1994.

(**196**) *Billboard,* May 18, 1996, "Cher Changes Approach for Her 'Man's World' on Reprise," Jim Bessman.

(**197**) *Cher Live in Concert,* August 29, 1999, concert performance broadcast and taped live from Las Vegas via HBO-TV.

(**198**) *San Francisco Examiner,* April 3, 1996, review of *Faithful* entitled *"Faithful* Can Be Truly Confusing," Barbara Shulgasser.

(**199**) *USA Today,* 1996, review of *Faithful* entitled *"Faithful* Plods a Misguided Course," Mike Clark.

(**200**) *San Francisco Chronicle,* August 30, 1996, review of *Faithful* entitled, "Even Cher's Good Looks Can't Save *Faithful,"* Peter Stack.

(**201**) *Tucson Weekly,* April 4, 1996, review of *Faithful* by Stacey Richter.

(**202**) *If These Walls Could Talk,* film, 1996, HBO Pictures.

(**203**) *New York Times,* January 11, 1998, "The World According to the Guy Who Wore the Furry Vest," Tom Kuntz. NOTE: This article quoted material from several other publications, including the *Los Angeles Times,* the *Chicago Tribune,* and minutes from the Washington Press Club Foundation.

(204) *USA Today,* February 2, 1995, "He's Got Guts, Babe: Bono in Role of Rebel," Jessica Lee.

(205) *USA Today,* January 7, 1998, "Bono's Death Ends American Odyssey—Soft Reputation Belied Hard Reality of a Success Story," Jill Lawrence.

(206) *New York Post,* January 7, 1998, "Left Behind a Rift with Daughter," Corky Siemaszko. NOTE: This article quoted material from the British publication *OK* magazine.

(207) *New York Post,* January 7, 1998, "Tearful Ex-Wife Cher Jets to Daughter's Side," Bill Hoffman and Ward Morehouse.

(208) Mark Bego's telephone interview with Anne Bego, January 5, 1998.

(209) *New York Post,* January 10, 1998, "He Planned to Buy Helmet—Next Time," Associated Press wire service story.

(210) *New York Post,* January 7, 1998, "Family Had No Idea of Horror," Denise Buffa, Brendan Bourne, and Tracy Connor.

(211) *New York Post,* January 7, 1998, "Bono Is Killed in Ski Accident," Michelle Caruso, Virginia Breen, and Corky Siemaszko.

(212) *New York Post,* January 10, 1998, "Two of Sonny's Wives Are Sisters in Grief" (incorporating quotes from the Palm Springs newspaper the *Desert Sun*), Larry Sutton.

(213) *New York Post,* January 10, 1998, "Bono's Humor & Vision Honored," Michelle Caruso and Larry Sutton.

(214) *Rolling Stone,* April 15, 1999, "Q&A Cher," Mim Udovitch.

(215) *USA Today,* January 15, 1998, "Bono's Wives Share Memories."

(216) *National Enquirer,* January 27, 1998, "Sonny's Widow & Cher How They Are Mending Their Broken Hearts . . . Together/Cher Helps Sonny's Shattered Widow Pick Up The Pieces," John South, Jeffrey Rodack, and Larry Haley.

(217) *USA Today,* January 26, 1998, "In Politics, The Beat Goes On," Larry King.

(218) *New York Times,* March 29, 1998, "The Widow's Run," Frank Bruni.

(219) *Star,* December 8, 1998, "Mystery of Autopsy Report: Who Killed Sonny Bono?" Bob Smith. NOTE: This article quoted material from *TV Guide* magazine.

(220) *Capital Style,* September 1998, "Partly Sonny and Hot/Pro Bono," Susan Crabtree. NOTE: This article quoted material from *People* magazine.

(221) *Entertainment Weekly,* February 19, 1999, "The Sonny Side," Ken Tucker.

(222) *VH1 Divas Live '99,* VH1 television coverage, April 13, 1999, Cher interviewed backstage at the event.

(223) *San Francisco Chronicle,* May 14, 1999, "*Tea* Illuminates Early Inspiration of an Artist," Mick LaSalle.

(224) *Chicago Sun Times,* May 14, 1999, *Tea with Mussolini,* review by Roger Ebert.

(225) *Tucson Weekly,* June 14, 1999, *Tea with Mussolini,* review by James Di Giovanna.

(226) *CDNow,* Internet music service, July 30, 1999, "Cher Breaks More Dates," Kevin Raub.

(227) *Entertainment Weekly,* August 31, 1999, "Cher Wear," Ken Tucker.

(228) *Hollywood Reporter,* February 2000, "Cher," review of her show at the Staples Center, Tony Gieske.

(229) *Star,* November 28, 2000, "Lonely Cher Butters Up Bagel Boy," Jennifer Pearson.

(230) *Daily Variety,* August 24, 2000, "Streisand Won't Play Mame" from the "Dish" column, by Michael Fleming.

(231) *Entertainment Weekly,* daily newswire, website, posted November 6, 2000, "Cher Wares: She Doesn't Surf the Web, but She Embraces It," Chris Willman.

(232) *Not.Com.mercial,* album liner notes by Cher, Artist Direct Records, 2000.

(233) *People,* November 27, 2000, "Cher, Nuns & Trouble."

(234) *New York Post.com,* newspaper website, November 3, 2000, "Cher Catches Holy Hell," Chris Wilson and Bill Hoffmann.

(235) *New York Times,* November 16, 2000, "Guest Role on NBC for Cher, the Doll," Stuart Elliott.

(236) *America Online,* music section, "Stars New Year's Resolutions," January 4, 2001.

(237) Mattel Toys, website, description of the Cher Doll, 2000.

(238) Mark Bego's interview with Mary Wilson, Los Angeles, California, April 26, 2000.

CHER MOVIE QUOTES

"Snap out of it!"⁓*Moonstruck*

"Drink up—because the champagne's on me!"⁓*Tea with Mussolini*

"If we're gonna have it, let's have it all!"⁓*The Witches of Eastwick*

"You must be confusing me with someone who gives a shit."⁓*Mask*

"When a woman comes to me and says that she doesn't know what she would have done without my help, I know I'm doing the right job."⁓*If These Walls Could Talk*

"Ma, I love him awful."⁓*Moonstruck*

"Yeah, well, at least someone's getting something once a week."⁓*The Witches of Eastwick*

"Well, if you're gonna be in the newspaper, then I wanna be in there too."⁓*Silkwood*

"Bad luck, that's it—is that all I'm ever gonna have?"⁓*Moonstruck*

"You take their money, you gotta take their shit."⁓*Mask*

"You are gonna be up there on the movie screen, with Jimmy Dean."⁓*Come Back to the Five and Dime, Jimmy Dean, Jimmy Dean*

"I need my family around me now."⁓*Moonstruck*

"I'm your lawyer, anything you tell me is confidential."⁓*Suspect*

"I don't think that men are the answer to everything."⁓*The Witches of Eastwick*

"I suppose you think this is divine providence."—*Mermaids*

"I think it's not about what you put on your body. I think it's more about what you are on the inside."—*Ready to Wear*

"I always see snakes—hundreds of them, and they're crawling all over me, and I disappear, and then I'm just not there anymore."—*The Witches of Eastwick*

"Well, are we having fun yet?"—*The Player*

DISCOGRAPHY

NOTE: On albums originally released from 1965 to 1986, these listings are configured as per their original two-sided vinyl lineup. From 1987 forward, the album listings are configured as per one-sided CD release. Configuration and record company listed is as per original American release, unless otherwise noted. The songwriters' names appear as they appeared on the original releases. First names have been added when available, or whenever provided.

The playing time of each of these cuts is provided whenever possible. Occasionally the song lengths will differ from album to album. This is especially true in songs like "Take Me Home," which was originally over six minutes long. Some of the "Greatest Hits" albums are comprised only of shorter single versions of songs. Original album times may differ from the later CD versions.

This discography is compiled of the original American albums, release dates, and original label. Also included are the most successful and most readily available import albums from around the world. Some of the album titles are identical, although their contents are completely different. For example, there are three separate albums entitled *Cher,* one in the 1960s, one in the 1970s, and one in the 1980s.

There is also a discrepancy in the way the word "Gypsys" is spelled in "Gypsys, Tramps and Thieves." The original album and single was spelled "Gypsys," while later albums spelled it as "Gypsies." For the sake of continuity, it is spelled throughout as "Gypsys."

Cher Solo Albums

1. *ALL I REALLY WANT TO DO* (Imperial Records) 1965
   Producer: Sonny Bono

   Side One
   1. "All I Really Want to Do"
      (Bob Dylan) 2:56
   2. "I Go to Sleep"
      (Ray Davies) 2:28
   3. "Needles and Pins"
      (Sonny Bono, Jack Nitzsche) 2:26

   Side Two
   1. "The Bells of Rhymney"
      (Seeger, Davies) 3:07
   2. "Girl Don't Come"
      (Chris Andrews) 2:05
   3. "See See Rider"
      (Sonny Bono, Greene, Stone) 2:38

4. "Don't Think Twice, It's All Right"
   (Bob Dylan) 2:25
5. "She Thinks I Still Care"
   (L. Lipscomb) 2:25
6. "Dream Baby"
   (Sonny Bono) 2:28

4. "Come Stay with Me"
   (Jackie DeShannon) 2:45
5. "Cry Myself to Sleep"
   (Mike Gordon) 2:18
6. "Blowin' in the Wind"
   (Bob Dylan) 3:24

2. *THE SONNY SIDE OF CHER* (Imperial Records) 1965
Producer: Sonny Bono

Side One
1. "Bang Bang (My Baby Shot
   Me Down)"
   (Sonny Bono) 2:40
2. "A Young Girl (*Une Enfante*)"
   (Aznavour, Chauvigny,
   O'Brown Jr.) 3:22
3. "Where Do You Go"
   (Sonny Bono) 3:12
4. "Our Day Will Come"
   (Hilliard, Garson) 2:12
5. "Elusive Butterfly"
   (Bob Lind) 2:30
6. "Like a Rolling Stone"
   (Bob Dylan) 3:45

Side Two
1. "Ol' Man River"
   (Kern, Hammerstein II) 2:50
2. "Come to Your Window"
   (Bob Lind) 2:48
3. "The Girl from Ipanema"
   (Jobim, Gimbel, V. DeMoraes) 2:09
4. "It's Not Unusual"
   (G. Mills, L. Reed) 2:08
5. "Time"
   (Michael Merchant) 3:16
6. "Milord"
   (G. Moustaki, B. Lewis, M. Monnot)
   2:43

3. *CHER* (Imperial Records) 1966
Producer: Sonny Bono

Side One
1. "Sunny"
   (Bobby Hebb) 3:06
2. "Twelfth of Never"
   (Livingston, Webster) 2:14
3. "You Don't Have to Say You Love
   Me"
   (Pallavicini, Wickham, Napier, Bell,
   Donaggio) 2:45
4. "I Feel Something in the Air"
   (Sonny Bono) 3:38
5. "Will You Love Me Tomorrow"
   (Gerry Goffin, Carole King) 2:55
6. "Until It's Time for You to Go"
   (Buffy Sainte-Marie) 2:45

Side Two
1. "Cruel War"
   (Peter Yarrow, Paul Stookey) 3:40
2. "Catch the Wind"
   (Donovan) 2:13
3. "Pied Piper"
   (A. Kornfield, S. Duboff) 2:22
4. "Homeward Bound"
   (Paul Simon) 2:52
5. "I Want You"
   (Bob Dylan) 2:53
6. "Alfie"
   (Burt Bacharach, Hal David) 2:48

4. *WITH LOVE, CHER* (Imperial Records) 1968
   Producer: Sonny Bono

Side One
1. "You Better Sit Down Kids"
   (Sonny Bono) 3:42
2. "But I Can't Love You More"
   (Sonny Bono) 3:34
3. "Hey Joe"
   (W. M. Roberts) 3:26
4. "Mama (When My Dollies Have
   Babies)"
   (Sonny Bono) 3:24
5. "Behind the Door"
   (Graham Gouldman) 3:36

Side Two
1. "Sing for Your Supper"
   (Richard Rodgers, Lorenz Hart)
   2:34
2. "Look at Me"
   (Keith Allison) 3:10
3. "There but for Fortune"
   (Phil Ochs) 3:25
4. "I Will Want for You"
   (N. Gimbel, M. LeGrand) 3:12
5. "The Times They Are A-Changin' "
   (Bob Dylan) 3:07

5. *BACKSTAGE* (Imperial Records) 1968
   Producers: Sonny Bono, Harold R. Battiste, Jr., and Denis Pregnolato

Side One
1. "Go Now"
   (Bennet, Banks) 3:56
2. "Carnival"
   (Perette, Creator, Weiss, Maria,
   Bonfa, DeArozamena) 3:26
3. "It All Adds Up to Now"
   (Douglas Sham) 2:57
4. "Reason to Believe"
   (Tim Hardin) 2:26
5. "Masters of War"
   (Bob Dylan) 4:09
6. "Do You Believe in Magic"
   (John B. Sebastian) 2:36

Side Two
1. "I Wasn't Ready"
   (Dr. John Creaux, Jessie Hill) 2:59
2. "A House Is Not a Home"
   (Burt Bacharach, Hal David) 2:14
3. "Take Me for a Little While"
   (Trade Martin) 2:40
4. "The Impossible Dream"
   (Joe Dorion, Mitch Leigh) 2:25
5. "The Click Song"
   (Miriam Makeba) 2:53
6. "A Song Called Children"
   (Bob West) 3:35

6. *CHER'S GOLDEN GREATS* (Imperial Records) 1968
Producer: Sonny Bono

Side One
1. "You Better Sit Down Kids"
   (Sonny Bono) 3:42
2. "Sunny"
   (Bobby Hebb) 3:06
3. "Come and Stay with Me"
   (Jackie DeShannon) 2:45
4. "Alfie"
   (Burt Bacharach, Hal David)
   2:48
5. "Take Me for a Little While"
   (Trade Martin) 2:40
6. "All I Really Want to Do"
   (Bob Dylan) 2:56

Side Two
1. "Bang Bang (My Baby Shot Me
   Down)"
   (Sonny Bono) 2:40
2. "Needles and Pins"
   (Sonny Bono, Jack Nitzsche) 2:26
3. "Dream Baby"
   (Sonny Bono) 2:58
4. "Elusive Butterfly"
   (Bob Lind) 2:26
5. "Where Do You Go"
   (Sonny Bono) 3:12
6. "Hey Joe"
   (William M. Roberts) 3:26

7. *3614 JACKSON HIGHWAY* (ATCO Records) 1969
Producers: Jerry Wexler, Tom Dowd, and Arif Mardin

Side One
1. "For What It's Worth"
   (Stephen Stills) 2:20
2. "(Just Enough to Keep Me) Hangin'
   On"
   (Buddy Mize, Ira Allen) 3:16
3. "(Sittin' On) The Dock of the Bay"
   (Otis Redding, Steve Cropper) 2:43
4. "Tonight I'll Be Staying Here with
   You"
   (Bob Dylan) 3:06
5. "I Walk on Gilded Splinters"
   (Dr. John Creaux) 2:30
6. "I Threw It All Away"
   (Bob Dylan) 2:44

Side Two
1. "Lay Baby Lay"
   (Bob Dylan) 3:28
2. "Please Don't Tell Me"
   (Grady Smith, Carroll W. Quillen)
   3:35
3. "Cry Like a Baby"
   (Wallace Pennington, Dewey
   Oldham) 2:45
4. "Do Right Woman, Do Right Man"
   (Dan Penn, Chips Morman) 3:20
5. "Save the Children"
   (Eddie Hinton) 2:50

8. *CHER* (Kapp Records) 1971
   [Later re-released as *GYPSYS, TRAMPS AND THIEVES*]
   Producer: Snuff Garrett

   Side One
   1. "The Way of Love"
      (Al Stillman, Jack Dieval) 2:30
   2. "Gypsys, Tramps and Thieves"
      (Bob Stone) 2:36
   3. "He'll Never Know"
      (Gloria Sklerov, Harry Lloyd) 3:27
   4. "Fire & Rain"
      (James Taylor) 2:59
   5. "When You Find Out Where You're
      Goin' Let Me Know"
      (Linda Laurie) 2:18

   Side Two
   1. "He Ain't Heavy, He's My Brother"
      (Bobby Russell, Bob Stone) 3:30
   2. "I Hate to Sleep Alone"
      (Peggy Clinger) 2:28
   3. "I'm in the Middle"
      (Billy Gate) 2:45
   4. "Touch and Go"
      (Jerry Fuller) 2:01
   5. "One Honest Man"
      (Ginger Greco) 2:22

9. *FOXY LADY* (Kapp Records) 1972
   Producer: Snuff Garrett
   ° Producers: Sonny Bono and Snuff Garrett

   Side One
   1. "Living in a House Divided"
      (Tom Bahler) 2:57
   2. "It Might as Well Stay Monday
      (From Now On)"
      (Bodie Chandler) 3:00
   3. "Song for You" °
      (Leon Russell) 3:14
   4. "Down, Down, Down"
      (Ester Jack) 2:53
   5. "Don't Ever Try to Close a Rose"
      (Ginger Greco) 2:45

   Side Two
   1. "The First Time"
      (Sonny Bono) 3:10
   2. "Let Me Down Easy"
      (Al Stillman, John Simon) 2:29
   3. "If I Knew Then"
      (Bob Stone) 2:34
   4. "Don't Hide Your Love"
      (Neil Sedaka, Howard Greenfield)
      2:50
   5. "Never Been to Spain"
      (Hoyt Axton) 3:27

10. *CHER/SUPERPAK* (United Artists Records) 1972
Producer: Sonny Bono

Side One
1. "All I Really Want to Do"
   (Bob Dylan) 2:56
2. "The Bells of Rhymney"
   (Pete Seeger, Idris Davies) 3:08
3. "Girl Don't Come"
   (Chris Andrews) 1:50
4. "Come and Stay with Me"
   (Jackie DeShannon) 2:38
5. "Blowin' in the Wind"
   (Bob Dylan) 3:30
6. "Needles and Pins"
   (Sonny Bono, Jack Nitzsche)
   2:35

Side Two
1. "Bang Bang (My Baby Shot Me
   Down)"
   (Sonny Bono) 2:40
2. "Elusive Butterfly"
   (Bob Lind) 2:26
3. "Time"
   (Michael Merchant) 3:14
4. "Where Do You Go"
   (Sonny Bono) 3:12
5. "Until It's Time for You to Go"
   (Buffy Sainte-Marie) 2:48
6. "Will You Love Me Tomorrow"
   (Carole King, Gerry Goffin) 2:55

Side Three
1. "Alfie"
   (Hal David, Burt Bacharach) 2:47
2. "Homeward Bound"
   (Paul Simon) 2:24
3. "Catch the Wind"
   (Donovan) 2:14
4. "Reason to Believe"
   (Tim Hardin) 2:25
5. "A House Is Not a Home"
   (Burt Bacharach, Hal David) 2:14
6. "You Don't Have to Say You Love
   Me"
   (Wickham, Donaggio, Napier, Bell)
   2:45

Side Four
1. "You'd Better Sit Down Kids"
   (Sonny Bono) 3:42
2. "Sunny"
   (Bobby Hebb) 3:08
3. "There but for Fortune"
   (Phil Ochs) 3:23
4. "Do You Believe in Magic"
   (John B. Sebastian) 2:37
5. "Mama (When My Dollies Have
   Babies)"
   (Sonny Bono) 3:24
6. "The Click Song"
   (Miriam Makeba) 2:54

11. *CHER/SUPERPAK VOLUME II* (United Artists Records) 1972
Producer: Sonny Bono

Side One
1. "Our Day Will Come"
   (Hilliard, Garson) 2:12
2. "The Times They Are A-Changin' "
   (Bob Dylan) 3:07
3. "Come to Your Window"
   (Bob Lind) 2:45
4. "I Wasn't Ready"
   (M. Rebennack, J. Hill) 3:00
5. "Hey Joe"
   (W. M. Roberts) 3:00
6. "Milord"
   (G. Moustaki, B. Lewis, M. Monnot) 2:33

Side Two
1. "Don't Think Twice, It's All Right"
   (Bob Dylan) 2:24
2. "She Thinks I Still Care"
   (D. L. Lipscomb, S. Duffy)
3. "The Cruel War"
   (Peter Yarrow, Paul Stookey) 3:20
4. "A Young Girl"
   (Aznavour, O. Brown Jr.) 3:22
5. "A Song Called Children"
   (Bob West) 3:35
6. "The Girl from Ipanema"
   (Jobim, Gimbel, DeMoraes) 2:10

Side Three
1. "Ol' Man River"
   (Jerome Kern, Oscar Hammerstein II) 2:47
2. "The Impossible Dream (The Quest)"
   (J. Darion, M. Leigh) 2:25
3. "Cry Myself to Sleep"
   (M. Gordon) 2:20
4. "Carnival"
   (Perette, Creatore, Weiss, Bonfa) 3:26
5. "Twelfth of Never"
   (J. Livingston, P. F. Webster) 2:14
6. "Like a Rolling Stone"
   (Bob Dylan) 3:53

Side Four
1. "It's Not Unusual"
   (G. Mills, L. Reed) 2:07
2. "I Want You"
   (Bob Dylan) 2:49
3. "I Will Wait for You"
   (N. Gimbel, Michel LeGrand) 3:03
4. "Take Me for a Little While"
   (T. Martin) 2:40
5. "Sing for Your Supper"
   (T. Martin) 2:40
6. "Go Now"
   (Bennet, Banks) 3:56

12. *BITTERSWEET WHITE LIGHT* (MCA Records) 1973
    Producer: Sonny Bono

Side One
1. "By Myself"
   (Howard Dietz, Arthur Schwartz)
   3:24
2. "I Got It Bad and That Ain't Good"
   (Paul Francis Webster, Duke
   Ellington) 3:47
3. "Am I Blue"
   (Grant Clark, Harry Akst) 3:43
4. "How Long Has This Been Going
   On"
   (George and Ira Gershwin) 4:20
5. "The Man I Love"
   (George and Ira Gershwin) 4:27

Side Two
1. "Jolson Medley" 4:12
   (A) "Sonny Boy"
       (Al Jolson, B. G. DeSylva, Lew
       Brown, Ray Henderson)
   (B) "My Mammy"
       (Sam M. Lewis, Walter
       Donaldson, Joe Young)
   (C) "Rock-a-Bye Your Baby with a
       Dixie Melody"
       (Sam M. Lewis, Joe Young,
       Jean Schwartz)
2. "More Than You Know"
   (Vincent Youmans, Edward Elisou,
   William Rose) 3:41
3. "Why Was I Born"
   (Jerome Kern, Oscar Hammerstein
   II) 2:45
4. "The Man That Got Away"
   (Harold Arlan, George Gershwin)
   4:13

13. *HALF BREED* (MCA Records) 1973
    Producer: Snuff Garrett

Side One
1. "My Love"
   (Paul McCartney, Linda
   McCartney) 3:31
2. "Two People Clinging to a Thread"
   (Gloria Sklerov, Harry Lloyd) 2:40
3. "Half Breed"
   (Mary Dean, Al Capps) 2:40
4. "The Greatest Song I Ever Heard"
   (Dick Holler) 2:48
5. "How Can You Mend a Broken
   Heart"
   (Barry Gibb, Robin Gibb) 3:21
6. "Carousel Man"
   (John Durrill) 3:20

Side Two
1. "David's Song"
   (David Paich) 3:24
2. "Melody"
   (Cliff Crofford, Thomas L. Garrett)
   3:34
3. "The Long and Winding Road"
   (John Lennon, Paul McCartney)
4. "This God-Forsaken Day"
   (Jack Segal) 2:43
5. "Chastity Sun"
   [originally "Ruby Jean & Billie
   Lee"]
   (James Seals, Dash Crofts) 4:14

14. *DARK LADY* (MCA Records) 1974
    Producer: Snuff Garrett

Side One
1. "Train of Thought"
   (Alan O'Day) 2:34
2. "I Saw a Man and He Danced with
   His Wife"
   (John Durrill) 3:13
3. "Make the Man Love Me"
   (Cynthia Weil, Barry Mann) 3:19
4. "Just What I've Been Lookin' For"
   (Kenny O'Dell) 2:36
5. "Dark Lady"
   (John Durrill) 3:26

Side Two
1. "Miss Subway of 1952"
   (Mary F. Cain) 2:16
2. "Dixie Girl"
   (John Durrill) 3:26
3. "Rescue Me"
   (Carl Smith, Raynard Miner) 2:22
4. "What'll I Do"
   (Irving Berlin) 2:28
5. "Apples Don't Fall Far from the
   Tree"
   (Bob Stone) 3:21

15. *CHER/GREATEST HITS* (MCA Records) 1974
    Producer: Snuff Garrett

Side One
1. "Dark Lady"
   (John Durrill) 3:26
2. "The Way of Love"
   (Al Stillman, Jack Dieval, Michael
   Revgauche) 2:30
3. "Don't Hide Your Love"
   (Neil Sedaka, Howard Greenfield)
   2:50
4. "Half Breed"
   (Mary Dean, Al Capps) 2:42
5. "Train of Thought"
   (Alan O'Day) 2:34

Side Two
1. "Gypsys, Tramps and Thieves"
   (Bob Stone) 2:36
2. "I Saw a Man and He Danced with
   His Wife"
   (John Durrill) 3:02
3. "Carousel Man"
   (John Durrill) 3:02
4. "Living in a House Divided"
   (Tom Bahler) 2:57
5. "Melody"
   (Cliff Crofford, Thomas L. Garrett)
   2:34

16. *STARS* (Warner Brothers Records) 1975
Produced by Jimmy Webb

Side One
1. "Love Enough"
(Tim Moore) 3:11
2. "Bell Bottom Blues"
(Eric Clapton) 3:11
3. "These Days"
(Jackson Browne) 4:11
4. "Mr. Soul"
(Neil Young) 3:05
5. "Just This One Time"
(Jimmy Webb) 4:50

Side Two
1. "Geronimo's Cadillac"
(Michael Martin Murphey) 3:00
2. "The Bigger They Come the
Harder They Fall"
(Jimmy Cliff) 3:30
3. "Love Hurts"
(Boudleaux Bryant) 4:20
4. "Rock & Roll Doctor"
(Lowell George, Fred Martin) 3:12
5. "Stars"
(Janis Ian) 5:17

17. *THE VERY BEST OF CHER* (United Artists Records) 1975
Producer: Sonny Bono

Side One
1. "All I Really Want to Do"
(Bob Dylan) 2:55
2. "Needles and Pins"
(Sonny Bono, Jack Nitzsche) 2:34
3. "Hey Joe"
(W. M. Roberts) 3:25
4. "Come Stay with Me"
(Jackie DeShannon) 2:38
5. "Where Do You Go"
(Sonny Bono) 3:07

Side Two
1. "Bang Bang (My Baby Shot Me
Down)"
(Sonny Bono) 2:41
2. "Will You Love Me Tomorrow"
(Carole King, Gerry Goffin) 2:55
3. "Alfie"
(Burt Bacharach, Hal David) 2:48
4. "Cruel War"
(Peter Yarrow, Paul Stookey)
5. "Mama (When My Dollies Have
Babies)"
(Sonny Bono) 3:24
6. "You Better Sit Down Kids"
(Sonny Bono) 3:40

18. *I'D RATHER BELIEVE IN YOU* (Warner Brothers Records) 1976
    Producers: Steve Barri, Michael Omartian

Side One
1. "Long Distance Love Affair"
   (M. Price, D. Walsh) 2:43
2. "I'd Rather Believe in You"
   (S. Omartian, M. Omartian) 3:46
3. "I Know (You Don't Love Me)"
   (B. George) 3:00
4. "Silver Wings & Golden Rings"
   (G. Sklerov, M. Leikin) 3:23
5. "Flashback"
   (A. Wayne, Alan O'Day) 3:55

Side Two
1. "It's a Cryin' Shame"
   (D. Lambert, B. Potter) 2:52
2. "Early Morning Strangers"
   (Barry Manilow, Hal David) 3:41
3. "Knock on Wood"
   (E. Floyd, S. Cropper) 3:31
4. "Spring"
   (J. Tipton) 4:27
5. "Borrowed Time"
   (J. Hill, B. Soden, J. Weber,
   S. Wichlin) 2:57

19. *CHERISHED* (Warner Brothers Records) 1977
    Producer: Snuff Garrett

Side One
1. "Pirate"
   (Stephen H. Dorff, Larry
   Herbstritt, Gary Harju) 3:07
2. "He Was Beautiful"
   (Gloria Sklerov, Harry Lloyd) 2:53
3. "War Paint and Soft Feathers"
   (C. K. Miller, Sandy Pinkard, Al
   Capps) 3:01
4. "Love the Devil Out of Ya"
   (John Durrill, Doc Pomus) 2:14
5. "She Loves to Hear the Music"
   (Peter Allen, Carole Bayer Sager)
   3:09

Side Two
1. "L.A. Plane"
   (Gary Harju, Larry Herbstritt) 3:09
2. "Again"
   (Joe Allen) 2:33
3. "Dixie"
   (John Durrill, Sandy Pinkart) 2:28
4. "Send the Man Over"
   (Cliff Crofford, T. Garrett) 3:51
5. "Thunderstorm"
   (John Durrill, Sandy Pinkard) 2:40

20. *TAKE ME HOME* (Casablanca Records) 1979
Producer: Bob Esty

° Producer: Ron Dante
Side One
1. "Take Me Home"
   (Michele Aller, Bob Esty) 6:47
2. "Wasn't It Good"
   (Michele Aller, Bob Esty) 4:40
3. "Say the Word"
   (Michele Aller, Bob Esty) 5:01
4. "Happy Was the Day We Met"
   (Peppy Castro) 3:58

Side Two
1. "Git Down (Guitar Groupie)"
   (Michele Aller, Bob Esty) 3:43
2. "Pain in My Heart"°
   (Richard T. Bear) 3:24
3. "Let This Be a Lesson to You"
   (Tom Snow) 3:13
4. "It's Too Late to Love Me Now"
   (Rory Bourke, Gene Dobbins, Jay
   Wilson)
5. "My Song (Too Far Gone)"
   (Cher, Mark Hudson)

21. *PRISONER* (Casablanca Records) 1979
Produced by Bob Esty

Side One
1. "Prisoner"
   (David Paich, David Williams) 5:50
2. "Holdin' Out for Love"
   (Cynthia Weil, Tom Snow) 4:23
3. "Shoppin' "
   (Bob Esty, Michele Aller) 4:30
4. "Boys & Girls"
   (Billy Falcon) 3:54

Side Two
1. "Mirror Image"
   (Michael Brooks, Bob Esty) 4:52
2. "Hell on Wheels"
   (Bob Esty, Michele Aller) 5:38
3. "Holy Smoke"
   (Bob Esty, Michele Aller) 4:56
4. "Outrageous"
   (Bob Esty, Michele Aller) 3:10

22. *I PARALYZE* (Columbia Records) 1982
    Producer: David Wolfert
    ° Producer: John Ferrar

Side One
1. "Rudy"
   (Jacques Morali, Henri Belolo, D.
   Frederiksen, H. Epstein, J. Hunter,
   M. Maierhoffer) 3:30
2. "Games"
   (A. Farber, V. Melamed) 3:50
3. "I Paralyze" °
   (John Ferrar, S. Kipner) 3:47
4. "When the Love Is Gone"
   (Desmond Child) 4:01
5. "Say What's on Your Mind"
   (J. Gottschalk) 4:06

Side Two
1. "Back on the Street Again"
   (D. Bugatti, F. Musker, J. Waite)
   3:15
2. "Walk with Me"
   (D. Wolfert, Desmond Child) 3:32
3. "The Book of Love"
   (Desmond Child) 3:25
4. "Do I Ever Cross Your Mind"
   (M. Smotherman, B. Burnette) 4:11

23. *CHER* (Geffen Records) 1987
    Producer: Michael Bolton
    ° Producers: Desmond Child, Jon Bon Jovi, Richie Sambora
    °° Producers: Jon Bon Jovi, Desmond Child, Richie Sambora
    °°° Producer: Desmond Child
    °°°° Producer: Peter Asher
    °°°°° Producer: Jon Bon Jovi

1. "I Found Someone"
   (Michael Bolton, Mark Mangold)
   3:42
2. "We All Sleep Alone" °
   (Jon Bon Jovi, Richie Sambora,
   Desmond Child) 3:53
3. "Bang Bang" °°
   (Sonny Bono) 3:51
4. "Main Man" °°°
   (Desmond Child) 3:48
5. "Give Our Love a Fightin'
   Chance" °°°
   (Desmond Child, Diane Warren)
   4:06

6. "Perfection" °°°
   (Desmond Child, Diane Warren)
   4:28
7. "Dangerous Times" °°°°
   (Susan Pomerantz, Roger Bruno,
   Ellen Schwartz) 3:01
8. "Skin Deep" °°°°°
   (Jon Lind, Mark Goldenberg)
   4:16
9. "Working Girl" °°°
   (Desmond Child, Michael Bolton)
   3:57
10. "Hard Enough Getting over You"
    (Michael Bolton, Doug James) 3:48

24. *HEART OF STONE* (Geffen Records) 1989
    Producer: Peter Asher
    °Producer: Michael Bolton
    °° Producer: Desmond Child
    °°° Producer: Jon Lind
    °°°° Producers: Diane Warren, Guy Roche

1. "If I Could Turn Back Time" °°°°
   (Diane Warren) 4:16
2. "Just Like Jesse James" °°
   (Desmond Child, Diane Warren)
   4:06
3. "You Wouldn't Know Love" °
   (Michael Bolton, Diane Warren)
   3:30
4. "Heart of Stone"
   (Andy Hill, Pete Sinfield) 4:21
5. "Still in Love with You" °
   (Michael Bolton, Bob Halligan Jr.)
   3:08
6. "Love on a Rooftop"
   (Desmond Child, Diane Warren)
   4:22
7. "Emotional Fire" °°
   (Desmond Child, Michael Bolton,
   Diane Warren) 3:53
8. "All Because of You" °°°
   (Jon Lind, Sue Schifrin) 3:30
9. "Does Anybody Really Fall in
   Love Anymore?" °°
   (Jon Bon Jovi, Richie Sambora,
   Desmond Child, Diane Warren)
   4:12
10. "Starting Over" °
    (Michael Bolton, Jonathan Cain)
    4:09
11. "Kiss to Kiss" °°°
    (Jon Lind, J. D'Astugues, Phil
    Galdston) 4:23
12. "After All (Love Theme from
    Chances Are)," duet with Peter
    Cetera
    (Tom Snow, Dean Pitchford) 4:07

25. *CHER: TAKE ME HOME/PRISONER* (Spectrum Records—GERMANY) 1990
    Producer: Bob Esty
    Producer: Ron Dante

1. "Take Me Home"
   (Michele Aller, Bob Esty) 6:42
2. "Wasn't It Good"
   (Michele Aller, Bob Esty) 4:21
3. "Say the Word"
   (Michele Aller, Bob Esty) 4:56
4. "Happy Was the Day We Met"
   (Peppy Castro) 3:55
5. "Git Down (Guitar Groupie)"
   (Michele Aller, Bob Esty) 3:43
6. "Pain in My Heart"
   (Richard T. Bear) 3:23
7. "Let This Be a Lesson to You"
   (Tom Snow) 3:14
8. "It's Too Late to Love Me Now"
   (Rory Bourke, Gene Dobbins, Jay
   Wilson) 3:38
9. "My Song (Too Far Gone)"
   (Cher, Mark Hudson) 3:54
10. "Prisoner"
    (David Paich, David Williams)
    5:49
11. "Holdin' Out for Love"
    (Cynthia Weil, Tom Snow) 4:24
12. "Shoppin' "
    (Bob Esty, Michele Aller) 4:28

13. "Boys & Girls"
    (Billy Falcon) 3:55
14. "Mirror Image"
    (Michael Brooks, Bob Esty) 4:52
15. "Hell on Wheels"
    (Bob Esty, Michele Aller) 5:34

16. "Holy Smoke"
    (Bob Esty, Michele Aller) 4:56
17. "Outrageous"
    (Bob Esty, Michele Aller) 3:11

26. *LOVE HURTS* (Geffen Records) 1991
Producer: Peter Asher
°Producer: Richie Zito
°° Producer: Bob Rock
°°° Producers: Guy Roche, Diane Warren
°°°° Producer: Steve Lukather

1. "Save Up All Your Tears" °°
   (Diane Warren, Desmond Child)
   4:00
2. "Love Hurts" °
   (Boudleaux Bryant) 4:19
3. "Love and Understanding" °°°
   (Diane Warren) 4:43
4. "Fires of Eden"
   (Kit Bain, Kate Goldenberg) 3:43
5. "I'll Never Stop Loving You" °°
   (Sue Griffin, David Cassidy, John
   Wetton) 3:57
6. "One Small Step" duet with
   Richard Page
   (Barry Mann, Wendy Waldman,
   Brad Parker) 3:28

7. "A World without Heroes" °°°°
   (Paul Stanley, Bob Ezrin, Lou
   Reed, Gene Simmons) 3:09
8. "Could've Been You"
   (Arnie Roman, Bob Balligan Jr.)
   3:30
9. "When Love Calls Your Name"
   (Tom Snow, Jimmy Scott) 3:32
10. "When Lovers Become Strangers" °°°
    (Diane Warren) 4:46
11. "Who You Gonna Believe" °
    (Steve Fortano, Joe Marquez,
    Jerry Marquez, Kevin Chalfant)
    4:47

27. *CHER'S GREATEST HITS 1965–1992* (Geffen Records—
ENGLAND/GERMANY) 1992

1. "Oh No Not My Baby"
   (Carole King, Gerry Goffin) 3:13
   Producer: Peter Asher
2. "Whenever You're Near"
   (Tommy Shaw, Jack Blades) 4:06
   Producer: Ron Nevison
3. "Many Rivers to Cross" [Live at the
   Mirage]
   (Jimmy Cliff) 4:10
   Producer: Cher

4. "Love and Understanding"
   (Diane Warren) 4:45
   Producer: Guy Roche and Diane
   Warren
5. "Save Up All Your Tears"
   (Diane Warren, Desmond Child) 4:00
   Producer: Bob Rock, Richie Zito
6. "The Shoop Shoop Song"
   (Rudy Clark) 2:52
   Producer: Peter Asher

7. "If I Could Turn Back Time"
   (Diane Warren) 4:02
   Producers: Guy Roche, Diane
   Warren
8. "Just Like Jesse James"
   (Desmond Child, Diane Warren)
   4:08
   Producer: Desmond Child
9. "Heart of Stone"
   (Andy Hill, Pete Sinfield) 4:18
   Producer: Peter Asher
10. "I Found Someone"
    (Michael Bolton, Mark Mangold)
    3:44
    Producer: Michael Bolton
11. "We All Sleep Alone"
    (Jon Bon Jovi, Richie Sambora,
    Desmond Child) 3:56
    Producers: Desmond Child, Jon
    Bon Jovi, Richie Sambora

12. "Bang, Bang"
    (Sonny Bono) 3:55
    Producers: Jon Bon Jovi,
    Desmond Child, Richie Sambora
13. "Dead Ringer for Love" duet with
    Meatloaf
    (Jim Steinman) 4:24
    Producers: Meatloaf, Stephan
    Galfas
14. "Dark Lady"
    (John Durill) 3:29
    Producer: Snuff Garrett
15. "Gypsys, Tramps & Thieves"
    (Robert Stone) 2:39
    Producer: Snuff Garrett
16. "I Got You Babe"
    (Sonny Bono) 3:12
    Producer: Sonny Bono

28. *HALF BREED* (MCA Records) 1992
    Producer: Snuff Garrett
    °Producers: Sonny Bono, Snuff Garrett

1. "Gypsys, Tramps and Thieves"
   (Bob Stone) 2:36
2. "Don't Hide Your Love" °
   (Neil Sedaka, Howard Greenfield)
   2:50
3. "The First Time" °
   (Sonny Bono) 3:10
4. "Let Me Down Easy"
   (John Simon, Al Stillman) 2:29
5. "Half Breed"
   (Mary Dean, Al Capps) 2:42

6. "Dark Lady"
   (John Durrill) 3:26
7. "Carousel Man"
   (John Durrill) 3:02
8. "Song for You"
   (Leon Russell) 3:14
9. "Train of Thought"
   (Alan O'Day) 2:34
10. "The Way of Love"
    (Al Stillman, Jack Dieval) 2:30

29. *BANG BANG AND OTHER HITS* (EMI/Capitol Special Markets) 1992
    Producer: Sonny Bono

1. "Bang Bang (My Baby Shot Me
   Down)"
   (Sonny Bono) 2:46
2. "All I Really Want to Do"
   (Bob Dylan) 3:00
3. "Needles and Pins"
   (Sonny Bono, Jack Nitzsche) 2:39
4. "Alfie"
   (Burt Bacharach, Hal David) 2:51
5. "Like a Rolling Stone"
   (Bob Dylan) 4:07

6. "Where Do You Go"
   (Sonny Bono) 3:12
7. "You Better Sit Down Kids"
   (Sonny Bono) 4:09
8. "Sunny"
   (Bobby Hebb) 3:06
9. "Hey Joe"
   (W. M. Roberts) 3:26
10. "Elusive Butterfly"
    (Bob Lind) 2:30

30. *CHER/ORIGINAL HITS* (Discy Records—HOLLAND) 1995
    Producer: Sonny Bono

1. "You Better Sit Down Kids"
   (Sonny Bono) 4:09
2. "I Go to Sleep"
   (R. Davies) 2:41
3. "Needles and Pins"
   (Sonny Bono, Jack Nitzsche) 2:50
4. "Like a Rolling Stone"
   (Bob Dylan) 4:07
5. "A Young Girl"
   (Aznavour, Chauvigny,
   O. Brown Jr.) 4:07
6. "Blowin' in the Wind"
   (Bob Dylan) 3:16
7. "I Feel Something in the Air"
   (Sonny Bono) 3:45
8. "Sunny"
   (Bobby Hebb) 3:06
9. "Come and Stay with Me"
   (Jackie DeShannon) 2:39
10. "The Bells of Rhymney"
    (Seeger, Davies) 3:20

11. "Our Day Will Come"
    (Hilliard, Gerson) 2:27
12. "Mama (When My Dollies Have
    Babies)"
    (Sonny Bono) 3:24
13. "Bang Bang (My Baby Shot Me
    Down)"
    (Sonny Bono) 2:43
14. "Until It's Time for You to Go"
    (Buffy Sainte-Marie) 2:41
15. "It's Not Unusual"
    (Mills, Reed) 2:08
16. "You Don't Have to Say You Love
    Me"
    (V. Wickham, S. Napier-Bell, P.
    Donaggio, V. Pallavicini) 2:45
17. "Don't Think Twice, It's All
    Right"
    (Bob Dylan) 2:50
18. "Cry Myself to Sleep"
    (M. Gordon) 2:27

31a. *IT'S A MAN'S WORLD* [ENGLAND/EUROPEAN VERSION] (WEA Records)
1995
°Producer: Christopher Neil
°° Producer: Greg Penny
°°° Producer: Stephen Lipson
°°°° Producer: Trevor Horn
+Song missing from U.S. version of the album

1. "Walking in Memphis" °
(Marc Cohn) 3:56
2. "Not Enough Love in the World" °°°
(Don Henley, Benmont Tench,
Daniel Korchmar) 4:21
3. "One by One" °°°
(Anthony Griffiths) 5:03
4. "I Wouldn't Treat a Dog (The Way
You Treated Me)" °° +
(Daniel Walsh, Steve Barri,
Michael Price, Michael Omartian)
5. "Angels Running" °
(Patty Larkin) 4:37
6. "Paradise Is Here" °°°
(Paul Brady) 5:03
7. "I'm Blowin' Away" °°°
(Eric Kaz) 4:03

8. "Don't Come around Tonite" ° +
(Maia Sharp, Mark Addson) 4:34
9. "What about the Moonlight" °
(Kathleen York, Michael Dorian)
10. "Same Mistake" °°
(Marc Jordon, John Capek) 4:26
11. "The Gunman" °°°°
(Paddy McAloon) 5:03
12. "Sun Ain't Gonna Shine
Anymore" °°°°
(Robert Gaudio, Bob Crewe) 5:12
13. "Shape of Things to Come" °°°°
+
(Trevor Horn, Lol Creme) 4:06
14. "It's a Man's Man's World" °°°
(James Brown) 4:37

31b. *IT'S A MAN'S WORLD* [American Version] (Reprise Records) 1996
Producer: Sam Ward
°Producer: Christopher Neil
°° Producer: Greg Penny
°°° Producer: Stephen Lipson
°°°° Producer: Trevor Horn

1. "One by One"
(Anthony Griffiths, Cher) 4:06
2. "Not Enough Love in the World"
(Don Henley, Benmont Tench,
Daniel Kortchmar) 4:24
3. "Angels Running" °
(Patty Larkin) 4:34
4. "What about the Moonlight"
(Kathleen York, Michael Dorian)
4:17
5. "Paradise Is Here"
(Paul Brady) 4:30

6. "The Same Mistake" °°
(Mark Jordan, John Capek) 4:25
7. "I'm Blowin' Away" °°°
(Eric Kaz) 4:02
8. "Walking in Memphis" °
(Marc Cohn) 3:58
9. "The Sun Ain't Gonna Shine
Anymore" °°°°
(Robert Gaudio, Bob Crewe) 5:13
10. "The Gunman" °°°°
(Paddy McAloon) 5:08
11. "It's a Man's Man's World" °°°
(James Brown, Betty Newsome) 4:36

32. *CHER: THE CASABLANCA YEARS* (Casablanca Records) 1996
    Producer: Bob Esty
    °Producer: Ron Dante

1. "Take Me Home"
   (Michele Aller, Bob Esty) 6:45
2. "Wasn't It Good"
   (Michele Aller, Bob Esty) 4:19
3. "Say the Word"
   (Michele Aller, Bob Esty) 4:59
4. "Happy Was the Day We Met"
   (Peppy Castro) 3:59
5. "Git Down (Guitar Groupie)"
   (Michele Aller, Bob Esty) 3:42
6. "Pain in My Heart (Love and Pain)" °
   (Richard T. Bear) 3:24
7. "Let This Be a Lesson to You"
   (Tom Snow) 3:15
8. "It's Too Late to Love Me Now"
   (Rory Bourke, Gene Dobbins, Jay
   Wilson) 3:38

9. "My Song (Too Far Gone)"
   (Cher, Mark Hudson) 3:54
10. "Prisoner"
    (David Paich, David Williams) 5:47
11. "Holdin' Out for Love"
    (Cynthia Weil, Tom Snow) 4:19
12. "Shoppin' "
    (Bob Esty, Michele Aller) 4:33
13. "Boys & Girls"
    (Billy Falcon) 3:54
14. "Mirror Image"
    (Michael Brooks, Bob Esty) 4:51
15. "Hell on Wheels"
    (Bob Esty, Michele Aller) 5:31
16. "Holy Smoke"
    (Bob Esty, Michele Aller) 4:54
17. "Outrageous"
    (Bob Esty, Michele Aller) 3:11

33. *CHER/THE ULTIMATE COLLECTION* (MCA Universal Records—EUROPE)
    1997
    Producer: Snuff Garrett

1. "Dark Lady"
   (John Durrill) 3:26
2. "The Way of Love"
   (G. Sklerov, H. Lloyd) 3:27
3. "Don't Hide Your Love"
   (Neil Sedaka, Howard Greenfield)
   2:50
4. "Half Breed"
   (Mary Dean, Al Capps) 2:42
5. "Train of Thought"
   (Alan O'Day) 2:34
6. "Fire and Rain"
   (James Taylor) 2:59
7. "He Ain't Heavy He's My Brother"
   (B. Russell, B. Scott) 3:30
8. "Never Been to Spain"
   (Hoyt Axton) 3:27

9. "Gypsys, Tramps and Thieves"
   (B. Stone) 2:36
10. "I Saw a Man and He Danced
    with His Wife"
    (John Durrill) 3:13
11. "Carousel Man"
    (John Durrill) 3:02
12. "Living in a House Divided"
    (T. Bahler) 25:7
13. "Melody"
    (C. Crofford, T. L. Garrett) 2:34
14. "Rescue Me"
    (C. Smith, R. Miner) 2:22
15. "I Hate to Sleep Alone"
    (P. Clinger) 2:28
16. "The Long and Winding Road"
    (John Lennon, Paul McCartney) 3:10

34. *BELIEVE* (Warner Brothers Records) 1998
    Executive Producer: Rob Dickens
    Producers: Mark Taylor, Brian Rawling
    °Producer: Junior Vasquez
    °° Producer: Todd Terry

1. "Believe"
   (Higgins, Barry, Torch, Gray,
   McLennon, Powell) 4:00
2. "The Power" °
   (Tommy Sims, Judson Spence) 3:56
3. "Runaway"
   (Paul Berry, Mark Taylor) 4:47
4. "All or Nothing"
   (Paul Berry, Mark Taylor) 3:59
5. "Strong Enough"
   (Paul Berry, Mark Taylor) 3:44

6. *"Dov'è L'Amore"*
   (Paul Berry, Mark Taylor) 4:18
7. "Takin' Back My Heart"
   (Diane Warren) 4:33
8. "Taxi, Taxi" °°
   (Todd Terry, Mark Jordan) 5:04
9. "Love is the Groove" °°
   (Betsy Cook, Bruce Wooley) 4:31
10. "We All Sleep Alone" °°
    (Desmond Child, Diane Warren)
    5:11

35. *SUNNY* (Magic Records—FRANCE) 1998
    Producer: Sonny Bono

1. "Sunny"
   (Bobby Hebb) 3:08
2. "The Twelfth of Never"
   (Livingston, Webster) 2:16
3. "You Don't Have to Say You Love
   Me"
   (Donaggio, Wickham, Napier, Bell)
   2:47
4. "I Feel Something in the Air"
   (Sonny Bono) 3:50
5. "Will You Still Love Me Tomorrow"
   (Gerry Goffin, Carole King) 2:57
6. "Where Do You Go"
   (Sonny Bono) 3:19
7. "Bang Bang (My Baby Shot Me
   Down)"
   (Sonny Bono) 2:45
8. "Homeward Bound"
   (Paul Simon) 2:26
9. "Pied Piper"
   (Kornfeld, Duboff) 2:17

10. "I Want You"
    (Bob Dylan) 2:48
11. "Alfie"
    (Hal David, Burt Bacharach) 2:51
12. "Milord"
    (Moustaki, Lewis, Monnot) 2:41
13. "All I Really Want to Do"
    (Bob Dylan) 2:57
14. "Come and Stay with Me"
    (DeShannon) 2:48
15. "I Go to Sleep"
    (Davies) 2:39
16. "Girl Don't Come"
    (Andrews) 2:18
17. "Come to Your Window"
    (Bob Lind) 2:59
18. "Dream Baby"
    (Sonny Bono) 3:00
19. "Mama (When My Dollies Have
    Babies)"
    (Sonny Bono) 3:26
20. "Behind the Door"
    (Gouldman) 3:44

36. *IF I COULD TURN BACK TIME/CHER'S GREATEST HITS*
    (Geffen Records—AMERICA) 1999

1. "Don't Come Crying to Me"
   (Diane Warren) 4:02
   Producers: Guy Roche, Thom Russo
2. "Love and Understanding"
   (Diane Warren) 4:43
   Producers: Guy Roche, Diane
   Warren
3. "Save Up All Your Tears"
   (Diane Warren, Desmond Child)
   4:03
   Producers: Rob Rock, Richie Zito
4. "The Shoop Shoop Song (It's in
   His Kiss)"
   (Rudy Clark) 2:50
   Producer: Peter Asher
5. "After All" duet with Peter Cetera
   (Tom Snow, Dean Pitchford) 4:04
   Producer: Peter Asher
6. "If I Could Turn Back Time"
   (Diane Warren) 4:14
   Producers: Guy Roche, Diane
   Warren
7. "Just Like Jesse James"
   (Desmond Child, Diane Warren)
   4:06
   Producer: Desmond Child
8. "Heart of Stone"
   (Hill, Sinfield) 4:16
   Producer: Peter Asher
9. "I Found Someone"
   (Michael Bolton, Mark Mangold)
   3:42
   Producer: Michael Bolton
10. "We All Sleep Alone"
    (Jon Bon Jovi, Richie Sambora,
    Desmond Child) 3:53
    Producers: Jon Bon Jovi, Richie
    Sambora
11. "Bang Bang"
    (Sonny Bono) 3:51
    Producers: Desmond Child, Jon
    Bon Jovi, Richie Sambora
12. "Take Me Home"
    (Michele Aller, Bob Esty) 3:28
    Producer: Bob Esty
13. "Dark Lady"
    (John Durrill) 3:27
    Producer: Snuff Garrett
14. "Half Breed"
    (Mary Dean, Al Capps) 2:44
    Producer: Snuff Garrett
15. "The Way of Love"
    (Al Stillman, Jack Dieval, Ruiz)
    2:31
    Producer: Snuff Garrett
16. "Gypsys, Tramps and Thieves"
    (Bob Stone) 2:37
    Producer: Snuff Garrett
17. "I Got You Babe," Sonny & Cher
    (Sonny Bono) 3:09
    Producer: Sonny Bono

37. *BITTERSWEET—THE LOVE SONGS COLLECTION* (MCA Records) 1999
Producer: Sonny Bono
°Producer: Snuff Garrett

1. "By Myself"
(Howard Dietz, Arthur Schwartz)
3:24
2. "I Got it Bad and That Ain't Good"
(Paul Francis Webster, Duke
Ellington) 3:47
3. "Am I Blue"
(Grant Clark, Harry Akst) 3:43
4. "How Long Has This Been Going
On"
(George and Ira Gershwin) 4:20
5. "The Man I Love"
(George and Ira Gershwin) 4:27
6. "Jolson Medley" 4:12
(A) "Sonny Boy"
(Al Jolson, B. G. DeSylva,
Lew Brown, Ray Henderson)
(B) "My Mammy"
(Sam M. Lewis, Walter
Donaldson, Joe Young)
(C) "Rock-a-Bye Your Baby with a
Dixie Melody"
(Sam M. Lewis, Joe Young,
Jean Schwartz)
7. "More Than You Know"
(Vincent Youmans, Edward Elisou,
William Rose) 3:41

8. "Why Was I Born"
(Jerome Kern, Oscar
Hammerstein II) 2:45
9. "The Man That Got Away"
(Harold Arlan, George Gershwin)
4:13
10. "What'll I Do" °
(Irving Berlin) 2:28
11. "The Long and Winding Road" °
(John Lennon, Paul McCartney)
3:10
12. "The Greatest Song I Ever Heard" °
(Dick Holler) 2:48
13. "David's Song" °
(David Paich) 3:24
14. "It Might As Well Stay Monday" °
(Ward Leslie Chandler) 3:00
15. "Don't Try to Close a Rose" °
(Ginger Greco) 2:45
16. "He'll Never Know" °
(Gloria Sklerov, Harry Lloyd) 3:27
17. "The Way of Love" °
(Al Stillman, Jack Dieval) 2:30

38. *BANG, BANG—THE EARLY YEARS* (Imperial Records) 1999
Produced by Sonny Bono

1. "Dream Baby"
(Sonny Bono) 2:54
2. "All I Really Want to Do"
(Bob Dylan) 3:00
3. "I Go to Sleep"
(Davies) 2:39
4. "Come and Stay with Me"
(DeShannon) 2:42

5. "Where Do You Go"
(Sonny Bono) 2:17
6. "You Don't Have to Say You Love
Me"
(V. Wickham, S. Napier-Bell, P.
Donaggio, V. Pallavicini) 2:48
7. "Bang Bang (My Baby Shot Me
Down)"
(Sonny Bono) 2:46

8. "Needles and Pins"
   (Sonny Bono, Jack Nitzsche) 2:39
9. "Elusive Butterfly"
   (Bob Lind) 2:31
10. "Alfie"
    (Burt Bacharach, Hal David) 2:51
11. "Sunny"
    (Bobby Hebb) 3:12
12. "Behind the Door"
    (Gouldman) 3:45
13. "Magic in the Air"
    (Sonny Bono) 3:51

14. "Mama (When My Dollies Have Babies)"
    (Sonny Bono) 3:27
15. "Hey Joe"
    (Roberts) 3:28
16. "You Better Sit Down Kids"
    (Sonny Bono) 3:44
17. "Girl from Ipanema"
    (Jobim, Gimbel, deMoraes) 2:15
18. "It's Not Unusual"
    (Mills, Reed) 2:19

39. *TAKE ME HOME* (Universal Music Records) 1999
    Producer: Bob Esty
    °Producer: Ron Dante
    °° Producer: Sonny Bono

1. "Bang Bang (My Baby Shot Me Down)" °°°
   (Sonny Bono) 2:42
2. "You Better Sit Down Kids" °°°
   (Sonny Bono) 3:41
3. "Take Me Home"
   (Michele Aller, Bob Esty) 3:26
4. "Pain in My Heart" °
   (Richard T. Bear) 3:24
5. "Wasn't It Good"
   (Michele Aller, Bob Esty) 3:50

6. "Git Down (Guitar Groupie)"
   (Michele Aller, Bob Esty) 3:43
7. "Happy Was the Day We Met"
   (Peppy Castro) 3:55
8. "It's Too Late to Love Me Now"
   (Rory Bourke, Gene Dobbins, Jay Wilson) 3:38
9. "Let This Be a Lesson to You"
   (Tom Snow) 314
10. "My Song (Too Far Gone)"
    (Cher, Mark Hudson) 3:54

40. *WITH LOVE, CHER* (Magic Records—FRANCE) 1999
    Producer: Sonny Bono

1. "You Better Sit Down Kids"
   (Sonny Bono) 4:10
2. "But I Can't Love You More"
   (Sonny Bono) 3:52
3. "Hey Joe"
   (Roberts) 3:27
4. "Mama (When My Dollies Have
   Babies)"
   (Sonny Bono) 3:26
5. "Behind the Door"
   (G. Gouldman) 3:45
6. "Sing for Your Supper"
   (Richard Rodgers, Lorenz Hart)
   2:36
7. "Look at Me"
   (K. Allison) 3:12
8. "There but for Love"
   (Phil Ochs) 3:26
9. "I Will Wait for You (Love Theme
   from *The Umbrellas of
   Cherbourg*)"
   (Michel Legrand) 3:16
10. "The Times They Are A-Changin' "
    (Bob Dylan) 3:09
11. "The Click Song"
    (Miriam Makeba) 2:57
12. "Take Me for a Little While"
    (T. Martin) 2:43
13. "Song Called Children"
    (B. West) 3:41
14. "Reason to Believe"
    (T. Hardin) 2:29

41. *CHER/GUEST SONNY* (The Entertainers/Sarabandas Records—EUROPE) 1999
    Producer: Sonny Bono

1. "Sunny"
   (Bobby Hebb) 3:06
2. "The Beat Goes On"
   (Sonny Bono) 3:21
3. "Bang Bang (My Baby Shot Me
   Down)"
   (Sonny Bono) 2:42
4. "Where Do You Go"
   (Sonny Bono) 3:15
5. "She's No Better Than Me"
   (Sonny Bono) 2:37
6. "Alfie"
   (Bacharach / David) 2:56
7. "I Got You Babe"
   (Sonny Bono) 3:06
8. "Come to Your Window"
   (Lind) 3:07
9. "Mama (When My Dollies Have
   Babies)"
   (Sonny Bono) 3:23
10. "Dream Baby"
    (Sonny Bono) 2:56
11. "I Go to Sleep"
    (Davies) 2:35
12. "The Click Song"
    (Makeba) 2:54
13. "Magic in the Air (I Feel
    Something in the Air)"
    (Sonny Bono) 3:47
14. "All I Really Want to Do"
    (Bob Dylan) 2:54
15. "You Better Sit Down Kids"
    (Sonny Bono) 4:06
16. "Needles and Pins"
    (Bono, Nitzsche) 2:46
17. "See See Blues (C.C. Rider)"
    (Bono, Greene, Stone) 3:00
18. "Behind the Door"
    (Gouldman) 3:42
19. "Come and Stay with Me"
    (DeShannon) 2:45
20. "Little Man"
    (Sonny Bono) 3:13

42. *CHER/THE GREATEST HITS* (WEA/Universal Records—GERMANY) 1999
Producers: Various

1. "Believe"
(Higgins, McLennan, Barry,
Torch, Gray, Powell) 3:58
Producers: Mark Taylor, Ben
Rawling

2. "The Shoop Shoop Song (It's in
His Kiss)"
(Rudy Clark) 2:51
Producer: Peter Asher

3. "If I Could Turn Back Time"
(Diane Warren) 3:59
Producers: Guy Roche, Diane
Warren

4. "Heart of Stone"
(Hill, Sinfield) 4:15
Producer: Peter Asher

5. "Love and Understanding"
(Diane Warren) 4:42
Producers: Guy Roche, Diane
Warren

6. "Love Hurts"
(Bryant) 4:16
Producer: Richie Zito

7. "Just Like Jesse James"
(Desmond Child, Diane Warren)
4:06
Producer: Desmond Child

8. "I Found Someone"
(Michael Bolton, Mark Mangold)
3:43
Producer: Michael Bolton

9. "One by One"
(Anthony Griffiths) 5:03
Producer: Stephen Lipson

10. "Strong Enough"
(Paul Barry, Mark Taylor) 3:44
Producers: Mark Taylor, Brian
Rawling

11. "All or Nothing"
(Paul Barry, Mark Taylor) 3:58
Producers: Mark Taylor, Brian
Rawling

12. "Walking in Memphis"
(Marc Cohn) 3:44
Producer: Christopher Neil

13. "Love Can Build a Bridge" Cher
with Chrissie Hynde and Neneh
Cherry
(Naomi Judd, J. Jarvis, Paul
Overstreet) 4:13
Producer: Peter Asher

14. "All I Really Want to Do"
(Bob Dylan) 2:37
Producer: Sonny Bono

15. "Bang Bang"
(Sonny Bono) 3:50
Producers: Desmond Child, Jon
Bon Jovi, Richie Sambora

16. "Gypsys, Tramps and Thieves"
(Bob Stone) 2:37
Producer: Snuff Garrett

17. "The Beat Goes On," Sonny &
Cher
(Sonny Bono) 3:28
Producer: Sonny Bono

18. "I Got You Babe," Sonny & Cher
(Sonny Bono) 3:12
Producer: Sonny Bono

19. *"Dov'è L'Amore"* (Emilio Estefan,
Jr. Mix)
(Paul Barry, Bark Taylor) 3:44
Producers: Mark Taylor, Brian
Rawling

43. *THE BEST OF CHER/THE MILLENNIUM COLLECTION* (MCA Records—
AMERICA) 2000
Producer: Snuff Garrett
°Producer: Bob Esty

1. "Gypsys, Tramps and Thieves"
   (Bob Stone) 2:37
2. "The Way of Love"
   (Jack Dirval, Michel Rivgauche,
   Al Stillman) 2:32
3. "Take Me Home" °
   (Michele Aller, Bob Esty) 6:46
4. "Dark Lady"
   (John Durrill) 3:27
5. "Half Breed"
   (Al Capps, Mary Dean) 2:46
6. "Train of Thought"
   (Alan O'Day) 2:36

7. "Living in a House Divided"
   (Tom Behler) 2:58
8. "Don't Hide Your Love"
   (Howard Greenfield, Neil Sedaka)
   2:49
9. "I Saw A Man and He Danced
   with His Wife"
   (John Durrill) 3:14
10. "Carousel Man"
    (John Durrill) 3:04
11. "All I Ever Need Is You," Sonny &
    Cher
    (Jimmy Holiday, Eddie Reeves)
    2:38

44. *CHER—MILLENNIUM EDITION* (Geffen/Universal Records—GERMANY)
2000
Producers: Various

1. "The Way of Love"
   (Jack Dieval, Al Stillman) 2:31
2. "Carousel Man"
   (John Durill) 3:03
3. "Living in a House Divided"
   (Tom Bahler) 2:56
4. "Melody"
   (Clifton T. Crofford, Thomas
   Garrett) 2:35
5. "Rescue Me"
   (Carl Smith, Raymond Miner) 2:22
6. "Dark Lady"
   (John Durrill) 3:27
7. "Don't Hide Your Love"
   (Neil Sedaka, Howard Greenfield)
   2:49
8. "Half Breed"
   (Al Capps, Mary Dean) 2:45
9. "Train of Thought"
   (Alan O'Day) 2:35

10. "Fire and Rain"
    (James Taylor) 3:00
11. "Never Been to Spain"
    (Hoyt Axton) 2:38
12. "Gypsys, Tramps and Thieves"
    (Robert Stone)
13. "The Shoop Shoop Song (It's in
    His Kiss)"
    (Rudy Clark) 2:51
14. "When Love Calls Your Name"
    (Tom Snow, Jimmy Jean Scott)
    3:31
15. "After All (Love Theme from
    Chances Are)"
    (Tom Snow, Dean Pitchford) 4:06
16. "Love on a Rooftop"
    (Diane Warren, Desmond Child)
    4:26
17. "The Long and Winding Road"
    (John Lennon, Paul McCartney) 3:13

45. *NOT.COM.MERCIAL* (Artist Direct Records) 2000
    [NOTE: This album is only available on the Internet, through Cher's own website:
    www.cher.com]
    Producers: Cher and Bruce Roberts

1. "Still"
   (Cher, Bruce Roberts, Bob Thiele)
   6:15
2. "Sisters of Mercy"
   (Cher, Pat McDonald, Bruce
   Roberts) 5:01
3. "Runnin' "
   (Cher, Pat McDonald, Bruce
   Roberts) 3:56
4. "Born with the Hunger"
   (Shirley Eikhard) 4:05
5. "The Fall (Kurt's Blues)"
   (Cher, Bruce Roberts, Pat
   McDonald) 5:17

6. "With or Without You"
   (Cher) 3:45
7. "Fit To Fly"
   (Cher, Kevin Savigar, Doug
   Millett) 3:53
8. "Disaster Cake"
   (Cher, Pat McDonald, Bruce
   Roberts) 3:25
9. "Our Lady of San Francisco"
   (Cher, Michael GavRvin, Rich
   Wayland) 2:15
10. "Classified 1A"
    (Sonny Bono) 2:55

46. *THE WAY OF LOVE* (MCA Records) 2000
    Producer: Snuff Garrett
    °Producer: Sonny Bono
    °° Producers: Sonny Bono, Snuff Garrett
    °°° Producer: Denis Pregnoloto
    °°°° Producer: Bob Esty

Disc 1
1. "The Way of Love"
   (Al Stillman, Jack Dieval) 2:31
2. "All I Really Want to Do" °
   (Bob Dylan) 2:58
3. "Bang Bang (My Baby Shot Me
   Down)" °
   (Sonny Bono) 2:44
4. "You Better Sit Down Kids" °
   (Sonny Bono) 3:42
5. "Gypsies, Tramps and Thieves"
   (Bob Stone) 2:37
6. "All I Ever Need Is You" Sonny &
   Cher
   (Eddie Reeves Jimmy Holiday) 2:40
7. "He'll Never Know"
   (Gloria Sklerov, Harry Lloyd) 3:29

Disc 2
1. "Half Breed"
   (Al Capps, Mary Dean) 2:45
2. "A Cowboy's Work Is Never Done,"
   Sonny & Cher °°°
   (Sonny Bono) 3:17
3. "Never Been to Spain"
   (Hoyt Axton) 3:26
4. "My Love"
   (Paul McCartney, Linda
   McCartney) 3:34
5. "The Greatest Song I Ever Heard"
   (Dick Holler) 2:50
6. "Carousel Man"
   (John Durrill) 3:03
7. "David's Song"
   (David Paich) 3:26

8. "When You Find Out Where You're Goin', Let Me Know" (Linda Laurie) 2:18
9. "I Hate to Sleep Alone" (Peggy Clinger) 2:28
10. "Touch and Go" (Jerry Fuller) 2:01
11. "Living in a House Divided" (Tom Bahler) 2:58
12. "It Might As Well Stay Monday (From Now On)" (Bodie Chandler) 3:01
13. "Song for You" (Leon Russell) 3:16
14. "When You Say Love," Sonny & Cher (Jerry Foster, Bill Rice, Steve Karman) 2:28
15. "Don't Ever Try to Close a Rose" (Ginger Greco) 2:47
16. "Don't Hide Your Love" (Neil Sedaka, Howard Greenfield) 2:49
17. "How Can You Mend a Broken Heart" (Barry Gibb, Robin Gibb) 3:22
18. "Two People Clinging to a Thread" (Gloria Sklerov, Harry Lloyd) 2:42
19. "Don't Pull It on Me" PREVIOUSLY UNRELEASED ON ALBUM ° (Sonny Bono) 2:38
20. "Classified 1A" ° (Sonny Bono) 2:58

8. "Melody" (Cliff Crofford, Thomas L. Garrett) 2:34
9. "Chastity Sun" (a/k/a "Ruby Jean & Billy Lee") (James Seals, Dash Crofts) 4:15
10. "Dark Lady" (John Durrill) 3:28
11. "Train of Thought" (Alan O'Day) 2:35
12. "I Saw a Man and He Danced with His Wife" (John Durrill) 3:14
13. "Make the Man Love Me" (Barry Mann, Cynthia Weil) 3:18
14. "Dixie Girl" (John Durrill) 3:24
15. "I Got It Bad and That Ain't Good" ° (Paul Francis Webster, Duke Ellington) 3:53
16. "Am I Blue?" ° (Grant Clark, Harry Akst) 3:45
17. "What'll I Do?" ° (Irving Berlin) 2:29
18. "The Beat Goes On" (Live), Sonny & Cher °°° (Sonny Bono) 9:41
19. "I Got You Babe" (Live), Sonny & Cher °°° (Sonny Bono) 3:26
20. "Take Me Home" °°°° (Michele Aller, Bob Esty) 6:46

47. *BEHIND THE DOOR 1964–1974* (Raven Records) AUSTRALIA 2000
    Produced by Sonny Bono
    °Produced by Snuff Garrett

1. "Dream Baby"
   (Sonny Bono) 2:52
2. "I Go to Sleep"
   (R. Davies) 2:40
3. "I Wasn't Ready"
   (Dr. John, Jesse Hill) 3:00
4. "A Song Called Children"
   (Bob West) 3:35
5. "I Want You"
   (Bob Dylan) 2:48
6. "It All Adds Up to Now"
   (Douglas Sham) 2:58
7. "Magic in the Air (I Feel
   Something in the Air)"
   (Sonny Bono) 3:24
8. "Until It's Time for You to Go"
   (Buffy Sainte-Marie) 2:42
9. "Behind the Door"
   (Gouldman) 3:44
10. "Come to Your Window"
    (Bob Lind) 3:07
11. "A House Is Not a Home"
    (Burt Bacharach, Hal David) 2:14
12. "Take Me For a Little While"
    (T. Martin) 2:42
13. "Reason to Believe"
    (Tim Hardin) 2:23

14. "She Thinks I Still Care"
    (L. Lipscomb) 2:15
15. "She's No Better Than Me"
    (Sonny Bono) 2:38
16. "I Hate to Sleep Alone" °
    (Peggy Clinger) 2:28
17. "I Saw a Man and He Danced
    with His Wife" °
    (John Durrill) 3:13
18. "Touch and Go" °
    (Jerry Fuller) 2:01
19. "If I Knew Then" °
    (Bob Stone) 2:34
20. "Song for You" °
    (Leon Russell) 3:14
21. "Never Been to Spain" °
    (Hoyt Axton) 3:27
22. "Rescue Me" °
    (C. Smith, R. Miner) 2:22
23. "The Greatest Song I Ever Heard" °
    (Dick Holler) 2:48
24. "Chastity Sun" (a/k/a "Ruby Jean
    & Billy Lee") °
    (James Seals, Dash Crofts) 4:14
25. "This God-Forsaken Day" °
    (Jack Segal) 2:43

Sonny & Cher Albums

NOTE: Configuration and song times below refer to original vinyl LPs, up until 1989; at that point, the albums and song times refer to the compact disc release. The song running times on the 1974 album *Sonny & Cher's Greatest Hits*, in absence of an original album, were taken from other albums, but should be accurate within a few seconds. Later CD releases of previously released vinyl albums are listed again only if they vastly differ (i.e., *Look at Us*, *The Wondrous World of Sonny & Cher*, and *Just in Case You're in Love*).

1. *LOOK AT US* (ATCO Records) 1965
Producer: Sonny Bono

Side One
1. "I Got You Babe"
   (Sonny Bono) 3:09
2. "Unchained Melody"
   (North, Zaret) 3:48
3. "Then He Kissed Me"
   (Spector, Greenwich, Berry) 2:51
4. "Sing *C'est La Vie*"
   (Sonny Bono, Greene, Stone) 3:37
5. "It's Gonna Rain"
   (Sonny Bono) 2:23
6. "500 Miles"
   (Hedy West) 3:48

Side Two
1. "Just You"
   (Sonny Bono) 3:25
2. "The Letter"
   (Harris, Terry) 2:06
3. "Let It Be Me"
   (Curtis, Becaud) 2:27
4. "You Don't Love Me"
   (Tommy Raye) 2:26
5. "You've Really Got a Hold on Me"
   (William "Smokey" Robinson) 2:14
6. "Why Don't They Let Us Fall in Love"
   (Spector, Greenwich, Barry) 2:31

2. *THE WONDROUS WORLD OF SONNY & CHER* (ATCO Records) 1966
Producer: Sonny Bono

Side One
1. "Summertime"
   (Dubose Heyward, George Gershwin) 2:35
2. "Tell Him"
   (Bert Russell) 2:34
3. "I'm Leaving It All up to You"
   (Don Bowman Harris, Dewey Terry) 2:18
4. "But You're Mine"
   (Sonny Bono) 3:02
5. "Bring It on Home to Me"
   (Sam Cooke) 3:04
6. "Set Me Free"
   (Ray Davies) 2:20

Side Two
1. "What Now My Love"
   (Carl Sigman) 3:28
2. "Leave Me Be"
   (Chris White) 2:03
3. "I Look for You"
   (Sonny Bono) 2:40
4. "Laugh at Me"
   (Sonny Bono) 2:50
5. "Turn Around"
   (Malvina Reynolds, Alan Greene, Harry Belafonte) 2:47
6. "So Fine"
   (Jim Gribble) 2:20

3. *IN CASE YOU'RE IN LOVE* (ATCO Records) 1967
   Producer: Sonny Bono

Side One
1. "The Beat Goes On"
   (Sonny Bono)
2. "Groovy Kind of Love"
   (Toni Wine, Carole Bayer) 2:20
3. "You Baby"
   (Phil Spector) 2:45
4. "Monday"
   (Sonny Bono) 2:55
5. "Love Don't Come"
   (Sonny Bono) 3:02
6. "Podunk"
   (Sonny Bono) 2:53

Side Two
1. "Little Man"
   (Sonny Bono) 3:15
2. "We'll Sing in the Sunshine"
   (Gale Garnett) 2:40
3. "Misty Roses"
   (Tim Harden) 3:05
4. "Stand by Me"
   (Ben E. King, Elmo Glick) 3:40
5. "Living for You"
   (Sonny Bono) 3:30
6. "Cheryl's Goin' Home"
   (Bob Lind) 2:40

4. *GOOD TIMES* Original Film Soundtrack (ATCO Records) 1967
   Producer: Sonny Bono

Side One
1. "I Got You Babe" (Instrumental)
   (Sonny Bono) 4:48
2. "It's the Little Things"
   (Sonny Bono) 3:31
3. "Good Times"
   (Sonny Bono) 5:15
4. "Trust Me"
   (Sonny Bono) 4:40

Side Two
1. "Don't Talk to Strangers"
   (Sonny Bono) 2:43
2. "I'm Gonna Love You"
   (Sonny Bono) 2:33
3. "Just a Name"
   (Sonny Bono) 6:28
4. "I Got You Babe"
   (Sonny Bono) 2:15

5. *THE BEST OF SONNY & CHER* (ATCO Records) 1967
Producer: Sonny Bono

Side One
1. "The Beat Goes On"
(Sonny Bono) 3:23
2. "What Now My Love"
(Carl Sigman, Gilbert Becaud,
Pierre Delanoe) 3:15
3. "I Got You Babe"
(Sonny Bono) 3:09
4. "Little Man"
(Sonny Bono) 3:15
5. "Just You"
(Sonny Bono) 3:25
6. "Let It Be Me"
(Mann Curtis, Gilbert Becaud) 2:27

Side Two
1. "A Beautiful Story"
(Sonny Bono) 2:51
2. "It's the Little Things"
(Sonny Bono) 3:31
3. "But You're Mine"
(Sonny Bono) 3:00
4. "Sing *C'est La Vie*"
(Sonny Bono) 3:37
5. "Laugh at Me"
(Sonny Bono) 2:50
6. "Living for You"
(Sonny Bono) 3:30

6. *SONNY & CHER LIVE* (Kapp Records) 1971
Producer: Denis Pregnolato

Side One
1. "What Now My Love"
(Carl Sigman, Gilbert Becaud,
Pierre Delanoe) 3:15
2. "The Beat Goes On"
(Sonny Bono) 9:00
3. "Once in a Lifetime"
(Anthony Newley, Leslie Bricusse)
2:08
4. "More Today Than Yesterday"
(Upton) 2:32
5. "Got to Get You into My Life"
(John Lennon, Paul McCartney)
6. "Someday (You'll Want Me to Want
You)"
(Jimmy Hodges) 4:00

Side Two
1. "Danny Boy"
(Traditional) 5:53
2. "Laugh at Me"
(Sonny Bono) 2:46
3. "Something"
(George Harrison) 4:00
4. "Hey Jude"
(John Lennon, Paul McCartney)
7:30
5. "I Got You Babe"
(Sonny Bono) 2:25

7. *ALL I EVER NEED IS YOU* (Kapp Records) 1972
   Producer: Snuff Garrett

Side One
1. "All I Ever Need Is You"
   (Reeves, Holiday) 2:38
2. "Here Comes That Rainy Day
   Feeling"
   (McCauley, Greenway, Cook) 2:33
3. "More Today Than Yesterday"
   (Upton) 2:30
4. "Crystal Clear/Muddy Waters"
   (Laurie) 2:39
5. "United We Stand"
   (Hilller, Simmons) 2:35

Side Two
1. "A Cowboy's Work Is Never Done"
   (Sonny Bono) 3:14
2. "I Love You More Than Yesterday"
   (Laurie, Tucker) 2:20
3. "You Better Sit Down Kids"
   (Sonny Bono) 3:16
4. "We'll Watch the Sun Coming Up
   (Shining Down on Our Love)"
   (Roberts, Welch) 2:29
5. "Somebody"
   (Sonny Bono) 3:07

8. *MAMA WAS A ROCK & ROLL SINGER, PAPA USED TO WRITE ALL HER
   SONGS* (MCA Records) 1973
   Producers: Denis Pregnolato, Michael Rubini
   °Producer: Sonny Bono

Side One
1. "It Never Rains in Southern
   California"
   (A. Hammond, M. Hazelwood) 3:47
2. "I Believe in You"
   (Denis Pregnolato, Michel Rubini,
   Don Dunne) 2:57
3. "I Can See Clearly Now"
   (Johnny Nash) 3:30
4. "Rhythm of Your Heartbeat"
   (Tony Macaulay, Geoff, Stevens)
   3:30
5. "Mama Was a Rock & Roll Singer,
   Papa Used to Write All Her Songs" °
   (Parts 1 & 2)
   (Sonny Bono) 9:39

Side Two
1. "By Love I Mean"
   (Hod David, Wil Jacobs, Marc Allen
   Trujillo) 4:20
2. "Brother Love's Traveling Salvation
   Show"
   (Neil Diamond) 3:10
3. "You Know Darn Well"
   (Tony Macaulay) 3:16
4. "The Greatest Show on Earth"
   (Bob Stone) 3:45
5. "Listen to the Music"
   (Tom Johnston) 3:59

9. *SONNY & CHER LIVE IN LAS VEGAS, VOLUME 2* (MCA Records) 1973
   Producer: Denis Pregnolato

Side One
1. "All I Ever Need Is You"
   (Reeves, Holiday) 6:22
2. Music and Dialogue 7:58
   (A) "I Can See Clearly Now"
       (Johnny Nash)
   (B) "You've Got a Friend"
       (Carole King)
   (C) "Where You Lead"
       (Carole King, Toni Stern)

Side Two
1. Comedy Monologue 3:36
2. "Gypsys, Tramps and Thieves"
   (Bob Stone) 2:28
3. "Brother Love's Traveling Salvation
   Show"
   (Neil Diamond) 3:36
4. "You and I"
   (Stevie Wonder) 5:15

Side Three
1. "Superstar" and Monologue
   (Leon Russell) 10:21
2. "Bang Bang (My Baby Shot Me
   Down)"
   (Sonny Bono) 6:00

Side Four
1. Introduction 1:43
2. "You'd Better Sit Down Kids"/
   "A Cowboy's Work Is Never
   Done"
   (Sonny Bono) 6:00
3. "I Got You Babe"
   (Sonny Bono) 3:07

10. *THE TWO OF US* (ATCO Records) 1973
    Producer: Sonny Bono

Side One
1. "I Got You Babe"
   (Sonny Bono) 3:09
2. "Unchained Melody"
   (Alex North, Hy Zaret) 3:48
3. "Then He Kissed Me"
   (Phil Spector) 2:51
4. "Sing *C'est La Vie*"
   (Sonny Bono, Charlie Green, Brian
   Stone) 3:37
5. "It's Gonna Rain"
   (Sonny Bono) 2:23
6. "Baby Don't Go"
   (Sonny Bono) 3:05

Side Two
1. "Just You"
   (Sonny Bono) 3:25
2. "The Letter"
   (Don F. Bowman Harris, Dewey
   Terry, Jr.) 2:06
3. "Let It Be Me"
   (Mann Curtis, Gilbert Becaud) 2:27
4. "You Don't Love Me"
   (Willie Cobbs) 2:26
5. "You've Really Got a Hold on Me"
   (William "Smokey" Robinson) 2:14
6. "Why Don't They Let Us Fall in
   Love"
   (Phil Spector, Ellie Greenwich, Jeff
   Barry) 2:30

Side Three
1. "The Beat Goes On"
   (Sonny Bono) 3:23
2. "Groovy Kind of Love"
   (Toni Wine, Carole Bayer) 2:20
3. "You Baby"
   (Phil Spector, Barry Mann, Cynthia
   Weil) 2:45
4. "Monday"
   (Sonny Bono) 2:55
5. "Love Don't Come"
   (Sonny Bono) 3:02
6. "Podunk"
   (Sonny Bono) 2:53

Side Four
1. "Little Man"
   (Sonny Bono) 3:15
2. "We'll Sing in the Sunshine"
   (Gale Garnett) 2:40
3. "Misty Roses"
   (Tim Hardin) 3:05
4. "Stand by Me"
   (Ben E. King, Elmo Glick) 3:40
5. "Living for You"
   (Sonny Bono) 3:30
6. "Cheryl's Goin' Home"
   (Bob Lind) 2:40

11. *SONNY & CHER'S GREATEST HITS* (MCA Records) 1974
Produced by Snuff Garrett
°Produced by Denis Pregnolato
°°Produced by Sonny Bono

Side One
1. "All I Ever Need Is You"
   (Reeves, Holiday) 2:38
2. "When You Say Love"
   (Foster, Rice) 2:26
3. "You Better Sit Down Kids" °
   (Sonny Bono) 3:15
4. "Crystal Clear/Muddy Waters"
   (Laurie) 2:39
5. "I Got You Babe" °
   (Sonny Bono) 3:05

Side Two
1. "A Cowboy's Work Is Never Done"
   (Sonny Bono) 3:15
2. "United We Stand"
   (Hiller, Simmons) 2:35
3. "The Beat Goes On" °
   (Sonny Bono) 2:18
4. "What Now My Love" °
   (Sigman, Becaud, Delanoe) 3:15
5. "Mama Was a Rock & Roll Singer,
   Papa Used to Write All Her
   Songs" °°
   (Sonny Bono) 3:43

12. *THE BEAT GOES ON* (ATCO Records) 1975
Producer: Sonny Bono
°Producers: Jerry Wexler, Tom Dowd, Arif Mardin

Side One
1. "The Beat Goes On"
   (Sonny Bono) 3:27
2. "I Got You Babe"
   (Sonny Bono) 3:09
3. "Just You"
   (Sonny Bono) 3:33
4. "Laugh at Me"
   (Sonny Bono) 2:50
5. "Baby Don't Go"
   (Sonny Bono) 3:08

Side Two
1. "Little Man"
   (Sonny Bono)
2. "Tonight I'll Be Staying Here with
   You" °
   (Bob Dylan)
3. "I Walk on Gilded Splinters" °
   (Mac Rebennack) 2:30
4. "Sing *C'est La Vie*"
   (Sonny Bono)
5. "Do Right Woman, Do Right Man" °
   (Dan Penn, Chips Moman) 3:19

13. *THE HIT SINGLES COLLECTION* (MCA Records—GERMANY) 1989
    Producer: Snuff Garrett
    °Producer: Sonny Bono
    °° Producer: Denis Pregnolato
    °°° Producers: Sonny Bono, Snuff Garrett
    °°°° Producers: Denis Pregnolato, Michael Rubini

1. "A Cowboy's Work Is Never
   Done" °°°
   (Sonny Bono) 3:15
2. "All I Ever Need Is You"
   (Reeves, Holiday) 2:33
3. "Mama Was a Rock & Roll Singer,
   Papa Used to Write All Her
   Songs" °
   (Sonny Bono) 3:43
4. "Here Comes That Rainy Day
   Feeling Again"
   (McCauley, Greenway, Cooks) 2:37
5. "United We Stand"
   (Hiller, Simmons) 2:26
6. "I Got You Babe" [Live Version] °°
   (Sonny Bono) 3:14

7. "The Beat Goes On" [Live
   Version] °°
   (Sonny Bono) 2:18
8. "What Now My Love" [Live
   Version] °°
   (Sonny Bono) 2:48
9. "I Can See Clearly Now" °°°°
   (Johnny Nash) 2:35
10. "When You Say Love"
    (Jerry Foster, Bill Rice, Steve
    Karman) 2:26
11. "It Never Rains in Southern
    California" °°°°
    (A. Hammond, L. Hazelwood)
    3:41

14. *ALL I EVER NEED IS YOU* (MCA Special Products Records) 1990
    Producer: Snuff Garrett
    °Producer: Sonny Bono
    °° Producer: Denis Pregnolato
    °°° Producers: Sonny Bono, Snuff Garrett

1. "All I Ever Need Is You"
   (Reeves, Holiday) 2:30
2. "A Cowboy's Work Is Never
   Done" °°°
   (Sonny Bono) 3:14
3. "When You Say Love"
   (Jerry Foster, Bill Rice, Steve
   Karman)
4. "Mama Was a Rock & Roll Singer,
   Papa Used To Write All Her Songs" °
   (Sonny Bono) 9:39
5. "You Better Sit Down Kids," Sonny
   Bono solo
   (Sonny Bono) 3:15

6. "Crystal Clear/Muddy Waters"
   (Laurie) 2:37
7. "The Beat Goes On" [Live] °°
   (Sonny Bono) 9:00
8. "I Got You Babe" [Live] °°
   (Sonny Bono) 3:05
9. "United We Stand" [Live]
   (Hiller, Simmons) 2:35
10. "Bang, Bang (My Baby Shot Me
    Down)" °°
    (Sonny Bono) 6:00

15. *THE BEAT GOES ON—THE BEST OF SONNY & CHER* (ATCO Records) 1991
    Producer: Sonny Bono

1. "Baby Don't Go"
   (Sonny Bono) 3:09
2. "Just You"
   (Sonny Bono) 4:04
3. "Sing *C'est La Vie*"
   (Sonny Bono, Stone, Green) 3:39
4. "I Got You Babe"
   (Sonny Bono) 3:11
5. "Why Don't They Let Us Fall in
   Love"
   (Spector, Greenwich, Barry) 2:35
6. "Laugh at Me"
   (Sonny Bono) 2:50
7. "But You're Mine"
   (Sonny Bono) 3:03
8. "The Revolution Kind"
   '(Sonny Bono) 3:25
9. "What Now My Love"
   (C. Sigman, G. Becaud, P.
   Delanoe) 3:35
10. "Have I Stayed Too Long"
    (Sonny Bono) 3:42
11. "Leave Me Be"
    (C. White) 2:03

12. "Little Man"
    (Sonny Bono) 3:20
13. "Living for You"
    (Sonny Bono) 3:38
14. "Love Don't Come"
    (Sonny Bono) 3:02
15. "The Beat Goes On"
    (Sonny Bono) 3:27
16. "Beautiful Story"
    (Sonny Bono) 2:51
17. "It's the Little Things"
    (Sonny Bono) 3:03
18. "My Best Friend's Girl Is Out of
    Sight," Sonny Bono solo
    (Sonny Bono) 4:13
19. "Good Combination"
    (M. Barkan) 2:57
20. "I Got You Babe" [*Good Times*
    soundtrack version]
    (Sonny Bono) 2:17
21. "Hello"
    (Bono, Stone, Green) 3:12

16. *I GOT YOU BABE* (Rhino Records) 1993
    Produced by Sonny Bono

1. "I Got You Babe"
   (Bono) 3:12
2. "The Beat Goes On"
   (Bono) 3:25
3. "Just You"
   (Bono) 4:05
4. "But You're Mine"
   (Bono) 3:05
5. "What Now My Love"
   (Sigman, Becaud, Delanoe) 3:36

6. "Have I Stayed Too Long"
   (Bono) 3:43
7. "Let It Be Me"
   (Becaud, Delanoe, Curtis) 2:31
8. "Sing *C'est La Vie*"
   (Bono, Greene, Stone) 3:39
9. "Laugh at Me"
   (Bono) 2:53
10. "The Revolution Kind"
    (Bono) 3:27

17. *ALL I EVER NEED—THE KAPP/MCA ANTHOLOGY* (MCA Records) 1995
Disc One
Produced by Snuff Garrett
°Produced by Sonny Bono
°° Produced by Sonny Bono, Snuff Garrett
°°° Produced by Denis Pregnolato, Michel Rubini

1. "Classified 1A," Cher solo °
   (Sonny Bono) 2:55
2. "Real People," Sonny & Cher °
   (Paul Anka) 3:12
3. "Somebody," Sonny & Cher °
   (Sonny Bono) 2:54
4. "Gypsys, Tramps and Thieves,"
   Cher solo
   (Bob Stone) 2:39
5. "I Hate to Sleep Alone,"
   Cher solo
   (Peggy Clinger) 2:29
6. "When You Find Out Where
   You're Goin', Let Me Know,"
   Cher solo
   (Linda Laurie) 2:19
7. "The Way of Love," Cher solo
   (Al Stillman, Jack Dieval) 2:33
8. "All I Ever Need is You," Sonny &
   Cher
   (Eddie Reeves, Jimmy Holiday)
   2:40
9. "Crystal Clear/Muddy Waters,"
   Sonny & Cher
   (Linda Laurie) 2:41
10. "United We Stand," Sonny & Cher
    (Tony Hiller, Peter Simons) 2:38
11. "A Cowboy's Work Is Never
    Done," Sonny & Cher °
    (Sonny Bono) 3:17
12. "Living in a House Divided," Cher
    solo
    (Tom Bahler) 2:59

13. "When You Say Love," Sonny &
    Cher
    (Jerry Foster, Bill Rice, Steve
    Karman) 2:29
14. "By Love I Mean," Sonny &
    Cher °°°
    (Hod David, Will Jacobs, Marc
    Allen Trujillo) 4:24
15. "Mama Was a Rock & Roll Singer
    Papa Used to Write All Her
    Songs," Sonny & Cher °
    (Sonny Bono) 3:44
16. "The Greatest Show on Earth,"
    Sonny & Cher °°°
    (Bob Stone) 3:50
17. "Half Breed," Cher solo
    (Mary Dean, Al Capps) 2:46
18. "Chastity Sun," Cher solo
    (James Seals, Dash Crofts) 4:17
19. "How Can You Mend a Broken
    Heart," Cher solo
    (Barry Gibb, Robin Gibb) 3:23
20. "Dark Lady," Cher solo
    (John Durrill) 3:29
21. "Train of Thought," Cher solo
    (Alan O'Day) 2:38
22. "Make the Man Love Me," Cher
    solo
    (Barry Mann, Cynthia Weil) 3:18
23. "Rescue Me," Cher solo
    (Carl Smith, Raynard Miner) 2:22
24. "Classified 1A," Sonny solo °
    (Sonny Bono) 2:22

Disc Two
Producer: Denis Pregnolato
°Producer: Sonny Bono

1. "What Now My Love" [Live]
   (Carl Sigman, Pierre Delanoe,
   Gilbert Becaud) 2:58
2. "The Beat Goes On" [Live]
   (Sonny Bono) 9:08
3. (A) "Once in a Lifetime" [Live]
      (Anthony Newley, Leslie
      Bricusse)
   (B) "More Today than Yesterday"
       [Live]
       (Patrick Upton)
   (C) "Got to Get You into My Life"
       [Live]
       (John Lennon, Paul
       McCartney) 6:07
4. "Someday (You'll Want Me to Want
   You)" [Live]
   (Jimmy Hodges) 4:27
5. "Laugh at Me" [Live]
   (Sonny Bono) 4:03
6. "I Got You Babe" [Live]
   (Sonny Bono) 3:53
7. "All I Ever Need Is You" [Live]
   (Eddie Reeves, Jimmy Holiday)
   3:09

8. (A) "I Can See Clearly Now"
       [Live]
       (Johnny Nash)
   (B) "You've Got a Friend" [Live]
       (Carole King)
   (C) "Where You Lead" [Live]
       (Carole King, Toni Stern)
       11:10
9. "You and I" [Live]
   (Stevie Wonder) 4:54
10. "Superstar" [Live]
    (Leon Russell, Bonnie Bramlett)
    5:23
11. Dialogue 1:50
12. "You Better Sit Down Kids"
    [Sonny solo, Live]
    (Sonny Bono) 4:20
13. "Band Introduction/I Got You
    Babe" [Live]
    (Sonny Bono) 6:03
14. "Our Last Show" Sonny solo °
    (Sonny Bono) 3:31

18. *I GOT YOU BABE AND OTHER HITS* (Atlantic/Flashback Records) 1997
Producer: Sonny Bono

1. "I Got You Babe"
   (Bono) 3:11
2. "Little Man"
   (Bono) 3:20
3. "Just You"
   (Bono) 4:04
4. "Good Combination"
   (Barkan) 2:57
5. "But You're Mine"
   (Bono) 3:03

6. "The Beat Goes On"
   (Bono) 3:27
7. "Have I Stayed Too Long"
   (Bono) 3:43
8. "A Beautiful Story"
   (Bono) 2:51
9. "It's the Little Things"
   (Bono) 3:03
10. "What Now My Love"
    (Sigman, Becaud, Delanoe) 3:38

19. *SONNY & CHER GREATEST HITS* (UNI / MCA Records) 1998
    Producer: Snuff Garrett
    °Producer: Sonny Bono
    °° Producer: Denis Pregnolato
    °°° Producers: Sonny Bono, Snuff Garrett

1. "All I Ever Need Is You,"
   Sonny & Cher
   (Holiday, Reeves) 2:38
2. "Gypsys, Tramps & Thieves," Cher
   (Stone) 2:36
3. "I Hate to Sleep Alone," Cher
   (Clinger) 2:26
4. "The Way of Love," Cher
   (Dieval, Stillman) 2:30
5. "Crystal Clear/Muddy Waters,"
   Sonny & Cher
   (Laurie) 2:38
6. "United We Stand," Sonny & Cher
   (Hiller, Simons) 2:35
7. "A Cowboy's Work Is Never Done,"
   Sonny & Cher °°°
   (Sonny Bono)
8. "When You Say Love," Sonny &
   Cher
   (Jerry Foster, Bill Rice, Steve
   Karman) 2:26
9. "Mama Was a Rock & Roll Singer,
   Papa Used to Write All Her Songs,"
   Sonny & Cher (Single Edit) °
   (Sonny Bono) 3:41
10. "Living in a House Divided," Cher
    (Bahler) 2:56
11. "The Greatest Show on Earth,"
    Sonny & Cher (Album Version)
    (Bob Stone) 3:48
12. "When You Find Out Where
    You're Goin', Let Me Know,"
    Cher
    (Laurie) 2:17
13. "Half Breed," Cher
    (Al Capps, Mary Dean) 2:43
14. "Dark Lady," Cher
    (John Durrill) 3:26
15. "Train of Thought," Cher
    (Alan O'Day) 2:35
16. "I Got You Babe," (Live) Cher °°
    (Sonny Bono) 4:35

20. *LOOK AT US* (Sundazed Records) 1998
Producer: Sonny Bono
+Bonus Tracks on this CD

1. "I Got You Babe"
(Sonny Bono) 3:11
2. "Unchained Melody"
(North, Zaret) 3:50
3. "Then He Kissed Me"
(Spector, Greenwich, Berry) 2:53
4. "Sing *C'est La Vie*"
(Sonny Bono, Greene, Stone) 3:39
5. "It's Gonna Rain"
(Sonny Bono) 2:21
6. "500 Miles"
(Hedy West) 3:53
7. "Just You"
(Sonny Bono) 3:29
8. "The Letter"
(Harris, Terry) 2:07

9. "Let It Be Me"
(Curtis, Becaud) 2:31
10. "You Don't Love Me"
(Tommy Raye) 2:27
11. "You've Really Got a Hold on Me"
(William "Smokey" Robinson)
2:15
12. "Why Don't They Let Us Fall in Love"
(Spector, Greenwich, Barry) 2:33
13. "It's the Little Things" +
(Sonny Bono) 3:02
14. "Don't Talk to Strangers" +
(Sonny Bono) 2:43
15. "Hello" +
(Sonny Bono) 2:42

21. *THE WONDROUS WORLD OF SONNY & CHER* (Sundazed Records) 1998
Producer: Sonny Bono
+Bonus tracks on this CD

1. "Summertime"
(Dubose Heyward, George Gershwin) 2:54
2. "Tell Him"
(Bert Russell) 2:25
3. "I'm Leaving It All Up to You"
(Don Bowman Harris, Dewey Terry) 2:16
4. "But You're Mine"
(Sonny Bono) 3:02
5. "Bring It on Home to Me"
(Sam Cooke) 2:49
6. "Set Me Free"
(Ray Davies) 2:21
7. "What Now My Love"
(Carl Sigman) 3:40
8. "Leave Me Be"
(Chris White) 2:03

9. "I Look for You"
(Sonny Bono) 2:41
10. "Laugh at Me"
(Sonny Bono) 2:53
11. "Turn Around"
(Malvina Reynolds, Alan Greene, Harry Belafonte) 2:48
12. "So Fine"
(Jim Gribble) 2:25
13. "The Revolution Kind" (Sonny solo)
(Sonny Bono) 3:23
14. "Have I Stayed Too Long"
(Sonny Bono) 3:45
15. "Crying Time" (Previously Unreleased) +
(B. Owens) 3:13

22. *IN CASE YOU'RE IN LOVE* (Sundazed Records) 1998
Producer: Sonny Bono
+Bonus tracks on this CD

1. "The Beat Goes On"
   (Sonny Bono) 3:26
2. "Groovy Kind of Love"
   (Toni Wine, Carole Bayer) 2:18
3. "You Baby"
   (Phil Spector) 2:53
4. "Monday"
   (Sonny Bono) 2:57
5. "Love Don't Come"
   (Sonny Bono) 3:01
6. "Podunk"
   (Sonny Bono) 2:54
7. "Little Man"
   (Sonny Bono) 3:20
8. "We'll Sing in the Sunshine"
   (Gale Garnett) 2:39
9. "Misty Roses"
   (Tim Harden) 3:03
10. "Stand by Me"
    (Ben E. King, Elmo Glick) 3:41
11. "Living for You"
    (Sonny Bono) 3:32
12. "Cheryl's Goin' Home"
    (Bob Lind) 2:40
13. "Beautiful Story" +
    (Sonny Bono) 2:51
14. "Good Combination" +
    (Sonny Bono) 2:54
15. "Plastic Man" +
    (Sonny Bono) 3:33

Cher and Gregg Allman as "Allman & Woman"

1. *TWO THE HARD WAY* (Warner Brothers Records) 1977
Producers: Johnny Sandlin, Gregg Allman, John Haeny

Side One
1. "Move Me"
   (S. Beckmeier, F. Beckmeier, V. Cameron) 2:57
2. "I Found You Love"
   (A. Gordon) 3:55
3. "Can You Fool"
   (M. Smotherman) 3:19
4. "You Really Got a Hold on Me"
   (William "Smokey" Robinson) 3:16
5. "We Gonna Make It"
   (Davis, Smith, Miner, Barge) 3:12
6. "Do What You Gotta Do"
   (Jimmy Webb) 3:27

Side Two
1. "In for the Night"
   (E. Sanford, J. Townsend) 3:30
2. "Shadow Dream Song"
   (J. Browne) 3:43
3. "Island"
   (Ilene Rappaport) 4:26
4. "I Love Makin' Love to You"
   (B. Weisman, E. Sands, R. Germinero) 3:51
5. "Love Me"
   (J. Leiber, M. Stoller) 2:49

Cher and Les Dudek & band as "Black Rose"

1. *BLACK ROSE* (Casablanca Records) 1980
   Producer: James Newton Howard

Side One
1. "Never Should've Started"
   (J. N. Howard, D. Paich, D. Foster,
   V. Carter) 4:14
2. "Julie"
   (B. Taupin, M. Chapman) 3:21
3. "Take It from the Boys"
   (Carol Bayer Sager, Bruce Roberts)
   4:59
4. "We'll All Fly Home"
   (J. Vastano, V. Poncia) 3:56

Side Two
1. "88 Degrees"
   (P. A. Brown) 5:57
2. "You Know It"
   (Les Dudek) 3:20
3. "Young and Pretty"
   (A. Willis, R. "T" Bear Gernstein)
   4:03
4. "Fast Company"
   (F. Mollin, L. Mollin) 3:47

Cher Cuts or "Guest Vocals" on Other Albums

1. *GENE SIMMONS* by Gene Simmons (Casablanca Records) 1978

   1. "Living in Sin," Gene Simmons and
      Cher
      (Simmons, Delaney, Marks) 3:50

2. *FOXES* [Movie Soundtrack] by Various Artists (Casablanca Records) 1980

   1. "Bad Love," Cher
      (Cher, Giorgio Moroder) 5:25

3. *DEAD RINGER* by Meatloaf (Epic Records) 1981

   1. "Dead Ringer for Love," Meatloaf
      and Cher
      (Jim Steinman) 4:21

4. *MERMAIDS* Original Soundtrack album by Various Artists (Geffen Records) 1990

   1. "The Shoop Shoop Song" by Cher
      (Rudy Clark) 2:51

   2. "Baby I'm Yours" by Cher
      (Van McCoy) 3:19

5. *BEAVIS AND BUTT-HEAD* (Geffen Records) 1993

    1. "I Got You Babe" by Cher and
    Beavis and Butt-head
    (Sonny Bono) 4:40

6. *THE GLORY OF GERSHWIN* by Various Artists (Mercury Records) 1994

    1. "It Ain't Necessarily So," Cher with
    Larry Adler
    (George Gershwin, Debose and
    Dorothy Heyward, Ira Gershwin)
    4:02

7. *FOR OUR CHILDREN TOO* by Various Artists (Kid Rhino Records) 1996

    1. "A Dream Is a Wish Your Heart
    Makes," Cher
    (Mack David, Al Hoffman, Jerry
    Livingston) 2:46

8. *SING AMERICA* by Various Artists (Warner Brothers Records) 1999

    1. "Star Spangled Banner," Cher
    (Francis Scott Key, John Stafford
    Smith) 2:01

9. *VH1 DIVAS LIVE '99* by Various Artists (Arista Records) 1999

    1. "Proud Mary," Tina Turner, Elton
    John, and Cher
    (John Fogarty) 6:02

    2. "If I Could Turn Back Time," Cher
    (Diane Warren) 4:13

10. *A ROSIE CHRISTMAS* by Rosie O'Donnell (Columbia Records) 1999

    1. "Christmas (Baby Please Come
    Home)," Cher and Rosie O'Donnell
    (Phil Spector, Ellie Greenwich, Jeff
    Barry) 3:10

CHER SINGLES

Cher as "Bonnie Jo Mason"
1. "Ringo I Love You" (Sceptor Records) 1965

Cher as "Cherilyn"
1. "Dream Baby" (Imperial Records) 1965

Cher as "Cher"
1. "All I Really Want to Do" (Imperial Records) 1965
2. "Where Do You Go" (Imperial Records) 1965
3. "Bang Bang (My Baby Shot Me Down)" (Imperial Records) 1966
4. "Alfie" (Imperial Records) 1966
5. "Behind the Door" (Imperial Records) 1966
6. "Mama (When My Dollies Have Babies)" (Imperial Records) 1966
7. "Hey Joe" (Imperial Records) 1967
8. "You Better Sit Down Kids" (Imperial Records) 1967
9. "The Click Song" (Imperial Records) 1968
10. "Take Me a Little While" (Imperial Records) 1968
11. "Chastity's Song" (ATCO Records) 1969
12. "For What It's Worth" (ATCO Records) 1969
13. "Put It on Me" (Kapp Records) 1971
14. "Classified 1A" (Kapp Records) 1971
15. "Gypsys, Tramps and Thieves" (Kapp Records) 1971
16. "The Way of Love" (Kapp Records) 1972
17. "Living in a House Divided" (Kapp Records) 1972
18. "Don't Hide Your Love" (Kapp Records) 1972
19. "Am I Blue" (MCA Records) 1973
20. "Superstar" (MCA Records) 1973
21. "Half Breed" (MCA Records) 1973
22. "Dark Lady" (MCA Records) 1974
23. "Train of Thought" (MCA Records) 1974
24. "I Saw a Man and He Danced with His Wife" (MCA Records) 1974
25. "A Woman's Story" / "Baby I Love You" (Warner/Spector Records) 1974
26. "A Love Like Yours," Cher & Harry Nilsson (Warner/Spector Records) 1974
27. "Rescue Me" (MCA) 1975
28. "Geronimo's Cadillac" (Warner Brothers Records) 1975
29. "Long Distance Love Affair" (Warner Brothers Records) 1976
30. "Pirate" (Warner Brothers Records) 1976
31. "War Paint and Soft Feathers" (Warner Brothers Records) 1977
32. "Take Me Home" (Casablanca Records) 1979

33. "Wasn't It Good" (Casablanca Records) 1979
34. "It's Too Late to Turn Back Now" (Casablanca Records) 1979
35. "Hell on Wheels" (Casablanca Records) 1979
36. "Prisoner" (Casablanca Records) 1979
37. "Rudy" (Columbia Records) 1982
38. "I Found Someone" (Geffen Records) 1987
39. "Skin Deep" (Geffen Records) 1988
40. "We All Sleep Alone" (Geffen Records) 1987
41. "After All," Cher & Peter Cetera (Geffen Records) 1989
42. "If I Could Turn Back Time" (Geffen Records) 1989
43. "Just Like Jesse James" (Geffen Records) 1989
44. "Heart of Stone" (Geffen Records) 1990
45. "You Wouldn't Know Love" (Geffen Records) 1990
46. "The Shoop Shoop Song" (Geffen Records) 1990
47. "Love and Understanding" (Geffen Records) 1991
48. "Save Up All Your Tears" (Geffen Records) 1991
49. "Love Hurts" (Geffen Records) 1991
50. "Oh No Not My Baby" (Geffen Records) 1992
51. "Many Rivers to Cross" (Geffen Records) 1993
52. "Whenever You're Near" (Geffen Records) 1993)
53. "Love Can Build a Bridge," Cher, Chrissie Hynde, Neneh Cherry (London Records) 1995
54. "Walking in Memphis" (Reprise Records) 1995
55. "One by One" (Reprise Records) 1996
56. "Paradise Is Here" (Reprise Records) 1996
57. "Believe" (Warner Brothers Records) 1998
58. "Strong Enough" (Warner Brothers Records) 1999
59. "All or Nothing"/"*Dov'è L'Amore*" (Warner Brothers Records) 1999

SONNY & CHER SINGLES

Sonny & Cher as "Caesar & Cleo"
1. "Do You Wanna Dance" (Reprise Records) 1965
2. "Love Is Strange" (Reprise Records) 1965
3. "Let the Good Times Roll" (Reprise Records) 1965

Sonny & Cher as "Sonny & Cher"
1. "Baby Don't Go" (Reprise Records) 1965
2. "The Letter" (Vault Records) 1965
3. "Just You"/"Sing *C'est La Vie*" (ATCO Records) 1965
4. "I Got You Babe" (ATCO Records) 1965
5. "But You're Mine" (ATCO Records) 1965
6. "What Now My Love" (ATCO Records) 1966

7. "Have I Stayed Too Long"/"Leave Me Be" (ATCO Records) 1966
8. "Little Man" (ATCO Records) 1966
9. "Living for You" (ATCO Records) 1966
10. "The Beat Goes On" (ATCO Records) 1967
11. "Beautiful Story" (ATCO Records) 1967
12. "Plastic Man" (ATCO Records) 1967
13. "It's the Little Things" (ATCO Records) 1967
14. "Don't Talk to Strangers" (ATCO Records) 1967
15. "Good Combination"/"You and Me" (ATCO Records) 1967
16. "Real People" (Kapp Records) 1971
17. "Somebody" (Kapp Records) 1971
18. "All I Ever Need Is You" (Kapp Records) 1971
19. "A Cowboy's Work Is Never Done" (Kapp Records) 1972
20. "When You Say Love" (Kapp Records) 1972
21. "Mama Was a Rock & Roll Singer, Papa Used to Write All Her Songs" (MCA Records) 1972

FILMOGRAPHY

1. *WILD ON THE BEACH* (1965)
   Director: Maury Dexter
   Cast: Frankie Randall
      Sherry Jackson
      Jackie & Gayle
      Sonny & Cher
      Sandy Nelson

2. *GOOD TIMES* (1967) [DVD]
   Director: William Friedkin
   Cast: Sonny & Cher
      George Sanders
      Norman Alden
      Larry Duran
      Edy Williams

3. *CHASTITY* (1969)
   Director: Alessio de Paola
   Cast: Cher
      Barbara London
      Tom Nolan
      Stephen Whittaker

4. *COME BACK TO THE FIVE AND DIME, JIMMY DEAN, JIMMY DEAN* (1982) [video]
   Director: Robert Altman
   Cast: Cher
      Karen Black
      Sandy Dennis
      Sudie Bond
      Kathy Bates
      Marta Heflin

5. *SILKWOOD* (1983) [video/DVD]
   Director: Mike Nichols
   Cast: Meryl Streep
      Kurt Russell
      Cher
      Craig T. Nelson
      Diana Scarwid
      Fred Ward
      Ron Silver
      Sudie Bond

6. *MASK* (1985) [video/DVD]
   Director: Peter Bogdanovich
   Cast: Cher
      Sam Elliott
      Eric Stoltz
      Estelle Getty
      Richard Dysart
      Laura Dern
      Micole Mercurio
      Harry Carey, Jr.

7. *THE WITCHES OF EASTWICK* (1987) [video/DVD]
   Director: George Miller
   Cast: Jack Nicholson
      Cher
      Susan Sarandon
      Michelle Pfeiffer
      Veronica Cartwright

8. *SUSPECT* (1987) [video]
    Director: Peter Yates
    Cast: Cher
        Dennis Quaid
        Liam Neeson
        John Mahoney
        Joe Mantegna

9. *MOONSTRUCK* (1987) [video/DVD]
    Director: Norman Jewison
    Cast: Cher
        Nicolas Cage
        Olympia Dukakis
        Vincent Gardenia
        Danny Aiello
        John Mahoney
        Anita Gillette

10. *MERMAIDS* (1990) [video/DVD]
    Director: Richard Benjamin
    Cast: Cher
        Bob Hoskins
        Winona Ryder
        Christina Ricci
        Michael Schoeffling
        Jan Miner

11. *THE PLAYER* (1992) [video/DVD]
    Director: Robert Altman
    Cast: Tim Robbins
        Whoopi Goldberg
        Greta Scacchi
        Peter Gallagher
        Sally Kellerman
        Dina Merrill
        Cher
        Sally Kirkland
        Steve Allen
        Jayne Meadows

12. *READY TO WEAR* (1994)
    [video/DVD]
    Director: Robert Altman
    Cast: Sophia Loren
        Marcello Mastroianni
        Julia Roberts
        Linda Hunt
        Tracy Ullman
        Kim Basinger
        Lyle Lovett
        Cher

13. *FAITHFUL* (1996) [video]
    Director: Paul Mazursky
    Cast: Cher
        Ryan O'Neal
        Chazz Palminteri
        Paul Mazursky

14. *IF THESE WALLS COULD TALK*
    (1996) [video/DVD]
    Directors: Nancy Savoca and Cher
    Cast: Sissy Spacek
        Diana Scarwid
        Demi Moore
        Anne Heche
        C. C. H. Pounder
        Shirley Knight
        Jada Pinkett
        Cher

15. *TEA WITH MUSSOLINI* (1999)
    [video/DVD]
    Director: Franco Zeffirelli
    Cast: Cher
        Judi Dench
        Joan Plowright
        Maggie Smith
        Lily Tomlin

TELEVISION

SERIES

1. *The Sonny & Cher Comedy Hour*
   CBS-TV (1971–74)
2. *Cher*
   CBS-TV (1975–76)
3. *The Sonny & Cher Show*
   CBS-TV (1976–77)

TV SPECIALS

1. *Cher*
   CBS-TV (February 12, 1975)
2. *Cher . . . Special*
   ABC-TV (April 3, 1978)
3. *Cher . . . And Other Fantasies*
   NBC-TV (April 7, 1979)
4. *Cher—A Celebration at Caesar's Palace*
   Showtime Cable-TV (April 21, 1983)
5. *Cher: Extravaganza at the Mirage* [video]
   CBS-TV (February 4, 1991)
6. *Sonny & Me . . . Cher Remembers*
   CBS-TV (May 20, 1998)
7. *VH1 Divas Live '99* [video / DVD]
   VH1 Cable TV (April 13, 1999)
8. *Cher Live in Concert* [video / DVD]
   HBO Cable-TV (August 29, 1999)

ALBUMS AND SINGLES CERTIFIED "GOLD" AND "PLATINUM" IN THE UNITED STATES

(For a single, "Gold" signifies a million copies sold. For an album, "Gold" signifies 500,000 copies sold, "Platinum" signifies a million copies sold.)

ALBUMS

Sonny & Cher
Look at Us (1965) Number 2/Gold
Sonny & Cher Live (1971) Number 35/Gold
All I Ever Need Is You (1972) Number 14/Gold

Solo
Cher [a.k.a. Gypsys, Tramps & Thieves] (1971) Number 16/Gold
Half Breed (1973) Number 28/Gold
Take Me Home (1979) Number 25/Gold
Cher (1987) Number 32/Platinum
Heart of Stone (1989) Number 10/Double Platinum
Love Hurts (1991) Number 48/Gold
Believe (1998) Number 4/Triple Platinum

SINGLES

Sonny & Cher
"I Got You Babe" (1965) Number 1/Gold

Solo
"Gypsys, Tramps & Thieves" (1971) Number 1/Gold
"Half Breed" (1973) Number 1/Gold
"Dark Lady" (1974) Number 1/Gold
"Take Me Home" (1979) Number 8/Gold
"After All" (1989) Number 6/Gold
"If I Could Turn Back Time" (1989) Number 3/Gold
"Believe" (1998) Number 1/Platinum

AWARDS

GRAMMY AWARDS
Best Dance Recording (1999) [Awarded in 2000] "Believe"

ACADEMY AWARDS
Best Actress (1987) [Awarded in 1988] *Moonstruck*

GOLDEN GLOBE
Best Supporting Actress (1983) *Silkwood*

CANNES FILM FESTIVAL
Best Actress (1985) *Mask*

BOYFRIENDOGRAPHY

WARREN BEATTY, actor
—dated (1962)

SONNY BONO, record producer,
    singer
—lived with (1964–69)
—married to (1969–75)

BILL HAMM, guitar player with
    Sonny & Cher
—dated (1972–73)

DAVID PAICH, conductor,
    keyboard player with Sonny & Cher
—dated (1973)

BERNIE TAUPIN, songwriter
—dated (1973)

DAVID GEFFEN, record producer
—dated (1973–75)

GREGG ALLMAN, rock star, the
    Allman Brothers
—dated (1975)
—married to (1975–78)

GENE SIMMONS, rock star, KISS
—dated (1978–80)

LES DUDEK, rock & roll guitarist
—dated (1980–82)

RON DUGUAY, hockey player
—dated (1982)

JOHN HEARD, actor
—dated (1982)

JOHN LOEFFLER, singer
—dated (1982–83)

VAL KILMER, actor
—dated (1982–84)

ERIC STOLTZ, actor
—dated (1984)

JOSH DONEN, television executive
—dated (1984–86)

TOM CRUISE, actor
—dated (1985–86)

ROB CAMILLETTI, bagel baker,
    actor
—dated (1986–89)

RICHIE SAMBORA, rock star, Bon
    Jovi
—dated (1989–90)

ERIC CLAPTON, rock star
—dated (1991)

THE SONNY & CHER COMEDY HOUR, EPISODE-BY-EPISODE

Note: *The Sonny & Cher Comedy Hour* was originally a six-episode summer replacement series on CBS-TV. It was such a success that it returned in December 1971 as a regularly broadcast series. In the beginning of 1974 Sonny & Cher divorced, and the last episode of *The Sonny & Cher Comedy Hour* was broadcast in May 1974. In the interim, ABC-TV broadcast *The Sonny Comedy Review* (1974), and CBS-TV produced the short-lived *The Cher Show* (1975). Neither show worked successfully. The duo, now divorced, returned with their retooled show, now known as *The Sonny & Cher Show*, broadcast from February 1976 to August 1977.

THE ORIGINAL SIX SUMMER 1971 EPISODES

1. Guest Star: Jimmy Durante
   Songs: "It Don't Come Easy," "Go Ahead Sock It to the People," "They Said I Sing Like a Frog" (Sonny), "Mrs. Robinson," "You're Gonna Miss Me" (Durante), "You Made Me Love You" (Cher), "Ain't No Mountain High Enough" (Sonny & Cher), "Suspicious Minds" [Cher dressed as a Good 'n' Plenty candy], "I Got You Babe" [closing song, with an explanation of the song].

2. Guest Star: Phyllis Diller
   Songs: "Proud Mary," "Georgia," "We'll Meet Again," "On Our Own" (Sonny & Cher).

3. Guest Stars: Harvey Korman, Robert Merrill, Carroll O'Connor
   Songs: "All I Ever Need Is You" (Sonny & Cher), "Gypsys, Tramps and Thieves," "Nobody Knows," "It Came upon a Midnight Clear" (Cher), "Listen Children" (animated).

4. Guest Stars: Dinah Shore, Tony Curtis, Glen Campbell, Carol Burnett, George Burns
   Songs: "Sooner or Later" (opening), "I'm Gonna Love You," "I've Got a Song" (Shore solo), "Mr. Tambourine Man" (Sonny & Cher), "Joy to the World" (Sonny & Cher, and Dinah Shore).

5. Guest Star: Carroll O'Connor
   Songs: "Good Day Sunshine" (Sonny & Cher), "What a Difference a Day Makes," "Rip It Up," "Remembering You."

6. Guest Star: Kate Smith
   Songs include "How Long Has This Been Going On."

REGULARLY SCHEDULED EPISODES

December 1971 to May 1974

7. Guest Star: Tony Randall, Honeycomb
   Songs: "I Love You More Today Than Yesterday" (opening), "The Way of Love" (Cher), "One Monkey Don't Stop No Show" (Honeycomb), "Brand New Key" (video), "We'll Sing in the Sunshine" (Sonny & Cher).

8. Guest Star: Art Carney
   Songs: "You're Too Good to Be True" (Sonny & Cher), "Ain't Misbehavin' " (Cher), You've Got a Friend" (Sonny & Cher).

9. Guest Star: Burt Reynolds
   Songs: "Cry Like a Baby," "Am I Blue," "Bad Moon Rising," "I Got You Babe" (Sonny & Cher).

10. Guest Stars: Mike Connors, Jean Stapleton
    Songs: "People Got to Be Free" (opening), "Together/It's So Easy" (Sonny & Cher).

11. Guest Stars: George Burns, David Clayton Thomas
    Songs: "The Beat Goes On," "We're on Our Way Home" (Sonny & Cher).

12. Guest Stars: The Jackson Five, Ronald Reagan
    Songs: "Let Me Down Easy" (Cher), "Looking through the Window" (Jackson Five), "Say It Isn't So," "Run Along Show."

13. Guest Stars: Chad Everett, Bobby Sherman
    Songs: "Happy Together" (opening), "Marching to the Music" (Bobby Sherman), "Simple Song of Freedom," "Look What They've Done to My Song" (Sonny & Cher).

14. Guest Stars: Jerry Lewis, the Supremes
    Songs: "A Little Help from My Friends," "It's Funny That Way" (Cher), "Your Wonderful Sweet, Sweet Love" (Supremes), "I Got You Babe" (Sonny & Cher).

15. Guest Stars: Robert Goulet, the Temptations
    Songs: "On Our Way Home," Temptations Medley "Smiling Faces Sometimes," "Look Around," "Superstar" (The Temptations), "Don't

Mess around with Jim"/"Can't Help Lovin' That Man of Mine" (Cher), "I Got You Babe" (Sonny & Cher).

16. Guest Stars: William Conrad, Rick Springfield
Songs: "With Love, from Me to You," "He Ain't Heavy, He's My Brother" (Cher), "My Little Girl" (William Conrad), "What Will the Children Think" (Rick Springfield).

17. SONNY & CHER CHRISTMAS SHOW
Guest Star: William Conrad (as Santa Claus)
Songs: Various Christmas carols by Sonny & Cher: "Jingle Bells" etc., and a medley of songs: with Chastity.

18. Guest Stars: Jean Stapleton, Lyle Waggoner
Songs: "Love Grows" (opening).

19. Guest Stars: Mark Spitz, Jerry Lewis (cameo)
Songs: "All I Really Want to Do" (Sonny & Cher), "You've Got a Friend" (Cher), "I Can See Clearly Now" (Sonny & Cher).

20. Guest Star: Mike Connors
Songs: "Jackson," "Rockin' Pneumonia and the Boogie Woogie Flu," "Bridge over Troubled Waters," "Something."

21. Guest Stars: Larry Storch, Merv Griffin
Songs: "Lodi," "Happy Song" (Merv Griffin).

22. Guest Star: Jim Nabors
Songs: "Just For a Thrill," "Listen to the Music" (Sonny & Cher).

23. SONNY & CHER VALENTINE'S DAY SHOW
Guest Stars: Joe Namath, Playboy Playmates
Songs: "On the Bayou," "It Never Rains in Southern California," "My Funny Valentine" (Cher), "I Got You Babe" (closing with Chastity).

24. Guest Stars: Danny Thomas, Miss Universe
Songs: "Put a Little Love in Your Heart" (opening), "Makin' Music"/"Put Your Hand in the Hand."

25. Guest Star: Don Adams
Songs: "Got to Get You into My Life" (opening), "I've Never Been in London" (Cher).

26. Guest Star: John Byner
Songs: "Personality" (opening), "Crocodile Rock" (Sonny & Cher), "Black & White" (video), "Alfie" (Cher).

27. Guest Stars: Carol Burnett, Lyle Waggoner
Cameos by William Conrad, Jean Stapleton, Tennessee Ernie Ford, Chad Everett
Songs: include "Sunshine, Lollipops and Rainbows."

28. Guest Stars: Jack Palance, Ed McMahon
    Songs: "Tie a Yellow Ribbon," "Honky Tonk Woman."

29. Guest Stars: Danny Thomas, Telly Savalas
    Songs: "I Couldn't Live without Your Love," "Get Ready," "Make It with
    You" (Cher).

30. THE SONNY & CHER YEARS, PART ONE (rock & roll show)
    Guest Stars: Dick Clark, Ed Burns, Chuck Berry, Jerry Lee Lewis, Bobby
    Vinton, Franki Valli and the Four Seasons
    Songs: "Rock & Roll Is Here to Stay," "Whole Lotta Shakin' Going On,"
    "Sherry," "Blue Velvet," "Go Johnny Go," two psychedelic 1960s medleys.

31. Guest Stars: Howard Cosell, Chuck Connors, Miss U.S.A., Miss Universe,
    Super Dave Osborne
    Songs: "Games People Play," "Bad, Bad Leroy Brown" (animated),
    "Without Love Where Would We Be" (Sonny & Cher), "Half Breed"
    (Cher).

32. Guest Stars: Jim Nabors, Lassie, Telly Savalas (cameo)
    Songs: "Everything Is Beautiful," "Cry Me a River," "Delta Dawn,"
    "Green Green Grass of Home" (Jim Nabors).

33. Guest Stars: Douglas Fairbanks, Jr., Rita Coolidge, Kris Kristofferson
    Songs: "Say, Has Anybody Seen My Sweet Gypsy Rose?" (Sonny & Cher),
    "That'll Be the Day," "All My Love and All My Kissin'," "You're
    Nobody 'Til Somebody Loves You."

34. Guest Stars: Andy Griffith, Bob Guccione, *Penthouse* magazine Pet of the
    Year
    Songs: "Yesterday," Rockin' Down the Highway."

35. THE SONNY & CHER YEARS, PART TWO (rock & roll show)
    Guest Stars: Wolfman Jack, Paul Anka, the Coasters, Neil Sedaka, Peter
    Noone (Herman's Hermits)
    Songs: "Rock & Roll Is Here to Stay," "Breakin' Up Is Hard to Do,"
    "Diana," "Charlie Brown," "Gypsys, Tramps and Thieves," "Calendar
    Girl," "Something Good," "Baby," "Yakety Yak," "Happy Birthday
    Sweet 16," "I Got You Babe."

36. Guest Stars: Danny Thomas, George Foreman, Ken Berry
    Songs: "Heartbreak," "Dark Lady" (Cher), closing number with Chastity.

37. Guest Stars: Merv Griffin, the Supremes, Miss World U.S.A.
    Songs: "I Couldn't Live without Your Love," "On My Own" (Cher), "All I
    Really Want" (Supremes).

38. Guest Stars: Sally Struthers, the Jackson Five, Tennessee Ernie Ford
    Songs: "Make Life a Little Easier," "Dancing Machine" (the Jackson Five).

39. Guest Stars: Ricardo Montalban, Jeanette Nolan, the DeFranco Family
    Songs: "Hey, What about Me," "Abracadabra" (the De Franco Family),
    "Midnight Hour," "Dark Lady" (animated).

THE SONNY & CHER SHOW

February 1976 to August 1977

40. Guest Stars: Joe Namath, the Righteous Brothers
    Songs: "Will You Still Love Me Tomorrow," "Lupe Lu" medley (Righteous
    Brothers), "Brother Louie" (Cher), "Didn't We Almost Make It This
    Time" (closing).

41. Guest Stars: Joel Grey
    Songs: "Beautiful Day" (opening), "Mockingbird," "Energy Shortage"/"I
    Got You Babe" (closing, with Chastity).

42. Guest Star: Raymond Burr
    Songs: "You Make Me Feel Brand New," "I Can See Clearly Now,"
    "Windmills of Your Mind" (Raymond Burr).

43. Guest Stars: Neil Sedaka, Evil Kneivel
    Songs: "I Love You More Today Than Yesterday"; Neil Sedaka medley
    "Hungry Years," "Breakin' Up Is Hard to Do," "Sad Eyes," "Calendar
    Girl," "Laughter in the Rain," "The Music Takes Me" (with Sonny &
    Cher); "I Got You Babe" (closing).

44. Guest Star: Don Knotts
    Songs: "Make Life a Little Easier," "United We Stand," "King of Hearts"
    (Cher).

45. Guest Star: McLean Stevenson
    Songs: "You Are the Sunshine of My Life," "Hang on in There Baby,"
    "How Long Has This Been Goin' On?" (Cher), "I Got You Babe"
    (closing).

46. Guest Stars: Gabriel Kaplan, Frankie Avalon
    Songs: "Venus" (Frankie Avalon), "How Sweet It Is to Be Loved by You,"
    "We're on Our Way Home"/"Try to See It My Way," "Say It Isn't So."

47. Guest Stars: Debbie Reynolds, the Smothers Brothers
    Songs: "Can't Take My Eyes Off of You" (with Tommy Smothers), "I
    Write the Songs" (Sonny with the Smothers Brothers), "I'm Gonna
    Make You Love Me."

48. Guest Stars: Diahann Carroll, Tony Randall
    Songs: include "God Bless the Child" (Diahann Carroll).

49. Guest Stars: Barbara Eden, the Smothers Brothers
    Songs: include "Heaven Must Be Missing an Angel."

50. Guest Stars: Bob Hope, the Jacksons, Bernadette Peters, Jim Nabors
    Songs: include "Enjoy Yourself" (Jacksons).

51. Guest Stars: Shields and Yarnell, Charo, Barbara Eden, the Smothers
    Brothers, Bob Hope, Don Knotts, Ruth Buzzi
    Songs: include "I Love You" (Sonny & Cher), "Desperado" (Cher).

52. Sonny & Cher HALLOWEEN/ELECTION DAY EPISODE
    Guest Stars: The Hudson Brothers, Shields and Yarnell, Jim Nabors
    Songs: "Still the One" (opening), "Things That Go Bump in the
    Night."

53. Guest Stars: Ruth Buzzi, Donny & Marie Osmond
    Songs: "That'll Be the Day," "I Love You" (Sonny & Cher, Donny &
    Marie), "It Had to Be You" (Cher).

54. Guest Stars: Ed McMahon, the Silvers, Betty White
    Songs: "Get Right Back" (open), "Boogie Fever"/"Hotline" (Silvers).

55. Sonny & Cher CHRISTMAS EPISODE
    Guest Stars: Bernadette Peters, Captain Kangaroo, Shields and Yarnell
    Songs: "Jingle Bells," "Send in the Clowns"/"Be a Clown" (Bernadette
    Peters), Christmas medley closing number.

56. Guest Stars: John Davidson, Karen Valentine
    Songs: "Make Your Own Sunshine"; "As Time Goes By" (Cher);
    medley/parody of 1970s TV show theme songs: "Movin' on Up,"
    "Welcome Back Kotter," "Maude," "Chico and the Man," "Laverne &
    Shirley," "Happy Days," "Baretta," "The Mary Tyler Moore Show,"
    "The Carol Burnett Show."

57. Guest Stars: Joey Heatherton, Don Knotts, Karen Valentine
    Songs: "Don't Pull Your Love Out on Me," "Yesterday" (Cher), "What I
    Did for Love."

58. Guest Stars: Andy Griffith, Twiggy
    Songs: "More Than You'll Ever Know," "Never Can Say Goodbye."

59. Guest Stars: Charo, George Gobel
    Songs: "You Are the Sunshine of My Life," "Come Rain or Come Shine,"
    "Bad, Bad, Leroy Brown."

60. Guest Stars: Farrah Fawcett, Debbie Reynolds, Don Knotts, Jim Nabors
    Songs: "All I Want to Do" (opening), "He & She" (with Farrah Fawcett
    and Don Knotts), "Dance to the Music" (with Debbie Reynolds),
    "Don't Go" (the couple's first song recorded as Sonny & Cher).

61. Guest Stars: Barbi Benton, William Conrad, Ruth Buzzi, Englebert
    Humperdinck
    Songs: "Come On Step Out with Me" (opening), "After the Lovin' "
    (Englebert Humperdinck), "We Almost Made It" (Cher), "Nights on
    Broadway" (Sonny, Cher, Barbi Benton, and Englebert Humperdinck).

62. Guest Stars: Betty White, Ken Berry, Flip Wilson
    Songs: include "Let It Be Me."

63. Guest Stars: Farrah Fawcett, Don Knotts, Glen Campbell
    Songs: "You Make Me Feel Like Dancing" (Sonny & Cher), "What a
    Difference" (Glen Campbell and Cher).

64. Guest Stars: Lyle Waggoner, Muhammad Ali, Marilyn McCoo & Billy
    Davis Jr.
    Songs: "Ain't That Peculiar"; "You Don't Have to Be a Star"/"Your Love"
    (Marilyn McCoo & Billy Davis Jr.); Medley "It Takes Two," "Where Is
    the Love," "You've Lost That Lovin' Feelin'," "Ain't Nothin' Like the
    Real Thing" (Sonny & Cher, Marilyn McCoo & Billy Davis Jr.); "I Got
    You Babe."

65. Guest Stars: Tina Turner, David Steinberg, Shields & Yarnell
    Songs: include "Teach Me Tonight" (Sonny & Cher).

COSTUME CHANGES ON THE 1999–2000 "BELIEVE" TOUR

1. Bronze-colored Viking outfit and headdress; red curly wig

2. Pirate hat and coat with body stocking; Louise Brooks bobbed hair

3. White sheer dress with mesh front for "The Way of Love"

4. Bugle-beaded dress and beaded skull cap for "Take Me Home"

5. Black pants; silver top

6. Nuevo Flamenco dress and train for *"Dov'è L'Amore"*

7. Black lace pants; red hair for "Strong Enough"

8. Silver pants; moon boots; wig with clear plastic tubing for "Believe"

INDEX

Lovin' Spoonful, 43
Lukather, Steve, 74

MacDowell, Andie, 233, 241
MacGraw, Ali, 237
Mackie, Bob, 77, 102, 175, 178;
Academy Award costume by,
171–72; *Cher* show costumes,
101, 102, 110–11; on design
purposes, 217; doll wardrobes,
119, 305; "Half Breed" cos-
tume, 89–90; press conference
costume, 214; TV show cos-
tumes by, 65, 68, 75–76, 78.
See also costumes; fashion
MacLaine, Shirley, 306
Madonna, 4, 195, 202, 293;
Cher's dislike of, 226, 230–31;
wedding, 1, 169–70
Mahoney, John, 180, 185
makeup, 20, 29, 65, 119, 156
Maltin, Leonard, 51
*Mama Was a Rock & Roll Singer,
Papa Used to Write Her Songs*
(album), 81–81
"Mama Was a Rock & Roll
Singer, Papa Used to Write All
Her Songs" (song), 80–81
The Mamas & the Papas, 44, 54
managers, 286–87
Manson, Marilyn, 308–9
Mantegna, Joe, 185
Mardin, Arif, 58
marriages: to Allman, 3, 5, 108; of
Cher's mother, 10; effect of,
170; lying about, 33, 43; pro-
posal from Dudek, 143; same-
sex, 271; to Sonny, 33–34, 61,
81, 83–86

Martin, George, 255, 256
Martin, Ricky, 203
Martin, Steve, 67, 133
Mask, xv, 4, 163–68, 310
Mason, Bonnie Jo, 28. *See also*
Cher
Mastroianni, Marcello, 254
Mathews, Jack, 167
Matlin, Marlee, 233
Mature, Victor, 13
The Maury Povich Show, 229
Mazursky, Paul, 262
MCA Records, 80, 82, 87; Cher
solo recordings, 94; record
deal, 96; rereleases, 291, 295,
303
McCallum, David, 52
McCartney, Paul, 36
McCoo, Marilyn, 68
McDonald, Pat, 301
McGuinn, Roger, 40
McGuire, Dorothy, 132
McIntosh, Robbie, 104
McQueen, Steve, 74, 185
Meadows, Jayne, 233
Meatloaf, 153
Mego Corporation, 118–19
Melcher, Melissa, 21
Melle Mel, 260
Mellen, Polly, 156
memoirs and biographies, 175, 282
Mercovich, Paul, 290
Mermaids, 4–5, 223–25, 227, 262,
287
The Merv Griffin Show, 65
Meyer, Ronnie, 238
Midler, Bette, 82, 88, 94, 101,
134; impersonators, 135; musi-
cal style, 201

ABOUT THE AUTHOR

Mark Bego is the author of several best-selling books on rock and roll and show business, with forty books published and over ten million books in print. His biographies include some of the biggest stars of rock, soul, pop, and country music. His first Top 10 *New York Times* bestseller was *Michael!* [Jackson] (1984). Since that time he has written about the lives of Rock Hudson, Aretha Franklin, Jewel, and Madonna.

In the 1990s Bego branched out into country music books, writing *Country Hunks* (1994), *Country Gals* (1995), *I Fall to Pieces: The Music and the Life of Patsy Cline* (1995), *Alan Jackson: Gone Country* (1996), *George Strait: The Story of Country's Living Legend* (1997), *LeAnn Rimes* (1998), and *Vince Gill* (2000). In 2000, his Patsy Cline biography was rated by *E! Online* as one of the Top 10 music bios of all times.

Bego has coauthored books with several rock stars, including Martha Reeves's *Dancing in the Street: Confessions of a Motown Diva*, which spent five weeks on the *Chicago Tribune* bestseller list in 1994. He worked with Micky Dolenz of the Monkees (*I'm a Believer*, 1993), Jimmy Greenspoon of Three Dog Night (*One Is the Loneliest Number*, 1991), and Mary Wilson (*Dreamgirl: My Life as a Supreme*, 2000 edition).

His writing has also been featured in several record albums and compact discs. In 1982 he wrote the interior notes to the Columbia House five-record boxed set *The Motown Collection*. His liner notes can also be found in the CDs Mary Wilson, *Walk the Line* (1992) and Martha Reeves & the Vandellas, *Lost and Found* (Motown Records 2001).

In 1998 Mark wrote books about three of the hottest leading men in late 1990s cinema. His *Leonardo DiCaprio: Romantic Hero* spent six weeks on the *New York Times* bestseller list. He followed it up with *Matt Damon: Chasing a Dream* and *Will Smith: The Freshest Prince*.

In 1998 Melitta Coffee launched *Mark Bego: Romantic Hero* blend coffee as part of their Celebrity Series. Mark divides his time between New York City, Los Angeles, and Tucson, Arizona. Visit his website at www.MarkBego.com

OTHER
COOPER SQUARE PRESS
TITLES OF INTEREST

MADONNA
Blonde Ambition
Mark Bego
Updated Edition
416 pp., 57 b/w photos
0-8154-1051-4
$18.95

DREAMGIRL & SUPREME
FAITH
My Life as a Supreme
Mary Wilson
Updated Edition
732 pp., 150 b/w photos, 15 color
photos
0-8154-1000-X
$19.95

ROCK SHE WROTE
Women Write About Rock, Pop,
and Rap
Edited by Evelyn McDonnell & Ann
Powers
496 pp.
0-8154-1018-2
$16.95

FAITHFULL
An Autobiography
Marianne Faithfull with David Dalton
320 pp., 32 b/w photos
0-8154-1046-8
$16.95

ROCK 100
The Greatest Stars of Rock's
Golden Age
David Dalton and Lenny Kaye
with a new introduction
288 pp., 195 b/w photos
0-8154-1017-4
$19.95

LIVING WITH THE DEAD
Twenty Years on the Bus with
Garcia and The Grateful Dead
Rock Scully with David Dalton
408 pp., 31 b/w photos
0-8154-1163-4
$18.95

FREAKSHOW
Misadventures in the
Counterculture, 1959–1971
Albert Goldman
416 pp.
0-8154-1169-3
$18.95

LENNON IN AMERICA
1971–1980, Based in Part on the
Lost Lennon Diaries
Geoffrey Giuliano
320 pp., 68 b/w photos
0-8154-1157-X
$17.95

DID THEY MENTION THE MUSIC?
The Autobiography of Henry Mancini
with a new afterword
Henry Mancini with Gene Lees
312 pp., 44 b/w photos
0-8154-1175-8
$18.95

DEPECHE MODE
A Biography
Steve Malins
280 pp., 24 b/w photos
0-8154-1142-1
$17.95

COLONEL TOM PARKER
The Curious Life of Elvis Presley's Eccentric Manager
James L. Dickerson
310 pp., 35 b/w photos
0-8154-1088-3
$28.95

GOIN' BACK TO MEMPHIS
A Century of Blues, Rock 'n' Roll, and Glorious Soul
James L. Dickerson
284 pp., 58 b/w photos
0-8154-1049-2
$16.95

DESPERADOS
The Roots of Country Rock, 1963–1973
John Einarson
370 pp., 24 b/w photos
0-8154-1065-4
$19.95

MICK JAGGER
Primitive Cool
Christopher Sandford
Updated Edition
352 pp., 56 b/w photos
0-8154-1002-6
$16.95

THE BLUES
In Images and Interviews
Robert Neff and Anthony Connor
152 pp., 84 b/w photos
0-8154-1003-4
$17.95

SUMMER OF LOVE
The Inside Story of LSD, Rock & Roll, Free Love and High Times in the Wild West
Joel Selvin
392 pp., 23 b/w photos
0-8154-1019-0
$15.95

ANY OLD WAY YOU CHOOSE IT
Rock and Other Pop Music, 1967–1973
Robert Christgau
Expanded Edition
360 pp.
0-8154-1041-7
$16.95

HE'S A REBEL
Phil Spector—Rock and Roll's Legendary Producer
Mark Ribowsky
368 pp., 35 b/w photos
0-8154-1044-1
$18.95